METRIC TABLE 5
U.S. and Metric Equivalents

U.S. to Metric	Metric to U.S.
1 in. = 2.54 cm (exact)	1 cm = .394 in.
1 ft = 0.305 m	1 m = 3.28 ft
1 yd = 0.915 m	1 m = 1.09 yd
1 mi = 1.61 km	1 km = .62 mi
1 in.^{3} = 16.387 cm^3	1 cm^3 = .06 in.^{3}
1 ft^3 = 0.028 m^3	1 m^3 = 35.315 ft^3
1 qt = 0.946 ℓ	1 ℓ = 1.06 qts
1 gal = 3.785 ℓ	1 ℓ = .264 gal
1 oz = 28.35 g	1 g = .035 oz
1 lb = 0.454 kg	1 kg = 2.205 lbs

Teaching Secondary Mathematics through Applications
Second Edition

HERBERT FREMONT
Queens College of The City University of New York

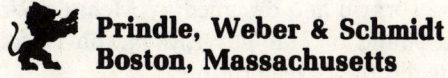
Prindle, Weber & Schmidt
Boston, Massachusetts

To Joseph, Sandy, Jay, David, and Jessica.

© Copyright 1979 by Prindle, Weber & Schmidt,
Statler Office Building, 20 Providence St., Boston, Massachusetts 02116.

All rights reserved. No part of this book may be reproduced or transmitted in any form or by any means, electronic or mechanical, including photocopying, recording, or any information storage and retrieval system, without permission, in writing, from the publisher.

Printed in the United States of America.

Library of Congress Cataloging in Publication Data

Fremont, Herbert, 1924-
    Teaching secondary mathematics through applications.

    Originally published in 1969 under title: How to teach mathematics on secondary schools.
    1. Mathematics—Study and teaching (Secondary)
I. Title.
QA11.F768   1978   510'.7'12   78-13380
ISBN 0-87150-256-9

This book was composed in English Times on the Editwriter 7500 by Carol Trowbridge. The text was designed by Eileen Katin and the staff of Prindle, Weber & Schmidt. Technical art was drawn by Phil Carver and Friends; part and chapter openings were drawn by Lydia Wunsch; and the cover was drawn and designed by Melinda Wooster. The book was printed and bound by Halliday Lithograph Corp. New England Book Components did the cover printing.

PREFACE

The second edition of *Teaching Secondary Mathematics through Applications* emphasizes (1) the need for teachers to show students there is no reason to fear mathematics and (2) the ways mathematics is integrated into their daily lives. This goal is accomplished through a problem-solving approach, which utilizes a wide variety of applications and puzzles that illustrate why mathematics is so important. (The wedge symbol "►" in the outer margins indicates sample problems.)

There are three parts in *Teaching Secondary Mathematics through Applications*. They are I) Preparing to Teach Mathematics, II) The Teaching of Mathematics, and III) Measuring Progress in Mathematics. Part II forms the heart of the text—methods of presenting mathematical content. The five sections that make up Part II are I) Mathematics and the Environment, II) Mathematics and Science, III) Mathematics and Society, IV) Mathematics: An Abstract System, and V) Mathematics and Finding Patterns. Parts I and III (Chapters 1, 2, and 20) present basic skills every teacher must have.

The mathematical concepts are not presented in any prescribed order, but specific suggestions are provided to show where a particular notion may be used in the classroom and how it fits into the curriculum. With the material presented in this text, teachers at the junior or senior high school level should be confident that they can develop appreciation and enthusiasm for mathematics in their students.

The impact of several colleagues on the original text has continued and influenced the preparation of the second edition. With this in mind, I would like to once again thank Dr. Gladys Crosby, Professor Morris Kline, Dean Marvin Taylor and my first editor, Professor Nathan Washton, for their help and guidance in completing this work.

Preface

Of those who provided direct assistance with this revision, I would like to express my gratitude to the many students in my graduate courses at Queens College. They often taught me as much as I did them, and added several of the activities included here. Ms. Anne Schick, my editor, provided patience, understanding and support to help make this revision a reality. For this I am grateful. And, finally, I would like to correct a serious oversight of the first edition. Professor John Kinsella, my teacher and mentor, helped me to begin to understand what the teaching of mathematics is all about. He provided the foundation for much of my later work, and I cannot thank him enough.

Herbert Fremont

CONTENTS

▶ **PART I   Preparing to Teach Mathematics**   1

1   *The Significance of Mathematics*   2

    1.1   Mathematics Helps Us to Understand Our Environment   3
    1.2   Mathematics is the Language of Science   3
    1.3   Mathematics and Society are Interdependent   3
    1.4   Mathematics is an Abstract System of Ideas   4
    1.5   Mathematics is the Study of Patterns   4
        For Investigation and Discussion   5
        For Further Reading   5

2   *Planning for Learning*   7

    2.1   Unit Planning   8
    2.2   Day-to-Day Planning   13
    2.3   A Restatement and the Four Freedoms   18
        For Investigation and Discussion   20
        For Further Reading   21

▶ **PART II   The Teaching of Mathematics**   23

SECTION I   Mathematics and the Environment   24

3   *Mathematics and Our Limited Resources*   24

    3.1   Mathematics of the Air Supply   24
    3.2   Mathematics of Water Conservation   28
    3.3   The Metric System   30
    3.4   Mathematics and the Conservation of Energy   34
        Footnotes   36
        For Investigation and Discussion   36
        For Further Reading   37

4 Natural Laws and Mathematics — 38

    4.1 Motion Experiments — 38
    4.2 Mirrors and Mathematics — 45
    Footnote — 54
    For Investigation and Discussion — 55
    For Further Reading — 55

5 The Mathematics of Living Things — 56

    5.1 Nature's Polygons — 56
    5.2 The Growth of Area and Volume — 58
    5.3 Symmetry — 62
    5.4 Maintaining Body Temperature and the Use of Percent — 66
    5.5 Warm-Blooded Animals and Inequalities — 69
    5.6 The Mathematics of Dieting — 75
    Footnotes — 76
    For Investigation and Discussion — 77
    For Further Reading — 77

6 Mathematics and Space Exploration — 78

    6.1 Periods of the Planets — 79
    6.2 Circle Properties and Planets — 81
    6.3 Time in Space Travel — 84
    6.4 How Far and How Much Can You See? — 88
    6.5 Tangents in Space — 90
    6.6 In Conclusion — 95
    Footnotes — 95
    For Investigation and Discussion — 95
    For Further Reading — 96

SECTION II Mathematics and Science — 97

7 Mathematics: The Language of Science — 97

    7.1 Simple Experiments — 98
    7.2 Algebra as a Language — 102
    7.3 Further Explorations of Algebra — 105
    7.4 The Equality Axioms — 106
    7.5 Vocabulary and Definitions — 109
    7.6 Mathematics or Physics? — 109
    7.7 Algebra as a Language—In Conclusion — 110
    Footnotes — 110
    For Investigation and Discussion — 111
    For Further Reading — 111

Contents vii

8 Mathematics as a Tool — 112

- 8.1 Distance, Rate, Time, and Beginning Quadratics — 112
- 8.2 Finding Square Roots — 115
- 8.3 Distance and the Quadratic Function — 118
- 8.4 A Word About Graphing — 124
- Footnote — 127
- For Investigation and Discussion — 127
- For Further Reading — 127

9 The Mathematics of Motion — 128

- 9.1 Speed-Time Graphs — 128
- 9.2 Distance as Area — 130
- 9.3 Rates of Change and Derivatives — 134
- 9.4 The Limit — 140
- 9.5 Integration — 141
- 9.6 The Motion of Springs — 147
- 9.7 Vectors in Trigonometry — 150
- Footnotes — 152
- For Investigation and Discussion — 152
- For Further Reading — 152

10 Light, Sound, and Mathematics — 154

- 10.1 Eclipses — 154
- 10.2 Circle Relationships — 157
- 10.3 Reflections and Conic Sections — 158
- 10.4 Mathematics and Science—In Conclusion — 166
- Footnote — 167
- For Investigation and Discussion — 167
- For Further Reading — 167

SECTION III Mathematics and Society — 168

11 Mathematics as a Model of Reality — 168

- 11.1 Crossing Bridges and Mathematics — 169
- 11.2 Euclid and the "Real World" — 173
- 11.3 Kepler's Laws of Motion — 175

11.4	Linear Programming and Mathematical Models	178
	Footnotes	184
	For Investigation and Discussion	184
	For Further Reading	185

12 Making Decisions: Statistics — 187

12.1	Collecting Data and Sketching Graphs	188
12.2	Other Types of Graphs	190
12.3	Sampling and Decision Making	193
12.4	Mean, Median, and Mode	197
12.5	Using Spinners	202
12.6	Measures of Dispersion	203
	Footnotes	206
	For Investigation and Discussion	206
	For Further Reading	206

13 Probability — 208

13.1	Expecting the Unexpected	208
13.2	Probability: Theory vs. Practice	211
13.3	The Normal Curve	212
13.4	Monte Carlo Methods	216
13.5	Computers	217
	Footnotes	221
	For Investigation and Discussion	221
	For Further Reading	222
	For Further Reading on Computers	223

SECTION IV Mathematics: An Abstract System — 224

14 Abstraction is Power — 224

14.1	Flips to Groups	224
14.2	Transformations and Living Things	230
14.3	Trigonometry: Ratios or Functions?	232
	Footnotes	237
	For Investigation and Discussion	237
	For Further Reading	237

15 Mathematical Thinking, Problem Solving, and Proof — 239

15.1	Solving Verbal Problems	239
15.2	Flashes of Insight	241
15.3	Trial and Error	243
15.4	Finding a Simple Equivalent	243
15.5	Mathematical Thinking and Drawing Generalizations	245
15.6	Mathematical Thinking and Proof	247
15.7	The Role of Diagrams	247
15.8	Proof, Logic and Rigor	248
	Footnotes	251
	For Investigation and Discussion	252
	For Further Reading	252

SECTION V Mathematics and Finding Patterns — 254

16 Patterns in Numbers — 254

16.1	Odd and Even	255
16.2	Prime and Composite	257
16.3	Perfect Squares	258
16.4	Basic Number Facts	261
16.5	Graphing Multiplication Tables	264
16.6	Directed Numbers	265
16.7	Number Patterns—In Conclusion	271
	Footnotes	272
	For Investigation and Discussion	272
	For Further Reading	272

17 Patterns in Algebra — 274

17.1	Patterns from Experiments	274
17.2	Rolling Circles	276
17.3	Discovery and Factoring	282
17.4	Operations on Polynomials	283
17.5	Variation	289
	Footnote	295
	For Investigation and Discussion	295
	For Further Reading	295

18 Patterns in Geometry — 296

- 18.1 Pythagorean Patterns — 296
- 18.2 Patterns and Indirect Proof — 301
- 18.3 Tesselations — 303
- Footnotes — 306
- For Investigation and Discussion — 306
- For Further Reading — 306

19 Paradoxes, Puzzles, and Patterns — 308

- 19.1 Sum the Series — 308
- 19.2 Fill the Jug — 309
- 19.3 Magic Squares — 312
- 19.4 In Conclusion — 316
- Footnotes — 316
- For Investigation and Discussion — 317
- For Further Reading — 317
- For Further Reading on Magic Squares — 317

▶ PART III Measuring Progress in Mathematics — 319

20 Evaluation — 320

- 20.1 Testing — 320
- 20.2 Making Tests — 321
- 20.3 Validity and Reliability — 325
- 20.4 Construction of Items — 325
- 20.5 Scoring — 326
- 20.6 Other Evaluation Techniques — 326
- 20.7 Standardized Tests — 329
- Footnotes — 333
- For Investigation and Discussion — 334
- For Further Reading — 335

21 Epilogue — 337

Index — 339

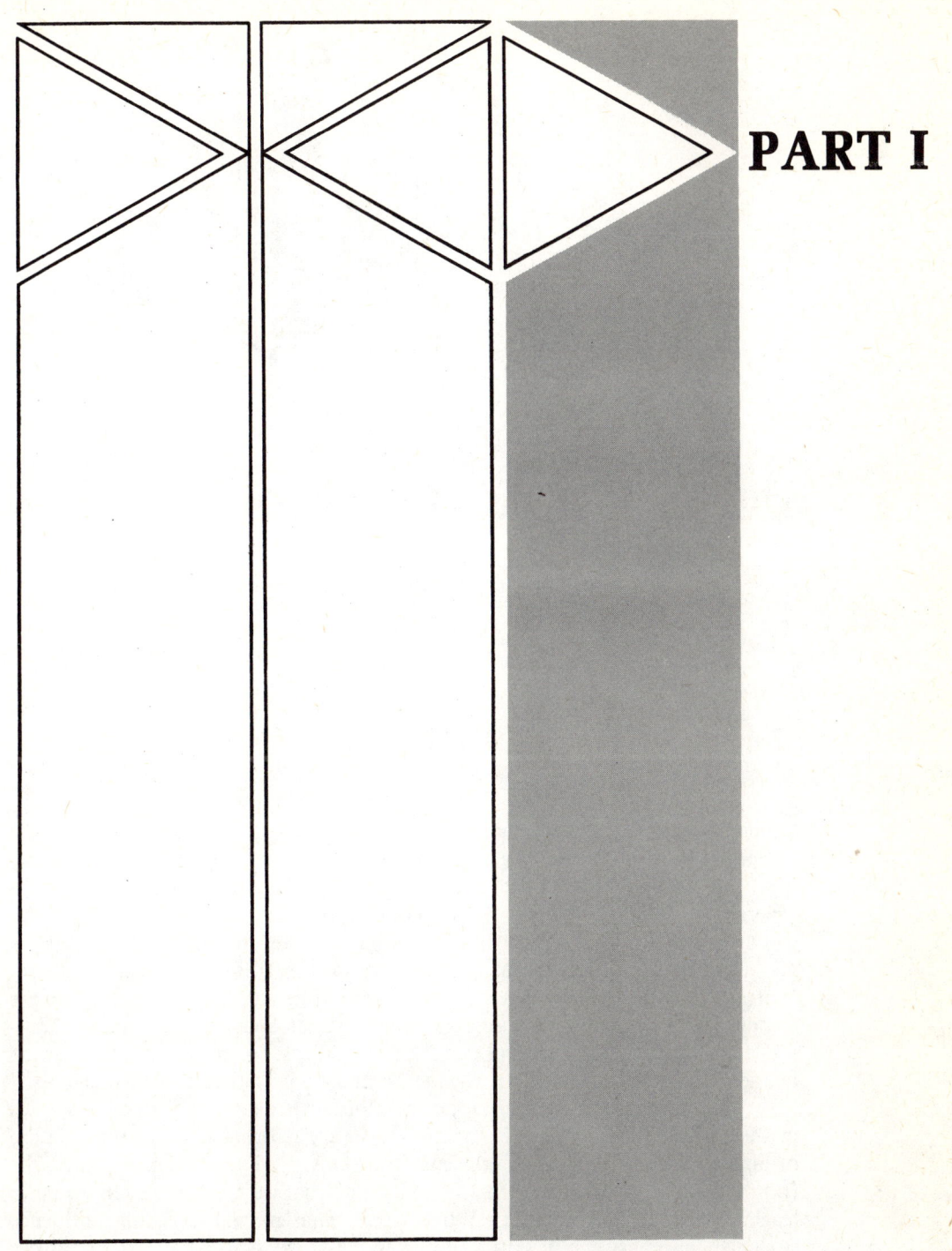

Preparing to Teach Mathematics

CHAPTER 1

The Significance of Mathematics

Mathematics holds a rather unique place in our society today. While most people accept the fact that mathematics is vital to the continued growth of our country, these same people feel completely inadequate in the subject. What's more, this general feeling of inadequacy is not accompanied by any loss in self-esteem. Apparently it is the oddball who can work successfully in mathematics, and the mathematician is often seen as a person withdrawn from the world, unable to relate well to other people. After all, what kind of person can find pleasure in the complex notions of mathematics? In short, mathematics has become an "antisocial" subject. This general attitude of people in our society towards mathematics is an interesting consequence of school mathematics experiences.

How could so many people develop such negative attitudes towards mathematics? Certainly teachers are making every effort to develop appreciation of mathematics as they teach concepts and skills. Perhaps one problem results from the way we look at mathematics and from what we feel is most important in teaching school mathematics. What we emphasize will certainly influence students' concept of mathematics. For example, if we focus on drill to excess, we may expect a particular idea of mathematics to develop. If we focus on applications, we may construct a completely different feeling about mathematics. Of course, we are not at liberty to choose one route at the exclusion of the other since drill and applications are both necessary in any mathematics course. Our chosen points of emphasis, however, influence student attitudes. What will be the important emphasis of the material presented here? Let us examine our goals and purposes.

1.1 Mathematics Helps Us to Understand Our Environment

Our first statement of purpose is to develop student awareness that *mathematics helps us to understand our environment*. It is not an oversight that the words "control" and "master" have been omitted from the statement. There are many who firmly believe that the two go together: Understand and control nature. While our understanding of the physical world can assist us in controlling certain events, our primary purpose should be to understand nature in order that we may better learn to share the bountiful awards of nature and coexist on this planet with all living things. We have all too often seen the results of man's attempt to "master" his environment: the cutting of timber, the damming of rivers, and the poisoning of the waters with insecticides and the air with pollutants. It would seem that a greater understanding of nature would prevent the destruction of redwood forests and the contamination of natural resources, and so the notion of "mastery" is seriously questioned. But in understanding this world in which we live, mathematics is an invaluable tool. Imagine trying to describe and work with physical relationships without the use of the symbolic language of algebra. Imagine trying to investigate form and function in nature, and thereby in man-made objects as well, without the concepts and visual images of geometry. And how would we have advanced technologically without the power that we have to study phenomena that are offered by the calculus?

Somehow this chapter in the story of mathematics must be shared with students of the subject. This means that our students will have to participate in a great number of experiences that will enable them to one day remark to themselves, "Look what I can do with mathematics!"

1.2 Mathematics is the Language of Science

Mathematics is the language of science, and therefore the means for communication between scientists. The close, natural ties between mathematics and science need to be exploited in school mathematics. By what better means could teachers of mathematics give importance and immediacy to the concepts considered in the classroom? Too often the work that may be observed today appears to be unrelated to anything of significance outside the walls of the school building. If we emphasize the language role that mathematics is fulfilling, we not only add interest and importance to the subject but we also point up important considerations for the learning of the subject. How does one learn a "language"? If a student is conversant with the symbolism of mathematics and what it represents, he has a good head start on learning how to explore the variety of concepts that await him. Therefore, we must focus upon this notion and concentrate upon helping our students to "speak the language."

1.3 Mathematics and Society are Interdependent

In addition to helping us understand our environment, mathematics has had an important effect upon the development of the society in which we live, an effect that is a reciprocal one. The society has in turn influenced the development of mathematics. We have an excellent example of this in the progress made in the launching of space vehicles. Many years of development in science and mathematics enabled the Russians to launch their first Sputnik. The western world in general, and the United States in particular, concerned about Russian progress, increased public spending for research in mathematics and science. The consequence has been accelerated growth and additional knowledge in both areas.

Our knowledge of mathematics influences our view of the world. We are at this very moment living through untold and unforseen changes in our society and in mathematics as a consequence of the refinement of the electronic computer. What part of our daily existence remains untouched?

If we are to impress students with the vibrant, growing side of mathematics, we must find ways to involve them in experiences that emphasize the interaction of mathematics and society.

1.4 Mathematics is an Abstract System of Ideas

We must not be mislead by the first three goals. Emphasizing the interaction of mathematics with the culture, as well as its role as a tool for, and the language of, science does not mean that we shall mask its true identity and nature. Whatever else it may be, mathematics is still an abstract system of ideas and must be seen as such by our students. Thus, as the students use mathematics to solve problems, we shall have to be prepared to indicate clearly how the mathematics "thing" and the physical "thing" are not one and the same. This becomes particularly important in the study of geometry, as it is easy to confuse the visual representations of the mathematical concepts with the concepts themselves. At the same time however, we will not minimize the important use that will be served by the visual representations. But if the student of mathematics is to gain some insight into the very heart of things mathematically, we shall somehow have to organize experiences to bring out the abstract nature of mathematical systems. The role played by mathematics is of primary importance. Helping students begin to formulate concepts of the nature of mathematics is equally important. Mathemathics stands as an example of what heights man may reach when he relies upon his powers of reason. The use of deduction in mathematics provides this discipline with the unique quality of determining the validity of propositions and the elimination of doubt. The use of logic alone would serve to establish an unusual position for mathematics among the many fields of endeavor in modern society.

1.5 Mathematics is the Study of Patterns

Finally, we must consider mathematics as the study of all possible patterns, both in the world around us and in the structure of the discipline of mathematics itself. It has already been mentioned that there are regularities and similarities in nature that would escape us entirely if it were not for the mathematical descriptions available to us. Thus $v = 32t$ and $s = 3w$, describing completely different physical situations, fit the same mathematical pattern: $y = ax$, the simple linear function. Internally, within the field of mathematics itself, this same search for and classification of patterns is always taking place. We classify all two-dimensional things, three-dimensional things, and even move into a world beyond our senses and do the same for four-, five-, and eventually n-dimensional spaces. We say that if $x^2 + y^2 = r^2$ is the equation of a two-dimensional circle, and if $x^2 + y^2 + z^2 = r^2$ is the equation of a three-dimensional sphere, we could almost expect $x^2 + y^2 + z^2 + u^2 = r^2$ to become the equation of a four-dimensional sphere—whatever that may be! Of course, the most remarkable fact about all this is that the study of problems in the real world triggers the development of new mathematics that frequently goes far beyond the problem at hand and into such areas as four-dimensional spaces. Despite the fact that new mathematics frequently has little apparent application to anything in the physical world, just as often some later use is found that assists man in his continued quest for progress. The four-dimensional geometry, for example, has become an important tool for the study of Einstein's theory of relativity. Thus, in the teaching of school mathematics we may be able to make an important beginning in helping students to realize the importance of the search for patterns through their own participation in the search.

The five principles just presented will form our intellectual goals. They will formulate the basis upon which the work in the classroom will be developed in succeeding chapters. The program that follows is a direct out-growth of the creation of experiences to develop these five principles:

Mathematics helps us to understand our environment.

Mathematics is the language of science.

Mathematics and society are interdependent.

Mathematics is an abstract system of ideas.

Mathematics is the study of patterns.

For Investigation and Discussion

1. Select an incident from history to demonstrate how the test "does it work?" led to a mathematical developement.
2. Give specific examples of how algebra and geometry add to our understanding of our environment.
3. In what ways may mathematics be considered a language? How might this influence classroom instruction in mathematics?
4. Give one example from each of arithmetic, algebra, and geometry to indicate how mathematics enables you to do something otherwise difficult to achieve.
5. Discuss the difference between a mathematical formulation of the area of a triangle and the physical area itself.
6. If the study of physical problems generates the development of new mathematics, how is it that this "new" mathematics is often highly abstract and has no physical counterpart?

For Further Reading

Books

Hawkins, David. "Nature, Man and Mathematics," *Developments in Mathematical Education*. A. G. Howson, ed. New York: Cambridge University Press, 1973, pp. 115–135.

Sawyer, W. W. *Mathematician's Delight*. New York: Penguin Books, 1946.

Periodicals

Adler, Irving. "Criteria of Success in the Seventies," *The Mathematics Teacher.* Vol. 65 (January 1972), pp. 33–41.

Fawcett, Harold P. "The Reflections of a Retiring Teacher of Mathematics," *The Mathematics Teacher.* Vol. 57 (November 1964), pp. 450–456.

Fitzgerald, William M. "The Role of Mathematics in a Comprehensive Problem Solving Curriculum in Secondary Schools," *School Science and Mathematics.* Vol. 75 (January 1975), pp. 39–47.

Greenberg, Herbert J. "The Objectives of Mathematics Education," *The Mathematics Teacher.* Vol. 67 (November 1974), pp. 639–643.

Wilcox, A. B. "England was Lost on the Playing Fields of Eton: A Parable for Mathematics," *The American Mathematical Monthly.* Vol. 80 (January 1973), pp. 25–40.

Wilder, R. L. "Mathematics and Its Relations to Other Disciplines," *The Mathematics Teacher.* Vol. 66 (December 1973), pp. 679–685.

CHAPTER 2

Planning for Learning

We hear a good deal today about starting new developments in the field of education that will revolutionize the classroom as we have traditionally conceived it. We find automated programs, teaching machines, learning cubicles, closed-circuit television, single-concept teaching films, and computerized instructional sequences among some of the recent developments. It is virtually impossible to attend a conference of mathematics teachers, read a journal, or discuss mathematics learning without hearing the word "discovery" mentioned over and over again. Everyone is talking about new methods, new techniques, and new materials, to aid the learning of mathematics, but one may well question how much is actually being done about it. Moreover, it seems even more important to ask how much has been done to help teachers who would like to do something about improving the learning of their students.

It is one thing to study the best available clues to the learning of mathematics, but it is quite another thing altogether to build classroom experiences making use of such knowledge. While there is a good deal of literature about the difficulties that youngsters encounter transferring what they have learned to new situations, the notion that teachers may experience these same difficulties has not received sufficient attention. In this chapter we will attempt to keep clearly before us the important ideas developed about learning, as well as those related to the nature and importance of mathematics, as we approach the vital task of preparing effective learning experiences for students.

Our mathematics goals, or principles, are stated in Chapter 1. As far as the principles of learning that guide the organization of classroom experiences are concerned, we will try to build upon these ideas:

1.   The "life cycle" of learning a mathematical idea dictates that learning must proceed from active involvement with concrete objects toward analysis with abstractions.

2. Throughout this process the student must be free to think about things and draw his own conclusions.
3. Opportunities for adventurous thinking in spurts and starts should precede analytical logical thought.
4. Children can abstract a mathematical principle if presented with a broad variety of situations in which the principle is inherent.
5. Visual images are necessary for students to be able to understand and use abstract concepts.

These five statements and the five principles presented in Chapter 1 may be thought of as assumptions in the manner of the postulates of geometry. In the true sense of postulates in mathematics, let us not consider the 10 assumptions to be "self-evident" truths. They do result, however, from a good deal of observation and investigation, which also is consistent with the formulation of mathematical postulates. These 10 notions are the basis upon which we will build our plans for helping students to learn mathematics. We shall investigate the mechanics of the planning process itself on both a long- and short-term basis. Most importantly, by the term **planning** we mean the careful development of a general approach to the creation of classroom learning experiences. Thus we are striving here for a framework for the teaching of mathematics. This is a far more significant undertaking than the mechanics of making plans, although plan construction is an important part of this process and will also be considered.

With our goals and our direction clear, let us select a sample topic and see in specific terms how we may proceed.

2.1 Unit Planning

The introduction to linear functions and equations from elementary algebra is a good starting point. If we were to plan a 2 to 3 week unit in this area, based upon our 10 assumptions, how would we proceed? Here are some suggested headings that may enable us to keep the important ideas uppermost in our minds as we work:

I. Objectives
II. Introduction
III. Overall development and content
IV. Summary and evaluation

Using this outline as a guide, we proceed to build our unit, "An Introduction to Algebra."

Objectives

What do we want our students to know?
What understandings should they have gained?
What skills do we want them to have when this unit is completed?

Since algebra is the language of the scientist and is of greatest importance because of the power it provides for the description of relationships in the physical world, the notion of function must be central in this development. Specifically, we would want students to understand what a linear function is by being able to recognize one when they see it.

As for skill development, the solution of simple linear equations would be of primary importance, as would the beginning development of skills in translating the language of algebra. The discovery of patterns in tables of values, the drawing of accurate graphs of functions, and the use of a new vocabulary are additional skills to be achieved.

The specific content of this unit will be listed in the section on development.

Introduction

How can we actively involve our students in experiences that are interesting and germane to the mathematics concepts of this unit?

We have assumed that the use of concrete representations in some active process will speed the understanding of mathematical concepts. In this instance, each member of the class will conduct some physical experiment involving a basic linear relationship. Such an experiment would yield data that could be organized in tables, and the students could seek out any patterns inherent in these tables. To add to their understanding of the relationship, graphs could be made of the particular function and predictions could then be attempted and checked. In this way, we could immerse our students in the idea of function actively and quickly.

There are many situations that involve linear relationships: the stretch of a spring, the perimeter of a square, and the velocity of a dropped object, to name a few. Let us begin with a simple machine that can be made easily and that is rather consistent in the results that it yields, such as W. W. Sawyer's platform and rollers (Figure 2.1).

Figure 2.1

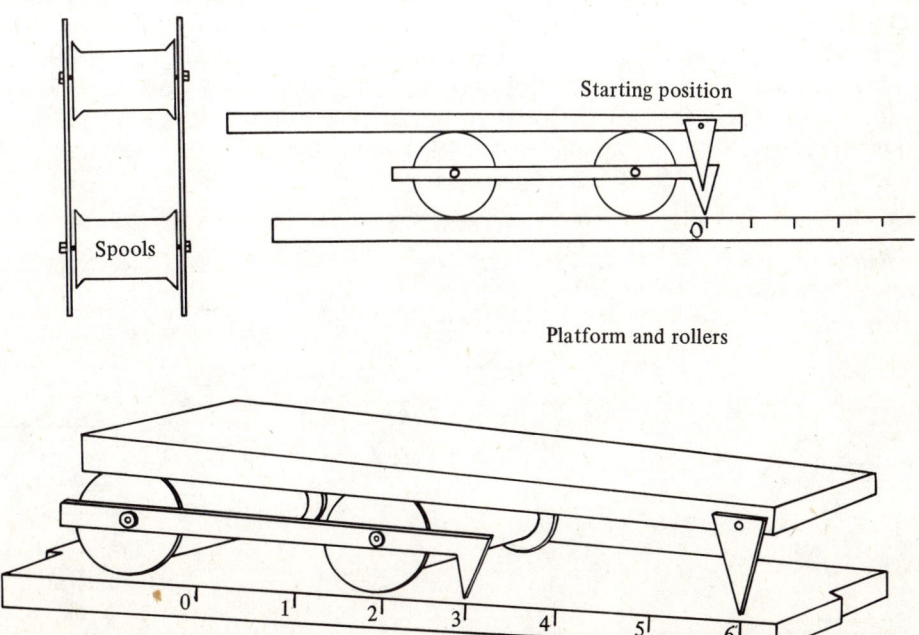

How far does the platform go as compared with the distance moved by the rollers?

With enough platform and roller sets, we can form groups of five or six students. Each group can conduct the experiment a number of times, collect and place the data in tables, search for patterns, and then describe the pattern using words. Later this description can be shortened to a formula, and the graph of the function can be drawn. The process of prediction enables the students to check with the apparatus. All the important mathematical ideas are inherent in such an experience. In addition, we have made a beginning that has our students "doing" rather than "watching and listening." At the same time, we have proceeded with an activity that directly relates to our stated goals.

Overall Development and Content

What will the students do after the introductory work?
How shall we maintain interest?
How shall we arrange the content?
What resource materials will help the students?
How can we provide a change of pace?
What are some possible trouble spots?

Once the students have conducted brief experiments that yield simple collections of data, what will they do next? Since the purpose of the experimentation is to involve the students with pertinent mathematical ideas, we must provide many such experiments. Thus, at least two or three experiments can be conducted as just described—two that are actually performed and a third that will perhaps be in a representational form: pictures or diagrams of a spring being stretched as weights are hung from it. At this point, instead of dealing with the concrete objects the student will turn to a representation of such objects and place a ruler on the photos or diagrams in order to derive their data (Figure 2.2). Later, diagrams of experiments will be presented to students with the data already stated on the diagram (Figure 2.3, see page 11). This will be followed by giving the students tables of data related to familiar objects and will culminate in work done with tables of numbers that do not refer to any concrete objects at all. Thus, our overall plan is to work from an active, real situation through a representation of such a situation to a final, completely abstract form.

Figure 2.2
An experiment in spring stretch.

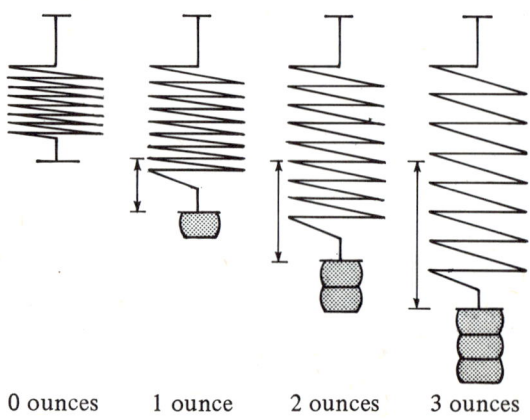

0 ounces   1 ounce   2 ounces   3 ounces

Figure 2.3
The speed of falling objects (ft/sec).

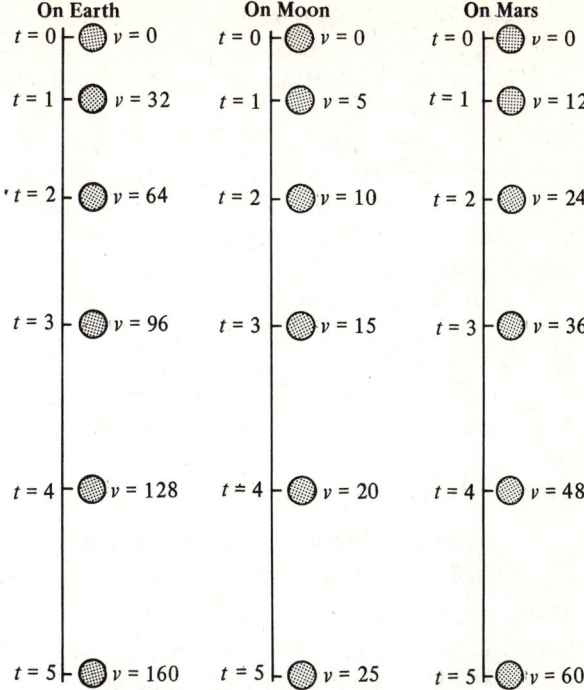

Our aim is to help students understand the linear function of form $y = ax$ and the ways in which such a function is described. We also want to introduce the solution of linear equations derived from such functions. Repetitive or drill experiences will help fix these ideas in student's minds. Regardless of the degree of abstraction, each time an experiment is considered (i.e., tables and graphs are made, followed by predictions that are later checked and equations are solved), students undergo a form of "drill." They work over and over again with the same mathematical concepts while the environment in which these concepts appear continually changes. Thus drill and boredom need no longer be synonymous.

In developing this unit of work, are there possible difficult areas that we may avoid or minimize by recognizing them at the planning stage, rather than waiting for them to occur in the classroom?

We should expect to encounter student trouble with the process of translating sentences into mathematical formulas. If this should develop, a statement by the teacher, at first, will help the students over this rough spot. Eventually, students will devise some plan of their own for stating these formulas.

Another possible difficulty may arise in the solution of equations. It is most important to emphasize, at this time, the translation of the symbolic language of algebra, rather than to become involved in formal techniques such as application of the equality axioms and balancing. For example:

Find the amount of weight necessary (w) to stretch the spring (s) 18 inches, if the relationship is described by $s = 3w$.

Solution: $s = 18$; thus I must solve $18 = 3w$. This says that 3 times some number is 18. The number must be 6, since $3 \times 6 = 18$.

To avoid the pitfalls that result from too much formal work, too soon, constant emphasis should be placed upon answering the questions, What does the equation say? and What do the symbols tell you? How to develop skill in handling more complex equations using more formal methods will be accomplished as the need arises.

As the students move from physical experiments through pictures and diagrams to abstract collections of data, the variation of activities will prevent student boredom. In addition, the freedom students have to construct their own formulas and to make and check their predictions also builds variety of activities into the unit.

As for the use of materials, we have already indicated that apparatus, pictures, and diagrams will all be involved in the unit as the class works in small groups as well as in whole-class groupings.

Thus the necessary repetition is provided, some anticipated trouble areas have been considered, and the activities of the unit carefully planned.

Summary and Evaluation

What are the important understandings and skills to be tested?

How shall we best determine how much has been learned?

The summary and evaluation should reflect back upon the objectives stated at the outset. In order to provide an overview of the work of the unit, the students have been asked to conduct a complete experiment from the collection of data to the solution of equations. The extent to which each student has been able to master the important ideas can be determined. In addition, tables of linear relationships ($y = ax$) have been presented. Students have attempted to find the patterns therein and describe their findings symbolically. Experiences have been developed to emphasize those areas in which the students have difficulty, and an examination has been administered. This test included collections of data that relate to physical objects as well as completely abstract data. This would conclude the unit of work. If we now join these separate sections together in outline form, the finished plan for the unit looks like this:

Unit: Introduction to Algebra: The Linear Function

Length: 2 to 3 weeks

    I. Objectives
        A. Beginning of student realization of the following concepts:
            1. Algebra is the language of science
            2. Algebra describes relationships in the physical world
            3. The meaning of function in general
            4. The linear function in particular
        B. Skills
            1. Solution of simple linear equations
            2. Pattern-finding and description
            3. Drawing of graphs of the linear function
            4. Use of new mathematical words
    II. Introduction
        A. Purpose: To seek out relationship between platform and rollers
        B. Procedures: Use five or six sets of platform and rollers; divide class into five or six groups to conduct experiments.

1. Perform and repeat experiment
2. Tabulate data
3. Search for patterns—describe verbally
4. Reduce description to formula
5. Draw graph
6. Make and test predictions

III. Overall development and content
  A. Additional experimentation
    1. By doing (apparatus)
      (a) Rotating wheels: rotations and distance
      (b) Balancing a lever with fixed weights
    2. By measuring (pictures and diagrams)
      (a) Spring stretch
      (b) Number of inches in feet, or number of millimeters in a centimeter
    3. By reading from data (pictures and diagrams)
      (a) Speed of falling objects—time
      (b) Distance of thunder: lightning flash—time
  B. Data presented in table form
    1. Familiar situations
      (a) Speed of falling objects on other planets
      (b) Varieties of spring—stretch experiments
      (c) Gasoline costs—gallons or liters
    2. Abstract collections of data—In each of the preceding situations:
      (a) Find a pattern — *How would you know*
      (b) Write a formula
      (c) Draw the graph
      (d) Compare with each other
      (e) Predict results from formula and graph
      (f) Check where possible against experiment or by alternate means
    3. Trouble spots
      (a) Writing formulas—provide many examples; check statement and formula; compare.
      (b) Solving equations—What does language mean? What do symbols tell us?

IV. Summary and evaluation
  A. Summary
    1. Weighing experiment: How many washers weigh a pound? 2 lbs.? 3 lbs.?
    2. Make a table-formula-graph. Prediction problems. How is this function like others? Unlike others?
  B. Examination

Day-to-Day Planning 2.2

Day-to-day planning procedures require different considerations from those of long-range planning. Our first task is to create interest in what we are doing. The beginning of a lesson or topic in general has too often been a consequence of a difficult paradox. Mathematics is a logical, sequential discipline. It begins with undefined terms, definitions, and postulates. Then, using the rules of logic, we proceed to prove propositions based upon these components, and we label as theorems those propositions with which we are successful. Thus, our mathematical structure grows. Since it grows in this fashion, many teachers have assumed this is how it should be taught—and "there's the rub." How often do teachers begin like this: "The topic we will discuss today is the isosceles triangle. Now what is an isosceles triangle?" After several student responses the teacher continues, "An isosceles triangle is defined to be . . ." This may sound like a sequential development, but what of the way in which children learn?

From what we know about learning, beginning with a definition of some unknown concept leaves students with a single choice: to *remember* what the teacher or some student has said. Since there has been no opportunity to work with these triangles before the stated definition, there is no opportunity to formulate one's own ideas or visual images regarding the topic. Beginning with a definition must result in rote memory work. On the other hand, if we would plan classroom activities to help children become actively involved with the pertinent ideas, *at the end* they should be able to provide us with a definition. In truth, this end product (the definition) may be somewhat different from ours. It will usually be substantially correct and will always reflect how the student is thinking.

The same general idea would apply to the development of methods for solving varieties of mathematical problems. If the way to do something mathematically is presented to students as a model, we are asking them to memorize and copy.

If, instead, we plan activities that will help a student to think and devise his own methods, we then have the greatest probability of successfully developing understanding. Thus, the point of view from which planning should proceed is to decide what to ask the students to do so that they can determine their own techniques for dealing with ideas. Some beginning that will attract their attention, get them involved, and whet their appetites for more is essential.

Beginning Activities

Generally, once the mathematical topic is clearly before us, we seek some interesting activity, being careful that the mathematics of concern at the moment is an integral part of that action. We are not concerned with creating interest for its own sake. Our desire is to find a setting for the mathematics to be learned that is of substance in order to help make the work meaningful. One interesting technique is to begin with a game. For example, in a "function" game, the teacher asks a student to say any number out loud. The teacher then responds with another number. For example,

Student	7
Teacher	9
Another student	14
Teacher	16
Another student	0
Teacher	2
Another student	9

At this point the teacher says, "How many know what number I am going to say next?" The teacher calls upon one student and indicates that the answer is correct but suggests continuing the game to be sure that the "trick" (function) is known. He then proceeds and the making of a rule passes to the first student who guesses correctly. Such an activity has all the elements of a game plus all the elements of the notion of function.

Other interesting beginnings may be made with puzzles, problems, stories, and applications. It has become customary in mathematics classes to teach skills and concepts and, once they are learned, to then present applications providing the student with an opportunity to make use of the newly learned ideas.

This progression of events is often mystifying. The application provides a reason for the student to learn whatever it is we want him to learn. Yet he only gets to this point *after* he has been taught the ideas. Thus, we may safely assume that he has learned whatever we have put before him without any reason other than his desire to please us. Is it any wonder that mathematics is so meaningless to so many?

"But wait," many teachers will say. "How can you possibly teach a student to work with an application if he lacks the necessary skills and understandings to carry out the desired calculations?" This is true, but we have lost sight of one crucial point: The teacher *knows* why the particular skills are needed because the teacher *knows* what is next on the agenda. The student, however, *does not know*. When he works to learn what we have set before him he has no purpose, no direction, and no feeling of a need to learn. He has already found out that he is required to do much in school that does not make sense, so one more such undertaking makes little difference! Turn the schedule around. Let us start with an application and place the student in a situation in which he is trying to find some result that has meaning to him. If he finds himself blocked in this, *then and only then* let us provide the new knowledge he needs.

Thus, the work is of consequence to the student because he *needs* and, what is more important, *wants* to know. Consequently, the teaching task, which is often thought of as preparing the student to deal with what is coming, becomes an act of creating situations in which the student will need and want to learn in order to successfully complete the tasks before him.

Young teachers often introduce a new topic in mathematics with a brief story of great interest to students. This is one way to gain student attention and involvement in a lesson. However, too often these situations of interest are only part of the first 5 minutes of the lesson. As soon as the mathematical statement is derived, the remainder of the lesson is devoted to work with mathematical abstractions. Who has not heard mathematics students give an audible groan of disappointment as a story of vital concern is eventually resolved in a symbolic mathematical statement? If such a tale is used to create interest, it is most important that a thread of the story continues throughout a major portion of the lesson. In this way we will not be in the position of "sugar coating" ideas for youngsters and encouraging their feelings of the uselessness of mathematics. As with games, stories involved in our lessons must have some important connection with the mathematics in question.

Development

Once we have developed a useful activity, involved the students and aroused their interest, we are faced with the problems of maintaining their interest and involvement and developing the lesson of the day. We then consider, What will the students be required to do as the lesson develops? We may assume that the greater the variety of activities, the greater the probability of realizing the desired learnings. Thus, we might ask ourselves: Will the students have to sit still and listen? Will they be required to listen and speak in answer to questions? Will they listen, speak, and work at their desks on the tasks provided? Will they manipulate materials or observe films or film strips? Will they construct some materials of their own?

There are endless possibilities. Sitting and watching may be satisfactory part of the time, but this is only one of the large variety of possible classroom actions. A change of pace in activity would also seem to offer a good opportunity to maintain a high level of student interest.

Whatever the topic, it would seem most important for each child to have the chance to come to grips with the ideas of the day by himself before he leaves the classroom—that is to say, before he attempts such work at home. How many times have we, as students, followed the clear, logical explanations of our mathematics professors only to sit down at home later to discover that we are unable to begin to attack the first problem! Explanations and developments of ideas by teachers are clear when they are observed, but unless the student has the opportunity to try to complete the work himself, he literally does not know what questions to ask. Offering work time in class provides the student with an opportunity to find out where he may need help—at a time when you are available to provide the help required. The teacher may circulate around the room and get direct "feedback" from students as to how much they have been able to grasp and offer individual assistance. Encouraging students to work together during this block of time also provides aid for those in need and builds the confidence of those offering the aid.

Upon the completion of such a work session, it may be useful for the students to take a look together at some of the areas that proved difficult. Thus, a rough spot is revisited with the hope that this additional discussion may clarify concepts that were not readily understood by all. Such findings may lead to the later development of additional lessons in the pertinent area.

Summary and Review

The class may be concluded with an activity which pulls together all the important ideas discussed and provides the basis for the suceeding day's work. Rather than a simple restatement of ideas, such an activity might involve the presentation of a problem that contains all the desired ingredients. Another such activity might be an oral or written true-false quiz that tests what has been learned and that is *not* used for grading. A game or group of puzzles that contain the mathematical ideas can also be played or replayed at this time. Moreover, it is possible that student-constructed problems could be presented for class consideration—depending upon the mathematics under consideration. Whatever is undertaken should provide something more than a simple rehashing of ideas.

An example of a typical daily lesson developed along these lines follows:

Sample Daily Lesson Plan

Topic: Congruence

Aims: 1. Knowledge of the corresponding parts of equal triangles that are sufficient to establish congruence.
2. The ability to use the concept of congruence.

Method:

Beginning Activity (time—10 min)

Problem: To find the distance across a pond, a boy put stakes at points A and B and at a convenient point, C. Walking along BC, he put another stake at D so that $BC = CD$. He did the same at E so that $AC = CE$. Will DE provide the distance wanted? (See Figure 2.4) Discuss to clarify what is happening. Discuss student-presented solutions.

Figure 2.4
Is $DE = AB$?

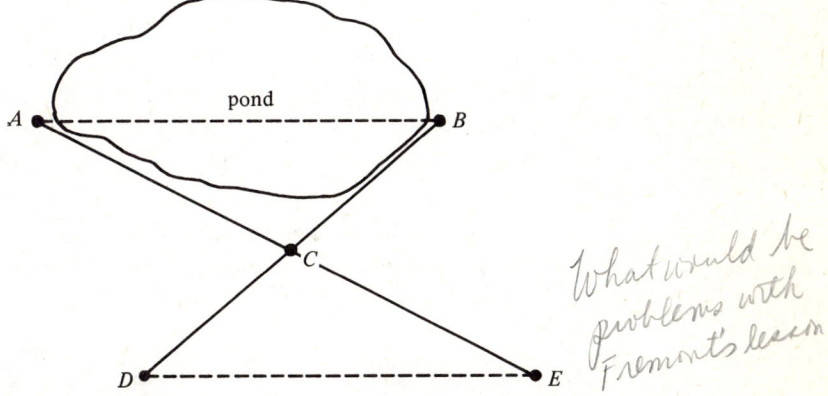

What would be problems with Fremont's lesson.

Development (time—25 min)
1. How can we solve the problem? Make a diagram of the geometric situation, construct triangles to scale using a compass and ruler, and measure.
2. Apply same method to new triangles—same situation but different measures. Does method still work?
3. Measure angles between equal sides. Conclusions?
4. Place a large scalene triangle on board. Ask students to make an accurate scale drawing. What measures do you want? Is one side enough? (Have a student measure this.) Are two sides enough? Are two sides and an angle between enough? Conclusions?

Summary and Review (time—10 min)
1. Will any three measures "fix" the triangle? Have students measure any desired parts of given triangle and attempt to construct desired congruent triangle.
2. Present oral true-false quiz.
   Sample questions:
   Can I construct the triangle on the board to scale if I have the following measures: Three sides? Three angles? Any two sides and any angle? Any two angles and any side? Two sides and the angle between?
3. After all questions are read and responded to, ask students to indicate question by question (by show of hands) whether they answered true or false.

2.3 A Restatement and the Four Freedoms

We have considered the development of a way of life for the daily operation of our mathematics classrooms. Among the ideas emphasized were the following:

1. Definitions should result from experiences with the concepts, rather than becoming a starting point.
2. Instead of teaching skills that will be needed later, we should place the student in a situation in which he feels the need. Then teach to satisfy that need.
3. Applications should be used in the beginning to arouse interest, as well as throughout the development.
4. Each lesson should begin with some attempt to create interest through the use of games, puzzles, and applications, provided that these activities have the desired mathematics as an inherent part.
5. The student should be involved in as many different kinds of activities (listening, speaking, writing, and doing, for example) as feasible to maintain a high degree of involvement and to provide for his abilities.
6. Time should be allowed for each student to work with the new ideas alone to aid him in asking intelligent questions.
7. We should develop summary activities that are more than mere restatements of ideas.

There are some additional "ground rules" that should be examined before we close this section. These considerations will not be found in lesson or unit plans, and yet they involve our daily interaction with our students. They are concerned with the climate of the room, and perhaps we may call these the four freedoms of the mathematics classroom. They are: the freedom to make mistakes, the freedom to ask questions, the freedom to think for one's self, and the freedom to choose methods of solution.

The Freedom to Make Mistakes

Whenever a student makes an error in a mathematics class, he feels that he has committed some mortal sin or, at the least, that he has done something terribly wrong. At all costs, he must try never to make mistakes. This is a rather curious notion, for if our students did not make mistakes and in fact knew all the correct answers, there really would not seem to be any purpose in their coming to class. They are in school to learn. Not knowing is, therefore, a natural state of being and not a wrong one. It is only through student declarations of what is not understood that we as teachers gain insight into what has to be done to help. Thus, we must be fairly certain that our classroom atmosphere, above all, poses no direct threat to the student so that he is free to err and that, in so doing, he aids the progress of all.

In addition, we want our students to feel free to guess, to try out ideas, and in short, to use their intuition without fear of recrimination. When a student feels that every answer he gives must be a correct one, he is much too guarded in his thinking. Let us be sure to keep our classroom atmosphere ripe for the development of "adventurous" thinking. To do this we honor and accept all thoughts and, at the least, congratulate the student for sharing a feeling of his with the class. In this way there shall be a minimum of limits placed by each student in the class upon his own imagination in dealing with mathematical problems.

Another way in which to assure this freedom is to do whatever possible to help students see the cause of their mistakes and to unobtrusively aid them in self-correction. By whatever means, students must feel that a mistake is but one step in the process that leads to learning.

The Freedom to Ask Questions

How many times have you been witness to a classroom situation in which a student is ridiculed because of a "silly" question? How many times have you seen a student virtually destroyed verbally because he has asked a question that was just answered by the teacher the moment before? Oftentimes, the very teacher who has done the ridiculing or who has wreaked verbal destruction upon a student makes periodical pleas to his students to be sure to ask questions, or else how will he know how his students are reacting to classwork? In this instance, as in many others, we cannot walk two sides of a street at the same time. If we are genuinely convinced that it is imperative for students to feel free to ask questions, then we must maintain an atmosphere conducive to questioning, an atmosphere that will allow each child to feel completely free to ask whatever may be of concern to him. One sure way to help develop such a climate is to honor each and every question posed—no matter how often repeated and no matter how minute a point may be involved. Make the questioner feel good for having asked. Everyone in your room will feel equally free to pose any question without fear of the question being silly or holding the class back. This is a vital freedom for effective, student-teacher relationships—effective in the sense of facilitating learning.

The Freedom to Think for One's Self

Earlier we discussed the effect of presenting model solutions to students with the resulting emphasis upon memorization. The student who is taught by use of these models is constantly asking himself, "How did the teacher do that one again?" rather than examining the information of the situation and trying to think through to the desired end. The unusually impossible answers that teachers find on test papers are one example of the fruits of this emphasis upon duplication. If we would, instead, devise situations in which the student is free to think for himself about the concepts contained therein, the student will then develop his own patterns of thought. This implies a readiness on the part of the teacher to not only accept but also reward the end product of this thought, even though it may not be of the same kind, quality, or preciseness as that of the teacher. This implies that the mathematical soundness of ideas will take precedent over elegance, precision, and conciseness of thought. Teachers are understandably reluctant to permit a student to struggle through a given situation on his own when tried and true short cuts can save time and energy. Certainly, this is well intentioned. But on the other hand, if one struggles with ideas, as one thinks for himself in attempts to solve whatever problem is before him and if his efforts result in his arriving at the desired end, a degree of satisfaction is present. This results in the strengthening of confidence in the ability to think through problems.

Rote memorization, necessary in some areas of mathematics, may be the greatest enemy of the continued development of mathematical thought in youngsters. It certainly gives our students a completely distorted view of the nature of mathematics itself. Encourage students to think by developing classroom situations that will afford the opportunity to do so.

The Freedom to Choose Methods of Solution

Closely allied with the freedom to think is the freedom to devise and employ one's own methods of solution in attacking mathematics problems. Most problems in mathematics can be approached in a wide variety of ways; no one way is necessarily better than any other. There seems to be an unwritten law that the fewer steps one requires to achieve a solution, the more elegant is that solution. It seems that the quickest route is thought to be best. This could be detrimental to the development of sound mathematical thought in youngsters. We often see teachers who are aware of the need of children to think for themselves putting many solutions to a given problem on the blackboard, side by side. This is an excellent technique for encouraging individual thought and adventurous thinking. But all too often this same teacher will then call the attention of the class to the solution that is completed in the fewest number of statements, indicating that since this is the shortest way; this is the way everyone should proceed! What makes a short solution better than a longer one? Placing solutions on the board together provides every student with an opportunity to see varieties of sound mathematical developments. Having done this, why not permit each student to choose for himself how he will approach this particular kind of problem? In this way, he is not forced into the position of having to recall what the teacher may say. He is free to fit the solutions to his own feelings of strength or weakness in mathematics. Allow each student to select his own path and you will be helping him to realize the importance of thinking about mathematics rather than trying to remember. Judge only the correctness of the mathematics and not the length of the demonstration. You may be rather pleasantly surprised at the quality and variety of student responses when students are free to think for themselves and devise their own appropriate solutions to problems.

Organizing classroom experiences that emphasize student originality in thought and problem solution will be developed in each area in the next section of this book.

For Investigation and Discussion

1. Write a lesson plan for the introduction of directed numbers to an average ninth grade class in elementary algebra.
2. Write a lesson plan for a topic in plane geometry of your own choosing.
3. Construct three ways in which a lesson for average eighth graders studying ratio and proportion may be started in order to catch student interest. Develop only the introductory part of the lesson.
4. Do the same for a topic of your own choosing from algebra or geometry.

5. Evaluate the plans just made by comparing with the general goals stated at the beginning of this chapter.
6. Discuss the use of applications and whether they should be introduced before, during or after skills and concepts are taught.
7. Devise ways in which to develop the *need to learn* on the part of the student.
8. Discuss the "four freedoms" described in this chapter and compare with your own experiences as a student.

For Further Reading

Books

Butler, Charles H.; F. Lynwood Wren, and J. Houston Banks. *The Teaching of Secondary Mathematics*. 5th ed. New York: McGraw-Hill, 1970, pp. 158-167.

Periodicals

Albrecht, Mary E. "A Teacher Plans Her Day," *The Arithmetic Teacher*. Vol. 3 (October 1956), pp. 151-156.

Brumfiel, Charles. "Using a Game as a Teaching Device," *The Mathematics Teacher*. Vol. 67 (May 1974), pp. 386-391.

Crouse, Richard. "Ripley's Believe It or Not—A Source of Motivational Incentives," *The Mathematics Teacher*. Vol. 67 (February 1974), pp. 107-109.

Eisenberg, T. A. and J. G. Van Beynen. "Mathematics Through Visual Problems," *The Arithmetic Teacher*. Vol. 20 (February 1973), pp. 85-90.

Farrell, Margaret A. "An Intuitive Leap or An Unscholarly Lapse?" *The Mathematics Teacher*. Vol. 68 (February 1975), pp. 149-152.

Fielker, David S. "Editorial," *Mathematics Teaching*. No. 77 (December 1976), pp. 2-3.

Giles, Geoff. "Does Teaching Inhibit Learning?" *Mathematics Teaching*. No. 65 (December 1973), pp. 33-38.

Johnson, David R. "The Element of Surprise: An Effective Classroom Technique," *The Mathematics Teacher*. Vol. 66 (January 1973), pp. 13-16.

Nemecek, Paul M. "Stimulating Pupil Interest," *School Science and Mathematics*. Vol. 65 (January 1965), pp. 47-48.

Ranucci, Ernest R. "Fruitful Mathematics," *The Mathematics Teacher*. Vol. 67 (January 1974), pp. 5-14.

Reys, Robert E. "Considerations for Teachers Using Manipulative Materials," *The Arithmetic Teacher*. Vol. 18 (December 1971), pp. 551-558.

Sobel, Max A. "Junior High School Mathematics: Motivation Versus Monotony," *The Mathematics Teacher*. Vol. 68 (October 1975), pp. 479-485.

White, Alvin M. "Beyond Behavioral Objectives," *American Mathematical Monthly*. Vol. 82 (October 1975), pp. 849-850.

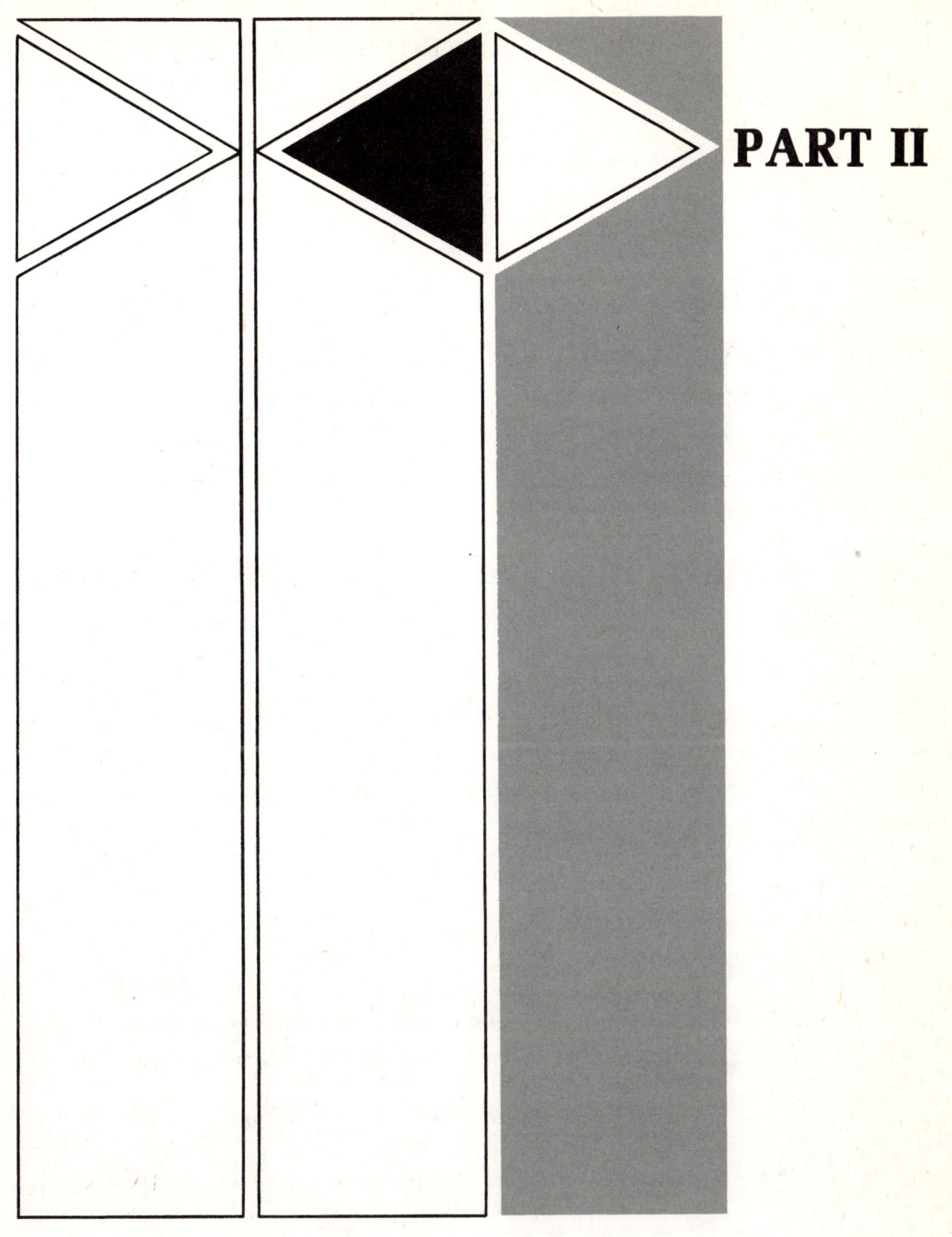

PART II

The Teaching of Mathematics

SECTION I

Mathematics and the Environment

CHAPTER 3

Mathematics and Our Limited Resources

Most of us are familiar with the need to protect our limited resources. A significant way for students to learn mathematics and to understand its vital role in our everyday lives is to study the environment. We will begin by examining air and water use and abuse.

When we think of running out of air or water, we encounter a concept that defies belief. Don't we have more air than we shall ever need? Doesn't water cover most of the surface of our planet? Aren't these resources infinite for all intent and purposes? Considering these questions, we have an excellent opportunity to make significant use of mathematical concepts and skills, including:

Calculations to determine how much of each resource we have;

Construction of tables and graphs to explore important aspects of these resources;

Clarification of the concept of infinity as opposed to a very large quantity;

Introduction to the concepts of scientific notation, exponents, metric measures, equation solution.

3.1 *Mathematics of the Air Supply*

How much useable air do we have?

We know that our planet is surrounded by a shield called the atmosphere, which screens the harmful ultraviolet rays out of the sunshine making life possible on Earth. Although the atmosphere may extend hundreds of miles into space, most of the useable air is contained in the troposphere, which averages about 8 miles in height above the Earth (Figure 3.1). We shall focus on this part of the atmosphere.

Figure 3.1
A picture of the troposphere (useable air).

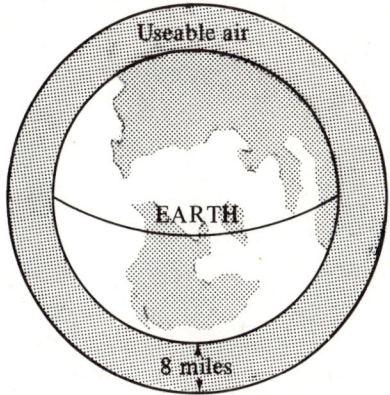

Radius of earth ≈ 4000 miles

Using 4000 miles as the radius of the earth and $V = \frac{4}{3}\pi r^3$ for the volume of a sphere, find the amount of useable air available to us.

How shall we proceed? One plan consists of finding the volumes of the two spheres and subtracting. In carrying out these calculations, the student quickly becomes aware of the tedious nature of operating with large numbers. This is an excellent time for the introduction of exponents and the use of scientific notation. Compare the solutions given in Table 3.1 (see page 26).

Throughout this process, it is important for students to be free to think through solutions on their own. In addition, the use of approximations in problem solving may be discussed and encouraged. Degree of accuracy is still another mathematical concept that may be considered.

Once an answer is calculated, we confront the question: What does it mean? In this case the answer is approximately $2.0 \times 10^9 \text{mi}^3$. Written out, this is a rather large number: 2,000,000,000 mi^3 which sounds like a lot of available air. But how can we make the figure more manageable? How many people live on the earth? How much air is that per person? Perhaps a better understanding will result from this comparison. World population is approaching 4 billion people, useable air is about 2 billion mi^3. Hence we have about ½ mi^3 of air per person! Does the amount of air now sound infinite in quantity? Other questions you might want to consider include:

> The air must be shared with other living things. What other life forms require air?
>
> Are there any other users of air? (Industry, utilities, transportation, etc.)
>
> How does the air over a large city compare with that over a farm area? Why?

The total weight of the entire atmosphere has been calculated to be 5×10^{15} tons. This is another way to examine quantity.

Table 3.1 Calculations for Volume.

Using Exponential Form	Without Exponents

Volume of Earth:

$V = \frac{4}{3}\pi r^3$	$V = \frac{4}{3}\pi r^3$
Use: $\pi = 3.14$, $r = 4000$	Use: $\pi = 3.14$, $r = 4000$
$V = \frac{4}{3}(3.14)(4000)^3$	$V = \frac{4}{3}(3.14)(4000)^3$
$= 4.18\ (4 \times 10^3)^3$	$= 4.18(64,000,000,000)$
$= 4.18 \times 64 \times 10^9$	$V = 267,520,000,000\ mi^3$
$V = 267.52 \times 10^9\ mi^3$	

Volume of Earth and Troposphere:

$V = \frac{4}{3}\pi r^3$	$V = \frac{4}{3}\pi r^3$
$V = \frac{4}{3}(3.14)(4008)^3$	$V = \frac{4}{3}(3.14)(4008)^3$
$\approx 4.18(64.38 \times 10^9)$	$= 4.18 \times 64,384,768,512$
$\approx 269.11 \times 10^9\ mi^3$	$= 269,128,463,380.16$
	$\approx 269,128,463,000\ mi^3$

Volume of Troposhere:

$V_{e+t} - V_e$	
$= 269.11 \times 10^9 - 267.52 \times 10^9$	$269,128,463,000$
$= 1.59 \times 10^9\ mi^3$	$- 267,520,000,000$
	$1,608,000,000\ mi^3$

▶ To get an idea of how the atmosphere thins out with its height above the Earth, half of its weight is within 3½ miles above the Earth. How much weight is that?

Seventy-five percent of the total weight of the atmosphere is within 7 miles of the Earth's surface. How much weight is that?

One percent of the total weight of the atmosphere lies above 20 miles over the Earth's surface. How much weight is that?

The atmosphere is made up of a mixture of nitrogen, about 77%, and oxygen, about 21%, plus small amounts of carbon dioxide, argon and some other gasses.

▶ If there is about ½ mi³ of air per person, and only 21% of that is oxygen, how much oxygen per person is available? (Do not count various uses.)

How much oxygen is contained in the troposphere (height about 8 miles)? How much nitrogen?

If you find student interest in this topic high, you may want to construct additional problems using the information in Table 3.2 and Figure 3.2. The study of our air offers a rich area for mathematical skill and concept development. In addition, it provides for an interplay of various branches of mathematics, allowing the student to become personally aware of the significance of mathematics as well as the importance of the problems themselves. This discussion can also lead to class and individual projects. Extensive use can be made of a variety of sources, and statistics can be given a prominent role in presenting findings. Most important, however, is the opportunity to teach students how to look at information, what questions to ask about information, and how to check out sources. Some references are listed at the end of the chapter. The work may be extended to other resources such as land, water, natural gas, oil, etc. The following example, concerning the use of water, involves a more personal kind of exploration than has been made with the study of air.

Table 3.2 Sources of Air Pollution.

Sources	Millions of Tons of Pollution Per Year				
	Carbon Monoxide	Sulphur and Nitrogen	Hydrocarbons	Particulants	Total
Motor vehicles (cars, trucks, . . .)	65	8	18	1	92
Factories and power plants (utilities, mills, . . .)	12	38	5	17	72
Garbage disposal and miscellaneous (each person creates approximately 1800 lb of waste per year)	17	2	4	4	27
Total	94	48	27	22	91

From *Pollution: Problems, Projects, Mathematical Exercises, Grades 6–9*. Wisconsin Department of Public Instruction and Wisconsin Mathematics Council, Bulletin No. 1082, pp. 71.

Figure 3.2 CO_2 budget of the Earth's atmosphere.

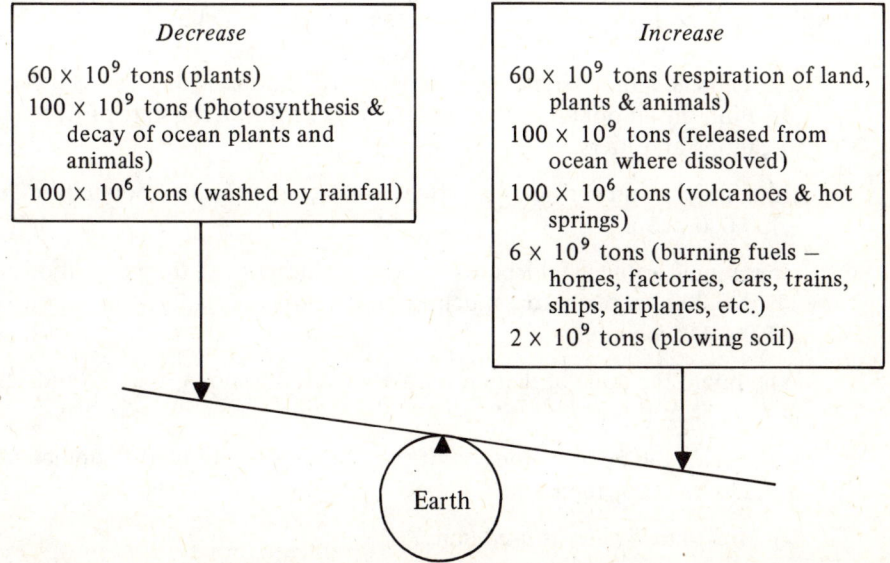

From Wisconsin Dept. of Public Instruction and the Wisconsin Mathematics Council. *Pollution: Problems, Projects, and Mathematical Exercises, Grades 6–9*. Bulletin No. 1082, p. 44.

3.2 Mathematics of Water Conservation

Are you wasting part of the water supply?

In the study of available air, we considered global conditions. We now make the work more personal and confront the student with wasteful practices that are individual responsibilities. Table 3.3 lists some everyday activities that involve the use of water. The water is given in liters and gallons, so that the student can gain experience with the metric system. Using Table 3.3, you may work on the following problems:

▶ What percent of the total daily use of water is spent for each item? Which has the largest percent? Which has the smallest?

Make a circle graph to represent the daily water use per person.

In what ways might you be able to save water?

How much water do you use in a week? A month? A year?

Table 3.3 Average Daily Water Use Per Person.

Purpose	Gallons	Liters
Flushing toilets	24.6	82
Washing, bathing	22.2	74
Kitchen use, drinking	6.6	22
Cleaning house, clothing	4.2	14
Washing car, watering garden	2.4	8
Total	60.0	200

Adapted from Thomas R. Brehman. *Environmental Demonstrations, Experiments and Projects for the Secondary School.* West Nyack, New York: Parker Publishing Co., 1973, p. 141. (This table uses 1 liter = .3 gal.)

Answers to these questions give information about one person. Imagine what will happen to the quantities of water on a nationwide basis.

▶ Use Table 3.3 and assume the population of Kansas to be 2,250,000 people. Find the amount of water used daily by people in the state of Kansas, in gallons and liters.

How much water would be used in Michigan if the population is 9,150,000 people?

How much water would be used daily in the U.S. if the population is 205,000,000 people? How much in North America if the population is 315,000,000 people?

Why might the table of daily water use (Table 3.3) not apply to countries in Europe and Asia?

If the chart did apply to the rest of the world and if the world population is 3,550,000,000, then:

(a) How much water is used daily?
(b) What percent of the world's use of water is taken up by the United States?

(c) What percent of all the water used in North America is taken up by the United States?

The numbers are staggering and begin to give students a sense of the enormity of the problem.

Table 3.4   Estimated Water Use 1940–1980 (Billions of Liters).

Year	Irrigation	Utilities	Domestic	Industrial	Total
1940	269	126	12	110	516
1950	379	227	17	144	767
1960	511	457	23	232	1222
1970	451	560	16	211	1239
1980 (projected)	514	859	18	284	1675

From *Statistical Abstract of the United States.* 96th Annual Edition. Washington, D.C.: Bureau of the Census, 1975, pp. 179.

Table 3.4 shows how much water is used for various purposes each day in the U.S. in billions of liters. We can see from this table that the huge amounts of water tallied in considering daily water use per person are only a small part of the total water use! The following problems may add a sense of perspective:

What percent of the water used in the U.S. in 1970 was for domestic use?

How does the change in domestic use from 1940 to 1970 compare with the change in total use?

In 1940, for what purpose was the greatest amount of water used? In 1970, for what purpose was the greatest amount of water used? How can you account for such a change?

By 1980, which of the 4 categories will show the largest percent increase over 1940? Which is the smallest? How can you explain why this happened?

In addition it may be well to consider the following:

For each year given, find the ratio of domestic use to use for irrigation and then for industry.

Why does the use of water generally continue to increase each year?

What percent of the projected use for 1980 will be for domestic use? Irrigation? Industrial? Utilities?

If domestic users save water will the total amount used be off sharply? Why?

Where does our water supply come from?

Mathematics can help students begin to gain a feel for exactly what the situation is with these vital life resources. What is more important for our purpose is that through this work the students can increase their skills in and understanding of

Multiplication and division of large numbers

Ratio, percent, and proportion

Interpreting and using data

Problem solving

to identify a few of the mathematical ideas encountered. The problems are real so the mathematics used becomes real. Table 3.5 offers additional information about which you can formulate your own problems.

Table 3.5 Facts Needed to Compute Each Person's Share of Earth's Water.

Earth's water supply:	109,000,000,000 gal = 4.12×10^{11} liters
World population:	3,616,000,000 people
Area of Earth covered by oceans:	139,356,000 mi^2 = 3.60×10^8 km^2
Average ocean depth:	12,451 ft = 3.79 km
Percent of Earth's water in oceans:	92%

The data in each of these charts is estimated data and will vary with the source, which enables us to emphasize another important concept: question the sources of information closely before using data to draw conclusions. Here are some additional projects to consider:

▶

Check your faucets at home. If there is a drip, place a measuring cup under it and see how much water you can collect in 10 minute intervals. Make a table of your results and draw a graph of the data. Try to find a pattern in the data and describe the relationship between time and water collected with a formula. Make predictions and check them by working with formulas.

If you let the water run while brushing your teeth, place a measuring cup under the faucet to see how much water is wasted. From this, figure out how much water you waste in a week, month and year. Figure out how much water your entire family may be wasting over the same time period. Make a table and graph of this information.

3.3   The Metric System

Most of the world uses the metric system of measurement rather than the English system currently in use in our society and in our schools. The U.S. Congress has passed laws that will eventually bring about the popular use of the metric system. Mathematics teachers have a major share of the responsibility for helping students gain familiarity and mastery of this system.

There has long been a unit in the junior high school mathematics curriculum concerned with conversions between the English and metric systems. This has not been one of the more popular units for students. Perhaps our obsession with the conversion of units has caused most of the grief students experienced. It may be better to organize experiences that require students to work in the metric system and deemphasize the conversion of units.

For example, we can begin by employing metric measures of familiar numbers:

> How tall are you?
> How long is your arm length?
> What is the size of your waist line?
> How long is your foot?
> What is your neck size?
> How long is your desk? How wide?
> How long is your math book? How wide?
> How high is a milk container?

These are a few of the kinds of questions that may be asked. Using metric tape measures, steel rules, meter sticks and rulers the students can work in the system and begin to develop a sense for lengths of common objects. We can extend these experiences by moving into ratio, percent, and proportion, as well as statistics and other topics by addressing such questions as:

> What is the ratio of your foot length to your height?
> How does your waist size compare with your height?
> What is the average height of the boys in the class? The girls?
> What is the average length of the girls' feet? The boys?
> What percent of the class is over 150 cm tall? What percent is under 150 cm tall?

This work may be followed by considering larger lengths and distance measures. Measures of the schoolroom, the building, distances drawn to scale making use of European road maps, teacher-made maps, and foreign guide books may all be employed to provide a rich collection of meaningful metric measures, as we move from centimeters to meters and kilometers. For example:

> How long is the classroom? How wide?
> How long is the school building? How wide?
> How long is a football field?
> What is the distance between bases on a baseball field?
> Select 2 cities on the map. How many kilometers is it from one to the other?
> Is it further from New York to Los Angeles or from New York to Shannon, Ireland?

Once distance measures have been established, it is natural to move into consideration of speeds in metric terms and a host of familiar motion problems. In doing this we encounter measures of meters per second (m/sec), meters per hour (m/hr), kilometers per hour (km/hr):

How fast does a person walk? (Use a stop watch and a fixed metric distance.)

Can a person ride a bicycle at the rate of 10 km/hr?

If a car on an interstate highway travels at 70 km/hr, is it over the speed limit?

Will an airplane flying at 800 km/hr break the sound barrier?

Students can be asked to make their own rulers containing both the metric and English measures side by side. (Figure 3.3). Stiff cardboard or heavy oaktag may be used. You will find that the construction of the ruler is an important learning experience in itself. Later the ruler may be used to answer questions and will offer students a ready reference for the meaning of a given metric measure in English units. Over the course of time, an intuitive sense for metric lengths will develop as the student begins to "think" metric.

Figure 3.3

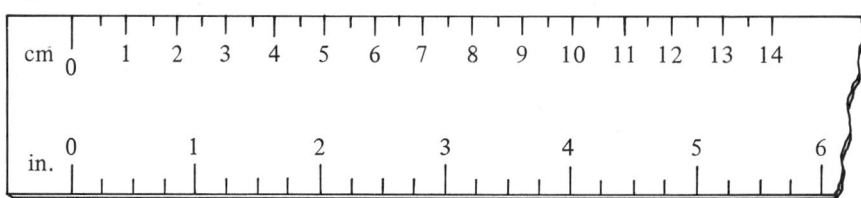

In much the same manner as that outlined above, we may develop activities with liquid measures and measures of weight. On a recent trip to Europe the following ready reference chart was given to American tourists:

1 cm	≈ .4 in.	$1 \text{ m}^2 \approx 11 \text{ ft}^2$
1 m	≈ 1.1 yd	$1 \text{ m}^3 \approx 35 \text{ ft}^3$
1 km	≈ 0.6 mi	
1 liter	≈ 0.3 gal	*Tire Pressure*
0.5 liters	≈ 1.1 pt	$1 \text{ kg/cm}^2 \approx 14.2 \text{ lb/in.}^2$
		$30 \text{ lb/in.}^2 \approx 2.1 \text{ kg/cm}^2$
100 g	≈ 3.5 oz	
1 kg	≈ 2.2 lb	

Using such a chart, the teacher may construct a broad variety of questions and activities. It is also an excellent practice to have students make up their own questions. To construct a question, the student must understand the units.

When our goal becomes an intuitive feel for the unit size and the ability to think metric as opposed to precise unit conversion, the nature of classroom experiences change. We can develop this "feel" by inviting students to test for the reasonableness of given measures.

Would you say each of these measures is reasonable or unreasonable?
(a) The cat's tail is 30 cm long.
(b) The husband is 20 cm taller than his wife.
(c) The heavyweight wrestler weighed 100 km.
(d) It was 25 °C outside, so I put on my overcoat.[1]

If these questions are answered using only metric measuring tools without conversion, students will begin to gain an intuitive sense of metrics. For example, although the initial reaction of American tourists abroad is to convert to English units, they soon begin to operate with the new metric measures.

Because measurement experiences are important as we measure particular things rather than as a topic in and of itself, all metric experiences are not grouped in a single section. Instead, metric measures will be highlighted as they occur in a multitude of mathematical experiences. For example, the work with water supply involved billions of liters of water. Later, as we explore the mathematics of dieting, we will find that the kilogram is a convenient unit. We use measurement rather than set it aside as a topic by itself. This approach was eloquently supported by King and Whitman in a recent study,

> Our experiences have convinced us that measurement should not, and in fact cannot, be 'taught.' Learning to measure is a gradual process related to the personal experiences of each learner.[2]

In the course of our work, measurement will occur naturally often enough to provide a multitude of important experiences to help students towards mastery.

One last word about metric measures. Students may more easily remember the relationships between units if we point out how consistent this system is with our base 10 numeration system. The prefixes of the metric names indicate this and apply to all metric measure:

*Kilo*meter = 1000 meters   *Milli*meter = .001 meter
*Kilo*gram = 1000 grams   *Milli*gram = .001 gram
*Kilo*liter = 1000 liters   *Milli*liter = .001 liter

If the students learn the meaning of the prefixes (many of which are familiar), they will be better able to deal with the units (see Figure 3.4). The variable base English system

12 in. = 1 ft
3 ft = 1 yd
1760 yd = 1 mi

is replaced with the consistent system of tens.

Figure 3.4

*kilo*meter	*hecto*meter	*deka*meter	*meter*	*deci*meter	*centi*meter	*milli*meter
1000	100	10	1	.1	.01	.001

To add to the importance of metrics and to ease some of the strangeness, we can point out some places where metric measures are currently in use in the U.S.:

- Science experiments and reports
- Auto parts and tools
- Track and field events
- Thermometers
- Medical prescriptions
- Electricity usage

Auto engine sizes

Postage stamp sizes

The students themselves may well add to this list once they are alerted to the metric system and know what to look for.

3.4 *Mathematics and the Conservation of Energy*

How much electricity do I use and what does it cost?

What role do students and their families play in the use of energy, particularly electricty?

We hear a good deal about conserving electricity, turning off lights, using fewer electrical applicances, keeping our homes cooler in winter. Just how much can we save? What does this mean in terms of the overall supply of electricity and in terms of dollars and cents? Table 3.6, which appeared in an interesting article in *The Arithemetic Teacher*[3], helps us to answer some of these questions.

We begin by asking students to list all appliances found in the home and to approximate the amount of electricity used by each. We describe usage in kilowatt hours. The use of this new unit of measure helps reenforce previous work with metric units. A 100-kilowatt bulb that burns for 10 hours uses 1 kilowatt of electricity. A 50-kilowatt bulb burns for 20 hours and also uses 1 kilowatt of electricity. The following questions may help students to better understand just what a kilowatt hour is.

▶
How long would a 25-watt bulb have to burn to consume 1 kilowatt? (40 hr)

A light bulb must burn 20 hours to use up 1 kilowatt of electricity. How many watts is the bulb?

Which uses more electricity, a 60-watt bulb that burns for 14 hours, or a 75-watt bulb that burns for 11 hours?

On the package for 100-watt bulbs, it states that the bulb has an average life of 750 hours. How many kilowatts will that bulb use on the average?

Once the students feel comfortable with the units, they may complete their survey of home use of electricity and organize their information into tables and graphs depending upon the area of mathematics emphasized. Students may be asked to find average usage over a period of time, compare uses with each other, combine data from the entire class and analyze. You may also discuss how to save and cut down energy usage. Such projected savings can be computed per student, per family, per class, among others. Since Table 3.6 offers both kilowatt and money data, the mathematical possibilities are plentiful. Some sample questions that may be posed using Table 3.6 are:

▶
How many kilowatts and how much money can be saved if a regular refrigerator is used instead of a frost-free type?

If you have a color and a black and white TV set, how much can be saved each month by using the black and white set all the time? By using it half the time?

Table 3.6 Consumption and Cost Per Month for Electricity

Usage	Appliance	Typical Energy Consumption (Kilowatt-Hours)	Cost
Heating, air conditioning	Home heating	1,930	$27.00
	Oil burner	50	1.50
	Furnace fan	100	3.00
	Room air conditioner	300	9.00
	Dehumidifier	67	2.00
	Humidifier	60	1.80
Lighting	5-room house (winter)	50	1.50
	6-room house (winter)	60	1.80
	8-room house (winter)	80	2.40
	Christmas lights	120	3.60
Cooking, refrigerating	Freezer (14 ft^2)	140	4.20
	Oven (microwave)	25	.75
	Oven (self-cleaning)	96	2.88
	Range	100	3.00
	Refrigerator	83	2.50
	Refrigerator/freezer (frostfree)	167	5.00
Laundry, hot water	Dryer	80	2.40
	Iron	13	.39
	Washer	9	.27
	Water heater (quick recovery)	183	5.50
TV, radio hi-fi	Hi-Fi	9	.27
	Radio	8	.24
	TV (black & white)	50	1.50
	TV (color)	100	3.00
Food preparation	Blender	1.25	.40
	Broiler	8	.25
	Carving knife	.66	.02
	Coffeemaker	8	.24
	Deepfryer	7	.21
	Dishwasher	30	.90
	Frying pan	15	.05
	Hot plate	7.5	.23
	Mixer	1	.03
	Toaster	3	.09
	Trash compacter	4	.12
	Waffle iron	2	.06
	Waste Disposer	2.5	.08
Health, beauty	Hair dryer	1	.03
	Heat lamp	1	.03
	Shaver	.15	.004
	Sun lamp	1.33	.04
	Electric toothbrush	.04	.001
Other	Battery charger	1	.03
	Blanket	22	.66
	Clocks (4)	6	.18
	Fan (circulating)	3.5	.11
	Fan (window)	14	.42
	Heating pad	1	.03
	Power tools (drill, sander)	3	.09
	Vacuum	4	.12
	Well pump (¾ hp)	20	.06

What does it cost to operate a room air conditioner for a week of 24 hour days? How much can you save if you only use it for sleeping (8 hours)?

What is the cost of operating Christmas lights for 5 hours a night for 10 days?

The students can construct questions of their own and eventually become involved in longer term projects should the interest warrant.

Besides illustrating how mathematics helps us to better understand our environment, these activities are designed to whet the appetite for more. For example, population growth, land use, food supply as well as other energy conservation areas such as natural gas, oil, coal, have not even been touched. The references provided offer you information in these areas as well as those described above.

When we present mathematics through the use of these problems, we involve many other disciplines: economics, biology, chemistry, physics, geology, sociology, to name a few. You may wish to arrange units of work together with teachers of other subjects. It is ironic that, in this age of specialization, we have rapidly become aware of the need for interdisciplinary cooperation to solve our most pressing problems. You will find that the only restriction on how much mathematics you can teach using the very real problems of pollution and conservation will be your own ingenuity.

Footnotes

1. See: Anton Glaser. *Neater by the Meter.* Published by Anton Glaser, 1237 Whitney Rd., Southhampton, Pa., 1974, p. 17.
2. See: Irv King and Nancy Whitman. "Going Metric in Hawaii," *The Arithmetic Teacher.* Vol. 20 (April 1973), p. 259.
3. Thomas R. Post. "The Energy Crisis: An Opportunity for Meaningful Arithmetical Excursions," *The Arithmetic Teacher.* Vol. 22 (January 1975), pp. 61-64.

For Investigation and Discussion

1. Select a topic from conservation and demonstrate how you would introduce this topic to students in order to emphasize basic mathematical skills.
2. Construct an outline for a lesson in air pollution that will clearly illustrate the importance of mathematics.
3. In the text it is stated that the branches of mathematics should be integrated for more effective learning. Devise a plan that gives a specific example of how this can be done.
4. Discuss the advantages and disadvantages of teaching mathematics emphasizing the relationship between different branches of mathematics.
5. State your opinion as to whether or not mathematics should be taught using an interdisciplinary approach. Provide specific reasons for your arguments.
6. You are to teach a unit on statistics at the junior high school level from data collection, to graphic presentation, to the drawing of conclusions. Describe how you would use home consumption of electricity to personalize the experience for each student.
7. Make a list of activities to help students gain experience with dry weights or liquid measures in the metric system similar to the examples of activities using distance and length measures offered in this chapter.

8. "Measurement should not be taught as a separate topic." Tell whether you agree or disagree with this statement and explain your reasons. Give specific illustrations.

For Further Reading

Books

Brehman, Thomas R. *Environmental Demonstrations, Experiments and Projects for the Secondary School.* West Nyack, New York: Parker, 1973.

De Bell, Garrett (ed.) *The Environmental Handbook.* New York: Ballantine Books, 1970.

Donovan, Frank. *Prepare Now for a Metric Future.* New York: Weybright and Talley, 1970.

Glaser, Anton. *Neater by the Meter.* Published by Anton Glaser, 1237 Whitney Rd., Southampton, Pa., 1974.

Leffin, Walter W. *Going Metric: Guidelines for the Mathematics Teacher, Grades K-8.* Reston, Va.: National Council of Teachers of Mathematics, 1975.

Leopold, Luna B. *Water, A Primer.* San Francisco: W.H. Freeman, 1974.

New York State Department of Environmental Conservation. *It Stacks Up!* Albany, New York. May, 1974.

Wisconsin Department of Public Instruction and the Wisconsin Mathematics Council. *Pollution: Problems, Projects, Mathematical Exercises. Grades 6-9.* Bulletin No. 1082.

Periodicals

The Arithmetic Teacher. Vol. 20 (April 1973), a special issue on Metrication.

Bracewell, Harry. "Using Water," *Mathematics Teaching.* No. 27 (Summer 1964), pp. 37-39.

Choate, Stuart A. "A Metric Bibliography," *The Mathematics Teacher.* Vol. 67 (November 1974), pp. 586-587.

Firl, Donald H. "The Move to Metrics: Some Considerations," *The Mathematics Teacher.* Vol. 67 (November 1974), pp. 581-584.

Hein, Harold C. "What's Your Share of the Earth's Air and Water Resources?" *School Science and Mathematics.* Vol. 72 (June 1972), pp. 469-470.

Henderson, George L. and Mary Van Beck. "Mathematics Educators Must Help Face the Environmental Pollution Challenge," *The Mathematics Teacher.* Vol. 64 (January 1971), pp. 33-36.

Henson, Kenneth T. "Principles of Conservation of Clean Air and Water Pertinent to the General Education Programs in Junior High School," *School Science and Mathematics.* Vol. 72. (January 1972), pp. 17-26.

Post, Thomas R. "The Energy Crisis: An Opportunity for Meaningful Arithmetic Excursions," *The Arithmetic Teacher.* Vol. 22 (January 1975), pp. 61-64.

Shumway, Richard J. and Larry Sachs. "Don't Just Think Metric—Live Metric," *The Arithmetic Teacher.* Vol. 22 (February 1975), pp. 103-110.

Yant, Sandra L. "Facing the Energy Crisis in a Mathematics Classroom," *The Arithmetic Teacher.* Vol. 23 (March 1976), pp. 223-224.

CHAPTER 4

Natural Laws and Mathematics

Mathematics, which brings complex relationships in nature to our attention, has often been called the "Queen and Servant of Science."[1] Let us explore this vital role played by mathematics with our students.

4.1 Motion Experiments

What child has not played with a ball, tossed it upward, let it drop, bounced it. Ask students to give some thought to what happens during this everyday activity.

▶
How fast does the ball fall?
Why is it that the ball comes down at all?
Why doesn't it keep on going up until it is out of sight?
What does it mean to say that the ball is falling?
Is it really falling or is it being pulled down?

Gravity and weightlessness are fascinating concepts to youngsters today in an era of moonwalks and space exploration. As we focus on the question of how fast things fall on or near the surface of the Earth, we have an excellent opportunity for scientific experimentation. A discussion of what scientists do, what is an experiment, how are experiments conducted, and what is meant by scientific observation should be a preamble to any such experiment. After the discussion, students can actually experiment to determine the speed of objects that are dropped.

Since this experiment is difficult to perform physically, we may use pictures or flip books (books whose pages are flipped to give the effect of motion) instead. If we decide to use flip books, they can readily be made on index cards. Each page should show a *t*-figure (time in seconds) and an *s*-figure (speed or velocity, used interchangeably here) in feet per second (Figure 4.1).

Figure 4.1

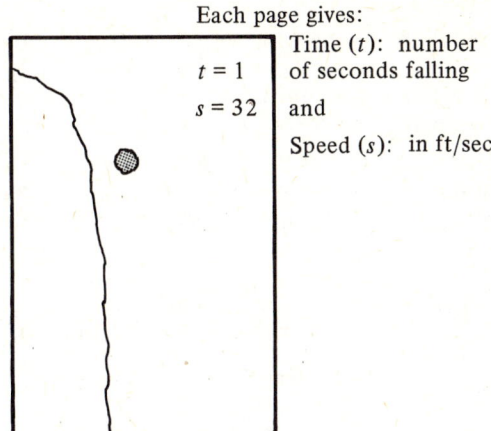

Each page gives:
Time (t): number of seconds falling
and
Speed (s): in ft/sec

If we choose pictures instead, the students may simply read the data from the pictures (Figure 4.2).

Figure 4.2
The speed of falling objects (ft/sec).

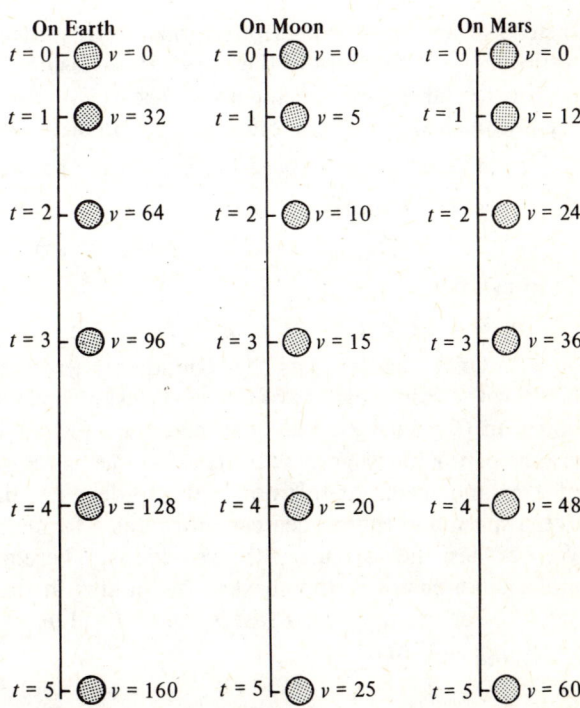

Whatever method is chosen, the problems and the procedures should be clear to all.

Assuming the use of flip books, flip the pages until you see the ball falling smoothly. Does it seem to go faster as it falls or slower? Guess. Now try to find out by checking the speed and time numbers on the pages.

How shall we record our data? (In a table.)

What values of time are convenient? ($t = 1, 2, 3, 4$)

What shall we do when we have the table of data? (Look for a pattern.)

How do we check patterns? (Test with table values for fit.)

If a pattern fits the table values, encourage students to describe the relationship in their table (Table 4.1) with words first and then with a formula. Any description is a good one if the table values fit. This is the only test to be made, and we emphasize the point that there is no one pattern that is best. The whole idea is to encourage students to think through these relationships for themselves.

Table 4.1

Time of Fall (in seconds) t	Speed (in ft/sec) n
0	0
1	32
2	64
3	96
4	128
5	160

Instead of any special description, take what students may find and put it to the test: does it fit the data in the table? Progressing from word description to formula often takes time for students to learn. Eventually it becomes easy if students are not pushed into it too quickly. One possible pattern is:

The amount of speed is 32 times the amount of time.

First cross out unnecessary words:

T̶h̶e̶ a̶m̶o̶u̶n̶t̶ o̶f̶ speed is 32 times t̶h̶e̶ a̶m̶o̶u̶n̶t̶ o̶f̶ time.

Then use symbols:

$$s = 32 \times t \quad \text{or} \quad s = 32t$$

Once a pattern has been found and described as a formula, a graph may be drawn to gain a picture of the relationship since pictures help us to see what is going on (Figure 4.3). This may be done by students in the manner of the line graphs of the lower grades. Little assistance is required except for identification of axes and scale. At this point, the student has described the relationship between speed and time in sentence form, as a formula, as a table, and as a graph. We now test the formula with predictions. These are carried out using the formula, table or graph and checked by looking at the flip book.

For example, how fast is the ball falling at 4½ seconds?

Using the formula:

$v = 32t$
$v = 32 \times 4½$
$v = 144$ ft/sec

Figure 4.3

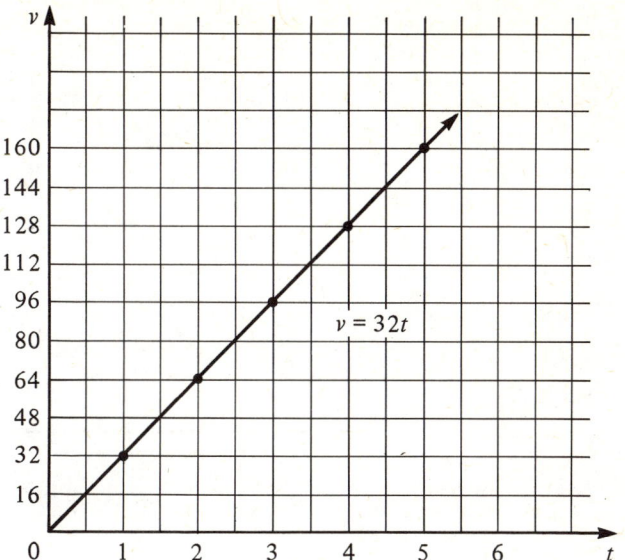

Using the table:

t	v
0	0
1	32
2	64
3	96

The table goes up by 32. So when $t = 4$,

$v = 96 + 32$ or   128.

Half of 32 is 16. For 4½ add 16 more.

```
   128
 + 16
   44  ft/sec
```

Using the graph (Figure 4.4; see page 42):

Find 4½ on the *t*-axis. Go up to the curve (Point *A*.) From this point, move across to the *v*-axis. You hit the *v*-axis at 144. Therefore,

$v = 144$ ft/sec

To check the work, find the flip book page with $t = 4½$ and read off the corresponding *v* value. It turns out to be 144, and the work checks. We have correctly predicted the outcome.

Metric measures may easily be used here. Instead of feet per second, we could make flip books using meters per second. Work with these units offers no greater difficulty than the English units.

Figure 4.4

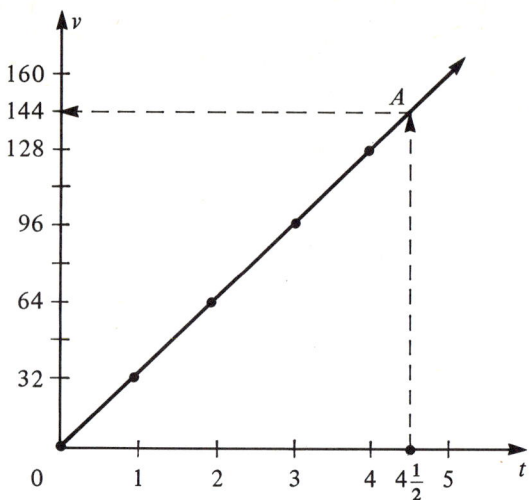

A beginning has been made in the solution of linear equations of form $y = ax$, and a rich bounty of mathematics evolves from the work. Other questions for prediction may include:

How fast is a ball falling after 2½ sec?
How fast is it falling after 5 sec?
How long will it take the ball to reach a speed of 24 ft/sec?
How long will it take to reach a speed of 112 ft/sec?

The student uses mathematics and as a result can predict how a falling object will behave! Incredible! Perhaps at last mathematics is coming alive.

After doing experiments, a discussion of the qualifications of the results is important so that students are not given a misleading impression. This experiment is a good case in point. As stated, the formula assumes that the object is falling in a vacuum, which is an idealized situation. The mathematical description itself is always an idealized description, and the teacher should remind students about these limitations as the work develops.

The motion experiment concerns one of the basic laws of nature on our planet. It also involves numbers that are larger and somewhat more difficult for computation and, therefore, can build student dissatisfaction with informal equation solution. In considering this relationship, some time should be devoted to a discussion of what the formula means, what is actually happening, what the symbols mean, and why the various symbols appear as they do. This should be true of any situation explored. As a new situation is considered and graphed and as linear equations are presented for solution, the teacher is providing built-in practice work for his students. For example, on Earth the acceleration due to gravity is approximately 32 ft/sec for each second of motion; hence the formula $v = 32t$. On the planet Mars, the formula for the speed of a dropped object would be $v = 12t$, since the pull of gravity is approximately 12 ft/sec for each second of motion. Table 4.2 gives the gravity figures for some of the better-known heavenly bodies. The teacher can build his own experiences using this information to assure a wealth of interesting practice experiences. For example:

If on Earth a boy drops a ball from the top of a building, how fast is the ball falling after 3 seconds? If the same motion is carried out on the moon, how fast is the ball falling?

On Earth a high school broad jumper can jump 17 feet. If he makes the identical jump on the moon, about how far would he jump? (Answer: about six times as far)

Table 4.2 Acceleration Due to Gravity.

Heavenly Body	Acceleration Due to Gravity, in ft/sec^2
Sun	900
Moon	5
Mars	12
Mercury	9
Venus	27
Saturn	35
Jupiter	80

Other problems of a similar nature can be constructed as needed.

An interesting question about the motion formula may also be considered:

If a ball of wood and a ball of steel were dropped from the top of a tall building, which would strike the ground first?

After some discussion and guessing, the following tables of data, which indicate the results of dropping the two balls in question, should be offered to students:

Wooden Ball

t	v
0	0
1	32
2	64
3	96

Steel Ball

t	v
0	0
1	32
2	64
3	96

Are there some mistakes? Why are the tables identical?

The mathematical formula includes everything important in the relationship. In this case, the velocity depends only upon the time of the fall. Whether the ball was made of a light or heavy substance has no effect. A sense of the significance of the formula and the symbols included is dramatically accomplished. The limitations mentioned earlier may be brought up here. A comparison can be made with the fall of a feather and a brick.

If student interest is high on these motion problems, the work may be extended into more advanced algebraic topics. The experimental procedures outlined above can be repeated, from the gathering of data to the making and checking of predictions. Some typical relationships follow:

$v = 32t + 10$ A ball thrown downward with initial speed of 10 ft/sec.

$v = 5t + 10$ A ball thrown downward on the moon with initial speed of 10 ft/sec.

$d = 16t^2$ The distance (d) traveled by a dropped object in t seconds.

$d = 16t^2 + 32t$ The distance traveled in feet (d) of an object thrown down with an initial velocity of 32 ft/sec after t seconds.

$v = 64 - 32t$ The speed (v) of an object tossed upward with initial speed of 64 ft/sec.

From this list, you can gain some insight into the mathematics of motion: introduction to linear and quadratic functions, the solution of linear and quadratic equations, and graphing these functions. The data of Table 4.2 provides the raw material for lots of practice. It makes possible the mathematical repetition necessary but with a changing locale that offers a fresh problem. A comparison of results offers additional understanding of these relationships since events on Earth can be compared with events on other planets.

Signed Numbers

The last formula offered, $v = 64 - 32t$, which describes the speed of an object thrown upward, deserves some special treatment. This is an interesting way to involve students with signed numbers.

If the ball is tossed at the rate of 64 ft/sec, it would continue to travel upward at that rate except for another force working on the ball, the force of gravity. We know that the acceleration due to gravity is about 32 ft/sec for each second the ball is in flight and that these two forces are operating in opposite directions. As a result, the pull of gravity will eventually slow the upward movement of the ball until it begins to fall back to earth. A downward throw resulted in an addition of forces. The upward thrust, therefore, results in their subtraction. The formula for this situation becomes $v = 64 - 32t$. Each second the ball is in the air, its upward motion is retarded 32 ft/sec. Eventually the motion will increase in speed *but in a downward direction* (Figure 4.5). We tabulate the velocities for this situation. Practice is provided with subtractions resulting in negative numbers:

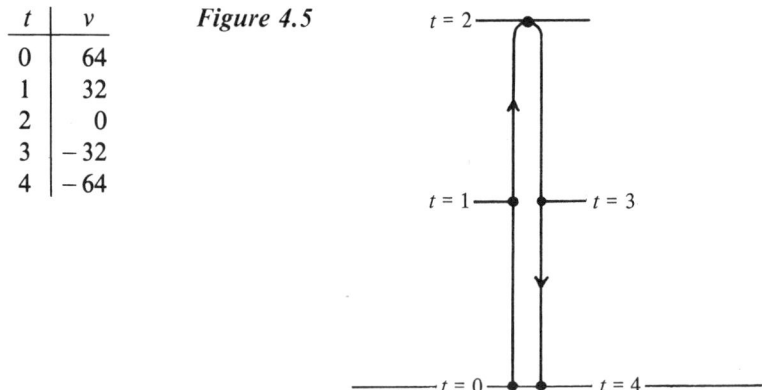

t	v
0	64
1	32
2	0
3	−32
4	−64

Figure 4.5

Some interesting questions arise. The ordered pair (2, 0) is included in the table; thus, the velocity is zero at the instant the ball has been in the air for 2 seconds. Where is the ball? Has it stopped? A lively discussion may develop.

Eventually, students will realize that the instant the direction of the ball changes from upward to downward it apparently has no velocity at all; it may be thought of as being suspended in space. Directly after that instant the ball begins to pick up speed again, this time in a downward direction. The mathematics used tells us precisely that, since these values are negative! A graph of the situation may be constructed; in this way students can get a "feel" for negative numbers.

Look at the motion of the ball as shown in Figure 4.5. How is the speed at 1 second different from that at 3 seconds? Both have the same magnitude (32) but they are different in direction (one positive, one negative). This concept of opposites should be emphasized with regard to negative numbers: The sign $-$, which we already know as an operation sign (subtraction), is now being used to indicate an opposite direction from the positive number of equal magnitude. What better way to emphasize the notion of opposites than to see positive used for upward motion and negative for downward?

We can explore other situations with the notion of opposites in mind: Above sea level is positive, below sea level is negative; profit is positive, losses are negative; temperature above zero is represented by positive numbers and temperature below zero is shown using negative numbers.

The number scale can be employed here to further emphasize the relationship of opposites. It may confuse students to see a familiar symbol of operation take on a new role, but after a while the interchangeability of uses for the subtraction sign will add to the student's power to use mathematics. Many textbooks and improvement programs in mathematics advocate a separation of operation and direction by changing the use of the symbol. One technique is to place a small addition or subtraction sign at the upper left-hand edge of the number; for example, $^+5$ or $^-8$; it is common to see examples such as $^+3 + {}^+9 =$. While this does eliminate the problem of two functions for a single sign, the use of these nonstandard symbols can become a crutch that is difficult to relinquish. But more important, this technique could inhibit the student's ability to decide whether the symbol is a sign of operation or a sign that indicates negative or positive.

The use of the number line at this point can dramatize the momentous step that has been taken by the introduction of negative numbers. We have extended our number system; that is, there are now as many negative numbers as positive ones. All of the arithmetic numbers are also called the positive numbers, with the two sets (the positives and the negatives) and zero forming the integers. If, at first, we introduce the arithmetic numbers as a subset of the integers rather than a completely new set, we are better able to build upon what the student already knows. Developing the skill necessary to use these numbers correctly will be done in Chapter 16.

The motion laws enable us to introduce students to a broad variety of important mathematics concepts and skills. At the same time, the student adds significant information to his understanding of the universe.

Mirrors and Mathematics   4.2

Another natural phenomenon that we experience but do not fully understand is the nature of light rays. Take a moment to reflect upon a world without the sun, or a world without the artificial light now available to us. Students will quickly realize the importance of light. The mathematics of light will offer a means for studying many concepts.

One successful approach is to think of light as traveling along in rays. Both sunlight through a window and the light from a flashlight seem to move through the air in straight lines that appear to be parallel. We can employ the tools of geometry to learn more about this basic natural phenomenon. We can also demonstrate directly an important reason for the study of geometry: The interaction of mathematics with the physical world results in advances in each area.

To clarify this, let us turn to some of the discoveries of the Greeks with regard to light as described by Euclid in his book *Optics*. Euclid observed what is now known as the law of reflection: If light rays strike a flat mirror, they are reflected so that the angle of incidence is equal to the angle of reflection. In Figure 4.6, a light ray from point A hits the mirror and is reflected to point B. Here $\angle 1$ is the angle of incidence (the angle made by the light ray and a perpendicular to the mirror surface as the light enters the mirror) and $\angle 2$ is the angle of reflection (the angle formed in the same manner as the ray leaves the surface of the mirror). Euclid observed that these angles were always equal. (Sometimes angles 3 and 4 are referred to as the angles of incidence and reflection. Since they too are equal, we may use either pair.)

Figure 4.6

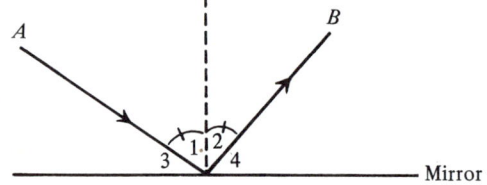

Using this basic law of light rays and the facts of geometry, we may add to our knowledge of each. When you look in a mirror, you see the reflection of objects. In the preceding situation, if you were at point B, as you looked into the mirror you would see the reflection of the object at A. The light rays from A spread out in all directions and strike the mirror at many points, each ray being reflected in accordance with the reflection law. How many rays are reflected from point A to you at point B? Here is a question that our knowledge of geometry can help us pursue. If fact, of all the rays only one such ray is reflected to point B. We may prove this using the indirect method:

Assume that there are many such rays reflected to the observer, and examine the logical consequences of this assumption. Using a geometric arrangement for this particular proposition, we proceed.

▶   *Prove:* There is but one light ray reflected from point A to the mirror to point B.

We Know: The angle of reflection must equal the angle of incidence. AP is a ray reflected to point B (Figure 4.7).

Assume there is another ray, AP', reflected to point B. Then $\angle 3 = \angle 4$ by the law of reflection. But this is impossible because $\angle 3$ is an exterior angle of $\triangle AP'P$; thus $\angle 3$ is greater than $\angle 1$. $\angle 2$ is an exterior angle of $\triangle BP'P$; thus $\angle 2$ is greater than $\angle 4$.

Figure 4.7

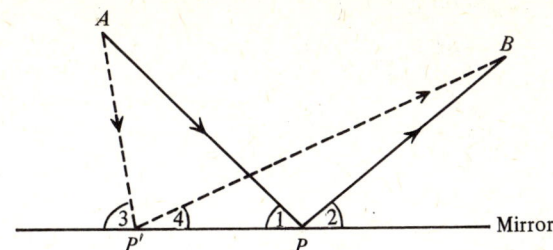

We now have contradictory statements:

∡3 > ∡1
∡2 > ∡4
∡1 = ∡2   (the reflection law)

So ∡3 must be greater than ∡4, and by the reflection law if ∡3 ≠ ∡4, $P'B$ cannot be the reflected ray of incident ray AP'.

We must therefore conclude that of all the rays from point A to the mirror, only one is reflected to you at point B because only one can satisfy the law of reflection!

> *Note:* The changes in notation resulting from the mathematics improvement programs of the late 1950's–early 1960's including
>
> $m∡A = m∡B$
>
> $\overrightarrow{AB}$: the ray with A as its end point and containing B.
>
> $\overleftrightarrow{AB}$: the line containing the two points A and B.
>
> $∡A \cong ∡B$: angle A is congruent to angle B.
>
> $\overline{BC} \cong \overline{DE}$: line segment BC is congruent to line segment DE.
>
> $d(A, C)$: the distance from point A to point C.
>
> will only be used here, as needed, to prevent misunderstandings.

We carry this investigation a step further and ask the following question about this light ray path: Of all the possible paths that may be followed to get from point A to the mirror to point B, how does this one compare? Is it the shortest? the longest? What do you think? Here is an excellent place to use measurement to gain insight into the relationship. The students may draw several different pathways from A to the mirror to B and measure each to see how they compare (Figure 4.8). The results are shown in a table such as Table 4.3.

Figure 4.8

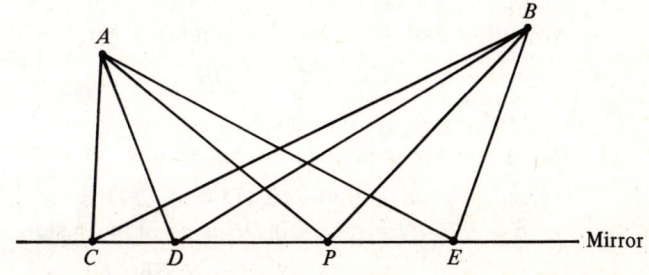

Table 4.3

Pathway	Measure
light ray *APB*	
ACB	
ADB	
AEB	
AFB	
etc.	

Of course, the student would have to construct the light ray path to be certain of the equality of the angles of incidence and reflection. This in itself is interesting practice. The other lines may be drawn with a straightedge. The diagram should also be large enough (cover an 8½ × 11 sheet) so that small differences of measure will be apparent. In this way the students may convince themselves of what the Greek mathematician Heron found (about 100 A.D.): The path of this ray is indeed the shortest path from the object to the mirror to a given point.

We find that nature is economical. Although it is somewhat involved, the proof developed by Heron may be of interest to teachers. It confirms what the students have established experimentally. In order to develop his proof, Heron took advantage of a keen observation: He noticed that if an observer at *B* sees an object at *A*, in the mirror he seems to see the object at *A'*. Thus, the image of the object appears to be as far behind the mirror as the object itself is in front (Figure 4.9). (This could be proved by showing that $\triangle ARP \cong \triangle A'RP$, an exercise the students could probably complete.)

Figure 4.9

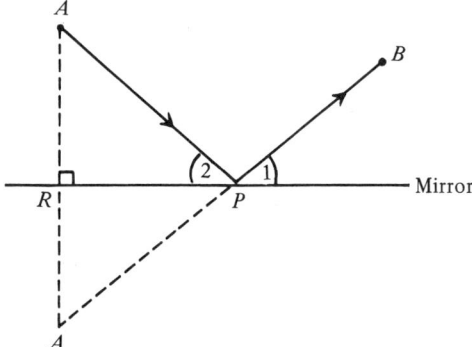

Heron's argument was developed along these lines:

Given: The path of the light ray from *A* to the mirror to *B* is $AC + CB$. Any other path is $AD + DB$ (Figure 4.10).

Prove: $AC + CB < AD + DB$

1. *F* is the image of *A* so that *AE* is $\perp m$, and $AE = EF$. (The image is as far behind the mirror as the object is in front.)

2. Heron concluded that $\triangle EAD \cong \triangle EFD$ by SAS: (S) $EA = EF$, (A) $\angle DEA = \angle DEF$, and (S) *DE* is a common side.

3. By the same reasoning $\triangle EAC \cong \triangle EFC$ by SAS.

Figure 4.10

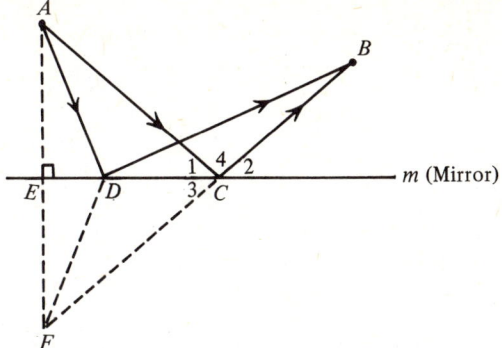

4. Thus our proof is complete if we can show that
   (a) $AC + CB < AD + DB$ or
   (b) $FC + CB < FD + DB$
   since $AC = FC$ and $AD = FD$ by congruent triangles.

5. Statement (b) is true if FCB is a straight line.

6. The mirror was represented by straight line m, thus $\angle 1 + \angle 4 + \angle 2 = 180°$.

   $\angle 1 = \angle 3$: congruent triangles
   $\angle 1 = \angle 2$: angles of incidence and reflection

7. Hence $\angle 3 + \angle 4 + \angle 1 = 180°$ or a straight angle by substitution of $\angle 3$ for $\angle 1$ and $\angle 1$ for $\angle 2$.

8. Thus FCB is a straight line $\Rightarrow FC + CB < FD + DB \Rightarrow AC + CB < AD + DB$. Q.E.D.

Let us step back a moment and take a good look at what we have done. On the face of it, it would seem that we have discussed some interesting applications of the inequality theorems. This is true, but we have accomplished much more. In physics, we have added two laws about the behavior of light rays. In geometry, we have added two theorems about the inequality of lines. These are listed here:

Theorem: Of all broken line paths from point A to any point P on line m, and then to B, only one path is such that AP and PB make equal angles with m.

Theorem: Of all broken line paths from point A to any point P on line m, and then to B, the path APB for which AP and PB make equal angles with m is the shortest path.

Physics Law: There is only one light ray from an object that is reflected from a mirror to an observer.

Physics Law: The lone light ray is the shortest path from the object to the mirror to the observer.

In effect we have provided a very real demonstration of the interaction of mathematics and the physical world. We have added to our knowledge in each field, as well as to our understanding of our environment. Mathematics shapes our understanding of the world and is in turn affected by the findings. This is a message that must be shared with students of mathematics at every level if we are to tell the whole story.

The work with the paths of light rays can be extended to include the converse of one of the previous theorems. Briefly the statement would be:

> **Theorem:** If the path from point A to a point P on a line m to point B is the shortest path from A to m to B, then the angles made with m by AP and BP are equal.

Physically, this theorem states that if the path of the light ray is the shortest path, then its angle of incidence is equal to the angle of reflection.

In addition, it is now possible to investigate a somewhat more complex reflection that we find in everyday use. Clothing stores sometimes have two mirrors hinged together (often three) so that a person can look at his side or back in order to see how well a suit or dress fits. If Figure 4.11 indicates the position of the mirrors, is it possible for a person standing at P to look into the mirror n and see the side of his body that faces the mirror m? If a person at P is to see his left side in the mirror n, the light ray would have to travel from P to mirror m to mirror n and back to P again, as shown in the diagram. How can we be sure that the light ray leaving P and striking the mirror at some point X will be reflected to mirror n? And if it should be so reflected, how can we be sure that it will be reflected in such in such a way that it will eventually return to P? This is far from obvious and is an interesting exercise for those who are able to consider it.

Figure 4.11

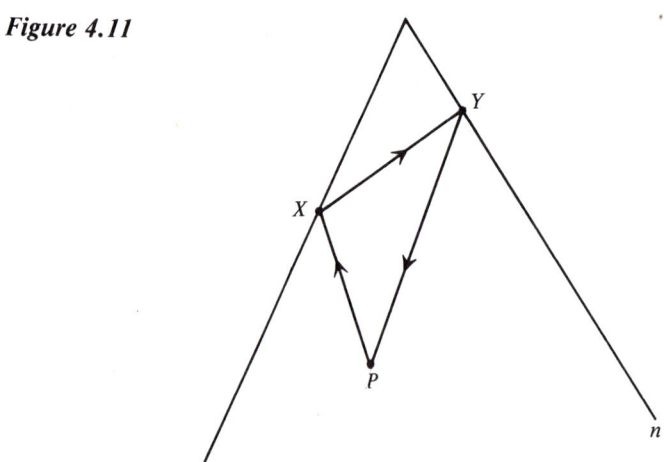

Many interesting problems can grow out of this discussion of light rays. The reflection laws do not apply only to light rays. They would, for example, explain the rebounding of a billiard ball on a pool table. Some sample problems follow:

▶ *1.* A trucking company delivers merchandise from boats on a river to two towns, A and B (Figure 4.12). If it wishes to build a single pier along the bank m to serve both towns, where should the pier be located so that the trucking distance will be shortest? (In this problem we may thank Heron for the solution. Build the pier at the point P on m that makes AP and BP form equal angles with m. How many such points are there?)

Figure 4.12

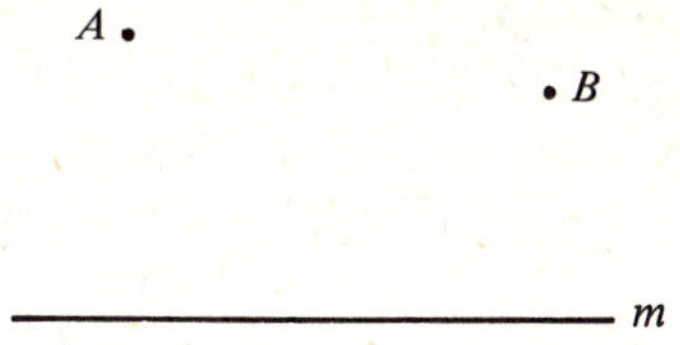

A •
                    • B

————————————— m

2. A telephone company wishes to build a central office on highway *h*, serving towns *A* and *B*. Where should it be located to keep the amount of wire needed as small as possible? (See Figure 4.13)

3. A dress shop mirror extends down to the floor so customers can see their entire body as they try on dresses. Must the mirror be full length? How long must it be to do the job? (Perhaps Figure 4.14 will help. *AB* represents the person looking into mirror *m*. *A'B'* is the person's image. Prove your answer is correct.)

Figure 4.13

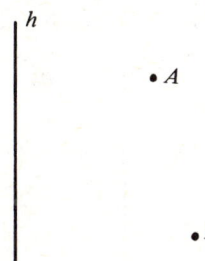

Figure 4.14

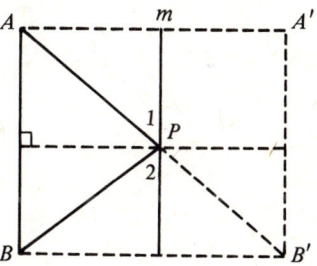

4. Two billiard balls are on the pool table as shown in Figure 4.15. Explain how the ball at *A* should be directed so that it will hit a side of the table and rebound to hit the ball at *B*.

5. An observer at *A* looks into mirror *m* and sees the image of a clock at *B*. Explain how to find the point *P* on the mirror where the ray of light from the object is reflected to the observer (Figure 4.16).

Figure 4.15

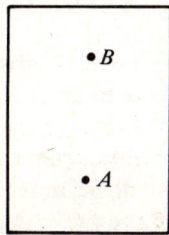

Figure 4.16

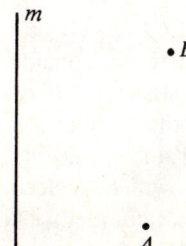

The reflection properties of light rays offer the student additional insights into how mathematics helps us to understand natural phenomena. This time, concepts of geometry came into play together with the notion of deductive proof. Proof is a most important and difficult idea and will be discussed in detail in Chapter 15. For now, it will suffice to point out the role that it plays in adding to our knowledge. The intuitive work that must precede the deductive demonstration is even greater in importance. This too will be considered later.

Light Rays and Parallels

Before leaving the notion of light, we explore one curious use of the reflection law, which involves a simple instrument called a periscope. The periscope offers us additional opportunities to add interest and importance to the ideas of geometry as we deal with parallel lines. It is an instrument simple enough to be made by the students in the class and yet useful enough to be an important precision instrument aboard a submarine. In order to make the periscope work, it is necessary to construct a situation resulting in parallel light rays. A light ray from an object at P is refelcted by a mirror (m) to a second mirror (n) to the eye of the observer at A (Figure 4.17). A long tube and two simple mirrors are all that is needed.

Figure 4.17

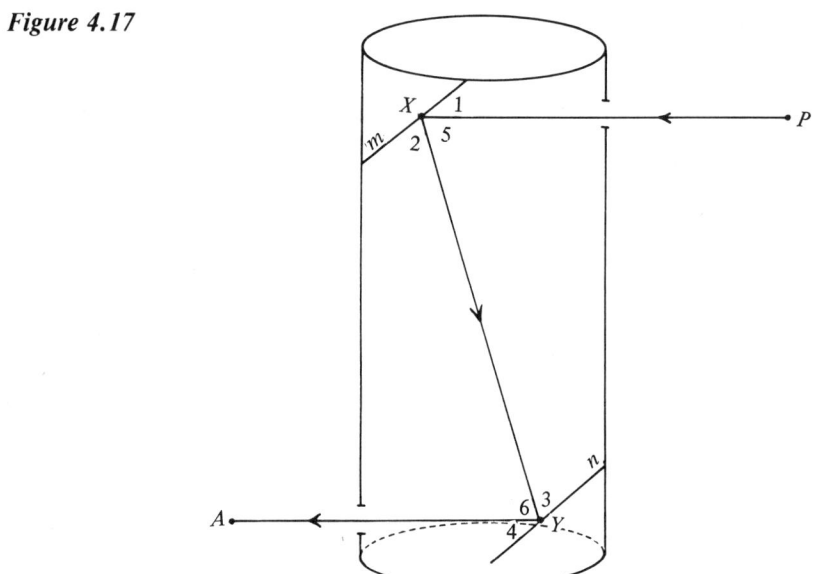

The problem to be considered, once the idea behind the periscope is understood, is: How shall the mirrors be placed so that the light ray that leaves the tube is parallel to the path it took upon entering? In our diagram, how can we be assured the $PX \parallel YA$? We have the reflection law available: but can we be certain that the mirrors will be placed so that the light ray will be reflected and observed as desired? Of course, we could use trial and error and move the mirror until it "works." Indeed this is undoubtedly what most students would actually do if they undertook the construction. But perhaps our knowledge of geometry can offer us some important assistance. Once again we ask students to focus upon the purely mathematical aspect of the situation.

We have two lines, *PX* and *YA*, and another line intersecting each of these lines at *X* and *Y*, respectively (Figure 4.18). Thus, we have two lines cut by transversal *XY*. Our aim here is to make *PX*∥*YA*.

As we examine the diagram, it begins to appear that ∡5 and ∡6 are the crucial angles. If they can be made equal to each other, it appears that the lines will be parallel. Let us examine a variety of situations involving parallel lines cut by a transversal and focus upon the angles located in a comparable position to test for some relationship. The adjustable quadrilaterals commercially available may be helpful here. Erector set strips, geo-strips, straight-line drawings, and protractors may serve equally well (Figure 4.19). Students can compare the measures of alternate interior angles for both parallel and intersecting lines.

Figure 4.18

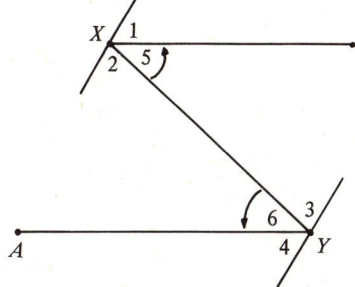

Figure 4.19

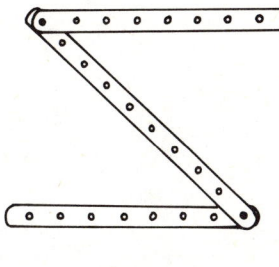

In this way added importance is given to the case in which the angles turn out to be equal. When experimentation has virtually convinced students that if the alternate interior angles are equal, the lines are parallel, we seek a proof of this proposition to confirm our findings:

>   ***Prove:*** *m* ∥ *n* (Figure 4.20).
>
>   ***Given:*** Lines *m* and *n* cut by transversal *t* so that ∡5 = ∡6.

Figure 4.20

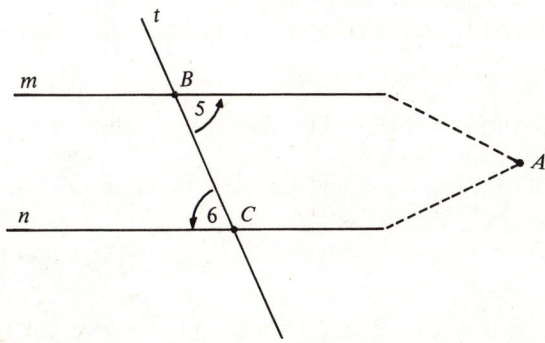

Let us assume that the lines are not parallel and see if a contradiction will result.

Assume that line *m* intersects line *n* at *A*.

We have thus formed triangle ABC, of which ∡6 is an exterior angle. ∡6 > ∡5 since ∡5 is an opposite interior angle. But this contradicts the given information: ∡6 = ∡5. Therefore lines *m* and *n* cannot intersect; it must be true that *m* ∥ *n*.

To return to the periscope, if we place the two mirrors so that ∡5 = ∡6, then we can be assured that the entering and departing rays will be parallel. In the actual construction of a periscope, it would be advisable to construct ∡1 = 45°. This would cause the light ray to travel straight down the length of the tube and would result in ∡5 = 90° (Figure 4.21). We could then use a narrower tube.

Figure 4.21

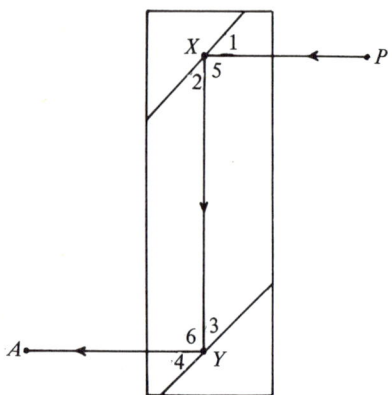

Another item of interest that results from this construction is that if ∡2 = ∡3, we would once again have an equal pair of alternate interior angles and, as a consequence, parallel lines. The parallel lines, in this case, are the two mirrors themselves. The work could be followed by exercises using the properties developed.

There are additional mathematics concepts that may be considered if we extend our study of the light properties. Some of these will be developed in Chapter 10, including:

How does light reflect off a parabolic mirror?

What is the principle behind the shape of an automobile headlight?

How does a telescope work?

Exploring light rays also adds to our understanding of sound, since sound waves have similar properties.

As you examine each question above more closely, you will find that mathematics is indeed intimately involved in our daily lives. Without mathematics, we would be handicapped in trying to gain a better understanding of nature.

Footnote

1. Eric T. Bell *Mathematics: Queen and Servant of Science.* New York: McGraw-Hill, 1951.

For Investigation and Discussion

1. Use Table 4.2 to develop a lesson on beginning equation solution for an eighth grade class.
2. Show how the facts of Table 4.2 can help provide drill work with a minimum of boredom.
3. List at least three experiences that may be used to enable students to learn how to construct formulas from collections of data involving familiar phenomena.
4. Demonstrate two different ways to introduce the addition and subtraction of signed numbers.
5. Using the relfection law as it applies to billiard balls, construct a lesson plan to help students begin to realize the interaction between mathematics and science.
6. Prove the converse of the theorem about the light-ray path being the shortest distance. See the statement on page 50.
7. Make a plan utilizing the construction of a periscope by the students, which emphasizes conditions necessary and sufficient for parallel lines.
8. Outline an investigation based upon two mirrors hinged at a 60° angle to determine whether or not the exiting and entering light rays are parallel.

For Further Reading

Books

Bell, E. T. *Mathematics: Queen and Servant of Science.* New York: McGraw-Hill, 1951.

Committee on Support of Research in the Mathematical Sciences, *The Mathematical Sciences. A Collection of Essays.* Cambridge: M.I.T. Press, 1969.

Engineering Concepts Curriculum Project, Polytechnic Institute of Brooklyn. *The Man Made World.* New York: McGraw-Hill, 1971.

Hogben, Lancelot. *Mathematics for the Million.* 4th ed. New York: W.W. Norton, 1968.

Kline, Morris. *Mathematics and the Physical World.* New York: Thomas Y. Crowell, 1959.

Land, Frank. *The Language of Mathematics.* New York: Doubleday, 1963.

Periodicals

Bates, Elsie. "Mathematics from the Environment," *Mathematics Teaching.* No. 47 (Summer 1969), pp. 12-14.

Bognato, Robert A. "Collaboration in the Mathematical Community," *The Mathematics Teacher.* Vol. 67 (December 1974), pp. 682-686.

Elkins, Richard L. and William A. Wockenfuss. "Graphical Mathematics for the Preengineering and Science Student," *The Mathematics Teacher.* Vol. 65 (December 1972), pp. 691-697.

Grant, Nicholas. "Mathematics on a Pool Table," *The Mathematics Teacher.* Vol. 64 (March 1971), pp. 255-257.

Hansen, David W. "The Dependence of Mathematics on Reality," *The Mathematics Teacher.* Vol. 64 (December 1971), pp. 715-719.

Johnson, David C. and Louis S. Cohen. "Functions," *The Arithmetic Teacher.* Vol. 17 (April 1970), pp. 305-311.

CHAPTER 5

The Mathematics of Living Things

The ability of mathematics to aid in our understanding of living things is great. The ability of living things to offer opportunities to make good use of mathematics is equally great. We examine one possibility.

5.1 Nature's Polygons

Why do bees and wasps build their honeycombs so that a cross section of the hive discloses that the cells are hexagonal in shape (Figure 5.1)? A British publication describes how this question was investigated by an 11-year old student. It is a fascinating question that has many implications. For example, why don't bees use square cells? A square is simpler than a hexagon. We immediately open up to two areas of investigation: (1) comparisons of squares and hexagons with equal perimeters, and (2) attempts to create patterns, called tessellations, by fitting together a variety of shapes using one polygon at a time. (We assume the use of regular polygons for this discussion).

Figure 5.1

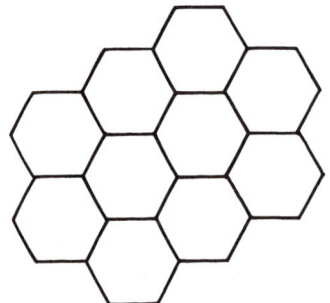

Ask students to place hexagons or squares on graph paper to simplify comparisons of area. Once the area of a hexagon of a fixed perimeter has been determined, the area of a square of equal perimeter may easily be considered. Table 5.1 gives some experimental results. It soon becomes apparent that given a hexagon and a square of fixed perimeters, the hexagon will enclose a greater area than does the square. Many questions may result from such an investigation:

> Does a triangle enclose greater area than a hexagon of equal perimeter?
>
> Does an octagon of equal perimeter with a hexagon enclose greater area?
>
> How do the other polygons relate to those studied in this respect?

If area seems to increase with an increase in the number of sides of a regular polygon (the perimeters fixed), why doesn't the bee construct the hive cells in an octagonal or decagonal shape, rather than hexagonal?

Table 5.1 Comparison of the Areas of Hexagons and Squares with Equal Perimeters.

Perimeter	Hexagon		Square	
	Side	A (Approx.)	Side	A
6	1	$2\frac{1}{5}$	$1\frac{1}{2}$	$2\frac{1}{4}$
12	2	$10\frac{1}{5}$	3	9
18	3	$23\frac{1}{5}$	$4\frac{1}{2}$	$20\frac{1}{4}$
24	4	$41\frac{1}{5}$	6	36

Invite students to attempt to fit together octagons and other polygons, and to construct sample hives. (Cutting out such pieces may be most instructional since students must figure out how to first make the various polygons.) As they try to make patterns (tessellations) using a given polygon, students will become sharply aware of the difficulty of building patterns that do not leave any spaces (Figure 5.2). We have the solution to our problem. The bee constructs his beehive cells in hexagonal form and they fit together and leave no spaces because, in the words of the 11-year old mentioned at the start, "with the same length of wall and the same amount of material the bee gets more area and therefore more volume in building a hexagonal honeycomb than if it builds a square one . . ."[1]

Figure 5.2

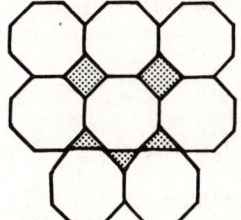 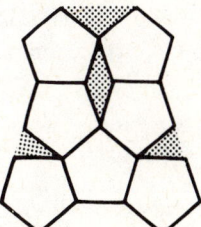

The students explored areas and perimeters of a broad assortment of polygons. After discussion of places other than hives where they may have seen this hexagonal cell construction (e.g., wallpaper, floor tiles, packaging, and large telescope lenses), additional examples could be presented comparing areas and perimeters. Eventually we can introduce triangular areas through the use of graph paper. If we begin with right-angled triangles, students quickly see that the area is half the completed rectangle or square (Figure 5.3). Other triangles then require careful consideration, as does the parallelogram resulting from placing two such triangles together. But use of the experimental approach will enable the students to build their own methods for finding area (eventually without the graph paper or squares) and will result in the invention of their own formulas. Symbols may be introduced to simplify their presentation. These activities may be followed by the exploration of circles—areas with a given perimeter—and the comparison of these with polygons. The work may then be extended to three dimensions, questioning why given shapes are used for various containers brought in from the supermarket. Finally, solids can be constructed using two-dimensional figures to focus upon the number of faces, number of edges, number of vertices, and so on.

Figure 5.3

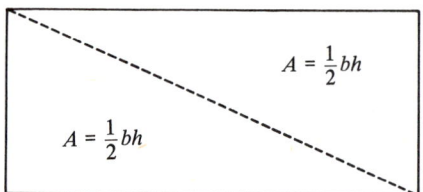

In addition to graph paper and squares, the student can make use of pegboards, Tinkertoys, erector sets, geo-strips and fold-up carpenters' rules. It is possible to construct solids out of Tinkertoys and a set of rods and connectors called D-Stix[2]. There seems to be an endless supply of interesting, active experiences available to aid student development of concepts and skills in a meaningful way.

Teachers will often say, "I'm teaching the area formula today." The statement itself points up a rote kind of teaching activity. Instead of "teaching" formulas, let us organize experiences for children that can result in their invention of formulas. Although it is not an easy task to develop these experiences, in the long run, it makes for efficient and effective learning.

Before we leave this development, let us be clear about its implications: If a circle gives greatest area for a fixed perimeter (or circumference) and a sphere gives greatest volume for a fixed surface area, we have an explanation for the shape of many manufactured products, as well as for the conditions under which many living things exist. We will deal with this further as we consider how perimeters, areas, and volumes grow.

5.2 The Growth of Area and Volume

Many years ago a book was written about a man named Gulliver who traveled to distant and strange lands[3]. On one of his voyages, Gulliver encountered a civilization of giants built just like him except that they were 12 times each of his dimensions. Gulliver was about 6 feet tall; the giants were 72 feet tall. On another voyage Gulliver encountered a nation of tiny people who were constructed much as he was but who were one-twelfth as large. The book goes on to describe

Gulliver's adventures with these strange people and becomes a fascinating tale that has been read for years. Let us take a brief but careful look at Gulliver's giants, for the idea of a race of giants has been with man ever since he has been able to dream.

If a giant existed who was like us in every way, except 10 times larger (we use 10 to simplify the work a bit), could he run as fast as we do?

It is known that the strength of a part of a structure (e.g., a girder of a bridge or a section of thigh bone) depends upon the area of a cross section. A cross section of thigh bone of a man is less than that of the giant; hence the giant's thigh can support more weight. But how much more weight can it support? To answer this question we will investigate how areas and volumes (used as an indicator of weight) change as the dimensions change. Let us do some simple experiments:

Area: As we double the dimensions of a two-dimensional object, what have we done to the area? Triple it? Quadruple it?

Volume: What happens to the volume as we double all the dimensions of a solid? Does it triple?

Using any materials that are necessary, or simply applying formulas, the students can tabulate the length of a side and the area of squares and the length of a side and the volume of cubes (Figure 5.4). To add to their understanding of these relationships, students draw line graphs to present a picture of them shown in Figure 5.5. The area grows with the square of the side, whereas the volume grows as its cube. Hence a surprising result becomes apparent: Double the length of a side of a square and you have increased the area by four times! Not only that, but you have increased a cube eight times in volume by doubling its side!

Figure 5.4

Square		Cube	
s	A	e	V
1	1	1	1
2	4	2	8
4	16	4	64
8	64	8	512

Figure 5.5

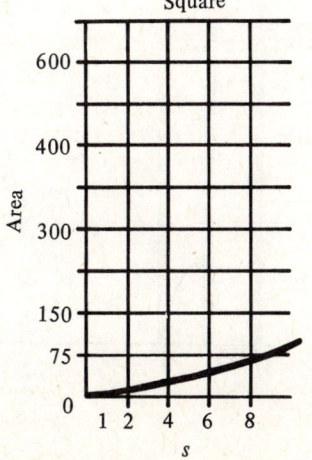
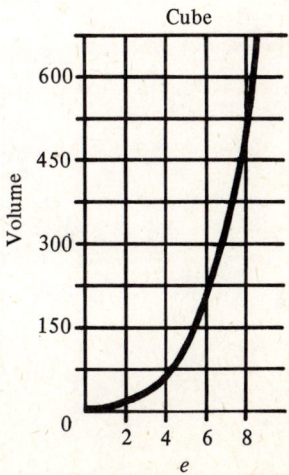

Volume grows a good deal more rapidly than area, which grows at a faster rate than the length of a side. This is shown rather dramatically by the graphs: We see the sharp upward climb of the line on the volume graph, as compared with that of the line on the area graph. Additional situations could be explored by constructing tables and graphs of the growth of particular rectangles, rectangular solids, and other figures. Among other advantages, we have some interesting practice with graphing.

The circle may be explored in a rather effective way by involving students in an experiment suggested in the British curriculum bulletin mentioned before[4]. The students may bring a variety of tin cans or jars to class and use these to determine the diameter-circumference ratio, π. Masking tape and a large sheet of graph paper are needed in addition to the cans. After guessing diameters, students fit tape around each can and cut to fit as closely as possible. The open end of the can is then placed upon the axes of the graph so that the diameter begins at the origin and coincides with the horizontal axis (Figure 5.6). Students mark the horizontal axis at the right-hand edge of the diameter, remove the masking tape, and stick it on the graph perpendicular to the axis at that point. We have the length of the diameter marked off on the horizontal axis and the length of the circumference represented by a vertical strip of tape. The students measure each,

Figure 5.6

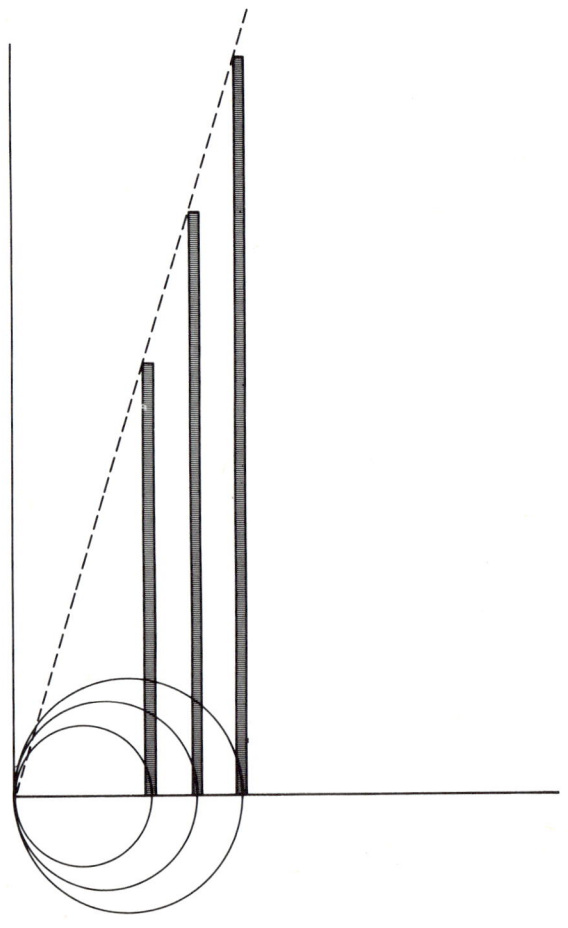

record the circumference and diameter in a table, and repeat the work for larger cans. Table 5.2 contains this information. After several measurements are completed, students notice that the tops of the verticle strips (bars) will lie in a straight line and are a little more than three times the distance from its foot to the origin. The table will show the ratio of C/D as computed. In terms of growth, doubling the diameter results in doubling the circumference. If we consider area, we find out that doubling a diameter increases the area four times, just as we saw before.

Table 5.2   A Comparison of Diameter and Circumference.

D (inches)	C (inches)	C/D
1	3¼	
2		
3		
4		
5		
.		
.		
.		

After experimentation we return well equipped to probe for answers to problem of the giant. Since the strength of the thigh bone depends upon the area of its cross section, if we increase all dimensions 10 times, how will the area of the cross section be affected? Its strength will go up as the square of 10, i.e., increase 100 times! That bone will certainly be stronger than its counterpart in man. But how much more weight will it have to support?

Since we are using volume measures to indicate weight, we must find out how much volume increases if all dimensions are increased 10 times. Our experimentation showed us that volume grows as the cube of the linear dimension; hence volume will increase 1000 times! Our big strong giant is a most unfortunate fellow! He has 100 times more strength in his thigh bones but must lift with it 1000 times more weight! Each time he gets to his feet, we can expect him to proceed to break both of his legs! Gravity has become a violent enemy. The implications of such a discussion are numerous. All kinds of changes in strength of arms and legs as well as lifting ability, may be considered. But most important of all is the role of these physical and mathematical laws and their effect upon the shape of all living things.[5]

There are many animals larger than man, such as the elephant and the rhinoceros, but their limbs are not proportional to those of man. Their thigh bones would be much thicker in order to compensate for the added weight. Haldane points out in a classic article on this subject that as we move from a gazelle to a rhino, the thickening of a leg becomes quite pronounced. Gravity, a mortal enemy of our mythical giant, has very little effect upon the smaller animals. It is quite common for a mouse to survive a fall from a 10-story building. Thompson and Haldane have made available to us the basic information necessary to carry out numerous fascinating and significant investigations involving the mathematical concepts of perimeter, area, volume, ratio and proportion, and percent, to list a few. The kinds of questions that may lead to investigations would include:

1. If a man coming out of swimming pool carries about 2 percent of his weight in water droplets upon him, what do you think happens to a fly which lands in the pool?

2. If you require a pound of meat a day and a quart of milk, how much would be needed to feed the giant who is 10 times us in every way? How much would be needed to feed the tiny man who is one tenth of us?

3. If we were to build an exact scale model of a bridge and make it 100 times smaller in all its dimensions, what is the ratio of the weights each should support?

4. If a rope with a 2-inch diameter was able to support 200 pounds before breaking, how much would be the maximum lifting power of a 4-inch diameter rope?

5. If 5000 mice weigh as much as one man, how would their combined surface area compare with that of the man?

5.3 Symmetry

We move on to the study of informal geometry and emphasize a transformational approach. The concept of symmetry and the transformation of reflection are of particular interest.

One of nature's trademarks is the symmetrical development of so many of her creatures. The exteriors of virtually all insects, animals and plants are constructed symmetrically; that is, they can be divided into two halves, one of which is the reflection of the other. While it is true (as any actor will quickly tell you) that each of us has a "better side," by and large, if a vertical line is drawn down our center, we would be left with two body halves whose outside appearances are very much alike (Figure 5.7). In addition to the many creatures of nature, we find symmetry in a multitude of man's constructions: automobiles, suits and dresses, tables and chairs, and even in the very letters used to form the alphabet (Figure 5.8).

Figure 5.7

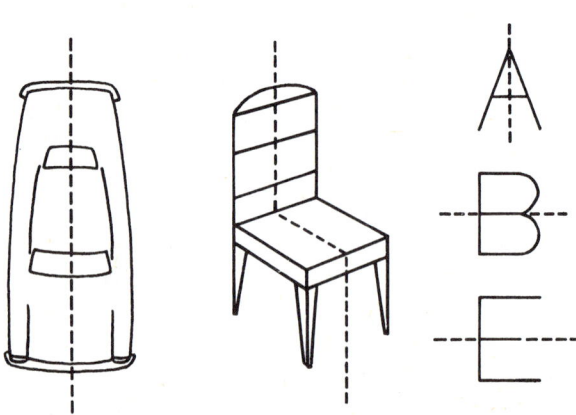

Figure 5.8

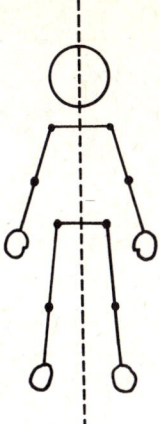

Many interesting classroom experiences can be organized around the concept of symmetry:

1. Paper folding illustrates line symmetry as does the cutting of designs into paper after folding. Students can vary the number of folds to show different kinds of symmetry.

2. Ink blots, or paint blots, can be made by dropping a spot of ink into the center of a piece of paper. Students can then fold the paper to form surprisingly symmetrical designs (Figure 5.9).

3. Some wallpaper designs contain symmetrical figures. Students can cut out designs thought to contain symmety along a suspected axis. They can then place one part upon the other to check for likeness. This kind of work is facilitated by using see-through paper or acetate. Tissue and wax paper may be held up to the light to check the superimposition of markings.

Figure 5.9

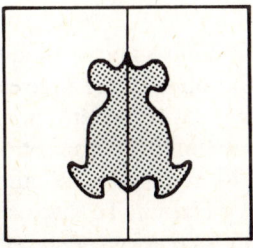 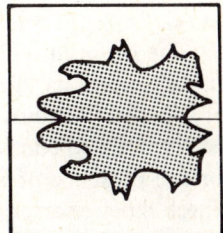

An interesting discussion of the use of mirrors to carry out activities involving symmetry appeared in an article by Marion Walter[6]. She has constructed "mirror" cards that require the students to place a mirror on a diagram to attempt to match a pattern shown in another diagram (Figure 5.10 see page 64). Safe, inexpensive metal mirrors may be obtained in any camping equipment store. These mirrors, in addition to the use just described, may offer students an interesting way to experiment with the reflection of light and to experimentally check the reflection law: The angle of incidence is equal to the angle of reflection[7]. Draw a solid line on a sheet of paper and intersect it at any angle with a broken line (Figure 5.11). Place a mirror vertically on the point of intersection so that the solid line and its reflection form a straight line. Use any straightedge to draw a continuation on the paper of the reflected dotted line. Compare angle measures with a protractor. You will undoubtably be able to think of many other uses for the mirrors.

Figure 5.10
Where must you place the mirror on Card 5 to see the pattern of Card 5A?

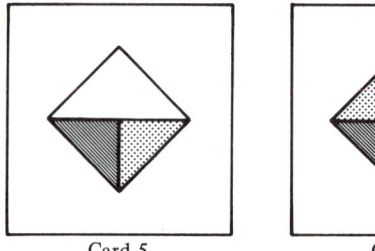

Figure 5.11

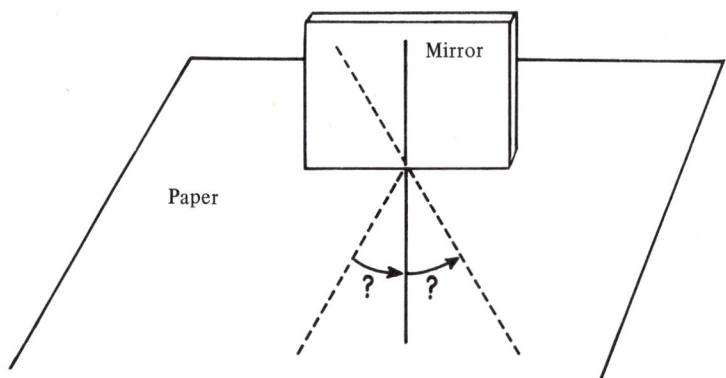

The different geometric regions may become subjects for the symmetry test. In fact, upon careful observation of these figures, students may find many axes of symmetry as shown in Figure 5.12. After numerous experiences, students may be prepared to consider a mathematical description of symmetry in order to test for the presence or absence of symmetry. Whatever they finally do derive from these experiences, one thing is certain: To discover this property called *symmetry* present in so many of nature's creations, gives one some significant insight into the apparent order in nature, an order that has become more understandable to us through mathematics.

Design-making combines the elements of construction and symmetry and has often fascinated students. How often have you seen a student condemned for having a "short interest span" sit for hours with a compass creating all sorts of intricate patterns and patiently coloring them. Offer designs to students and ask if the designs can be duplicated (Figure 5.13). Students will need little encouragement to try this and to move on to the invention of their own designs. The symmetric qualities of the designs are considered and tested to add to the mathematical side of these experiences.

Figure 5.12

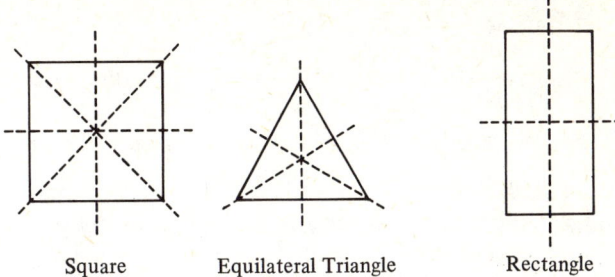

Square   Equilateral Triangle   Rectangle

Figure 5.13

One final word about symmetry. Today in our schools we are much more concerned about teaching a motion geometry, which involves all kinds of transformations, than we were in the past. In such an approach, symmetry is but one of the many kinds of transformations that may be made to a figure. Some other kinds of transformations would involve *rotating figures,* in which properties that remain constant, as well as those that change, are observed; *translation of figures,* in which a figure is moved in a particular direction without turning; and *reflection,* of which symmetry is a special case that results when the figure as a whole remains unchanged. These ideas will be considered in later chapters, as will the general area of geometry.

The references at the end of this chapter offer additional help. For our purposes, the study of symmetry as indicated offers increased appreciation for nature as an architect.

5.4 Maintaining Body Temperatures and the Use of Percent

Have you noticed how much more quickly soup will cool if it is in a bowl as compared to being placed in a cup?

Why does the soup remain hotter, longer, in a cup?

The explanation may open the door to many interesting properties of living things, which bring into play the use of relatively simple mathematical concepts.

Heat is lost through the surface of a body. In humans, heat is lost through the skin. The greater the surface area, the greater the heat loss, and the quicker the cooling process. Apply this to the soup bowl and observe and compare the surface areas of the bowl and the cup. It becomes apparent why the cooling process works so much quicker in the bowl. Briefly, the bowl has much greater surface area. Another dramatic example of this is the way a pizza cools so quickly. Heat loss is an important property of the bodies of all living things, and of particular importance to warm-blooded animals.

The bodies of warm-blooded animals have a fairly constant temperature. In man, normal temperature may vary from 98° to 99.5°, but most people have a normal temperature of 98.6°. If heat loss is constant, then to keep the body temperature constant, heat must be supplied. We do this by eating. The amount of food that is necessary varies with size, and leads to an interesting collection of percent problems. Percent can be very difficult for students. Some heat loss problems requiring the use of percent follow.

▶
> A man must eat roughly 2% of his weight per day in order to maintain his body heat. A mouse, on the other hand, requires food amounting to 50% of his weight; that is why mice seem to be continuously eating.
>
> How much food would a boy or girl weighing 75 lb need in order to maintain body heat?
>
> If a 110-lb boy eats 4 lb of food, will he have eaten enough to keep his body temperature up?
>
> A small mouse ate 4½ oz. of food one day. This was 50% of his weight. How much does he weigh?

The dual objectives of discovering how mathematics adds to our knowledge of living things and of creating a need to learn important mathematical concepts, are both satisfied by these problems. Such problems result in work with percent, practice with fundamental skills, as well as consideration of the relationship between surface area and volumes of solids. The mathematics shows clearly how the size of an animal is directly related to the amount that must be eaten. A mouse with a small stomach and still smaller intake tubes (esophagus) has to make eating a full time job. Man, on the other hand, is able to maintain body temperature on only 2% of his weight. Perhaps this is one reason why many people have trouble keeping their waist lines down. Since percent causes such widespread difficulty, let us examine in detail how this concept may be taught before continuing to explore the mathematics of living things.

Since the percent symbol is used in newspapers, in local stores, on TV, on test scores, and in almost every facet of student's lives, one would expect the concept of percent to be easily mastered. Unfortunately, ease of understanding is not necessarily a function of the frequency of occurrence in everyday lives.

Very few students cannot say "percent means hundredths." In spite of this, we have all encountered many students who find percent problems difficult. It seems that students are able to verbalize definitions with little functional comprehension. The words themselves fail to bring any pictures or notions to mind that enable the student to actually use the concept of percent.

In addition to the heat loss problems, we may consider comparisons relevant to the concept of percent:

> The best girl basket shooter had made 12 baskets in 20 tries. The best boy was able to sink 14 baskets in 25 tries. Who was the better shot?

> A seventh grade class had an average of 27 students present each day, out of 30 students in the class. An eighth grade class averaged 32 students attending each day, out of a total of 36 students. Which class had better attendance?

> Joe put 1 ounce of chocolate syrup into an 8 ounce glass and filled it with milk. Sandy made a big batch and put 5 ounces of syrup into a 36 ounce container and filled it with milk. Which drink had the stronger chocolate flavor?

Any of these problems could serve to get the students into situations that require the use of percent. After time for working, thinking, discussion, and evaluation of individual attempts at solution, writing all ratios with a common base may be offered as one way to resolve the issues. It is customary to use 100 as such a base, and so we introduce percent as the ratios written with a base of 100. The student finds that this common base makes comparisons easier. The method he uses to change the fractions into equivalent ones with 100 as a denominator should be of his own choosing. Certainly, finding equivalent fractions in order to carry out operations with common fractions will serve as a guide. The word and symbol for percent grows naturally out of the preceding discussion. There is little need for any formal statement of what percent represents, since this is basically an introduction.

Problems requiring the student to solve what has been known as the three classic cases of percent grow out of these beginning experiences. Years ago, much time was spent in mathematics classes drilling the students on memorization of how to solve each of the three cases:

> Finding the percentage: 50% of 80 = □
> Finding the percent (rate):   □% of 80 = 40
> Finding the number: 50% of □ = 40

This kind of separation becomes totally unnecessary once the proportion idea has been considered. A percent was seen as a special case of ratio. Finding any of the missing numbers of the preceding equations can be resolved by writing them as proportions and solving for the missing number. In this way the equations may be rewritten:

$$50\% \text{ of } 80 = \square \rightarrow \frac{50}{100} = \frac{N}{80}$$

$$\square\% \text{ of } 80 = 40 \rightarrow \frac{N}{100} = \frac{40}{80}$$

$$50\% \text{ of } \square = 40 \rightarrow \frac{50}{100} = \frac{40}{N}$$

The student simply solves the proportion. He does not attempt to memorize three different methods after recognition of which particular case he has before him.

Other methods that eliminate the need for three cases are available to the students. If a good deal of equation work has been done, the use of the formula

$$b \cdot r = p, \quad \text{base} \times \text{rate} = \text{percentage}$$

is a helpful approach. The net effect is similar to that of using proportion, but the thinking is very different. In this instance, the given members of the formula are substituted into it, and the resulting equation is solved for the unknown. Sometimes students may solve the equation for the unknown first and then complete the substitution process. What percent of 80 is 40? The problem may be solved by writing either

$$p = br \qquad\qquad p = br$$
$$40 = 80 \cdot r \quad \text{or} \quad r = \frac{p}{b}$$
$$\frac{40}{80} = r \qquad\qquad r = \frac{40}{80}$$

In any case, the student is making use of the fundamental relationship between base, rate, and percentage. Difficulties arise here in applying the knowledge.

There are other methods, too; which one is best is an irrelevant question. It is not important that we teach our students *the best way*. Rather, it is important that our students learn that they can use the knowledge they have already acquired to think through to the answer in a new situation. This is what mathematics is about—not finding *the* best method, but *thinking* and *reasoning*. All such methods that take you where you want to go are indeed *best methods*. When a problem is attempted, the student thinks about how the relationships in the problem can be arranged to work for a solution, not "How did we do that one in class yesterday?" Perhaps this is one way to avoid the glib but empty statement that "percent means hundredths."

We now return to the mathematics of living things. Note that the different four-footed animals are constructed so that they carry their weight differently[8]. Table 5.3 indicates approximately how the weight is borne by the front and hind legs of some animals:

Table 5.3

Animal	Total Weight	Percent of Weight on:	
		Front Legs	Hind Legs
Camel	1596 lb	67%	33%
Llama	308 lb	66⅔%	33⅓%
Elephant	4004 lb	58%	42%
Horse	924 lb	57½%	42½%

Some sample problems are:

How much weight is on the front legs of an average horse?

How much weight is carried by the rear legs of an average elephant?

If a cow carries 60% of its weight on its front legs and we know it has 720 lb on its front legs, how much does it weigh?

If a lion weighing 500 lb is constructed so that 225 lb is resting on its rear legs, what percent of its weight is upon the rear legs?

What percent of your weight is on your legs?

Still more such problems can be constructed from the following: Every animal's body is supported by a skeleton. The bones make up different parts of the body's total weight:

Mouse or wren	8%
Dog or goose	13%
Man	18%

A 200-lb man probably has bones that weigh how many pounds?

The bones of a dog weigh about 5 lb. How much is the dog likely to weigh?

A wren weighs 4.3 oz. About how much do its bones weigh?

Warm-Blooded Animals and Inequalities 5.5

The mathematics of warm-blooded animals can also provide students with an interesting beginning to the study of inequalities. There is much in nature that we may call upon. The amount of food (in pounds per day) that the body requires to maintain a constant temperature of 98.6° F is approximately described by the inequality

$$F \geq \frac{1}{50} W$$

where W = pounds of body weight and F = pounds of food. The following problem requires students to solve a linear inequality.

How much food must a 200-lb man eat in order to maintain his body temperature?

Using the relation, we get

$$F \geq \frac{1}{50} W$$

$$F \geq \frac{1}{50} \cdot 200$$

$$F \geq 4$$

The man in question must eat at least 4 lb of food. Thus, his body temperature is maintained by 4 lb of food as well as by any greater amount of food, e.g., 5, 6, or more pounds. In this case, our answers are a collection of numbers and so it is natural to describe them as a set of numbers. Indeed, since these numbers are the solution to the problem, we call them collectively a *solution set*. The nature of the problem dictates the possible numbers which may be used to select members of this solution set. This time (in the measurement of weights) the real numbers are the numbers from which we shall select our answers. Since the inequality contained a single variable, we may draw a one-dimensional graph (Figure 5.14, see page 70) to illustrate the answers.

Figure 15.4 A graph of the solution set F ≥ 4.

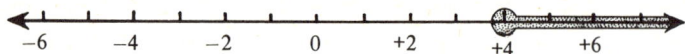

The graph indicates that any of the values from 4 to the right satisfy the inequality, including 4. (We shade in the circle at the left end of the graph, instead of using an unshaded circle if 4 were not included.) The graph is a line. This same graph might have been a collection of discrete points if the data had referred to discrete objects like people, tickets or cars.

We extend the study of inequalities by using problems from other areas.

▶ The maximum weight that an elevator can hold is 1500 lb. In a particular office building, it is determined that those using the elevator average 150 lb. How many people form a "safe load?"

The elevator operator cannot weigh the people, but he can count them. We are now dealing with the counting of natural numbers. The inequality that describes this situation and its solution is presented here:

$$1500 \geq 150n$$
$$\frac{1500}{150} \geq n$$
$$10 \geq n$$

A picture of the numbers that make up the solution set for this problem is included in Figure 5.15. Thus the elevator is safe for one person to ride alone and for two, three, and on up to, but not more than, 10 people. The graph is now a set of discrete points since we are referring to people rather than measurements. The solution set may also be represented by showing each element included using the set bracket notation:

$F \geq 4$ or $\{F \mid F \geq 4\}$
$n \leq 10$ or $\{1, 2, 3, 4, 5, 6, 7, 8, 9, 10\}$

Figure 5.15 A graph of the solution set 10 ≥ n.

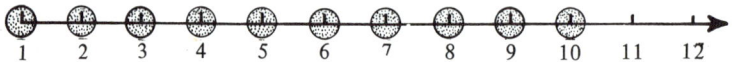

When the nature of the number system is clear because of the particular problem involved, we need not indicate this any further. If there is a question, however, it may be best to clearly indicate these possibilities called the universal or replacement set and make this a part of the symbolism used to present the problem. For example, the problems mentioned before may be written $\{F \in R \mid F \geq 4\}$ which is read:

The set of all F that belongs to the real numbers such that F is greater than or equal to 4.
$\{F \quad \in \quad R \quad F \quad \geq \quad 4\}$

By the same token:

$$\{n \in N \mid 1500 \geq 150n\}$$

The set of all n that belong to the natural numbers such that 1500 is greater than or equal to $150n$.

It is very important to use only those symbols that are needed to communicate the ideas. These forms should not be introduced where they may cloud rather than clarify the ideas.

Inequalities: Informal Solutions

How was the second inequality, $1500 \geqslant 150n$, solved? What methods were used?

If common sense reasoning fails to help students, we need to explore formal techniques. In the preceding problems, these seem hardly necessary. However, we may soon provide problems in inequalities that will surely create a need for more powerful techniques. Then we can consider the equality axioms and determine whether or not they may be applied to inequalities. But first, the two-dimensional graph of inequalities grows naturally out of the work done and poses some interesting questions. For this let us return to the relationship introduced earlier.

An approximate formula for the amount of food required for maintainance of human body temperature is

$$F \geqslant \frac{1}{50}W.$$

The minimum amount of food needed varies from animal to animal; thus, a mouse's food requirements would be described by the inequality

$$F \geqslant \tfrac{1}{2}W.$$

Although the mouse certainly requires less total food to maintain his body temperature than does man, proportional to his size, he requires a good deal more.

In studying this relationship we ask students to turn to the graph to picture the information. We have two variables so students can construct the familiar graph on the two-coordinate axes system. In this case we shall graph F as a function of W. It may be well to introduce the notation $F = f(W)$, which is to be read, "F depends upon, or is a function of, W." It is helpful to place $f(W)$ on the vertical axis as a label and begin to use this function notation in the table of values if one is to be made. But first, students are faced with a rather difficult problem:

How shall the graph of $F \geqslant \tfrac{1}{2} W$ be made?

Where are the values that satisfy this inequality?

How many are there?

At this point the students require time to think and wonder for themselves. The test for any suggested methods will be: Can we be sure that we have located all such values or ordered pairs? A suggestion about drawing the graph of the function described by the equation $F = \tfrac{1}{2}W$ is a good beginning.

Once the relation has been graphed, part of the desired picture is drawn. In the "greater than or equal to" statement students have provided for "equal to." But where are the "greater than" points? Here the students use the process of trial and error, selecting and testing points to determine the part of the coordinate plane that is included in the graph (Figure 5.16, see page 72). The shaded area is included, as is the line itself. When the graph is completed, it may be helpful to pause and consider carefully what was done.

Figure 5.16

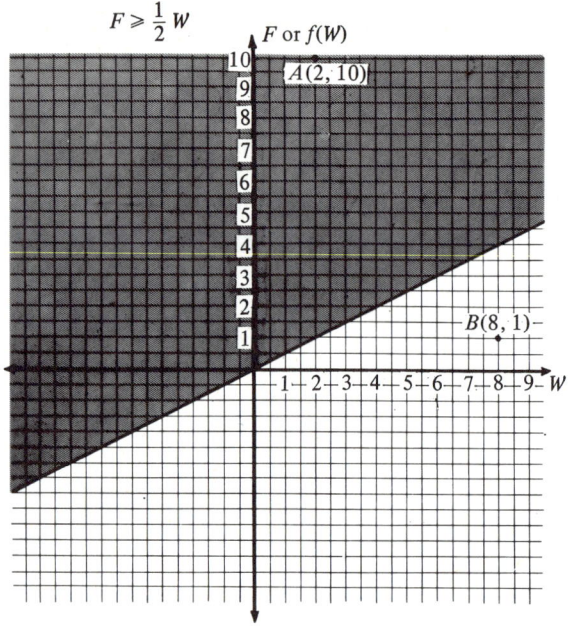

To graph the inequality, a graph of the equality was drawn. This line immediately divided the plane into three parts: the region above the line, the line itself, and the region below the line. We have the line and two half-planes created by the line. There are apparently three possibilities present to relate F and $½W$:

F is greater than (>) $½W$ or F is equal to (=) $½W$
or F is less than (<) $½W$

These would seem to correspond to the three divisions of the plane just described. In the inequality under consideration we see that we are required to illustrate two of these three possibilities: "equal to" and "greater than." The line provides the ordered pairs fitting the "equal to" description. Eventually, the two half planes above and below the line will satisfy the "greater than" and "less than" situations. But which is to be which? This question is resolved by using trial and error. A point in the upper half is selected and its coordinates (W, F) are tested to determine if the inequality is satisfied: Choose point A(2, 10). Substitution results in

$F > ½W$
$10 > ½(2)$
$10 > 1$ True

And, indeed the statement is true. The inequality is satisfied. For further assurance, we choose a point below the line and not in the upper half-plane and test it: Choose point $B(8, 1)$.

$F > ½W$
$1 > ½(8)$
$1 > 4$ False

As anticipated this point does not satisfy the inequality. The student may wish test many more points before becoming convinced that the upper half-plane is indeed the region they have been seeking.

To indicate the desired portions of the graph, shading lines are drawn and the line itself is kept as a solid line. Had the inequality been $F > \frac{1}{2}W$, without the equality, the equality line would appear as a broken line. By looking at the graph, we see instantly what is and what is not included.

It is important to note here that the graph is a mathematical description of the inequality under consideration. It has included in it many meaningless values as far as the situation generating the inequality is concerned. For example, negative values are meaningless in discussing amounts of food to be consumed. Consequently, we need only the first quadrant to satisfy the physical situation. In addition, many of the ordered pairs in this quadrant are without physical meaning: A mouse weighing in excess of 10 pounds is not likely to be found. We have a very real opportunity to keep clearly before the students the important differences between things mathematical and things physical.

The process of graphing may, in turn, be applied to each inequality considered, so that solutions are being found algebraically and graphically. The three divisions of the plane should be pointed out each time so that an intuitive feeling for the idea that the line is a boundary line of the two half-planes develops. After several such graphs, many students may attempt to abandon trial and error. All well and good. The only criterion to apply to such methods is the pragmatic "does it work" test. At this point, the elegance or lack of elegance, should not become part of judging the validity of a student-constructed idea.

Inequalities: Formal Solutions

An extention to the work with inequalities may result from further exploration of life on earth. For example:

1.   The percentage of bateria left in a culture (p) depends upon the number of seconds (t) it is exposed to ultraviolet rays. This relationship may be described as
$$p = 100 - \frac{19}{2}t$$

2.   A particular culture was not safe to use unless there was less than 24% bacteria remaining in it. What lengths of time render the culture safe?
$$24 > 100 - \frac{19}{2}t$$

Solving this particular inequality may require the use of a method more powerful than an understanding of the symbolism. Such a problem, or one equally difficult, creates a need for students to learn a new technique. When the students are thwarted, we turn to familiar forms and try to determine a strategy based upon our methods with previous work. How would we solve the equation $24 = 100 - \frac{19}{2}t$? May we use the axioms of equality here? That is, to cite but one case, if we employ the addition axiom, do we destroy the inequality or alter the sense of it?

Simple trial and error experimentation should be our guide as we operate upon simple numbers to clarify the outcome. For example, we know that $10 > 5$. If we add equal quantities

$$10 + 3 > 5 + 3$$
$$13 > 8 \quad \text{True}$$

After we have tested many different positive and negative numbers, a feeling that addition is permissable as described becomes entrenched. The same process should follow for each of the operations of subtraction, division, and multiplication. These activities are designed to result in some basic assumptions to be used in dealing with inequalities:

If $a > b$ and $c = d$, then
1. $a + c > b + d$
2. $a - c > b - d$

If $a > b$ and $c > 0$, then
3. $ac > bc$

If $a > b$ and $c < 0$, then
4. $ac < bc$

If $a > b$ and $c > 0$, then
5. $\dfrac{a}{c} > \dfrac{b}{c}$

If $a > b$ and $c < 0$, then
6. $\dfrac{a}{c} < \dfrac{b}{c}$

The inequality used before as an example may serve to illustrate the multiplication and division assumptions:

$$10 > 5 \qquad\qquad 10 > 5$$
$$2 \times 10 \;\boxed{?}\; 2 \times 5 \qquad -2 \times 10 \;\boxed{?}\; -2 \times 5$$
$$20 > 10 \qquad\qquad -20 < -10$$

$$10 > 5 \qquad\qquad 10 > 5$$
$$10 \div 5 \;\boxed{?}\; 5 \div 5 \qquad 10 \div -5 \;\boxed{?}\; 5 \div (-5)$$
$$2 > 1 \qquad\qquad -2 < -1$$

The students see that the inequality sign is reversed when the multiplication or division by a negative quantity is carried out. The original problem of the bacteria is therefore solved as follows:

$$24 > 100 - \frac{19}{2} t$$

Multiply by 2: $\qquad 48 > 200 - 19t$

Subtract 200: $\qquad -152 > -19t$

Divide by -19: $\qquad \dfrac{-152}{-19} < \dfrac{-19t}{-19}$

$$8 < t$$

More than 8 seconds of exposure is required.

This problem, as well as those completed earlier, helps to make many ideas more meaningful. The notion of the range and domain of variables may be explored.

▶ What are the values of t that have meaning in this situation? Can t, for instance, be negative?

What of the *p*-values. Can they be negative?

Is there a maximum or minimum value for each?

Since we are thinking of $p = f(t)$, t is the independent variable (horizontal axis on the graph) and we speak of its *domain*. The domain consists of the real numbers from zero and up: $t \geq 0$. The range consists of the real numbers from zero to 100:

$$0 \leq p \leq 100$$

The latter inequality indicates that 100% is the maximum amount of bacteria that may be present and zero is the least amount. In this way, the concepts of range and domain aid our ability to focus upon values that are meaningful in the physical situation.

The use of situations from nature has offered us the chance to introduce many mathematical topics at different levels. Throughout, students have used mathematics to find out more about living things.

The Mathematics of Dieting 5.6

In dealing with body weight and food intake, it is natural to begin thinking of dieting. There are probably very few students at the secondary level who have not heard about the need to count calories when dieting. Although some people prefer to regulate the weight of the foods they are eating rather than calories, which would be consistent with the previous development regarding body weight, most students would probably be familiar with calories.

The needs of various animals in terms of calories per day are given in Table 5.4. The table contains metric units which provides needed practice, but can be converted to the English system if so desired (1 kg. is about 2.2 lb). Discussion may center on questions like the following

What is a calorie? (The amount of heat needed to raise the temperature of 1 kg of pure water 1 °C or 1 lb of pure water 4 °F.)

How many calories are you now consuming?

Why does a horse require more calories than a man?

Which animal requires the most calories per kilogram of weight? The least? Compare their sizes. Explain.

Table 5.4 Daily calorie requirements.

	Weight in Kg.	Total Calories
Guinea Pig	0.7	156
Rabbit	2	116
Man	70	2,310
Horse	600	13,200
Elephant	4,000	52,000
Whale	150,000	255,000

Recalling the earlier discussion about the food necessary to maintain body temperature and the fact that heat is lost through the surface area, will help students to better analyze the given data. Adding a column to the table titles "Calories Per Kg" may help students to see that these results are consistent with earlier ones since smaller mammals have to eat a greater percent of their weight to maintain body temperature. Hence, it is logical to expect the amount of calories consumed per kilogram to also be greater for the smaller-sized animals.

Collecting data, making tables and graphs, working with metric units, working with rates, in addition practice with basic computation are all among the mathematical ideas inherent in this situation. In addition, an opportunity is present to alert students to the need for a healthy diet, the nature of a healthy diet, which foods are vital, and how to determine the ingredients of processed foods, among other things. There are numerous possibilities for a variety of significant mathematics projects.

One further consideration to be mentioned makes use of minimum areas and heat loss. As discussed earlier, we lose our body heat through our skin. The more skin surface we have, the more heat we will lose in a given time period of similar activity. (Exercising would result in greater heat loss than resting.) This notion of heat loss also underlies the design of tea and coffee pots, home heating equipment, and indeed any area concerned with dispensing or conserving heat. This brings us back to the beehive discussion in which we found that a circle offers maximum volume for a given amount of surface area. We may now attempt to answer the simple question: Why is a teapot made round?

We must minimize the surface area if the water in the pot is to stay as hot as possible. Furthermore, a manufacturer would like to minimize surface area because it means less material per pot and lower cost. What shape will maintain a volume of a quart and still satisfy these two objectives? The sphere. Flatten the bottom, add a handle, and you have a teapot.

The situations and relationships considered here are designed to whet the appetite, and the references provided offer additional classroom experiences. There is no shortage of ideas to help students realize the role of mathematics in understanding the environment and the living things inhabiting it.

Footnotes

1. The Schools Council, Her Majesty's Stationery Office. *Mathematics in Primary Schools,* Curriculum Bulletin No. 1. 1965, pp. 55–56.
2. "D-Stix." Manufactured by Geodestix, Spokane, Washington.
3. Jonathan Swift. *Gulliver's Travels.* New York: W.W. Norton. 1961.
4. The Schools Council, Her Majesty's Stationery Office, *Mathematics in Primary Schools,* Curriculum Bulletin No. 1. 1965, p. 154.
5. For an interesting discussion see: J. B. S. Haldane. "On Being the Right Size," *The World of Mathematics,* James R. Newman, ed. New York: Simon and Schuster, 1956, pp. 952–957.

    Also see: Sir D'Arcy Thompson. *On Growth and Form,* J. T. Bonner, ed. New York: Cambridge University Press, 1961.
6. Marion Walter. "An Example of Informal Geometry: Mirror Cards," *The Arithmetic Teacher.* Vol. 13 (October 1966), pp. 448–452.
7. Richard F. Thaw and John E. Morlan. *Experiences and Demonstrations in Elementary Physical Science.* Dubuque: William C. Brown, 1964, pp. 3.
8. See: Sir D'Arcy Thompson. *On Growth and Form,* J. T. Bonner, ed. New York: Cambridge University Press, 1961, p. 254.

For Investigation and Discussion

1. Make a list of common objects that contain examples of symmetry of one form or another. Devise a lesson to teach students about symmetry using these objects.
2. Read Chapter 2, "On Magnitudes" in *On Growth and Form* (see references) by Sir D'Arcy Thompson. Describe how to make use of the ideas herein in plane geometry classes.
3. How do you explain the fact that many students can say, "Percent means hundredths," and yet cannot solve problems involved with percent?
4. Compare two methods of teaching percent ideas and emphasize the difficulties and advantages of each.
5. Select a physical situation involving inequalities and outline the procedures to be used that establish a need for formal techniques of solution. Then illustrate how the need will be met. (Use linear inequalities.)
6. Show how the solution of a quadratic inequality may involve the concepts of intersection and union of sets.
7. Construct a plan of activities that asks students to explore the growth of the area of a particular rectangle and the volume of the prism (rectangular solid) formed with the given rectangle as a base.

For Further Reading

Books

The School's Council, Her Majesty's Stationery Office. *Mathematics in Primary Schools,* Curriculum Bulletin No. 1. 1965.

Konkle, Gail S. *Shapes and Perceptions.* Boston: Prindle, Weber and Schmidt, 1974.

Thompson, Sir D'Arcy. *On Growth and Form,* J. T. Bonner, ed. New York: Cambridge University Press, 1961.

Walter, Marion I. *Boxes, Squares and Other Things.* Reston, Va.: National Council of Teachers of Mathematics, 1970.

Periodicals

Bishop, Thomas D. and Judy Kay Fetters. "Mathematical Reflections and Reflections on Other Isometries," *The Mathematics Teacher.* Vol. 69 (May 1976), pp. 404–407.

Cole, Blaine L. and Henry S. Weissenfluh. "An Analysis of Teaching Percentages," *The Arithmetic Teacher.* Vol. 21 (March 1974), pp. 226–228.

Fransden, Henry. "The Last Word on Solving Inequalities," *The Mathematics Teacher.* Vol. 62 (October 1969), pp. 439–441.

Kerr, Donald R. Jr. "The Study of Space Experiences: A Framework for Geometry for Elementary Teachers," *The Arithmetic Teacher.* Vol. 23 (March 1976), pp. 169–174.

Sloyer, Clifford W. "A Quality Inequality," *The Mathematics Teacher.* Vol. 68 (February 1975), pp. 84–87.

Smith, Arthur F. "An Application of Functions and Graphs to Inequalities," *The Mathematics Teacher.* Vol. 68 (October 1975), pp. 510–513.

Usiskin, Zalman. "Transformations in High School Geometry Before 1970," *The Mathematics Teacher.* Vol. 67 (April 1974), pp. 353–360.

Wendt, Arnold. "Per Cent Without Cases," *The Arithmetic Teacher.* Vol. 6 (October 1959), pp. 209–214.

Herron, J. Dudley and Grayson H. Wheatley. "A Unit Factor Method for Solving Proportional Problems," *The Mathematics Teacher.* Vol. 71 (January 1978), pp. 18–21.

Schmalz, Rosemary, S. P. "The Teaching of Percent," *The Mathematics Teacher.* Vol. 70 (April 1977), pp. 340–343.

CHAPTER 6

Mathematics and Space Exploration

Thanks to television, virtually every child knows about the advances made in space technology, such as moon walks, satellites orbiting the Earth, and the link-ups in space by orbiting vehicles. As space trips begin to expand our environment and our understanding of it, we can introduce students to mathematical concepts related to space exploration.

To gain some perspective of the Earth's position in our solar system, we may ask students to examine the comparitive sizes and volumes of the planets, the sun, and the moon. A series of interesting problems may be constructed from the information given in Table 6.1 involving the computation of volume and surface area; ratio and proportion; the use of scientific notation; and the conversion of units. Students can also gain some perspective about the size of our universe.

Table 6.1 *Table of Radii.*

Planet	Radius in Meters	Circumference at Equator	Volume	Surface Area
Mercury	2.6×10^6			
Venus	6.31×10^6			
Earth	6.38×10^6			
Mars	3.4×10^6			
Jupiter	7.2×10^7			
Saturn	6.0×10^7			
Uranus	2.7×10^7			
Neptune	2.5×10^7			
Pluto	uncertain	?	?	?
Sun	7.0×10^8			
Moon	1.7×10^6			

Such problems, together with those done earlier regarding the various gravity accellerations of the planets, build an interesting reservoir of information about the universe. At the same time, we increase student's skills and their understanding of mathematical concepts.

Periods of the Planets 6.1

This work can be taken still further by considering the positions of the planets relative to Earth. An interesting problem in a sourcebook produced by NASA asks:

> How often will Jupiter and Saturn appear in the same direction in the night sky as seen from Earth?[1]

After discussion about the meaning of the problem, students can consider what information is necessary to find an answer. An examination of these ideas helps students gain insight into the movement of the planets and the position of Earth in the solar system. As the problem becomes more meaningful, the probability of a solution is increased.

The revolutions of the planets mentioned, their **periods**, must be known to solve the problem. Table 6.2 shows how some of the planets compare with Earth.

Table 6.2 Number of Earth Years to Make One Revolution About the Sun (Approx.).

Planet	Earth Years for One Period
Earth	1
Mars	2
Jupiter	12
Saturn	30
Uranus	84
Neptune	165
Pluto	250

Now try to work the problem. Students should be given only as much information as needed to help them progress. They should be encouraged to try the problem without any indication of how to proceed, if we are to maximize opportunities for individual thought. Once a single question is asked about a given problem the student's thinking is directed. Present the problem and let the students go. If they have difficulty, there will be time for assistance. In this way, each student has the opportunity to think through a problem for himself and, at the least, has the chance to find out what he does not know.

The given problem may be considered in a number of ways. Two possibilities are:

1. Let J and S represent the periods of revolution of Jupiter and Saturn respectively. What part of a revolution will Jupiter complete in one Earth year? Saturn?

Jupiter: $\frac{1}{12} J$ Saturn: $\frac{1}{30} S$

Since they are to appear in the same direction in the sky,

$\frac{1}{12} J = \frac{1}{30} S$

Eliminate fractions:

$5J = 2S$

Jupiter makes 5 revolutions to 2 for Saturn. You may complete the problem.

2. Another approach: The time required has to be a multiple of 30 (Saturn's period) and 12 (Jupiter's period). What is the least common multiple of 12 and 30?

The planets will line up in the Earth sky once every 60 years.

At this point, similar problems may be attempted:

▶
About how often will the three planets, Jupiter, Saturn, and Uranus appear in the same direction in the night sky of the Earth?

How often could we expect Saturn and Uranus to appear in line in the Earth's sky at night?

About how often will Mars and Jupiter be so aligned?

You can construct many additional problems.

The positions of the planets at any given moment is of the utmost importance to scientists planning space shots such as the Jupiter probe and the Mars landing. While only simple mathematics is required for the previous problems, more advanced mathematics is necessary to do others.

The calculation of the time it takes various planets to make a single trip about the sun (the number of days in their respective years, or what is called their *period*) offers an interesting situation that also serves as important introductory work to circles. For example, consider this problem:

▶
At a certain time, the Earth, Mars, and the sun are in a straight line. (Let us assume that the Earth and Mars travel in a circular orbit.) It takes 780 days for the sun, the Earth, and Mars to be in a straight line again. Compute the period of Mars (Figure 6.1).

Figure 6.1

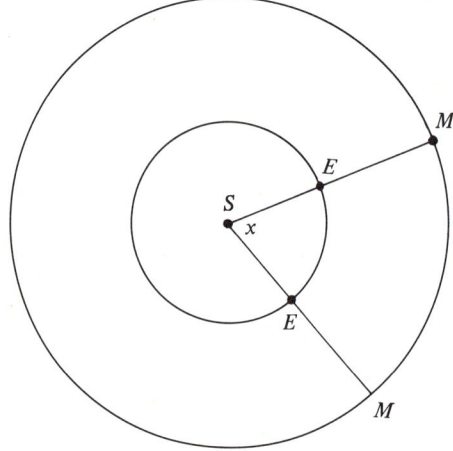

It will help the students to recall that in 780 days the earth completed 2 revolutions (730 days) and part of a third (50/365). In the same time, Mars completed one revolution and part of a second. If the students are unable to progress, they should be asked to find x. However they proceed, one solution involves two proportions in this manner:

$$\frac{x}{360} = \frac{50}{365} \quad \text{or} \quad x = 49°$$

Since Mars has made one revolution plus 49°, it has turned through 360° + 49°, or 409°.

$$\frac{360}{409} = \frac{p}{780} \quad \text{or} \quad p = 687$$

Thus, the period of Mars is about 687 days.

Circle Properties and Planets 6.2

The study of the circle itself is one of no small consequence. It is a common figure, seen everywhere and perphaps taken a bit for granted by students. The wheels of automobiles and trains are circles, and you can well imagine the consequences of using some other shape. What kind of ride would result from a car with square wheels? The shapes of coins and dishes, the cross sections of tree trunks and cans, and even the moon and sun suggest circles, as does the equator. There is no end of variety of physical objects that bring the circle to mind.

The mathematical properties of circles will shed light upon numerous problems from the physical world. If an auto tire is to fit the wheel properly, we become concerned with circumference. The size of the Earth at the equator and the distance around any of the planets and moons of our solar system also concern circumference. In machinery, one wheel is often used to make another wheel move. A circular shape helps to keep this motion smooth. When we are interested in the speed with which the wheels turn, we again need to know circumference. We immerse our students in the study of these concepts by asking questions.

> How would you go about finding the circumference of this earth upon which we live? Direct measurement would require a lot of string and a lot of walking! Yet back in about the third century B.C., a Greek mathematician was able to compute the earth's circumference. How did he do it?

The way in which Eratosthenes went about computing the circumference of the earth makes clear the power of mathematics! Perhaps the best way to help students realize the importance of this calculation is to place them in the position of Eratosthenes himself. Assume that the earth is shaped much like a sphere. If we cut through the sphere (like cutting through an orange) and pass our knife through the center, the surfaces of the two halves are circular. How would you go about trying to find the circumference of this circle, which is the length of the equator?

Many students have been led to believe that Columbus first thought the Earth to be round in 1490. They may be quite surprised to learn that more than 2000 years ago there were people who were aware of Earth's spherical shape!

But how did Eratosthenes proceed? He knew that Alexandria (point A) was due north of, and 500 miles from, the city of Syene (now called Aswan). This is point B in Figure 6.2. Thus, $\widehat{AB}$ is 500 miles. Eratosthenes also knew that on June 21 (summer solstice) at noon the sun shone directly down into a well at Syene. This meant that the sun's rays came directly along line BO at that time of the year. He also determined that the sun's rays made an angle of $7\frac{1}{2}°$ with line OAD, a line straight up from the surface of the Earth at point A.

Figure 6.2

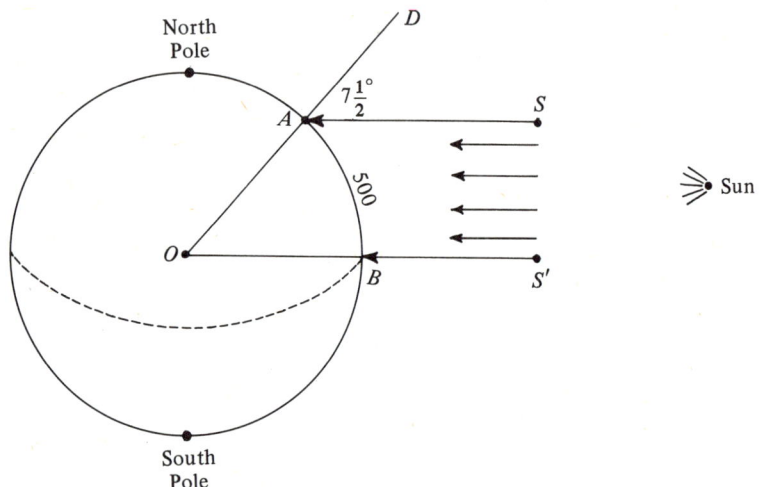

Since the sun is so far away, we may consider its rays to be parallel lines when they reach the Earth; that is, SA and $S'B$ are parallel. With this information, ask the students to do as Eratosthenes did and compute the circumference of the Earth. It is important to provide time for "groping" so that students have an opportunity to realize the satisfaction that comes from "cracking" a puzzling problem.

The solution presented by Eratosthenes involves the use of corresponding angles to establish $\angle AOB = 7\frac{1}{2}°$. He then solved the proportion,

$$\frac{7\frac{1}{2}}{360} = \frac{500}{x}$$

and finally arrived at the answer: 24,000 miles. This is a remarkable result when you consider that in the time of Columbus, geographers are reputed to believe that the correct figure for the circumference of the Earth was 17,000 miles. As a matter of fact, had Columbus known the correct figure (about 24,900) he might never have understaken to sail to India!

The brief work above with circles, circumference, etc. has been a demonstration of how, with a little mathematics, we have been able to determine approximations of the circumference of our planet as well as the periods of planets under certain conditions. What a remarkable return for our mathematical efforts. In this way we open new vistas to the role of mathematics in helping us to better "see" nature.

Many pertinent exercises are available. The following list is a sample:

1. What is the circumference of the path of a satellite that is in a circular orbit 500 mi above the surface of the Earth?

2. If a telephone line were constructed around the Earth and if the wire were 20 ft above the surface of the Earth at each point, how much longer would the wire be than the circumference of the Earth? ($r = 4000$ mi) (See Figure 6.3.)

3. Same problem as the preceding except based on the moon. ($r = 1080$ mi) Compare the answer here with that of problem 2.

4. A belt is wrapped tightly around two wheels, A, and B, each of which turns on an axle. The function of the belt is to transmit the motion of wheel A to wheel B. (Assume that the belt doesn't slip.) If the radius of wheel A is 6 in. and it revolves 1000 times a minute, what should be the radius of wheel B so that it will revolve 1500 times a minute? (See Figure 6.4.)

5. The sun, the Earth, and Venus are in a line every 579 days. In that time Venus makes more than two revolutions and the Earth more than one. Find the number of days in a year on Venus (Figure 6.5).

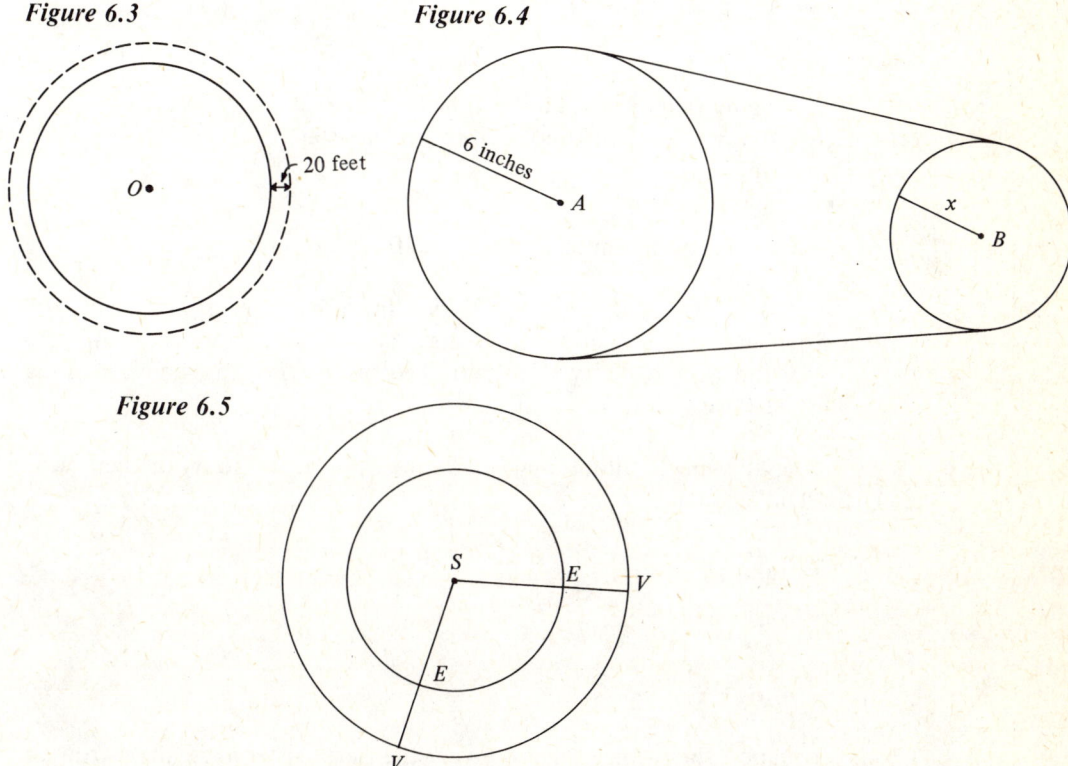

Figure 6.3

Figure 6.4

Figure 6.5

Notice how a given mathematical concept may have numerous uses in a variety of apparently unrelated situations. This is another significant quality of mathematics.

6.3 Time in Space Travel

If man were to be able to travel as fast as the speed of light, 186,300 miles per *second*, it would still take more than 4 years to travel to Alpha Centauri, the nearest star that is not in our solar system! Does this mean that man will never be able to travel the universe? Is it too vast to be spanned by a human being who lives to an average age of 70? Not exactly. The aging rate is not constant everywhere, strange as it may seem. Einstein's theory of relativity offers some fascinating ideas about aging. Most importantly for us, the mathematics of this situation involves the solution of radical equations in algebra. We once again offer students the opportunity to add to their understanding of the universe and the role played by mathematics in the process.

Einstein posed that if one system moves very fast with respect to another system, time will pass more slowly in the rapidly moving system. For example, if one sister of a set of twins went off into space at a rapid rate and came back to Earth after a while, she would actually be younger than her twin sister! The faster she traveled, the more the aging process would slow down. As a matter of fact, using mathematics and Einstein's equations you can figure out with accuracy what the age differences would be.[2] The aging rates are related to each other in accordance with the formula:

$$R_a = R_b \sqrt{1 - \left(\frac{v}{c}\right)^2}$$

where

R_a: aging rate of astronaut brother or sister
R_b: aging rate of earthbound brother or sister
v: speed of travel
c: speed of light

Let us see what this means in terms of a specific situation.

▶ An astronaut was on a spaceship traveling at half the speed of light. His sister on Earth was one year younger at the time of launch. How long must the astronaut travel so that he returns to Earth the same age as his sister? (Use $v = 0.5c$).

After allowing a suitable amount of time for students to try on their own, apply Einstein's equations:

$$R_a = R_b \sqrt{1 - \left(\frac{v}{c}\right)^2} \quad \text{since } v = 0.5c$$

$$R_a = R_b \sqrt{1 - \left(\frac{0.5c}{c}\right)^2}$$

$$= R_b \frac{\sqrt{3}}{2}$$

This last equation shows that for every year the Earth sister ages, the astronaut brother will only age $\sqrt{3}/2$ years. Imagine, the clocks on Earth have moved a year while the clock on the spaceship has advanced only $\sqrt{3}/2$ years, about .87 of a year! But we have not answered the question about their ages being the same. Let x be the time needed:

$$x = \frac{\sqrt{3}}{2}x + 1 \text{ year}$$
$$2x - \sqrt{3}x = 2$$
$$x(2 - \sqrt{3}) = 2$$
$$x = \frac{2}{2 - \sqrt{3}}$$
$$x = 4 + 2\sqrt{3} \text{ years}$$

In $4 + 2\sqrt{3}$ years of space travel, the astronaut will return to Earth and find himself at the same age as his sister who was a year younger when he left. This sounds incredible but, from all available evidence, apparently true. That's about 7½ years of travel at half the speed of light. To check the answer, let N be the sister's age. The astronaut's age is $N + 1$. After $4 + 2\sqrt{3}$ years of travel the ages are:

Astronaut

$$A_a = N + 1 + \frac{\sqrt{3}}{2}(4 + 2\sqrt{3})$$
$$= N + 1 + 2\sqrt{3} + 3$$
$$= N + 4 + 2\sqrt{3}$$

Sister

$$A_b = N + (4 + 2\sqrt{3})$$

The answer checks since both ages are identical.

A host of problems may now be attempted, first keeping the speed at $0.5c$ and later varying the speed. These problems not only aid in the realization of some startling facts about our world, but also provide opportunities to use a considerable amount of algebra. Here is some additional practice:

> Find the general equations necessary to solve the previous problem if the sister's age is N and the astronaut is d years older.

> At the same speed ($0.5c$) a female astronaut goes off in space. If she is 5 years older than her 20-year old brother, who remains on Earth, how long should she travel in order to return to Earth at the same age as her brother?

> An astronaut, who is 8 years older than his 18-year old brother, goes off in a rocket ship at half the speed of light. How long a trip should he make to return at the same age as his brother?

> At what velocity must an astronaut travel in order that he may age half as fast as a brother back on Earth?

> Twins are 10 years old. One twin, a girl, is placed on a space ship and sent off. The other, a boy, remains on Earth. If the speed of the ship is .94 of the speed of light, how long should the trip be so that the girl returns to Earth and finds her twin brother twice as old as she is?

> How would the rates of aging compare if the astronaut could travel at the speed of light?

From the solution of radical equations to the solution of linear equations, these space problems have involved the student with many mathematical notions, which have added to the understanding of the physical concepts themselves.

Special Units

In working with the magnitudes involved in space problems, it becomes necessary to introduce many new units. This adds to student understanding of measurement at the same time that it enlarges his knowledge of space.

For example, in the previous section, we encountered the speed of light: 186,300 mi/sec. How fast would this be in mi/hr? After students have had a chance to try to convert on their own and the problem is discussed, we see that methods of conversion, as well as scientific notation, come into play:

$$v = 186,300 \ \frac{\text{mi}}{\text{sec}} \times \frac{60 \text{ sec}}{1 \text{ min}} \times \frac{60 \text{ min}}{1 \text{ hr}}$$
$$= (1.863 \times 10^5)(6.0 \times 10)(6.0 \times 10) \text{ mi/hr}$$
$$= 6.707 \times 10^8 \text{ mi/hr or } 670,700,000 \text{ mi/hr}$$

You may now have a better idea of just how fast light travels. If a spacecraft were to escape from our solar system (leaving at a distance equal to the Earth's average distance from the Sun) it would need a speed of 94,200 mi/hr or more. That's quite fast compared to jetliners that fly at about 550 mi/hr. The speed of light is still more than 1000 times faster than that.

The use and conversion of units of measure sometimes causes stress for student and teacher. The physicist has a unique method for dealing with this problem that often strikes terror into the heart of mathematics teachers. Imagine how students might react to the physics teacher who "cancels" units. Cancellation is difficult enough; but when it is done with units rather than numbers, that is too much. Before exploring this idea, let us be clear that units, like most other concepts we have considered, are discussed as needed. There is no lesson on "units." The activities described have resulted from ample opportunities to convert various units.

Shall we accept the practice of

$$(5 \text{ ft}) \times (10 \text{ ft}) = 50 \text{ ft}^2$$

or

$$\frac{90 \text{ ft}}{\cancel{\text{sec}}} \cdot \frac{\overset{1}{\cancel{60 \text{ sec}}}}{1 \text{ min}} = \frac{5400 \text{ ft}}{\text{min}}$$

just as if we were multiplying and dividing units? The real question would seem to be, Why not? Physicists are quick to put these symbols to work for them, so why should math teachers be reluctant? The process makes good sense to students and, most importantly, it works! Indeed, we can carry this a bit further: How far will I drive if I average 30 mph (mi/hr) for 6 hr?

$$\frac{30 \text{ mi}}{\cancel{\text{hr}}} \times 6 \ \cancel{\text{hr}} = 180 \text{ mi}$$

The outcome is a natural one and the process should be acceptable. The conversion of units in speed-time situations may be greatly facilitated through the use of these techniques. Sixty miles per hour is equivalent to how many feet per second (ft/sec)?

$$\frac{60 \ \cancel{\text{mi}}}{\cancel{\text{hr}}} \cdot \frac{1 \ \cancel{\text{hr}}}{3600 \text{ sec}} \cdot \frac{5280 \text{ ft}}{1 \ \cancel{\text{mi}}}$$

The "fractions" we have introduced can be thought of as multiplication identity elements; thus our result should have the same value that we began with. In addition, we selected the multipliers by keeping clearly before us what we wanted our answer to be. This is a typical mathematical activity—putting the symbols to work for you. In this case the result is:

$$\frac{60 \text{ mi}}{\text{hr}} \cdot \frac{1 \text{ hr}}{3600 \text{ sec}} \cdot \frac{5280 \text{ ft}}{1 \text{ mi}} = \frac{\overset{1}{\cancel{60}} \cdot \overset{88}{\cancel{5280}} \text{ ft}}{\underset{1}{\cancel{3600}} \text{ sec}} = \frac{88 \text{ ft}}{\text{sec}} = 88 \text{ ft/sec}$$

Students who can negotiate this path are to be encouraged. Be especially careful, however, of destroying good student insight by forcing an answer about why it works. This is a most difficult question. It does work and we should in this case accept it at face value. Those who cannot master these ideas may use other techniques. We must not let words like "cancel" scare us. Our concern is with ideas, not words. If "cancel" can help students understand what is going on, let us be happy we have it to use.

You may also wish to reconsider this discussion using metric units, e.g. What is the speed of light in kilometers? This is an interesting use of metrics. Another problem follows:

Alpha Centauri, the nearest star, is about 4.3 light years away, (4.3 times the distance light can travel in one year). If a spaceship was able to maintain a speed of 94,200 mi/hr, how long would it take to make the trip?

Because of the vastness of space, we not only find scientific notation a necessity, but we also require special large units such as the light year. How many miles are contained in one light year? Using the speed of light to be 6.707×10^8:

$$1 \text{ light yr} = 6.707 \times 10^8 \frac{\text{mi}}{\text{hr}} \times \frac{24 \text{ hr}}{1 \text{ da}} \times \frac{365 \text{ da}}{1 \text{ yr}}$$

$$= 5.875 \times 10^{12} \text{ mi/yr} = 5.88 \times 10^{12} \text{ mi}$$

Now the problem solution can be completed:

$$t = \frac{4.3 \times 5.88 \times 10^{12} \text{ mi}}{94,200 \text{ mi/hr}}$$

$$= \frac{25.28 \times 10^{12} \text{ hr}}{9.42 \times 10^4}$$

$$= 2.68 \times 10^8 \text{ hr.}$$

The student can convert into years and will find the result to be 3.1×10^4 yr or 31,000 yr! Speeds approaching the speed of light are a necessity for successful space travel.

Other units you may wish to investigate through the study of space problems are:

1 astronomical unit (AU): average distance of Earth to sun, 92,960,000 mi

1 parsec: 2.06×10^5 AU or 3.26 light yr.

Mach number (M): ratio of vehicle speed to speed of sound at that altitude; e.g. aircraft at 30,000 ft flies at speed of sound, about 995 ft/sec. Flight is at Mach 1. Same altitude, speed 1990: Mach 2.

Some problems are listed below:

> In our solar system Pluto is the farthest planet from the sun. How long would it take sunlight to reach Pluto if maximum distance from the sun is 4.60 billion miles? Express the distance from Pluto to the sun in light years.
>
> What is the Mach number of an aircraft flying at an altitude where the temperature is 0 °C and the speed of sound is about 330 m/sec if the speed of the aircraft is 495 m/sec?
>
> Find the speed of an aircraft flying at Mach 2.3 if the speed of sound at this altitude is 1150 ft/sec. Express this speed in mi/hr.

6.4 How Far and How Much Can You See?

An astronaut in orbit around the Earth can see great distances and large portions of the Earth. If you stand at the seashore and look out to the ocean, you can see a much shorter distance than someone higher than you are, looking in the same direction. That's why the astronaut has such an advantage. He is really out of this world. We involve some important mathematics and interesting information about our world in asking ourselves, How far can you see? How far is it to the horizon?

> If the land is flat before you or if you were at the beach on either coast of our country, how far would you be able to see?

An application of the Pythagorean theorem and some approximation provides us with an interesting relationship (Figure 6.6). Since light rays can be assumed to travel in straight lines, if you were to stand at point A, you would be able to see to the horizon—a tangent line (d) from eye level to the curve of the earth. But how long is line d? If we use the Pythagorean theorem, since the radius of the earth forms a right angle with line d at point B, we find that

$$d^2 + r^2 = (r + h)^2$$

Figure 6.6

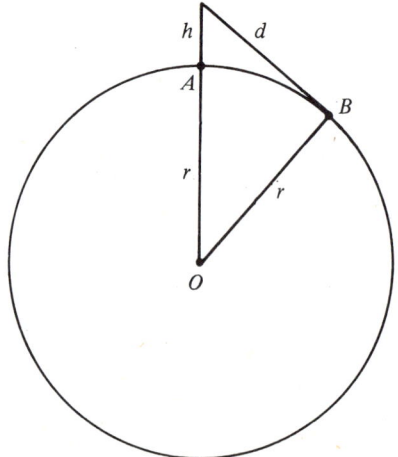

Solving for d,
$$d^2 = (r + h)^2 - r^2$$
$$d^2 = r^2 + 2hr + h^2 - r^2$$
$$d^2 = 2hr + h^2$$

By the distributive law,
$$d^2 = h(2r + h)$$

If your eyes were 5 ft above the earth, then $h = 5$ ft, or to be correct, with the radius of the earth in miles, $h = .00094+$ mi. Since h is so small in comparison with r, the value of $(2r + h)$ is extremely close to $2r$; so a good approximation of the distance that you can see to the horizon is $d^2 = 2rh$. If we take this formula, express the radius of the earth as 4000 miles, and change the height into units of feet, we can get a simple formula that will enable us to arrive at quick approximations:

$$d^2 = 2rh$$
$$d^2 = (2)(4000)\frac{h}{5280} = \frac{8000}{5280}h$$

or
$$d^2 = \frac{100}{66}h$$

which we can approximate to
$$d^2 = \frac{3}{2}h$$

and finally
$$d = \sqrt{\frac{3}{2}(h)}$$

We have arrived at a fairly close approximation of the distance (in miles) to the horizon when we know the height (in feet) above the surface of the earth:

$$d = \sqrt{\frac{3}{2}h}$$

This development is primarily for the teacher's understanding and is not necessarily intended to students.

The formula that is finally conceived offers an opportunity to introduce many problems involving radicals. For example:

If your eyes are 5 ft above the earth, how far can you see?

Since $d = \sqrt{\frac{3}{2}h}$, we solve and get

$$d = \sqrt{\frac{3}{2}(5)}$$
$$d = \sqrt{\frac{15}{2}} = \sqrt{7.5}$$
$$d = 2.7$$

If your eyes are 5 ft above the earth's surface, you can see about 2.7 mi.

If we are to concern ourselves with distances to the horizon from much larger heights, such as those of astronauts, we may return to the formula found earlier to add to our accuracy. For example:

▶ How far would an astronaut be able to see to the horizon if he were 25 mi high?

It may be appropriate in this instance to use

$$d^2 = 2rh + h^2$$
or $$d = \sqrt{2rh + h^2}$$

Not only is the accuracy of the result improved (and a larger h may require such a revision), but we now have before us the problem of finding the square root of a sum.

We now consider the question, Is $\sqrt{a + b} = \sqrt{a} + \sqrt{b}$? Thus, we reinforce the importance of the earlier processes since, in this instance, we must take the sum first or else our work will be incorrect. For example, is $\sqrt{9 + 16} = \sqrt{9} + \sqrt{16}$?

$$\sqrt{9 + 16} = \sqrt{25} = 5$$
$$\sqrt{9} = 3, \quad \sqrt{16} = 4, \quad 3 + 4 = 7$$

At this point the investigation might be extended to include subtraction. It would then be timely to present the students with a series of examples involving operations with numbers in radical form, emphasizing the process of simplification.

6.5 Tangents in Space

There are still further mathematical advantages to be drawn from the topic of space exploration. While algebraic concepts play an important role, the geometry is also of interest.

The idea of tangent is a difficult one to define exactly, but an idea that is intuitively quite accessible. A boy stands at the seashore and gazes out to sea. His line of vision is tangent to the earth at the horizon (Figure 6.7). The moon passes between the sun and the Earth, forming an eclipse; the shadow boundary lines are tangent lines (Figure 6.8). An inclined plane is tangent to a disc that is rolling down its length. These are some familiar situations involving the tangent. Let us recall a problem of the distance to the horizon:

▶ A lookout in the crow's nest of a ship is 100 ft above the sea. How far can he see?

Figure 6.7

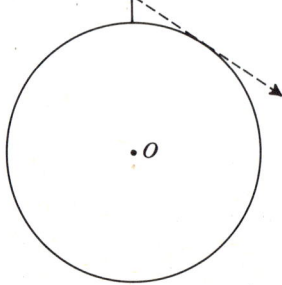

Figure 6.8

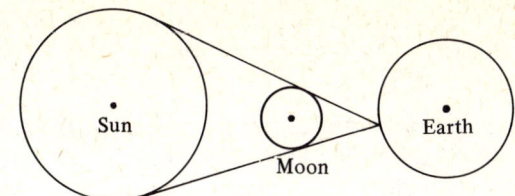

In dealing with this situation in algebra, we made several assumptions about the relationships present. We can now be a bit more precise in our explanation. As the sailor looks out over the sea, his line of vision extends to the horizon: a tangent from his lookout point to a great circle of the Earth (Figure 6.9). Before, we assumed that $\triangle AOB$ was a right triangle with a right angle at B. Can we be sure of this? If we attempt to make a drawing or construction of this situation, we find that since the lookout is on a pole vertical to the Earth's surface, if extended (AC), it should pass through the center of the Earth. Of course, we are assuming that the Earth is a perfect sphere, which it is not in acutality. It does approximate the sphere closely enough for our purpose. If we complete $\triangle AOB$ by drawing OB, it appears that $OB \perp AB$. If this is true, we may use the Pythagorean theorem to determine any desired lengths. But how can we be sure? Perhaps if the circle is of a particular size or if AC is made a certain length, the line OB (the radius) will not be perpendicular to the tangent AB at the point of contact. And so we attempt a proof by focusing upon the geometry alone.

Prove: $m \perp PQ$ at Q (Figure 6.10).

Given: Line m tangent to circle p at Q.

Figure 6.9   **Figure 6.10**

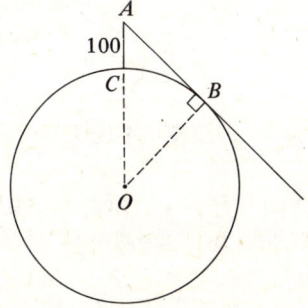   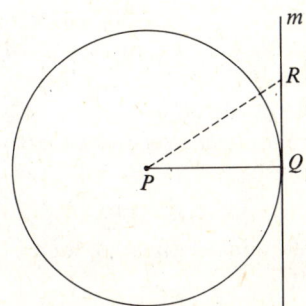

If we can show that PQ is the shortest distance from p to line m, then, since the shortest distance from a point to a line is the perpendicular, we will have shown $PQ \perp m$.

Compare PQ with PR, where R is any other point on line m. R must be outside the circle since m meets the circle at but one point, Q. Thus, R must be farther from the center than Q or $PR > PQ$. So PQ is the shortest line from p to m.

The converse of this theorem is also important and is developed in an interesting manner in the SMSG text[3]. A single proposition is considered that involves the three possible relationships between a circle and a line in the same plane: The line is outside the circle, on the circle, or inside the circle. The proposition is stated as follows:

> Given a line and a circle in the same plane (Figure 6.11), let P be the center of the circle; let F be the foot of the perpendicular from P to the line. Then either:
>
> **(a)** Every point of the line is outside the circle, or
>
> **(b)** F is on the circle, and the line is tangent to the circle at F, or
>
> **(c)** F is inside the circle, and the line intersects the circle in exactly two points, which are equidistant from F.

Figure 6.11

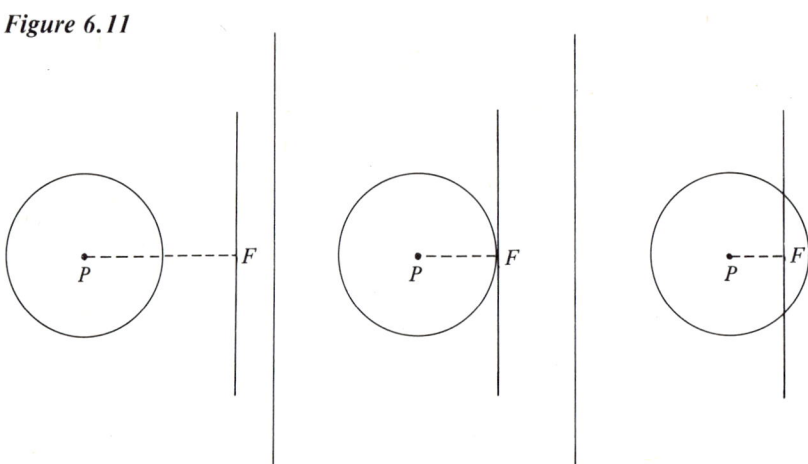

This is a rather long statement of a theorem and its proof is equally lengthy, but the text explains that the gains are worth the effort. Once this theorem has been established, all the other theorems about secants, chords, and tangents become corollaries.

Here, only the second case (b) is presented as it is pertinent to the problem under consideration.

> F is on the circle (Figure 6.12). Here we have $PF = r$. Thus, if Q is any other point on the line, then $PQ > r$. Hence the line is tangent to the circle at point F.

Figure 6.12

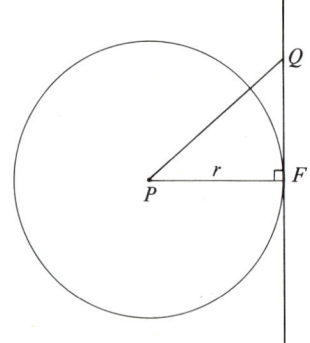

Now we have a solid basis upon which to make use of the Pythagorean theorem in order to find the distance that the sailor in the crow's nest can see. The solution is based on Figure 6.9. Since OB and OC are radii of the earth, we may use 4000 miles as an approximation for their length. (Changing to feet, we get 4000×5280, which gives 21,120,000 ft). The lengths of the sides of the triangle are as follows: $AO = 21,120,100$; $BO = 21,120,000$.

$$AB^2 + (21,120,000)^2 = (21,120,100)^2$$
$$AB = \sqrt{(21,120,100)^2 - (21,120,000)^2}$$
$$AB = \sqrt{100^2 \cdot (211,201)^2 - 100^2 (211,200)^2}$$

By factoring, we get

$$AB = 100\sqrt{(211,201)^2 - (211,200)^2}$$

Factoring again, we get

$$AB = 100\sqrt{(211,201 - 211,200)(211,201 + 211,200)}$$
$$AB = 100\sqrt{(1)(422,401)}$$
$$AB = 65,000 \text{ ft (approximately) or about 12 mi}$$

The sailor 100 ft above the sea is able to see about 12 mi in every direction. Students can imagine what will happen with an astronaut. Let us ask them to find out.

> A spacecraft at altitude of 100 mi is in orbit about the Earth. What will the distance to the horizon be for an astronaut in the spacecraft? (Use the formula for long distance.)

$$d = \sqrt{2rh + h^2}$$
$$= \sqrt{2(4000)(100) + 100^2}$$
$$= \sqrt{810,000}$$
$$= \sqrt{81 \times 10^4}$$
$$= 10^2 \times \sqrt{81}$$
$$= 900 \text{ mi}$$

That's quite a difference. You can clearly see how distance to the horizon is a function of height above the Earth. A variety of problems can be presented for practice in the solution of radical equations, finding square roots, and generally using the techniques of both algebra and geometry as the student works with circles and tangents.

The following application yields some interesting work in determining surface areas on a sphere:

> Gemini 11 achieved one of the highest orbit altitudes of its time, about 850 miles. What percent of the Earth's surface was visible to astronauts Conrad and Gordon from this altitude?

This time we are trying to find a portion of the Earth's surface (Figure 6.13 see page 94). The surface area of a sphere is found by

$$A_e = 4\pi r^2$$

but what about the zone that is shaded? Examine the Figure 6.13.

Figure 6.13

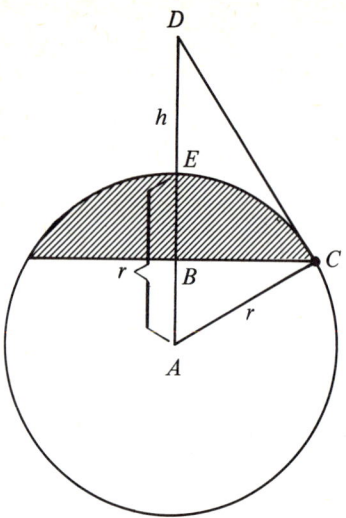

How are $\triangle ABC$ and $\triangle ACD$ related? (Are they similar triangles?) Therefore:

$$\frac{AB}{AC} = \frac{AC}{AD} \quad \text{and} \quad AB = \frac{(AC)^2}{AD} \quad \text{or} \quad AB = \frac{r^2}{r+h}$$

$$BE = r - AB$$
$$= r - \frac{r^2}{r+h} = \frac{r^2 + rh - r^2}{r+h}$$
$$= \frac{rh}{r+h}$$

Let the area of the region with altitude BE be A_z. Then

$$A_z = 2\pi r(BE)$$
$$= 2\pi r \left(\frac{rh}{r+h}\right)$$

The ratio of the area of the zone to the surface area of Earth:

$$\frac{A_z}{A_e} = \frac{2\pi r}{4\pi r^2}\left(\frac{rh}{r+h}\right)$$
$$= \frac{h}{2(r+h)}$$

If $h = 850$,

$$\frac{A_z}{A_e} = \frac{850}{2(4000 + 850)}$$
$$= \frac{85}{970} = 0.088$$

The astronauts can see 8.8% of the Earth's surface from their orbit. Some more sample problems:

▶ Gemini 10 with astronauts Collins and Young aboard flew in an orbit with a high point at 168 mi and a low point of 100 mi. What percent of the Earth's surface could they see from these altitudes? How far is their distance to the horizon from each altitude?

Discuss how the ratio $\frac{A_z}{A_e}$ varies with the altitude, h.

From what altitude will an astronaut be able to see 1/5 of the surface of the Earth?

What percent of the Earth's surface can be "seen" from a satellite whose altitude is 21,700 miles above the Earth?

From what altitude will an astronaut be able to see ½ of the Earth's surface?

In Conclusion 6.6

Mathematics will enable students to understand more about their environment. In dealing with the broad variety of physical situations from pollution to space exploration, we have encountered the need to make use of a multitude of mathematical skills and concepts. In the process, we often had to combine the use of several branches of mathematics and so began to develop, in students, a feeling for the unity in mathematics. We also saw how mathematics interacts with other disciplines as we seek solutions to problems.

Do not underestimate the value of placing mathematics into a living, breathing environment. Taking the time necessary to help students to understand situations in which mathematics is used will pay handsome dividends. You are offering the students a picture of mathematics all too often hidden from their view. Mathematics takes a good deal of its life's blood from the world in which we live. In return, mathematics offers us the ability to see more clearly how this world operates. It is a perfect union that somehow was torn apart as we constructed curriculum for youngsters. The time has come to reunite mathematics with reality. In this section we emphasized its role in the environment. We now turn to the use of mathematics as the language of science.

Footnotes

1. Developed at Duke University. *Space Mathematics. A Resource for Teachers.* Washington, D.C.: NASA, January 1972, p. 25.
2. See: Developed at Duke Univeristy. *Space Mathematics. A Resource for Teachers.* Washington, D.C.: NASA, January 1972, p. 48, Exercise 19.
3. School Mathematics Study Group. *Mathematics for High School: Geometry,* Part II, Student's Text. New Haven: Yale University Press. 1961, pp. 414–416.

For Investigation and Discussion

1. Use the table of information about the planets (Table 6.1) to develop a lesson comparing the volumes of planets in our solar system.
2. Construct three examples like those on page 78 designed to interest students in doing work using the concept of the circumference of a circle.
3. Make a lesson plan with the objective of developing the ability to solve radical equations. Use the Einstein relationship described in Section 6.3.
4. Indicate how the discussion of "units" on pages 86–87 might proceed using the metric system. Extend this to include the conversions on page 88.

5. In the discussion of tangents (Section 6.5), a theorem from the SMSG textbook was mentioned concerning the possible relationships between a line and a circle in the same plane. Of the three cases considered, only one was discussed. Describe how you would help students to learn the other two.

6. Plan a lesson to enable students to devise a formula for the distance that can be seen from the surface of the moon. (Use radius = 1000 mi).

For Further Reading

Books

Ahrendt, Myrl H. *The Mathematics of Space Exploration,* New York: Holt, Rinehart and Winston, 1965.

Glasstone, Samuel. *Sourcebook on the Space Sciences.* New York: Van Nostrand, 1965.

Kline, Morris. *Mathematics and the Physical World.* New York: Thomas Y. Crowell, 1959.

National Aeronautics and Space Admininstration. *Space Mathematics: A Resource for Teachers.* (Developed at Duke University.) Washington, D.C., 1972.

NASA. *The Shapes of Tommorrow.* Washington, D.C., 1957.

Woodby, Lauren G. "How Far Can You See?" *Enrichment Mathematics for the Grades,* 27th Yearbook. Reston, Va.: National Council of Teachers of Mathematics, 1963, pp. 269-273.

Periodicals

Ahrendt, Myrl H. "The Flight of Apollo II Analyzed with High School Mathematics," *School Science and Mathematics.* Vol. 70 (June 1970), pp. 549-562.

Fischer, Irene. "The Shape and Size of the Earth," *The Mathematics Teacher.* Vol. 60 (May 1967), pp. 508-516.

Graesser, R. F. "The Direction of Sunset," *The Mathematics Teacher.* Vol. 60 (February 1967), pp. 115-116.

Johnson, Donovan A. "Mathematics Outside the Classroom," *School Science and Mathematics.* February 1974, pp. 129-134.

Metz, Jim. "When Will We Meet Again? A Modified Answer," *The Mathematics Teacher* Vol. 70 (January 1977), pp. 41-45.

SECTION II

Mathematics and Science

CHAPTER 7

Mathematics: The Language of Science

Can you imagine what it would be like for a scientist to try to communicate the results of his work to another without the highly developed system of mathematics?

E. T. Bell in *Mathematics, Queen and Servant of Science*, makes this point especially clear. He indicates by example after example, how progress in science was only possible because of developments in mathematics:

> The revolution in modern physics which began with the work of W. Heisenberg (1901–) and P. A. M. Dirac (1902–) in 1925 could never have been started without the necessary mathematics of matrices invented by Cayley in 1858, and elaborated by a small army of mathematicians from then to the present time.[1]

Bell goes on to describe how mathematicians attempt to aid in the resolution of scientific problems. In so doing they may develop new, highly abstract mathematics, which have no present application whatsoever, only to find important uses later. Thus growth in both mathematics and science would seem to be dependent each upon the other, which explains Bell's apt title.

It is quite common to hear high school students talk about the wonder of science: how combined liquids magically change color, how the combination of certain elements causes an explosion, how we gain fantastic lifting power through the use of simple machines. Yet these same students are eager to share their common boredom and lack of interest in mathematics. How could mathematics be so intimately interwoven in the ideas of science from process to concepts, and yet appear to be so grossly unappreciated by students? Perhaps one important reason is a lack of emphasis upon the role of mathematics in science as students are learning mathematics. Too often mathematics is taught for its own sake, with a few applications introduced as a means of practice after concepts have been taught. How ironic. It would seem that the order should be exactly reversed since applications create the willingness and the need to learn. If our instruction is to have purpose and significance for students, then it would seem that students should be thrust into problems stemming from real life situations. The students' interest level and the desire and need to know may then be at its height. This same idea is expounded by Fitzgerald who writes:

> It is my contention that students in secondary schools are not provided with experience in grappling with real comprehensive problems affecting themselves, their lives, their communities and their environments. If students could have such experiences in schools, not only would mathematics become better understood and more appreciated, but school itself might become a more significant and appreciated institution.[2]

If we think of mathematics as a language, we must consider how a language is learned. There is a strong need for concrete anchors upon which to hook abstract ideas in the learning of a language, an abstract set of symbols. Think back to how you attempted to learn a foreign language. How did you learn the meanings of words? W. W. Sawyer has a fine example in the introduction to *Vision in Elementary Mathematics* where he confronts the reader with Chinese symbols.[3] After offering the symbols without explanation, Sawyer then explains what the pictures represent and how they came to be what they are. This explanation instantly makes the symbols easier to comprehend and remember. Teachers are often reluctant to present more problem solving situations because of the time involved. They say that allowing time for student exploration would make the task of "covering" a full syllabus an impossibility. However, consider the example of the Chinese symbols. This would seem to indicate that presenting the work with an emphasis on student understanding could save time by eliminating much repetitive drill. Both teachers and students could then complete the required work. In any case, here we offer the problem centered approach. Let us see how it might proceed with the emphasis upon mathematics as a language.

7.1 Simple Experiments

Science experiments yield data. Once we deal with collections of data, we become involved in the use of the language of mathematics. When we organize the data and seek patterns of relationship, the outcome is usually described as a mathematical formula. A spring-stretch experiment is a good example.

▶   How much will a spring stretch as weights are hung from it?

Springs are all around us. A few minutes of discussion with students about the use of springs will result in a sizeable list of uses, from watches to furniture.
Any kind of spring that is flexible enough to give meaningful results can be used, especially a slinky-toy spring. Small fishing scales may be convenient since they give a clear indication of the amount of weight added as well as an easy measure of the resulting extension of the spring. If weights are not available, or-

dinary hardware store nuts, bolts and washers will suffice. Before the students do the experiment, briefly discuss the process of scientific experiment and generally clarify this process as explained in Section 4.1. Consideration might be given to:

What do scientists do?

What is an experiment?

What is scientific observation?

In addition, it is important that the students guess about the outcome: What do you think is going to happen to the spring as we hang weights from it? The students' answers, together with their explanations, stimulate thinking about the situation and create interest in *wanting* to do the experiment. Everyone will be anxious to see if the results were anticipated with any degree of correctness. Guessing builds the desire to do the task.

How shall the students proceed? Hang weights from the spring one at a time (or 1 oz at a time, if your equipment permits), measure the resulting stretch, and record the results in a table of information such as this:

When we hang:	The spring stretches:
(weight in oz)	(stretch in in.)

The physical arrangement of the room will depend upon the amount of equipment the teacher has available. For the best results, 5 or 6 setups of springs and weights could be located in different areas of the room so that students could cluster about these in small groups. If only a single experiment is available, the experiment could be undertaken at the front of the room with several students coming up and doing the work. One student could record the results on the chalkboard while the others do the same at their seats; another student could actually place the weights on the spring; and perhaps a third student could read off the results after carrying out the measuring process. When the experiment is completed and the data collected, each child will have a table of data before him. If mulitple sets of equipment are used, we will have the results of 5 or 6 experiments readily available. If only one set was employed, the teacher might emphasize the need for repeating the experiment in order to be sure that the recorded results are the product of the weights and the springs rather than the experimenter.

We are now ready to examine the data. First, did things come out as you had expected? Compare your guesses with the results. Second, is there any pattern in the numbers of the table? The various patterns found by the students should be written out in sentence form on the chalkboard as the class explores each one in an attempt to determine if it actually does fit the data. If we assume that the spring in question yielded results that showed a stretch of 3 in for each ounce of weight added, the statements given by the students might include:

The stretch is three times the weight.

The weight is always one third of the stretch.

You add three to the last stretch to find the new one.

Whatever the description, at this point the only relevant question to be asked is "Does the description fit the data in the table?" It is most important to refrain from trying to correct student statements here despite the fact that it is necessary to differentiate, for example, between the thing and the number of units of the "thing." While no attempt is made to play down these important concepts, they are not considered at this time since they may detract from our main purpose. The main purpose is use of the language of mathematics to describe what happens. Precision will come later as needed.

After you write sentences on the chalkboard and check against the tables, shorten the statement to make it more manageable, in the manner described previously:

> The amount of stretch is three times the amount of weight.
> ~~The amount of~~ stretch is three times ~~the amount of~~ weight.
> Stretch is three times weight.

A brief discussion of formulas may follow, which offers students an opportunity to recall familiar formulas they have encountered earlier, such as:

$$A = s^2 \qquad C = 2\pi r \qquad I = PRT$$

Knowing the formula gives us an understanding of the relationships involved in the given situation. We emphasize language by saying: Look at the formula $s = 3w$. Whenever a symbol is written in a mathematical sentence, it has a definate purpose for being there:

▶
> What does the s represent?
> What does the w represent?
> What does the 3 represent?

The last question may puzzle students. They should consider the question: Would the 3 appear if we used a different spring? The teacher might want to repeat the experiment with a variety of springs to indicate that the constant will change. Hence, it has something to do with the nature of the spring itself—perhaps its thickness, the strength and elasticity of the metal of which it is made, or the number of coils it contains. This might be a fruitful area for further study. In any case, each symbol in the formula has an important reason for being there, an idea we emphasize repeatedly so that there is little mystery in the use of symbols. We are beginning to decode algebra.

We can add to our understanding by looking at a picture of the relationship, a graph. Since, in this instance, the strength depends upon the amount of weight, we identify the horizontal axis as the w-axis and the vertical as the s-axis. This is justified solely on the basis of tradition. When we plot points and draw the line, (only the first quadrant is needed), we have a picture of the relationship (Figure 7.1). Students might consider the following:

▶
> Examine the graph. What kind of curve is it? Does it go through the origin? Must the graph extend only as far as the points we have in the table?

When we know the relationship and have described it mathematically, we have gained some power to predict events. How much will the spring stretch if we hang 5 oz of weight upon it? If we hang 6 oz? What about 7 oz? Encourage the students to figure out the answers in any way they wish (trial and error, formula, or graph) and then to check these results with the springs themselves. Thus, the equipment first used to generate data is now used as a means for checking.

Figure 7.1
A graph showing the relationship of stretch to weight.

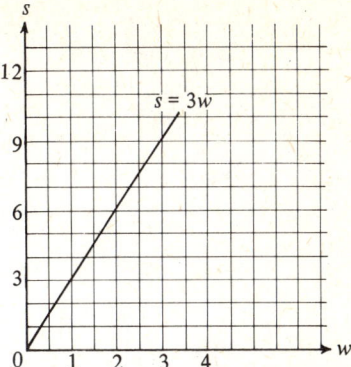

This elementary beginning to the study of the linear function and the solution of linear equations is carried out in a completely unstructured and informal manner. For the most part, we limit ourselves to finding the dependent variable when given the idependent variable (if $s = 3w$ and you are given w, find s). We should emphasize however, that in predicting through the use of mathematics we are completing a rather fantastic process. The information contained within the table was a result of observation. Now we are indicating what will happen without doing the experiment at all. Using paper and pencil, we can offer a description of what would take place in the physical situation, and *it works!*

Let us reexamine what we have done. The start we have made is an active one that poses a definite challenge. Yet it does not rely to any marked degree on previous work with mathematical concepts. Psychologically, we seem to be building upon a firm base. By deriving mathematical expressions from a physical experiment and using the symbolism to describe the inherent relationship, we help youngsters learn the language of mathematics based upon concrete experiences, with the emphasis upon the notion of function. The informal nature of the work done provides maximum opportunity for students' success. The hoped-for result is that they will begin to conclude that this "algebra" is not a formidable enemy after all and, perhaps, may be a good friend.

Experiments with Diagrams

A slight digression is in order before we continue. Should the proper equipment become a problem, the teacher might want to use drawings or diagrams of springs in series, illustrating how a spring is extended under a given amount of weight (Figure 7.2 see page 102). The only equipment necessary is a ruler, so that the students can measure on the diagrams to determine for themselves the amount of stretch in each case. While they are not active participants in the sense of carrying out the experiment, they are only one step removed because they *are* gathering their own data. Of course, the first-hand experience of working the experiment is preferable.

The process of using representations is important in the total development since our goal is to begin with the physical, concrete experience and work gradually toward abstraction. Gathering data from drawings is a step away from the concrete toward the abstraction and the eventual presentation of tables of data which involve only x and y with no concrete counterpart.

Figure 7.2
An experiment in spring stretch.

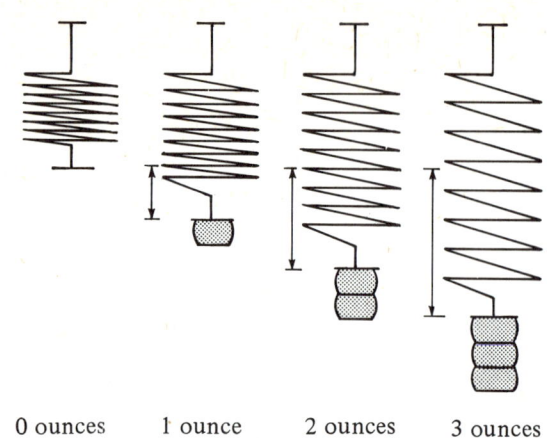

7.2 Algebra as a Language

To build the sense of algebra as a language, we proceed slowly. Instead of exploiting all the mathematical possibilities of this experiment, we go on to other relationships that will also result in the same type of linear function. We then repeat the same procedures of experimentation in this new environment:

▶
1. What do you think will happen? Guess.
2. How should we do the experiment?
3. How shall we keep a record of what occurs?
4. Do the experiment. Verify the data. Record the results.
5. Look for a pattern.
6. Write a sentence and reduce it to formula.
7. Draw the graph.
8. Attempt predictions and check with apparatus.

Some additional helpful relationships:

▶
1. Platform and rollers. Using this simple machine devised by W. W. Sawyer (see section 2.1) the students can explore the distance traveled by the platform as compared with that of the rollers, a relationship described by $P = 2R$ (Figure 7.3).

2. Motion problems. Investigating the speed of a dropped object as a function of the time it falls yields the description

   $v = 32t$ on Earth
   $v = at$ for any planet.

3. The distance of lightning based upon the time between the flash and the sound of thunder is approximately

   $D = \frac{1}{5}t.$

Figure 7.3

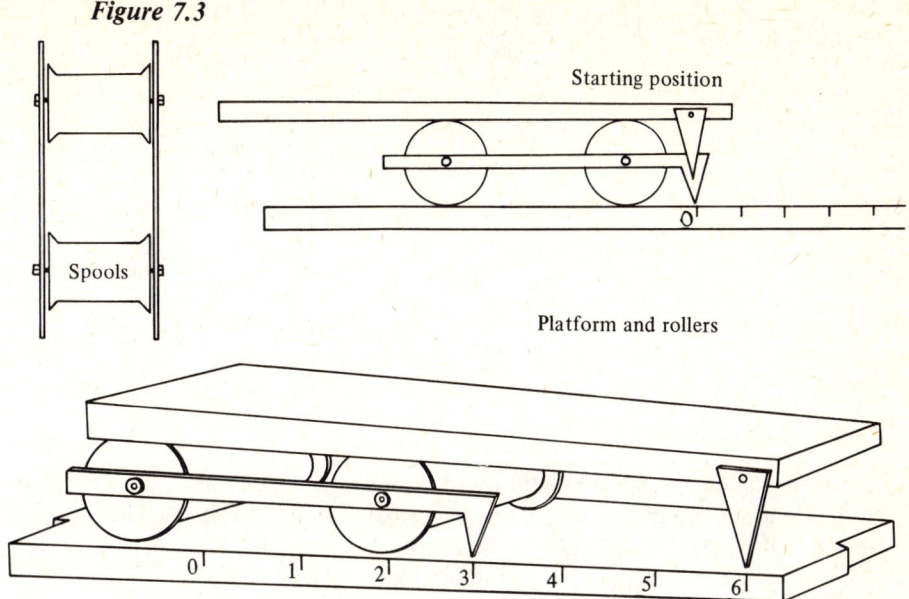

Solution of Equations

An important beginning is made when students use mathematics as the language of science. In addition, we have an interesting, meaningful introduction to the study of algebra. To increase the complexity of the work and introduce new mathematics concepts, we select situations accordingly, to make it necessary for students to extend their use of mathematics as a language.

Returning to spring-stretch experiments, the students do another experiment that yields perhaps $s = \frac{1}{2}w$. This time the emphasis is upon solving this linear equation; that is, given values of the dependent variable (s or stretch lenghts), the student is challenged to find the resulting value of the independent variable w or weight measures.

For example,

$6 = \frac{1}{2}w$

"One half of some number is 6. What is the number?"
"Half of 12 is 6, so $w = 12$."

$7 = \frac{1}{2}w$

"Seven is half of what number? 14, so $w = 14$."

Students should also be directed to check their findings with the graphs they have drawn. If 12 ounces of weight is necessary to extend the spring 6 inches, let us check the graph and see whether or not (12, 6) is a point on it (Figure 7.4 see page 104). As the graphs are used, the additional vocabulary necessary to describe what you are doing will be introduced as it comes up in the natural course of events. The words

| ordered pairs | coefficient | y-axis | origin | plotting |
| variable | x-axis | coordinate axes | coordinates | |

will all be in common use, as well as the necessary symbolism for the points (x, y). In this way, we extend our language.

Figure 7.4

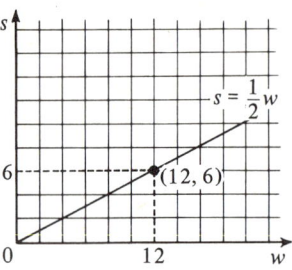

Experiments from Tables

The ready-made results involving other spring experiments may be presented to students, using different coefficients for w to provide a variety of practice situations (Table 7.1). This should be limited to a few cases since the spring law is only one example of the language of mathematics.

Table 7.1 Results of experiments with three different springs.

Spring A		Spring B		Spring C	
w	s	w	s	w	s
0	0	0	0	0	0
1	4	1	1½	1	2½
2	8	2	3	2	5
3	12	3	4½	3	7½
4	16	4	6	4	10

Additional examples offering practice in the use of language to solve linear equations can be constructed from the applications listed on page 109.

About Formal Solutions

No mention has been made of formal methods for solution of these equations. When do the students learn to solve equations in a more formal way? Formal methods do not have to be taught at this point since most of the students will be able to work through to the correct answer without such techniques. Why introduce unnecessary techniques? It is most important that each student have a clear understanding of the meanings of the symbols used. This is fundamental to all future work in algebra, and provides a firm foundation upon which to build mathematical ideas. Emphasis upon the language is one step toward the elimination of rote learning.

In addition to the gradual introduction of the need for more formal approaches, the teacher may provide a good deal of practice with basic computational skills by simply selecting those numbers that are of concern. Thus we slowly move away from the informal solution, but we have not yet introduced the application of equality axioms in solving equations. We can accomplish this after first establishing a need to use such ideas.

Further Explorations of Algebra 7.3

We can extend the mathematics being considered to more difficult examples through further work with the spring-stretch experiment. This time we ask students to focus on the total length of the spring rather than the stretch. For example, in one case, the resulting formula will be $L = 2w + 4$. In discussing the formula so that everything in it is understood, we emphasize that

> L and w represent the variables in the experiment, while 4 is the original spring length. The coefficient of w, 2, is a result of the properties of the spring itself, as discussed in the earlier spring experiments.

The solution of equations follows the pattern of the previous work based on understanding the language. Ask students:

> How much weight must be hung from the spring if it is to be extended until it is 14 in. long?

While they are free to proceed in any manner of their choice, most students will probably substitute into the formula. The thinking based on decoding the language would roughly go like this:

$$L = 2w + 4$$

If $L = 14$, the formula becomes

$$14 = 2w + 4$$

This says that twice a number with 4 added is 14. Since 4 added to 10 is 14, the "twice a number" must be 10 so

$$2w = 10$$

If twice a number is 10, then the number must be 5, so we write

$$w = 5$$

Therefore 5 oz of weight stretches the spring to a length of 14 in.

Through their knowledge of the language of algebra, students have considerable power to solve many linear equations. No formal techniques are necessary at this point. If we continue to provide students with a rich variety of equations, we will have built in the idea that when dealing with equations one first asks: What does the statement tell me?

The symbols are not mysterious chicken tracks on a piece of paper, which are manipulated rotely in accordance with memorized rules. Instead students are fully aware of where they are going and how they hope to get there. In the process, they also get a glimpse of how mathematics enables the scientist to deal with data collected from experimentation and how results are communicated to fellow students.

In households of students who are in their first algebra course, parents or friends will often ask the student to "say something in algebra!" The response is usually a grand bit of double-talk involving x's and y's, and everyone has a good laugh. The irony of it all is that if the students do indeed get a feel for algebra as a language, they not only will be able to "speak" algebra; they will also have an excellent technique to solve virtually any equation, not to mention an important step up on the ladder to higher mathematics.

7.4 The Equality Axioms

How will students learn to solve the "harder" equations? The ability to use the language will not always help to work to a solution. We now attempt to put the student in the position of *needing* to learn such methods. Any of the complete linear relationships would introduce such a situation, but the motion formula is a particularly good example. Here we may begin with pictures of the data (Figure 7.5) or the tables themselves:

t	v
0	10
1	18
2	26
3	34
4	42

t	v
0	32
1	64
2	96
3	128
4	160

Figure 7.5

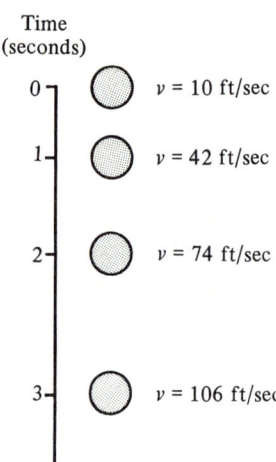

Time (seconds)

0 — $v = 10$ ft/sec

1 — $v = 42$ ft/sec

2 — $v = 74$ ft/sec

3 — $v = 106$ ft/sec

It is important that the students fully understand what is happening in the situation. For example:

▶ A baseball is thrown downward from the roof of the Empire State Building. Here is the speed of the ball for each second it is falling:

Time (sec.) t	Speed (ft/sec) v
0	16
1	48
2	80
3	112

When students are able to describe the relationship with a formula, they should sketch a graph of the information. The larger numbers here may cause some difficulties. In general, the students will probably note that

... the speed goes up by 32. Since the zero is 16, the formula should be $v = 32t + 16$. The coefficient of t appears to indicate the constant difference while the zero of t gives the constant.

Having found the formula and sketched its graph, the students should have no doubts as to its meaning. Some attention must be given to questions such as:

Why are the two terms in the formula ($32t$ and 16) added?

How is it that we have a value of $v = 16$ when $t = 0$? What does this mean?

After predictions are made, which determine the velocity at various instances in time, we ask the question: How many seconds will it take the baseball to reach a speed of 176 ft/sec? This question would require a solution of the equation

$$176 = 32t + 16$$

The size of the numbers here may result in student uncertainty as to how to proceed. It may be quickly noticed that "some quantity added to 16 yields 176; hence, that quantity must be 160." This fact is written as $32t = 160$, and the division process employed earlier may suffice. If the students are able to proceed in this manner, they should be encouraged to do so. Others may need additional instruction, however. This should be provided along the lines established previously, without any overconcentration on the development.

The question to be asked next would be: How many seconds will it take the ball to reach a speed of 224 ft/sec? These numbers should cause concern. If not, larger numbers or fractions can be employed. Eventually a discussion must follow of some more effective method of operation. At this juncture, we introduce the equality axioms and along with these axioms, a simple balance scale to aid student understanding (Figure 7.6).

Figure 7.6

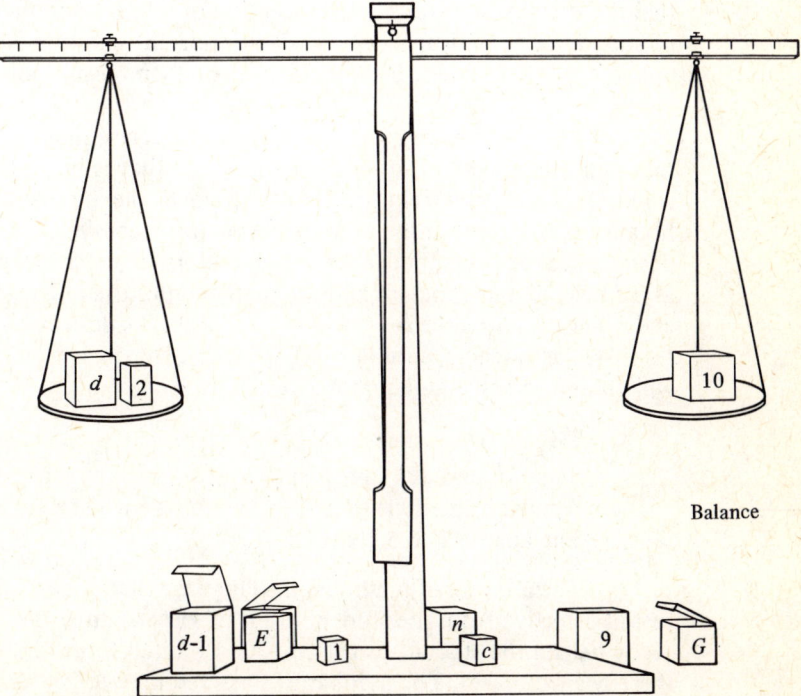

Balance

Balancing

The balance scales provide a physical representation that the process of "doing the same thing to both sides" does indeed maintain the equality. The immediate needs of the situation require the use of subtraction and division only. However, after the problem of a particular equation has been resolved, the question may well be asked: Would the equality be maintained if we added or multiplied both sides of it by equal quantities? In this way we are not only extending the "balancing" to include all four basic operations, but we are also building an understanding of how mathematical knowledge is extended. Often, a mathematician becomes interested in a physical problem and, in trying to find a solution, he develops many ideas and follows many hunches that go far beyond the immediate need. In this simple instance of "balancing," we can offer some insight into how mathematics is built.

Thus, the students are now in possesion of two basic approaches to the solution of equations: using the language and "balancing" or using the equality axioms; i.e.,

If $a = b$ and $c = d$, then $a + c = b + d$.
If $a = b$ and $c = d$, then $a - c = b - d$.
If $a = b$ and $c = d$, then $ac = bd$.
If $a = b$ and $c = d \neq 0$, then $\dfrac{a}{c} = \dfrac{b}{d}$.

The fact that the axioms have been learned and are now available to the students does not mean that henceforth each student will solve equations using only these axioms. It is important for the student to decide how to solve particular equations in the way best suited to himself. It is up to the teacher to be sure that the students approach to the solution of an equation involves the correct use of sound mathematical thinking. The important question is not, Which method did you use? but rather, Is your thinking mathematically sound and is the answer correct?

There has been a tendency lately to declare that the answer is unimportant and that it is the way the student works that is important. He must understand. This is not entirely true. To the student the answer is of vital importance because it is his indicator for correct or incorrect work. We should not try to deemphasize answers, but rather we should try to put the emphasis to work for us as we help students understand the mathematics used. The student has a desired end which is getting the right answer. From this he derives a good deal of satisfaction. We, as teachers, should share this goal. Hence, it may well be that a student will choose to solve an equation in this way:

$224 = 32t + 16$
Since 16 and 208 give a sum of 224, we may write $32t = 208$.
Applying the division axiom, dividing by 32, gives $t = 6.5$.
The answer is 6.5 seconds.

The mixture of methods, the language that is used and the axiom used, is just as effective from the student point of view as any other method. It has correctly helped the student to get where he wanted to go. Independent thinking is thereby encouraged. The number of steps required to get somewhere is of far less importance than using correct mathematical thinking, no matter how inelegant by someone else's standards. Freedom to think is in the spirit of mathematics.

A variety of relationships involving the complete linear function should then be explored in order to provide practice in equation solution without tiresome repetition. Among these we may find:

> Motion problems applied to other planets—for example, on Mars the problem just described would be:
> $v = 12t + 16$.

> Finding the Fahrenheit temperature from the speed of an ant:
> $T = 11s + 39$.

> The amount of money deducted from income tax by a married couple for dependents:
> $D = 1200 + 750n$.

> The number of diagonals in a polygon of s sides that can be drawn from any one vertex:
> $d = s - 3$.

Vocabulary and Definitions 7.5

All too often in mathematics classes, we find a lesson beginning with a definition of the new concept of the day. Teachers present this definition to students who have little, if any, idea about what the definition really means. It is the premise here that definitions, rather than being the starting point of a development, are actually its end product. If we develop effective classroom experiences, we may assume that in the end students will each be able to write a fairly accurate definition by themselves. While the organization of a mathematical system may begin with definitions, the teaching of mathematics is another thing altogether. Presenting a definition at the start leaves the student with but one task: remembering. Presenting him with a variety of activities involving new concepts and words leaves him with a very different task: thinking.

In the exploration of the linear function just completed, the concept of **variable** was an important notion. If $s = 3w$, we may speak of s and w as variables. The students, having collected the data from the spring experiments, have ample physical evidence of the varying nature of *these quantities*. The meaning of variable is observed in action. Each time a new experiment is undertaken, additional situations involving varying quantities are introduced. Little by little, bit by bit, the student begins to formulate his own concept of variable at this stage in terms of the dependency relationship. Later, it is expected that this idea will become a more abstract and generalized notion. It is intended that the experiences described will lay the foundation for the abstraction.

Mathematics or Physics? 7.6

Let us reexamine two functions developed earlier. First we look at $v = 32t$ and ask: If a ball is dropped from a building 144 ft high, how fast is the ball falling after 6 sec? When the answer 192 ft/sec is offered, we have to point out that after

3 sec the ball struck the ground! Its speed after 6 sec is therefore 0. How is it that mathematics provides an apparently incorrect answer? Is our mathematics wrong? Have we miscalculated? It is important to stress the difference between mathematics and the physical world. The mathematics world is a world of abstract ideas, whereas the physical world is a three-dimensional reality. Our answer of 192 ft/sec is mathematically correct but does not fit the physical situation, which has meaning only up to $t = 3$. Thus, we begin to intuitively develop the idea that mathematics is a model that matches reality remarkably well—albeit far from perfectly. As such, mathematics provides much information, but we must check our results in the physical situation to be sure they "work."

This important concept is reinforced by exploring a pool-filling situation. If a pool 8 ft deep is filled with water at the rate of 2 ft/hr, how deep will the water be after 2 hr? 3 hr? 4? 5? Of course, it is the 5-hr mark that interests us here. Mathematically, the situation is described by $h = 2t$, and if $t = 5$, then $h = 10$; thus the water in the pool is 10 ft deep. But the pool is only 8 ft deep. After we run the water for 5 hr, there may be a good deal of water in the area; but the depth of water in the pool will only be 8 ft. Once again we discuss the necessary restrictions on the variables ($0 \leq h \leq 4$) and the difference between mathematical "things" and physical "things." We point out that mathematics is only a model of the "real" world, and it is remarkable that it fits the environment as well as it does. The spring law may offer yet another example of this since the spring may well break if too much weight is hung from it. It will not stretch indefinitely. This vital notion about mathematics must be explored each time the occasion arises to help students grasp the subtle but basic differences.

7.7   *Algebra as a Language—In Conclusion*

Several science applications of mathematics have been presented in some detail as they are fundamental to an introduction of algebra. Such an introduction is intentionally designed to stress the role of mathematics as the language of science. Care was taken to consider how to make this language meaningful to the student. To this end, every symbol included in formulas derived from experimentation was discussed and explained so that any mystery would be dispelled. To aid in this process, students were encouraged to solve equations using their basic number knowledge and translations of the symbolic code we call algebra. Students may forget how to carry out certain algebraic operations, but once learned, it is unlikely that they will soon forget how to interpret an algebraic sentence. Such a beginning will offer a high probability that students will, at the least, know what is being asked of them.

Footnotes

1.   Eric T. Bell. *Mathematics, Queen and Servant of Science.* New York: McGraw-Hill, 1951, pp. 1–2.

2.   William M. Fitzgerald. "The Role of Mathematics in a Comprehensive Problem Solving Curriculum in Secondary Schools," *School Science and Mathematics.* Vol. 75 (January 1975), p. 42.

3. W. W. Sawyer. *Vision in Elementary Mathematics.* New York: Penguin Books, 1964, pp. 1-5.

For Investigation and Discussion

1. The introduction of a mathematics concept is completed with an important application from science. Compare the value of this approach with the primary use of science applications as practice.
2. Select a simple experiment from the chapter and describe in detail how you would use such an activity in a mathematics lesson.
3. Create a situation in which students find themselves unable to solve equations using the language of algebra and are in need of the axioms of equality.
4. Show how the axioms would be introduced to students, emphasizing student participation in the process.
5. Choose a situation from the list on page 109 and build a lesson designed to provide practice for students in solving linear equations.

For Further Reading

Books

Bell, Eric T. *Mathematics: Queen and Servant of Science.* New York: McGraw-Hill, 1951.

Fouch, Robert S. and Eugene D. Nichols. "Language and Symbolism in Mathematics," *The Growth of Mathematical Ideas, Grades K-12,* 27th Yearbook. Reston, Va.: National Council of Teachers of Mathematics, 1959.

Goals for the Correlation of Elementary Science and Mathematics. (Report of the Cambridge Conference on Teacher Training.) Published for Educational Services, Inc. by Houghton Mifflin, 1969.

Johnson, Donovan A. and Gerald R. Rising. *Guidelines for Teaching Mathematics.* 2nd ed. Belmont, Ca.: Wadsworth, 1972, pp. 274-297.

Kline, Morris. *Mathematics and the Physical World.* New York: Thomas Y. Crowell, 1959.

W. W. Sawyer. *Vision in Elementary Mathematics.* New York: Penguin Books, 1964.

Willerding, Margret F. and Ruth A. Hayward. *Mathematics: The Alphabet of Science.* New York: John Wiley and Sons, 1968.

Periodicals

Assad, Saleh. "From Graph to Formula," *The Mathematics Teacher.* Vol. 64 (March 1971), pp. 231-232.

Bausor, John. "Mathematics and Science: Uneasy Truce or Open Hostilities?" *Mathematics Teaching.* No. 68 (September 1974), pp. 32-41.

Bell, Max S. "Mathematical Models and Applications as an Integral Part of High School Algebra Class," *The Mathematics Teacher.* Vol. 64 (April 1971), pp. 293-300.

Bender, E. A. "Teaching Applicable Mathematics," *The American Mathematical Monthly.* Vol. 80 (March 1973), pp. 302-307.

Bowen, John J. "Mathematics and the Teaching of Science," *The Mathematics Teacher.* Vol. 59 (October 1966), pp. 536-542.

Bunch, Bryan. "Teaching Applications of Mathematics," *Mathematics Forum.* December 1967, pp. 1-2.

McCreery, Louis R. "Lively Functions for Algebra One," *The Mathematics Teacher.* Vol 62 (May 1969), pp. 365-368.

Wilder, R. L. "Mathematics and Its Relation to Other Disciplines," *The Mathematics Teacher.* Vol. 66 (December 1973), pp. 679-685.

CHAPTER 8

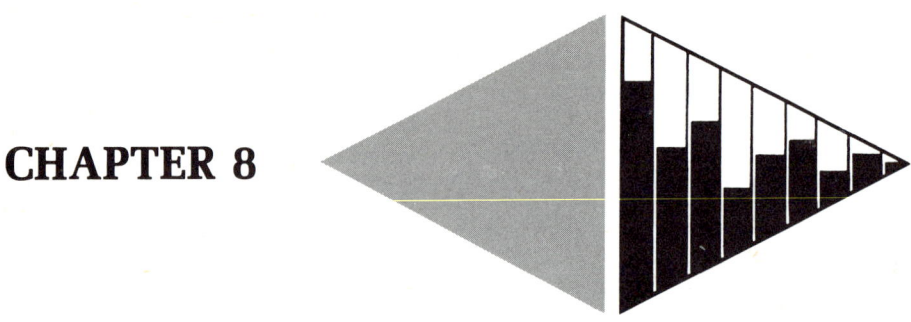

Mathematics as a Tool

In focusing upon mathematics as a tool, we are merely changing the point of emphasis. However, mathematics as language, mathematics as facilitator and aid to discovery, are two roles that continue to operate whenever we deal with any science applications. To get proper perspective, try to keep in mind how science might have proceeded without the use of mathematics. Progress would indeed have been slow, if not altogether at a halt.

8.1 Distance, Rate, Time, and Beginning Quadratics

We have explored the speed of objects at or near the surface of the Earth, but have not said anything about the distance traveled. The distance relationship is a particularly fruitful one to explore for a variety of reasons. Motion problems, if met earlier in the study of linear functions, are familiar. A continuing physical theme is present as the mathematical knowledge is extended. Since the formula, which holds at or near the surface of the Earth, changes if a different planet is considered, we have a rich supply of mathematically repetitive situations available. The flip books shown earlier, pictures or diagrams of objects falling through space, offer students the opportunity to gather their own distance-related data to tabulate.

An inclined plane and simple pendulum may also provide an active experience with variables that can illustrate the distance formula (a string 39 in. long has a period of about 1 sec). After some practice, students working in teams would begin to get fairly accurate results regarding the distance a ball would roll down an inclined plane in a given number of seconds as measured by the pendulum.

In any event, once the information is collected, the students will have before them a table of values. Here is one in seconds and feet:

t (sec)	d (ft)
0	0
1	16
2	64
3	144
4	256

Certainly the pattern of these numbers is not as readily observable as were the patterns of the linear relationships. A bit of reasoning comes to the aid of the student. From the velocity formula, he is able to determine the speed with which the object is falling at any unit of time ($v = 32t$). Thus, at 1 sec the velocity is 32 ft/sec; yet in the table the distance traveled is seen to be 16 ft. Is there some mistake? Shouldn't the distance traveled be 32? Did the ball drop with a speed of 32 ft/sec for the entire second? No. It reached this speed at precisely 1 sec in time. As a matter of fact, after ½ sec the speed of the ball was only 16 ft/sec. The speed goes from zero to 32 in 1 sec and in between it passes through all the intermediary speeds. In this way we turn the attention of the student toward using the average speed over the interval. We find this by any one of a variety of techniques, such as:

> To find the mean of any collection of numbers with a constant increase, such as 2, 4, 6, 8, 10, 12 . . . or 1, 2, 3, 4, 5, 6, 7 . . ., simply take the average of the first and last terms. For example, in the instances just mentioned:
>
> $$\frac{2 + 12}{2} = 7 \qquad Check: \begin{array}{l} 2 + 4 + 6 + 8 + 10 + 12 = 42 \\ 42 \div 6 = 7 \end{array}$$
>
> $$\frac{1 + 7}{2} = 4 \qquad Check: \begin{array}{l} 1 + 2 + 3 + 4 + 5 + 6 + 7 = 28 \\ 28 \div 7 = 4 \end{array}$$

Since the velocity changes at a constant rate from 0 to 32, the average speed for the first second interval is

$$\frac{0 + 32t}{2} = 16t$$

If this is the average speed for an interval of t-seconds, then the distance traveled is *rate* × *time* or

$$(16t)(t) = 16t^2$$

This is certainly not the only way in which the result can be arrived at, but it is one that will work. It also brings into sharp focus the symbolism of the quadradic function. While this concept has been met in arithmetic, the experiences here serve to reinforce what was done earlier, and to prepare for an extensive study of the use of radicals. We have derived the statement $d = 16t^2$ as a description of how the distance fallen by a dropped object varies with the length of time it has been falling. After graphing, prediction is undertaken to find the resulting distance fallen after various time periods. Eventually we arrive at predictions requiring the calculation of the number of seconds of time required for the object to fall any given distance. We turn to the solution of a simple quadraditc equation:

▶ How long would it take a ball dropped from the roof of the Yankee Stadium, 192 ft high, to strike the ground?

Although the table pattern and the graphs could be used to find the desired number, we also make use of the formula; hence,

$$d = 16t^2$$
If $d = 192$,
$$192 = 16t^2$$

If we translate the symbols, we are looking for a number that will be multiplied by itself and then mulitplied by 16 to give a final product of 192. This is a rather difficult equation to solve through our understanding of the language. Consequently, those who need to will make use of the division axiom to get to:

$$192 = 16t^2$$
$$\frac{192}{16} = \frac{16t^2}{16}$$
$$12 = t^2$$

The student finds that he encounters a number that is not a perfect square, an irrational number. At this point we make use of the radical sign to indicate what we want without computation: $t = \sqrt{12}$.

It is important to be clear about the meaning of the expression $\sqrt{12}$. The radical sign indicates that we are considering the principle square root of 12, which is the positive root. For example:

▶ When asked to find the square root of 16, the answer is ± 4. Both roots are necessary, $+4$ and -4. However, if the question reads $\sqrt{16} = $ _____, the answer is 4. The use of the radical sign ($\sqrt{}$) indicates that only the positive root is required.

It may be well to estimate the value of $\sqrt{12}$ for the time being, indicating that it is somewhere between 3 (whose square is 9) and 4 (whose square is 16) and somewhat closer to 3. We could say approximately 3.4 perhaps, and let it go at that. For all the student knows, this may be a rare occurrence and most numbers will be perfect squares.

Only after repeated introduction of these irrationals should time be taken to explore them in detail. Then you can indicate the significance of what has occurred and become involved with teaching radicals, as well as with the various ways of classifying the sets of numbers with which we have been working.

The important idea is the introduction of another axiom: If $a = b$ (a, b nonnegative real numbers), $\sqrt{a} = \sqrt{b}$. The reverse process of squaring may now be discussed. After careful discussion of the effects of these last two operations on the signs of the numbers, another axiom may be developed for squaring. It would not be necessary to become involved in an extended study of extraneous roots. On the contrary, it would be best simply to point out the possibilities and hold any extended analysis until a situation is introduced involving such roots.

The students are now solving these limited form quadradic equations involving motion problems. The numbers with radical signs are occuring frequently, and estimations are employed for the irrational numbers as predictions are carried out.

A change in celestial body provides a rich fund of simple quadradic equations, offering drill without tedium.

Finding Square Roots 8.2

Let us take a closer look at these "radical" numbers. Is there some way to be more exact about their values? How might we calculate $\sqrt{12}$ so that it is accurate to the nearest tenth, for example? While the process may have been developed in an earlier grade, lack of use sometimes results in almost complete forgetting. It may be well to proceed as if this were a new problem. We mention two simple methods here since they are based upon the meaning of square root itself. Both involve estimation.

Guess-Average Method

The idea behind this method is to guess what the square root will be and check by dividing the original number by your guess. In order to refine your guess, take the average of it and the result of the division. Repeat the process as often as necessary to gain accuracy to any desired place. This is an excellent place to make use of the mini-calculator. Here is an example:

Find $\sqrt{12}$ correct to the nearest tenth.

1. Guess: 3.3
2. Divide:

$$
\begin{array}{r}
3.63 \text{ (rounds off to 3.64)} \\
3.3\,\overline{\smash{\big)}\,12.0{,}000} \\
\underline{9\ 9} \\
2\ 1\ 0 \\
\underline{1\ 9\ 8} \\
1\ 20 \\
\underline{99} \\
210
\end{array}
$$

Carry your work to one place more than is contained in your guess.

3. Compare: guess 3.3, quotient 3.64
If your guess had been exact, what would the quotient be?
Since the quotient here is larger than the guess, what can you say about the guess? We know $\sqrt{12}$ is between 3.3 and 3.64. We halve the difference by finding the mean.
4. Average $3.3 + 3.64 = 6.94$
$6.94 \div 2 = 3.47$

5. We repeat the entire process using 3.47 as our new guess.
Divide:

$$3.47 \overline{)12.00.000} \quad \text{(quotient 3.458)}$$

Compare: $\sqrt{12}$ lies between 3.47 and 3.458

Average: 3.47 + 3.458 = 6.928
6.928 ÷ 2 = 3.464

If we are in need of $\sqrt{12}$ correct to the nearest tenth, the averaging process is really unnecessary. When we compare, we can see that to the nearest tenth $\sqrt{12}$ = 3.5. Should we require greater accuracy, the process may again be repeated with 3.464 as our new guess.

This method is suprisingly powerful and brings one close to the desired square root rather quickly, despite poor guessing. For example, if a student failed to see that $\sqrt{12}$ was between 3 and 4 and chose, say, 6 as a guess, he would not be in trouble at all:

Divide: $6\overline{)12.00}$ (quotient 2.0)

Compare: $\sqrt{12}$ lies between 2 and 6

Average: 2.0 + 6 = 8.0
8.0 ÷ 2 = 4.0

Repeating: 12 ÷ 4.0 = 3.00
3.00 + 4.0 = 7.00
7.00 ÷ 2 = 3.5

Repeating: 12.0 ÷ 3.5 = 3.43
3.43 + 3.5 = 6.93
6.93 ÷ 2 = 3.465

Thus, in three divisions we have gone from a completely out of range guess to a number that is correct in the tenths and hundredths places. This is a powerful method indeed.

Guess-Multiply Method

The second method of approximation may even be simpler. It, too, may be enhanced by using a mini-calculator. Here again we guess the desired root; this time we check our estimate by multiplying it by itself, i.e., square it. If we guessed correctly, the product will be the number that we are finding the square root of. If not, we refine our guess and multiply to check again. Here is an example of this method:

▶ Find $\sqrt{12}$ correct to the nearest tenth.

1. Guess: between 3 and 4, say 3.2.
2. Multiply: 3.2 × 3.2 = 10.24
3. Compare: 3.2 is too small, but 4.0 is too large:

$(3.2)^2 = 10.24; (4.0)^2 = 16.00$

Thus, our desired root is between 3.2 and 4.0.

4. Revised guess: 3.5. Repeat the process.
5. Multiply: 3.5 × 3.5 = 12.25
6. Compare: 3.5 is also too large. The root now lies between 3.2 and 3.5.
7. New Guess: 3.35 (halfway between)
8. Multiply: 3.35 × 3.35 = 11.2225
The root lies between 3.35 and 3.50.

Eventually, by repetition and examination of products, the desired accuracy is achieved.

Operations

A side road may be explored briefly here. All through their study of mathematics, students have been carrying out four basic operations: addition, subtraction, multiplication, and division. The processes of squaring and finding the square root are the first new operations introduced. The term *binary operation* can now take on meaning since, in contrast, the new operations are unary operations. In each of the four basic operations, one number describes the result of performing a given operation with *two* numbers; i.e., when you do addition with 2 and 5, the result is 7. These new operations, however, are carried out on but *one* number. We may square 10; we may find the square root of 12. Each time only one number is operated upon. Aside from the earlier work with arithmetic, this is the first time we have undertaken such operations. This is, therefore, an event of some consequence and should be appropriately recognized as such.

We also want to continue to build upon the ideas previously developed. Addition was rapid counting. Multiplication was rapid addition, repeated addition at that. Squaring may be thought of as rapid multiplication, and repeated multiplication too. Newly encountered ideas fit rather nicely into our overall framework.

It is appropriate at this point, if student interest warrants, to extend this discussion about operations into explorations of the abstraction of operation itself. The introduction of finite arithmetics, for example, could bring into focus arbitrarily defined operations and lend greater meaning to the entire process.

Other relationships that are examples of the quadradic function of form $y = ax^2$ and are suitable for investigation at this time are:

The weight (W) in 100-lb units that can be lifted by a rope of diameter d: $\qquad W = d^2$

The area of a projected picture (A) from a projector x ft away from the screen: $\qquad A = \frac{1}{9}x^2$

The weight (W) in 100-lb units that can be supported by a wood plank 6 ft long, 8 in. wide, and d in. thick: $\qquad W = d^2$

The lift generated by a wing (L) with wing area (S) with minimum forward speed v: $\qquad L = .0038Sv^2$

8.3 Distance and the Quadradic Function

The problems instigated by a study of motion laws, can be expanded to include the complete quadratic by a change of question. By adding some of the techniques used by the Greeks to study algebraic relationships through a geometric approach, we have an interesting way for students to visualize multiplication of polynomials and factoring.

If we investigate the height above ground of objects dropped from a balloon, airplane, or building top, we encounter a more complicated quadratic function. For example:

▶
A ballon 300 ft high dropped flares. How high above ground would the flares be at each second of their drop to the earth?

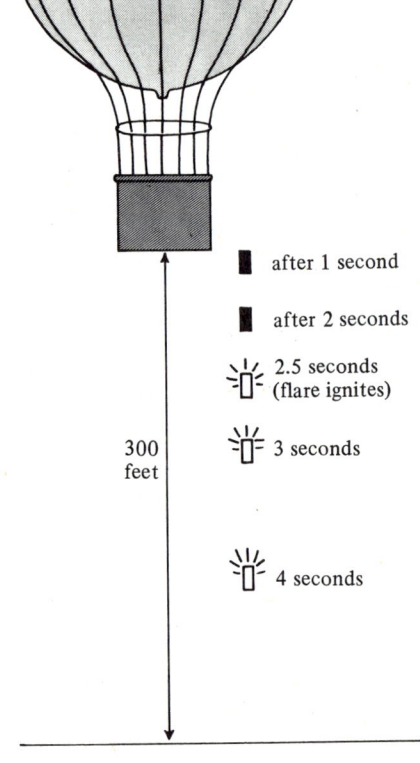

Figure 8.1

Earlier, we saw that all dropped objects under certain conditions fall in accordance with the formula $d = 16t^2$. This would tell us how far the object fell in a given time. If we subtract this from the 300 ft of height of the balloon, we can arrive at the height at any instant. (Figure 8.1). Consequently, the formula $d = 300 - 16t^2$ would seem to yield the function we seek. If we make tables and graphs, we have a good view of what is happening. The introduction of prediction problems (perhaps a fuse is set to ignite the flare at a specified height) requires the solution of more difficult equations:

▶
We would like the flare to ignite at a height of 200 ft. How many seconds should elapse before the flare ignites?

$$d = 300 - 16t^2$$
$$200 = 300 - 16t^2$$

It is possible to solve this equation and find its roots in the same manner as before. This requires using the axioms to eventually arrive at:

$$t^2 = \frac{100}{16}$$

$$t = \frac{10}{4} \quad \text{or} \quad 2\tfrac{1}{2} \text{ sec}$$

Would it be possible to solve this equation without invoking the equality axioms as we did previously?

At this point we introduce as a possible alternative the process of factoring known as **factoring the difference between two squares**: We first make one side zero. (The reason for this will be clear shortly.)

$$0 = 100 - 16t^2$$

Look at the right side. Both terms are special kinds of numbers: They are perfect squares. Since the left side is zero, this may help. To find factors that yield a zero product, we must know something about the factors; that is, we know that one or both must be zero. How else can we arrive at a zero product? Is this true of all numbers? If two numbers have a product of 6, must one of the numbers be 6? This is a special property of those factors whose product is zero. But can we find the factors of $100 - 16t^2$?

We may represent products as areas of rectangles and squares. Since both $16t^2$ and 100 are perfect squares, let us show these as areas (Figure 8.2).

Figure 8.2

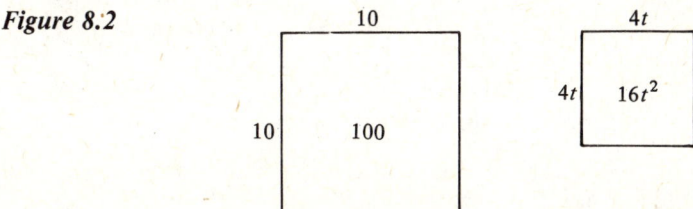

What is the length of each side? The statement $100 - 16t^2$ actually calls for the difference in area between these two squares. Place the smaller square inside the larger and see what is involved (Figure 8.3).

Figure 8.3

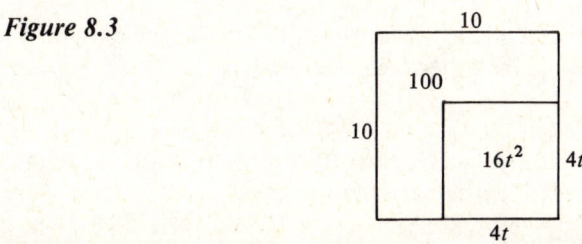

The total area we are interested in is the difference between the areas of the two squares. If we remove the area of the smaller square altogether ($16t^2$), we

Figure 8.4

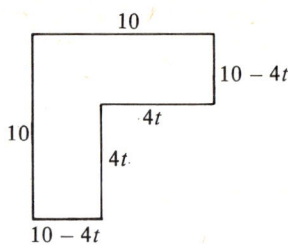

are left with the area indicated in Figure 8.4. This area is $100 - 16t^2$. Can we rearrange this area to form a rectangle? If we can, the length and width of that rectangle will give us the factors we seek. We proceed in the following manner: We cut off the shaded piece (Figure 8.5) and place it below the remaining rectangle. In this way we have not changed the total amount of area ($100 - 16t^2$), but we have changed the shape to one that is rectangular. (Notice how the side $10 - 4t$ is placed along a side of equal length.) The area is known; therefore the length and width of this newly formed rectangle must provide us with the factors whose product is this area. Reading from Figure 8.5, we find that

$$(10 - 4t)(10 + 4t) = 100 - 16t^2.$$

Figure 8.5

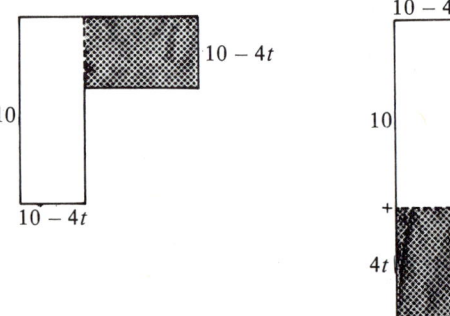

We have factored the difference of two squares and are ready to return to the original problem, $0 = 100 - 16t^2$. Substituting the factors gives:

$$0 = (10 - 4t)(10 + 4t)$$

How does this help? Now we can make use of the special property of factors with a zero product. We know that at least one of the two factors above *must be zero!* Let us assume that the first factor is zero:

$$10 - 4t = 0$$

What is the value of t? If $t = 2\frac{1}{2}$, then $10 - 4t = 0$. We have found a possible solution. What happens if the other factor is zero?

$$10 + 4t = 0$$

What is the value of t? If $t = -2\frac{1}{2}$, then $10 + 4t = 0$, a second solution.
The two roots of the original equation are
$\qquad t = 2\frac{1}{2} \qquad$ and $\qquad t = -2\frac{1}{2}$

The emphasis in this development has been somewhat different from that discussed previously. In this instance we are fixing things to happen the way that we want them to in order to work toward a desired outcome. (We set the factors of an expression equal to zero, for then we may be better able to determine the missing factors.) Often a mathematician manufactures a particular expression to help him get where he wants to go. In effect, he is working backward from his desired end. This is perfectly acceptable as long as the problems worked on are equivalent to the original one. Trial and error is a frequent and respectable partner in such a process.

Once a single quadratic expression has been factored, others are also, using the diagrams of squares and rearranging partial areas without altering the total area. After doing many such problems, the students may be directed to attempt to find the factors without the diagrams. Perhaps an examination of those already done correctly will generate relationships leading students to the desired factors, without the necessity of drawing and manipulating squares. The work with squares could, incidentally, be carried out by actually cutting pieces of cardboard.

Teachers must maintain flexibility as to the exact moment that each student can discard the use of squares (drawings or pieces of cardboard). All students cannot be expected to see relationships at the same time. If we attempt to help students to "discover" as many concepts as possible, we also assume that each student will have the opportunity to do so. This, in turn, implies differing lengths of time to reach certain guideposts in a given course.

Suffice it to say here that all students do not discover at the same instant, if at all. Permit students to use the squares as long as they feel the need, and encourage the discontinuance of such use. Later the squares can be used for checking or for testing ideas. Eventually a point will be reached when everyone proceeds without any representation.

The Complete Quadratic

We have seen how the difference between two squares can be factored. We turn now to physical situations that require the factoring of a trinomial and the introduction of functions in the complete quadratic form of

$$ax^2 + bx + c = 0$$

as well as the solution of the derivative equations.

We may continue the work with motion problems at this point; or if a change is desired, we may select other relationships. Here are some possible situations that may be introduced to involve students with the general quadratic and to establish the need for additional factoring techniques:

An object thrown down with an initial velocity of 32 ft/sec:	$d = 16t^2 + 32t$
Possible areas of a rectangular plot enclosed by 100 ft of fencing:	$A = 50x - x^2$
Surface area of a box 1 ft high with a square base of side x:	$S = 4x + x^2$

A variety of motion problems involving the computation of maximum heights are also available.

An object thrown upward with initial velocity of
96 ft/sec: $\qquad h = 96t - 16t^2$

If we select one of these situations to focus upon, the process may be clarified.

▶ An open box with a square base must contain a total of 5 ft². If the box is 1 ft high, what must be its dimensions?

Substitution in the formula yields:

$$S = 4x + x^2$$

If $S = 5$,

$$5 = 4x + x^2$$

We proceed as before and use the equality axioms to reduce one side to zero, and we arrive at

$$x^2 + 4x - 5 = 0$$

Once again, if we can find factors that give a product of $x^2 + 4x - 5$, we can work toward the solution on the same basis that we did earlier; one of the factors (or both) must be zero. But we cannot proceed for we no longer have before us the difference between two squares. We have a trinomial. The student is in need of help, since he cannot continue. We teach to satisfy this need and turn to factoring a trinomial.

Using squares and rectangles (drawings or cardboard pieces) as before, we find two binomial factors as shown in Figure 8.6. The final rectangle yields:

$$x^2 + 4x - 5 = (x + 5)(x - 1)$$

The problem is resolved as before. This work can be extended to include a wide variety of factorable trinomials. The work is done first with the geometric figures and later, as the need is developed, through student constructed methods. A detailed description of how these figures may be used can be found in Chapter 17. This approach can also offer a physical representation, which completes the square by actually using geometric squares and lays the foundation for the development of the quadratic formula.

We have been finding factors by making use of visual or manipulative materials. It is quite possible, at this stage, to put the algebra itself to work and make use of a brief algebraic analysis. Look at the original equation,

$$x^2 + 4x - 5 = 0$$

How shall we express the polynomial $(x^2 + 4x - 5)$ *as the product of two binomials?*

In other words, we would like to find two factors of form $(x + a)$ $(x + b)$, where a, b are integers. How shall we proceed? Perhaps we may learn more about the missing numbers a and b if we carry out the indicated multiplication. (We may also employ the distributive law.)

$$(x + a)(x + b) = x^2 + ax + bx + ab$$

Factoring yields:

$$x^2 + (a + b)x + ab$$

Figure 8.6

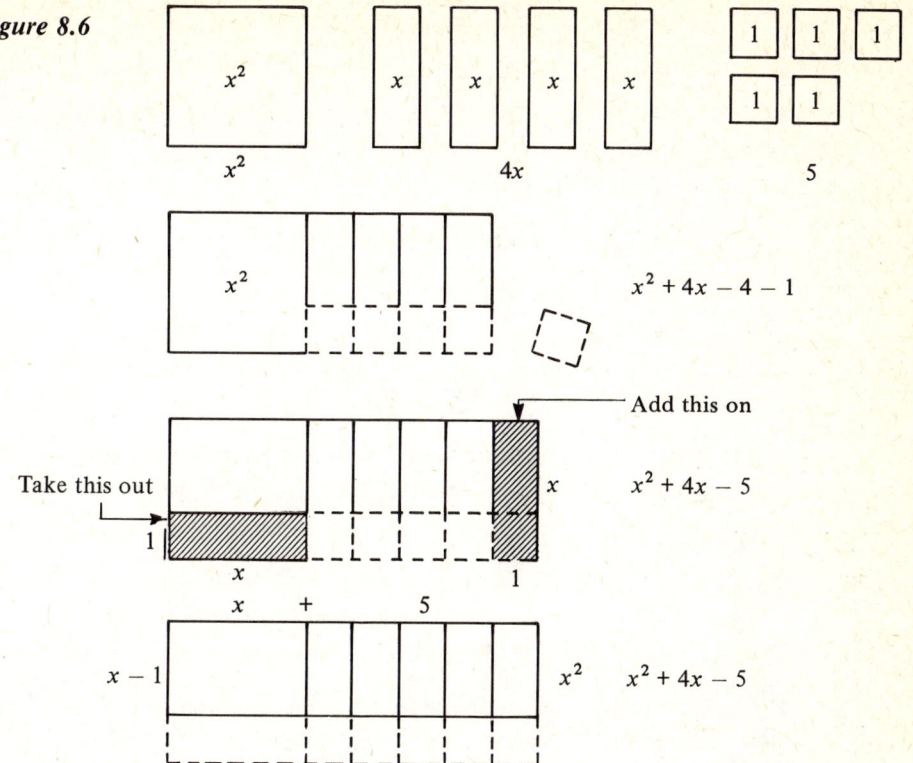

If this expression is compared with the original trinomial,

$x^2 + 4x - 5$ and $x^2 + (a + b)x + ab$

we see that $(a + b)$ must yield 4, while ab must total -5. Thus, we have learned a good deal about our missing numbers, a and b. We know their sum and their product. Trial and error, or any other method, may now be employed:

> For a sum of 4, we might use (2, 2), (3, 1), (4, 0), (5, -1), or a whole host of possibilities. For a product of -5, we might use (5, -1) or (-5, 1). The desired pair of numbers is a single pair satisfying both conditions. Checking the two conditions we see that one pair is common to both: 5 and -1. We let $a = 5$ and $b = -1$, and the factors are:

$(x + 5)(x - 1)$

If we multiply out as a check, we find that the factors do indeed "work." We then proceed as before. If the a and b values were reversed, the conditions would be satisfied. Would we have to correct the factors? The students might try this and discuss their findings.

This method has much to recommend it. Besides generalizing our approach, we let the symbols and the techniques do the work for us. If the symbols and techniques have resulted in new information about mathematics, they will certainly offer the same opportunity when we deal with mathematics having physical counterparts.

Using mathematics, the scientist adds to his knowledge of the physical phenomena he is studying. Here is a simple example. We found

1. $v = 32t$ velocity-time on Earth
2. $d = 16t^2$ distance-time on Earth

Without further experimentation, we use mathematics to find the distance-velocity relationship:

$$v = 32t$$
$$t = \frac{v}{32} \quad \text{substitute this into 2}$$
$$d = 16t^2$$
$$d = 16\frac{v^2}{32}$$
$$d = \frac{v^2}{64} \quad \text{or} \quad v = 8\sqrt{d}$$

We now see how distance and velocity are related. Mathematics has become more than a language of science, and is adding to our knowledge of the physical situation.

8.4 A Word About Graphing

Once students have learned how to complete the squares with quadratic expressions, they have a short cut to the drawing of graphs. The effect is similar to that achieved through the use of the slope-intercept form of the linear function when drawing linear graphs. This method was recommended by the Commission on Mathematics.[1]

We examine the graph of

$$x^2 + 4x - 5 = y$$

We begin by arranging the terms to facilitate the process of completing the squares, and then carry out the necessary adjustments:

$$x^2 + 4x - 5 = y$$
$$x^2 + 4x + 4 - 5 - 4 = y$$
$$(x + 2)^2 - 9 = y$$

This final form, $(x + 2)^2 - 9 = y$, enables us to learn a good deal about the graph. Since the first expression is squared, by inserting values for x we can make the entire expression $(x + 2)^2$ as large as we wish. How small can we make it? No matter what value of x is used, we cannot make the value less than zero. Hence this graph will have a minimum point and will open upward. What value of x will result in a zero value for the entire squared expression? Evidently $x = -2$ will reduce the expression inside the parentheses to zero and will result in the minimum value. In one quick stroke, we have found the equation of the axis of symmetry, as well as the abscissa of the turning point. How can we locate the y-value of the turning point? This value fairly jumps out at us: -9. In short order we know the general shape of the curve (opens upward), its axis of symmetry ($x = -2$), and its turning point $(-2, -9)$. If we now select any convenient value for x or y, we find not only one additional point but two, because of the symmetry of the parabola, and we may sketch the curve (Figure 8.7).

Figure 8.7

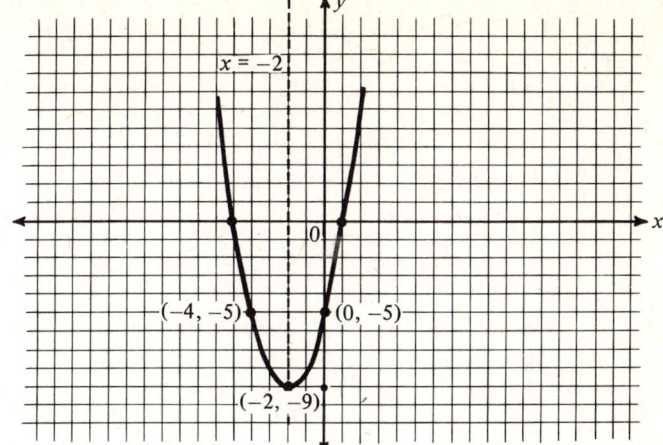

We have made a quick sketch of the desired curve. We may now also find the roots of the equation $y = x^2 + 4x - 5$ for any value of y simply by locating the x-values corresponding to the y-value in question. In the case of the equation $x^2 + 4x - 5 = +7$, we draw the graph of $y = 7$ (a straight line parallel to the x-axis, seven units above it) and mark the intersections of this line with the curve (Figure 8.8). The same process could be carried out for any other values of y. Frequently it is the zeros in which we have our interest: $y = 0$. In this case we simply observe the intersections with the x-axis.

Figure 8.8

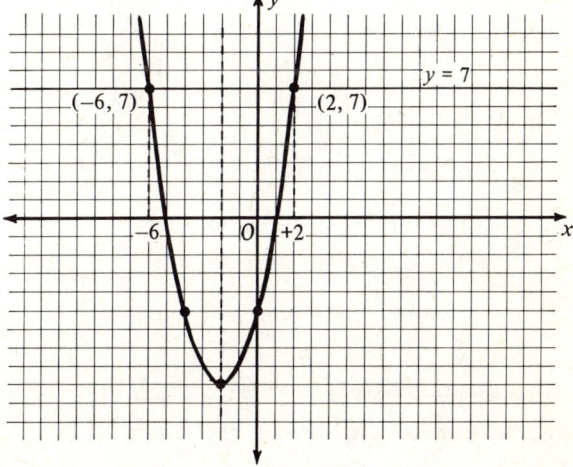

Perhaps this development eliminates some of the mystery frequently present in the minds of students as they solve quadratic equations by graphing techniques. In addition, the sudden appearance of y in the equation is most confusing. How often have you heard students cry in dismay "Where'd the y come from?" when they attempted to solve equations like $x^2 + 4x - 5 = 0$ by graphing? Where *does* the y come from? Using the ideas just presented, perhaps it will be somewhat more reasonable to students to find that we graph the function $x^2 + 4x - 5 = y$; then we seek out the particular y-values in which we have some interest.

We have a broad variety of relationships available that enable youngsters to realize how mathematics adds to our knowledge of science and provides practice with quadratics.

Automobile Functions

A car hitting a pole at r mph is equivalent to one falling h ft:
$$h = .0336r^2$$

The stopping distance, d, of a car moving r mph:
$$d = .055r^2 + 1.1r$$

The horsepower, H, generated by an auto engine at n rpm (revolutions per minute):
$$H = 15 - \frac{(n - 2000)^2}{150{,}000}$$

The spacing of autos (S) in feet on a busy road with average speed v ft/sec:
$$S = 18 + v + \frac{v^2}{32}$$

Miscellaneous Functions

The stopping distance (d) of a train t sec after braking:
$$d = 44t - 4t^2$$

The volume of a particular tree (v) in terms of its diameter (x):
$$v = 3.1x^2$$

The cost ($$y$) of producing x tons of metal in a particular factory:
$$y = 20 + 60x - .075x^2$$

Functions Involving Geometry

The rectangle considered most pleasing to the eye has length l and width w:
$$w^2 + wl - l^2 = 0$$

The number of diagonals (d) in a polygon of n sides:
$$d = \frac{n^2 - 3n}{2}$$

The total number of intersections (x) possible with n straight lines:
$$x = \frac{n(n - 1)}{2}$$

The greatest number of regions (R) created by the intersection of n straight lines:
$$R = \frac{n^2 + n + 2}{2}$$

The radius of a circular arch (r) whose span is $2s$ and whose crown is h (Figure 8.9):
$$r = \frac{s^2 + h^2}{2h}$$

Figure 8.9

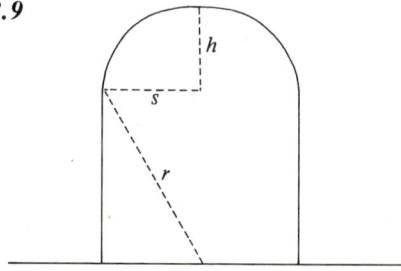

Footnote

1. See: *The Report of the Commission on Mathematics. Appendices.* New York: College Entrance Examination Board, 1959, pp. 47–57.

For Investigation and Discussion

1. Plan a lesson for the introduction of the quadratic function based upon the distance relation $d = 16t^2$.
2. Indicate how interesting practice experience may be provided by moving the locale of problems to other planets and the moon.
3. Plan a lesson that will result in the need to work with radicals by selecting a situation in which radicals are inherent.
4. Plan a lesson that enables students to make use of "completing the squares," in order to analyze the function for graphing purposes.
5. Demonstrate how rectangular areas may be used to aid student understanding of the process of factoring quadratic trinomials.
6. Select two physical situations and illustrate how mathematics plays the two roles of "queen" and "servant" of science.

For Further Reading

Books

Conference Board of the Mathematical Sciences. *Overview and Analysis of School Mathematics, Grades K-12.* National Advisory Committee on Mathematical Education. 1975, pp. 25–31.

Forsythe, George E. "Solving a Quadratic Equation on a Computer," *The Mathematical Sciences,* George A. Boehm, ed. Committee on Support of Research in the Mathematical Sciences (COSRIMS). Cambridge: M.I.T. Press, 1969, pp. 138–152.

Hooke, Robert and Douglas Schaffer. *Math and Aftermath.* New York: Walker. 1965.

Polya, George. *Studies in Mathematics, Mathematical Methods in Science.* Vol. XI, School Mathematics Study Group, Stanford University, Ca., 1963.

Periodicals

Edmonds, George F. "An Intuitive Approach to Square Numbers," *The Mathematics Teacher.* Vol. 63 (February 1970), pp. 113–117.

Farrell, Margaret A. and Ernest R. Ranucci. "On the Occasional Incompatibility of Algebra and Geometry," *The Mathematics Teacher.* Vol. 66 (October 1973), pp. 491–497.

Gabai, Hyman. "Graphcodes," *The Mathematics Teacher.* Vol. 69 (April 1976), pp. 276–279.

Ruchlis, Hy. "Putting Reality into Mathematics," *The Mathematics Teacher.* Vol. 64 (April 1971), pp. 369–371.

Sconyers, James M. "The Limits of Parabolas," *The Mathematics Teacher.* Vol. 67 (November 1974), pp. 652–653.

CHAPTER 9

The Mathematics of Motion

The motion laws and the study of springs have still further uses not mentioned, ranging from elementary mathematics to geometry, trigonometry, and calculus. This is a rather broad mathematical spectrum, but an interesting method of tying together the various branches of mathematics usually treated in isolation. We shall focus on change and rates of change.

9.1 *Speed-Time Graphs*

One way to study the motion laws (particularly $d = rt$) in using informal geometry and arithmetic is to consider speed-time graphs. We have already seen how graphing may be a natural outgrowth of the study of geometric concepts. The familiar motion relationship offers students another nice way to tie different concepts together.

▶   You get on your bike and ride at a steady rate of 12 mi/hr for 4 hr. Draw a graph showing the relationship between speed and time and use it to find the distance traveled (Figure 9.1). (Assume the speed at the first instance is 12.)

The graph is a horizontal line since the time is changing but the speed is not. Drop a perpendicular from its right end point down to the time axis, and you will have drawn a rectangle. But where is the distance in all of this? We have here the kind of visual representation that is useful throughout our mathematics work, a geometric model of a physical event. This model also constitutes a picture of multiplication. Distance (under constant rates of speed) is found by the familiar

Figure 9.1

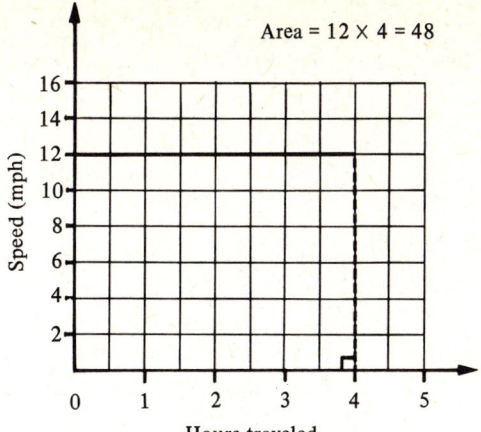

$d = rt$. Hence, it is the product of the speed and the time. The rectangle we have drawn has an area defined to be the product of its length and width. If we look at the graph, we find that the length and width of the rectangle are representations of speed and time. In this instance, the ideas are interchangeable. Therefore, the area of the rectangle—the area under the curve—will indicate the distance, 48 miles.

Let us alter the situation slightly.

You get on your bike and ride, increasing your speed at a steady rate so that the chart in Figure 9.2 describes your speed. What distance have you gone after 4 hr?

Figure 9.2

Hours	0	1	2	3	4
Speed	0	4	8	12	16

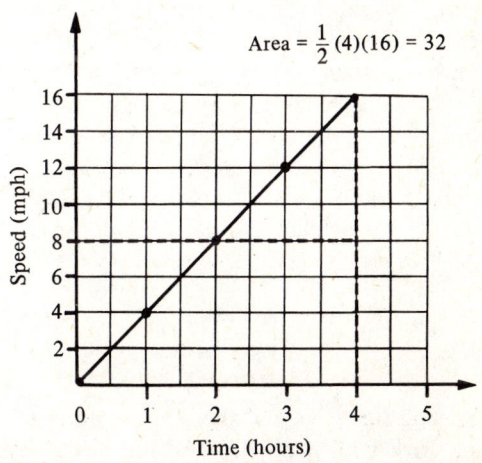

After the students draw the graph they should discuss ways to use the graph to find the answer. Alternative methods become valuable as checks. The graph is now a straight line that moves upward as it moves to the right. If students drop a perpendicular from the right end point, they enclose a triangular region under the curve. Using their knowledge of triangle area, they compute it and determine the distance, 32 mi. Is there a rectangle on our graph that has this same area? A horizontal line through the midpoint of the curve creates a rectangle equal in area to the triangle: 8 × 4 or 32 mi. Once again, students have found distance to be the area under the curve.

Finally, you get on the bike and take readings each half hour of a 4 hr ride and record the values found in the chart in Figure 9.3. Find the distance traveled in 4 hr.

Figure 9.3

Hours	0	1	2	3	4
Speed	0	5	8	6	10

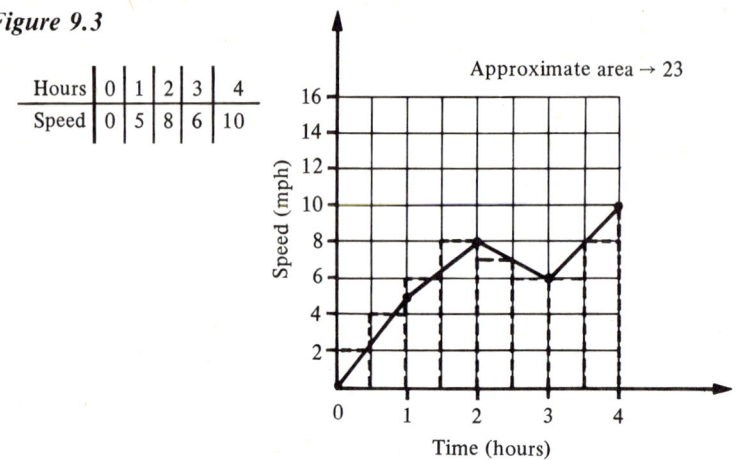

Here is a fine puzzle for the students. If they are encouraged to work together, they may offer some ingenious methods of solution. While this is no simple problem, it is an important one that has the seeds of the calculus planted within it.

How do they proceed? Earlier they found the areas of many irregular figures by counting squares. This is an excellent method. After counting the squares, we find the desired area. We may also construct rectangles of equal base with heights varying in accordance with the curve. Then approximate the area.

Many problems involving a wide range of motions can be presented for additional student experience. We are using our methods for graphing, our knowledge of motion, our geometric concepts of area, and untold arithmetic computations. We are preparing the ground for the study of algebra and the later study of the calculus.

9.2 Distance as Area

Carrying the work further, we take the formula $d = rt$ and move into more formal work with geometry and algebra. We utilize the relation between distance and area, using area as a model for distance. The mathematics applies equally well to each, as the elements of one situation are isomorphic to those of the other.

As we did with the bicycle rider, we represent the distance as the area of a rectangle (r and t are the measures of its sides) by placing the entire situation on the coordinate axes. For example, if an auto moved at a constant rate of speed, say 30 mi/hr, and traveled 6 hr, the auto would travel 180 mi. The graph, shown in Figure 9.4, is a straight line parallel to the horizontal axis (t-axis) at the level $v = 30$. The area of this rectangle is equal to the distance, 180. We follow this general plan but vary the speed and encounter some interesting ideas:

Figure 9.4

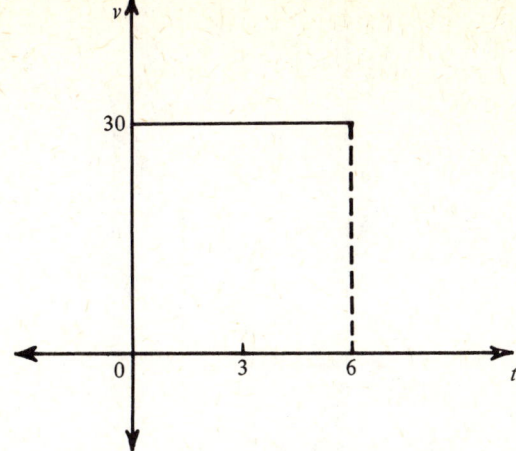

The auto travels 15 mi/hr for 3 hr and 30 mi/hr for 3 more hours (Figure 9.5). The areas of the two rectangles (3 × 15 = 45 and 3 × 30 = 90) represent the total distance traveled.

Figure 9.5

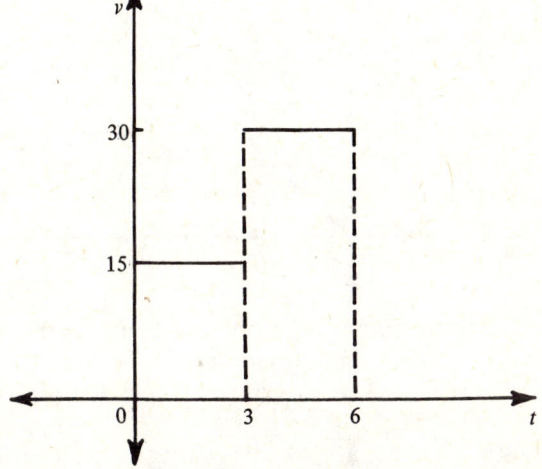

The auto starts at 2½ mi/hr and increases velocity in sudden jumps of 2½ mi/hr every half hour for 6 hr. Again the sum of the areas of all these rectangles would be the distance traveled as shown in Figure 9.6. (see page 132).

If we continue this pattern of reducing the time interval and the velocity for the corresponding interval but maintain the idea of sudden increases in speed, the graph of these separate velocities comes very close to being the graph of a straight line. The narrower the rectangle, the more the series of "steps approximates the straight line. Hence, the area under the straight line from $t = 0$ to $t = 6$ should represent the distance traveled during this time interval (Figure 9.7 see page 132). However, the area of the triangle formed is ½(30)(6) or 90 mi. Thus, 90 mi is the distance traveled.

Figure 9.6

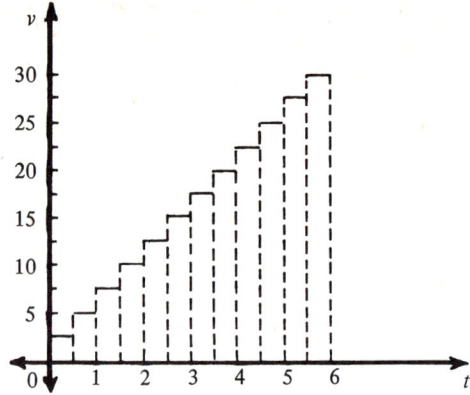

Figure 9.7

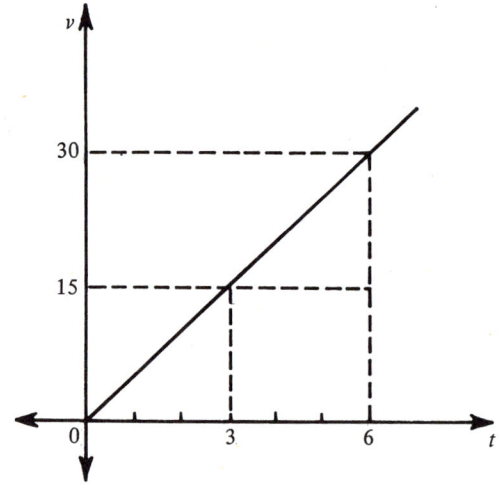

If we take the midpoint of the interval from $t = 0$ to $t = 6$, erect the perpendicular *BC*, and draw a line through *C* parallel to the *t*-axis, we obtain rectangle *ODEF* (Figure 9.8). The area of this rectangle equals the area of $\triangle OAF$.

Figure 9.8

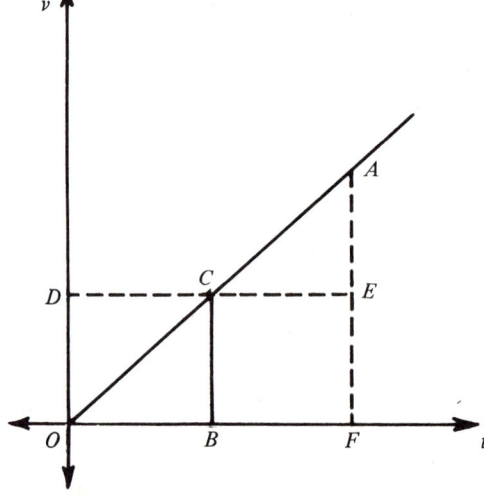

(Show that $\triangle OCD \cong \triangle ACE$.) We may then say that rectangle *ODEF* represents the distance traveled. Its base and height are 6 and 15, respectively; so once again 90 mi is the distance traveled. It appears, then, that a constant velocity of 15 mi/hr over the interval is equivalent to the continuously increasing velocity described by $v = 5t$.

Using both the geometry and the algebra, we may generalize this result. If an object moves with velocity $v = at$ from $t = 0$ to $t = T$, the area under the straight line from $t = 0$ to $t = T$ indicates the distance traveled. If we erect a perpendicular *BC* at $\frac{T}{2}$ and construct *DE*, we have a rectangle shown in Figure 9.9 whose area is equal to that of $\triangle OAT$. If we determine the area of this rectangle, we will, in effect, have found a statement for the distance covered in the given interval. But what is the height and base of this rectangle? In determining

Figure 9.9

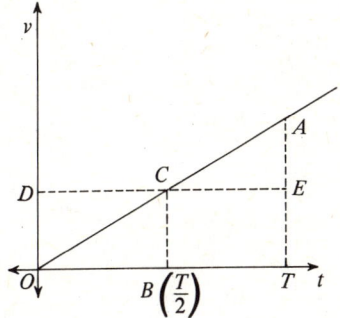

the height, we see that it is *BC*. Its length is the value of $v (v = at)$ at $t = \frac{T}{2}$. By substitution we get

$$v = a\left(\frac{T}{2}\right).$$

Thus, the constant velocity of $\frac{aT}{2}$ continued for *T* hours is equivalent to the changing velocity $v = at$. The velocity

$$\frac{aT}{2} = \frac{0 + aT}{2}$$

which is another way of saying that the equivalent constant velocity is the average of the initial (zero) and final (aT) velocities.

Since we were given that the length of the rectangle is *T*, the area becomes

$$bh = \left(\frac{aT}{2}\right)(T).$$

The distance in question is

$$d = \frac{aT^2}{2}$$

If we now substitute the acceleration of gravity ($a = 32$), we find that

$$d = 16T^2$$

This is precisely the way in which Galileo obtained the formula for the distance traveled by a falling body! (Compare this with the method in Chapter 8).

The preceding discussion serves many significant purposes. Concepts from geometry and algebra both were needed; and what is more, we have made an intuitive start on some of the ideas of the calculus.

It is possible, if interest warrants, to extend this work to include trapezoids. For example:

▶ If an object is thrown downward with a velocity of 10 ft/sec, the velocity is described as $v = 10 + 32t$. The object falls for 6 sec. Represent the distance traveled geometrically as an area and calculate the area (Figure 9.10).

Figure 9.10

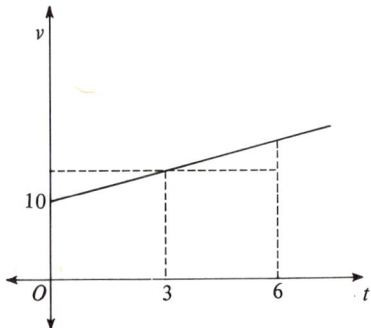

In solving such a problem, the students have a choice of finding the area of a trapezoid or a rectangle. These areas are equal and also provide the distance traveled. One figure can be used for finding an answer and the other can serve as a check.

The situation may be generalized, in the manner of the earlier work. Many problems involving the calculations of area and the determination of distances traveled, as well as proofs of originals may also be presented to students. Building on the preceding work, we now focus upon rates of change rather than change itself.

9.3 Rates of Change and Derivatives

A problem in motion is presented.

▶ A runner is timed over a measured 100 yd track. She starts before the starting line so that she may enter the course at top speed. Here is the time she reached different distance markers:

t (sec)	0	1	2	3	4	5	6	... 10
d (ft)	0	10	20	30	40	50	60	...100

We can tell at a glance where the runner is at any time, but can we tell how fast she is running? Perhaps a graph of this information will help (Figure 9.11). The graph turns out to be a straight line. Let us find her speed when $t = 4$. The rule for the function just described is easy enough to find: $d = 10t$. Since she seems to gain 10 ft each second, her speed seems to be just that, 10 ft/sec. Does this speed change as she runs? We know the speed is constant by examining the table and observing the steady increase in distance for each second. We can also tell that the speed is constant from the graph. The curve is a straight line. The formula $d = 10t$ indicates the constant speed as well. Her speed at $t = 4$ will therefore be the same as at $t = 2$ or 5 or any other number of seconds. It is a constant 10 ft/sec throughout.

Figure 9.11

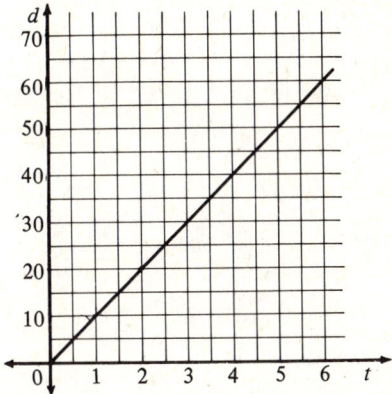

Could we find this speed from the distance-time graph? What is the speed? We may think of it as the change in distance for a given time interval. Look at the graph and determine how the distance changed in the 1-sec time interval from 2 to 3 sec. (Figure 9.12). The distance changed by 10 ft in the 1-sec time interval. From the graph, we can see that this is also the slope of the line.

Figure 9.12

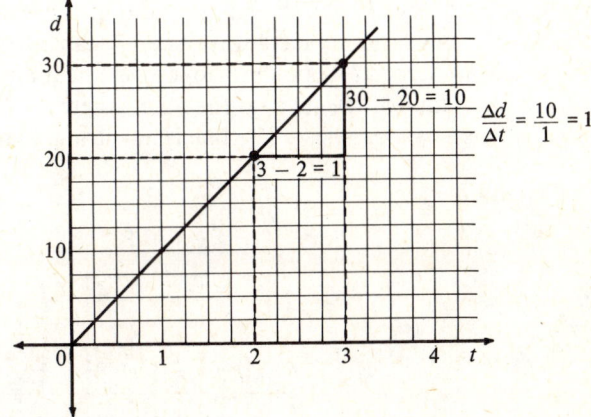

Thus, we find that

$$\frac{d_2 - d_1}{t_2 - t_1} = \frac{\Delta d}{\Delta t} = \frac{30 - 20}{3 - 2} = 10$$

We know that the slope of a straight line is constant at each point on the line, so once again we find the speed is constant and is 10 ft/sec. Despite the fact that our graph involves distance-time, we found the speed by determining the slope or steepness of the line. Will this always work? A look at other functions will enable us to find out.

At this point the students might pursue the answers to the same questions for other simple linear functions, such as:

$y = 3x$
$y = 2x + 5$
$y = -x - 3$, etc.

In each of these cases, the speed is constant and is represented by the slope of the straight line describing the function. We are concentrating on familiar information from a new point of view: exploring the rate of change of the distance with respect to the change in time. It is well for students to list the results shown in Table 9.1.

Table 9.1

Formula	Speed
$y = 10x$	$v = 10$
$y = 3x$	$v = 3$
$y = 2x + 5$	$v = 2$
$y = -x - 3$	$v = -1$

The slope of the line has provided us with the speed. We ask students to focus on a more complicated function:

A boy sledding down a hill passes distance markers as follows:

t	0	1	2	3	4	5
d	0	1	4	9	16	25

Can students answer the same questions as before? That is, since we know where the boy is at any instant, say $t = 3$, can we find how fast he is going at that particular second? If our previous work held any clues, draw the graph and seek out the slope of the curve at the point where $t = 3$ (Figure 9.13). Here we seem to have a bit of a problem. The line is not straight and may be recognized as

Figure 9.13

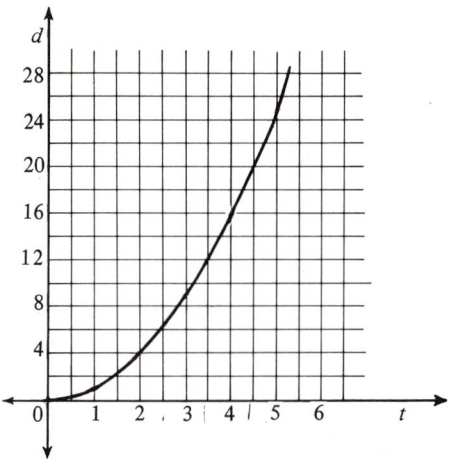

a portion of the familiar parabola. The formula for this motion (looking at the table) is $d = t^2$. The speed is not constant because the boy gains speed as his sled comes down the hill. Thus, the speed will be different at each point—as the graph indicates. Indeed, the graph curls upward to show that more distance is being covered in the same amount of time; hence, the speed is increasing. At the same instant where $t = 3$, the distance is 9 ft. Since it took 3 sec to cover the 9 ft, the speed appears to be 3 ft/sec. But wait, something is wrong here. If we declare the speed to be 3 ft/sec when $t = 3$ and if the speed is increasing continuously, in the time before $t = 3$, the speed must have been less than 3 ft/sec. But if this is so, then how could the sled have covered 9 ft in 3 sec? Something is amiss somewhere. We are having trouble because we are confusing two different ideas: average speed over an interval and speed at an instant in time or **instantaneous speed.** The sled went 9 ft in 3 sec. Its **average** speed is 3 ft/sec and not its speed at that instant. Indeed, its speed at the instant of 3 sec will undoubtably have to be greater than 3 ft/sec since it began at zero and gradually increased. If its average was 3, then somewhere in the interval it must have exceeded 3 to take care of the period when it was less than 3.

How shall we get at this elusive *instantaneous* speed? If students take a smaller interval around 3 and perhaps they will better see what is happening. Here they may embark upon the arithmetical exercises of finding the distance corresponding to $t = 2.9$ and $t = 3.1$. Our original table is expanded to include:

t	2.9	3	3.1
d	8.41	9	9.61

Computing average speed $\left(\frac{\Delta d}{\Delta t}\right)$ between 2.9 and 3 gives a change in distance (Δd) of .59 for a change in time (Δt) of .1, or $\frac{.59}{.1}$ or 5.9 ft/sec. If we carry out the same computation for the interval from 3 to 3.1, we get $\frac{.61}{.1}$ or 6.1 ft/sec. We begin to get a sense of the speed at the instant $t = 3$: It is somewhere between 5.9 and 6.1 ft/sec. The students should repeat these calculations for a shorter interval, $t = 2.99$ and 3.01, and then to $t = 2.999$ and $t = 3.001$. Eventually students become fairly well convinced that the speed at 3 itself must be 6 ft/sec. They begin a new table of instantaneous speeds and continue their investigation and calculation at the instant $t = 1$ through $t = 5$ or 6. Each time the speed is recorded in the new table so that a pattern may be observed:

t	1	2	3	4	5	6
v	2	4	6	8	10	12

It soon becomes clear that when the distance-time relationship is $d = t^2$, the speed-time counterpart is $v = 2t$. Going through the entire experience with other motion problems ($y = 2x^2$, $y = x^3$, $y = x^2 + x$, etc.) and listing the results as before leads to a general rule for answering the central problem of the calculus: Given a rule for finding where an object is at any instant in time, find how fast it is moving at that instant.

What of the graph? If we accept the fact that the reduction in the size of the interval of time eventually leads to the conclusion that the instantaneous speed at $t = 3$ is 6 ft/sec, what does this mean graphically? If we first clarify the meaning of average speed and then follow graphically the same process we

Figure 9.14

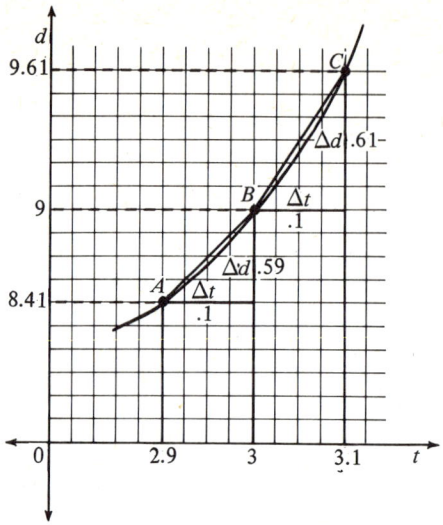

carried out arithmetically, we can see that the slope of the tangent to a point describes the instantaneous speed at that point (Figure 9.14.) The slope of *AB* is 5.9, the average speed for the given interval. The same is true of *BC,* whose slope is 6.1. As we move point *A* toward point *B*, we reduce Δ*t*. If we imagine this process being carried out until points *A* and *B* virtually merge, we can illustrate intuitively how the slope at the point *B* may be thought of as the slope of the tangent to the curve at that point. We also have begun to establish an intuitive foundation for the general description of the instantaneous speed. Using $y = x^2$, we chose a small interval about *x*: Δ*x*. This change in *x* brings about a corresponding change in *y*: Δ*y*.

$$y = x^2$$
$$y + \Delta y = (x + \Delta x)^2$$

Removing parentheses, we get

$$y + \Delta y = x^2 + 2x\Delta x + \Delta x^2$$

We are concerned with the change, so we subtract the original equation, $y = x^2$:

$$y + \Delta y - y = x^2 + 2x\Delta x + \Delta x^2 - x^2$$
$$\Delta y = 2x\Delta x + \Delta x^2$$

The average speed is $\frac{\Delta y}{\Delta x}$. We divide both sides by Δ*x*:

$$\frac{\Delta y}{\Delta x} = \frac{2x\Delta x + \Delta x^2}{\Delta x}$$

$$\frac{\Delta y}{\Delta x} = 2x + \Delta x \quad \text{(average speed)}$$

Now if we move point *B* toward *A* so that Δ*x* → 0,

$$\lim_{x \to 0} \frac{\Delta y}{\Delta x} = \frac{dy}{dx} = 2x \quad \text{(instantaneous speed)}$$

This process is not attempted until the students have calculated the results and drawn freehand tangents to curves in a vast number of cases. There is no hurry. We are struggling to build a "feel" for the process and if we provide sufficient examples, the general development just shown becomes an obvious "next step" rather than a mystery. But this can occur only if its formulation is at the end of the experiences described rather than at the beginning.

The notion of limit and the new symbolism are introduced *after* a rich variety of experiences has been undertaken. The important notion is that the derivative tells us the speed or steepness of the given formula at a point. We use the word "speed," but the functions to be explored need not be limited to motion. Since a function, by its nature, indicates changing values of variables, the derivative will tell us how fast changes are taking place, hence our focus upon *rates of change*. We may be concerned with spring stretch and time, area of a wound and time, pressure and height, price and time, or any other pair of variables. When we are concerned with *instantaneous rates of change,* we are concerned with the derivative. Repetition of the process takes us another step forward and indicates the rate at which *changes* are taking place. This process may be continued indefinitely. Thus, if we begin with $s = 16t^2$ we find the *instantaneous* rate of change to be $v = 32t$. Repetition of differentiation yields $a = 32$. The significance of the results may best be described as follows:

Distance: $\quad s = 16t^2$

Speed: $\quad$ The change in *distance* with respect to time is the speed or velocity.

$\quad v = 32t \quad$ (first derivative $\frac{ds}{dt}$ or s')

Acceleration: $\quad$ The change in *speed* with respect to time is the acceleration.

$\quad a = 32 \quad$ (second derivative $\frac{d^2s}{dt^2}$ or s'')

We have not discussed the vital concept of limits. We have only dealt with simple functions and assumed these functions to be continuous. We have not considered the inverse process to differentiation. This will be explored shortly. For the conclusion of this discussion, it is important to realize that our goal has been an introduction to the calculus based upon familiar functions and known processes. The remainder of work with differentiation involves working with more and more complicated functions. There are four basic principles that students must learn, in addition to what has already been discussed. Suitable problems are plentiful for the introduction of these principles of differentiation: If we let $f(x) = u$ and $g(x) = v$, then:

1. Sum and difference:

    $y = u + v \quad y' = u' + v'$
    $y = u - v \quad y' = u' - v'$

2. Product:

    $y = uv \quad y' = u'v + uv'$

3. Quotient

    $y = \frac{u}{v} \quad y' = \frac{u'v - uv'}{v^2}$

4. Function of a function (chain rule):

    If $y = f(u)$ and $u = f(x)$,

    $$\frac{dy}{dx} = \frac{dy}{du} \cdot \frac{du}{dx}$$

9.4 The Limit

The key idea in the preceding work was the notion of limit. It was intuitively dispatched by seeing that values tended in a certain direction and toward a given value. We said that as the size of the interval was made smaller and smaller and tended toward zero, the limit of the average rate became the instantaneous rate. Does the interval ever *become* zero; and if not, how could the speed at a point ever actually *become* the value we call the instantaneous rate? For example, $y = x^2$. The instantaneous rate at $x = 3$ is 2×3 or 6. The definition we use of this rate is

$$\lim_{x \to 0} \frac{\Delta y}{\Delta x}$$

Is the speed at the point $x = 4$ actually 8? Then does Δx ever actually take the value zero? No. If it did, we could not divide by it and all our work is fruitless. This problem has plagued mathematicians for years. Indeed, the inventors of the calculus, both Newton and Leibniz, did not have an exact formulation of limits. Is it any wonder, then, that our students find this concept so difficult to understand?

Only extended experience with the idea will render it meaningful, and this is not likely to occur in a single semester. We have already appealed to student intuition by considering values that the variable in question approached. We may offer some additional aid in the very situation that generated the idea initially and by following the same kinds of arithmetic procedures developed before. When we say that the limit of the average speed as x approaches 3 is 6, in effect we are declaring that we can make the average speed differ from the limit (instantaneous speed) by as little as we wish. In fact, we may consider it to be a challenge. If you select as small an interval as you like about the limit, there must be an average speed that differs from the limit by less than that amount. Let us turn to the calculations. The student should form a chart (Table 9.2) listing the succeeding x-values approaching 3, the resulting y-values, and the average speeds:

Table 9.2 $y = x^2$ as $x \to 3$.

x-values	Δx	y-values	Δy	Average speed $\frac{\Delta y}{\Delta x}$
3.1	.1	9.61	.61	6.1
3.01	.01	9.0601	.0601	6.01
3.001	.001	9.006001	.006001	6.001
3.0001	.0001	9.00060001	.00060001	6.0001

The average speed values are heading for 6. If 6 is truly the limit, then the challenge must be met. It goes like this: You select as small an interval as you wish close to 6 and, to beat off the challenge, I must find a number sufficiently close to 3 to yield an average speed that is between 6 and your value. For example,

> Your challenge: get closer than .1 from 6
> My reply: Let $x = 3.01$, because when $x = 3.01$, the average speed = 6.01; this is closer to 6 than .1

This challenge can only be met successfully by the number we call the limit. It must also be true that not only 3.01 satisfies the test, but all numbers between 3 and 3.01 also satisfy the test. In effect, we can say that if we think of the average speeds as a sequence of numbers (for example, 6.1, 6.01, 6.001, 6.0001, . . .), to call 6 the limit of this sequence is to indicate that as we keep taking terms we get closer and closer to 6, and we can get as close to 6 as we wish. Given the challenge in different terms, if an interval is selected (say, .1 from 6) and if 6 is the limit as described, there is a finite number of terms of the sequence outside the interval, but an *infinite* number inside! This is true despite the fact that the interval may be made as small as you desire! A remarkable idea is this notion of limit. To do more in high school would seem to be rushing things. We have tried to provide the student with some intuitive feeling about limits. This should be our chief goal at this level. College instruction will serve to refine the ideas only introduced here.

Integration 9.5

Every operation the student has met has involved an inverse operation. Differentiation is no exception. It is rather curious to observe how the inverse operation arises through a consideration of areas under a curve. What possible connection can there be between rates of change and the summation of areas? If we are going to develop an inverse process to differentiation, since the derivative is the speed calculated by knowing the distance relationship, we evidently will reverse this process. We will begin with a description of the speed in an attempt to find the distance formula. This is a familiar undertaking. Earlier we saw how speed-time graphs could help us to determine the distance traveled. An object falls on a strange planet as shown by the following data:

t	0	1	2	3	4	5	6
v	0	3	6	9	12	15	18

The graph is shown in Figure 9.15. How far has the object fallen in 4 sec?

Figure 9.15

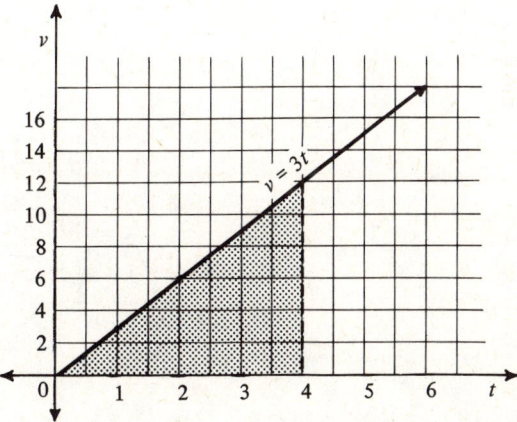

In our earlier work we found that the area under the curve provided us with the required distance. Briefly, the rationale for this consisted of finding the area of a rectangle equal to the area of the desired triangle. Since distance is defined by $d = rt$ and the rectangle area by $A = lw$, the parallel is clear. We can find the triangle area directly by use of the familiar triangle formula, $A = \frac{1}{2}bh$.

Figure 9.16

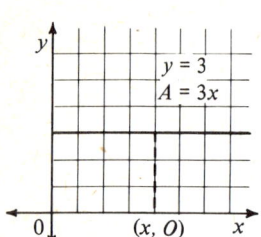 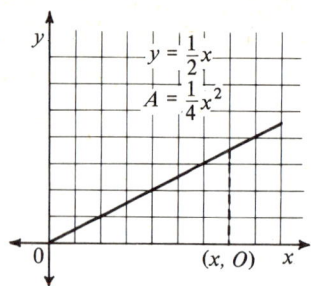 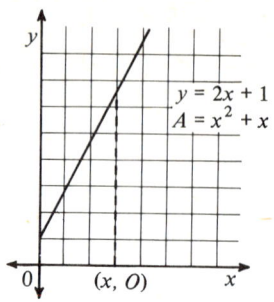

In the preceding problem, the solution may be arrived at as follows: $A = \frac{1}{2}(4)(12)$, where 12 is the value of $3x$ when $x = 4$. The distance traveled by the object in 4 sec is 24 ft. Or we may use average speed over the interval again:

$$\frac{0 + 12}{2} = 6$$

Then $6 \times 4 = 24$. The area under the curve and the distance traveled are indeed related. To build upon this idea and to allow time for the notion to develop, many additional problems may be solved by the students in this rudimentary way. Samples of such problems are shown in Figure 9.16. Each time the distance is calculated, the student has reversed the process of differentiation. We call this finding the **antiderivative.**

Perhaps we can find a general formula for the area under the curve in any interval, instead of dealing with each problem anew. Generalization can only result from a broad collection of experiences. If we investigate the curve $y = 4x$ and carry out the same ideas using a general point, what happens? (See Figure 9.17.) The area of the enclosed triangle becomes

$$A = \tfrac{1}{2}(x)f(x) = \tfrac{1}{2}x(4x) = 2x^2.$$

Figure 9.17

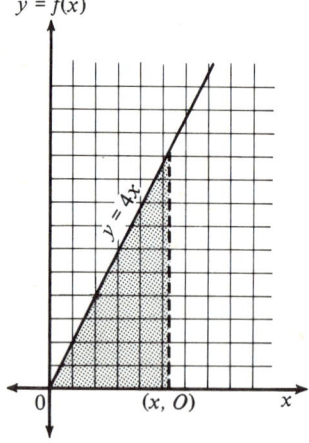

We have our first statement of the indefinite integral. We began with the formula for speed and determined the function—distance. A quick check on our results would be to differentiate the function and match the result with the speed formula:

$$\frac{d(2x^2)}{dx} = 4x$$

Figure 9.18

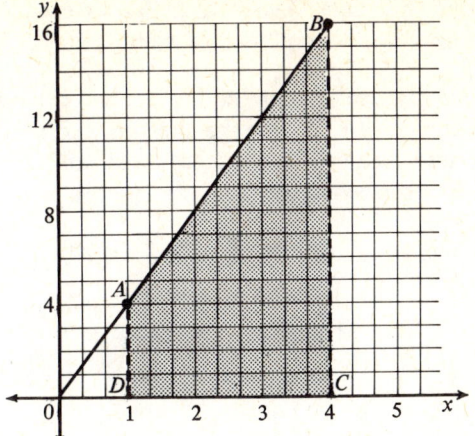

We have thus derived a general statement for finding the area bounded by the curve, the x-axis, and a perpendicular from a point on the curve to the x-axis. Will this result enable us to find the area under the curve in an interval that does not include the origin? (See Figure 9.18.) If we apply the function we just derived, the antiderivative of $y = 4x$ (that is, $2x^2$). If we make use of the right end point $x = 4$, we get

$$A = 2(4)(4) = 32$$

The area is 32 square units. But what exactly have we found? And why use the right end point and not the left end point? If the students are free to resolve these questions for themselves in their own way, they will have a good opportunity to realize that substitution of $x = 4$ into the antiderivative yields the area of $\triangle BOC$. But this contains more area than was intended. The extra piece is $\triangle AOD$, which also happens to be the area that results from substitution of the x-coordinate of the left end point. In effect we have carried out the following:

The desired area is area $\triangle BOC$ − area $\triangle AOD$.

$$2(4)^2 - 2(1)^2$$
$$32 - 2 = 30$$

The desired area is 30 square units.

The process employed here is most interesting. If we generalize to any function, assuming for the moment that the method will hold up, we find that we have done the following:

$$A = F(b) - F(a)$$

where a is the x-coordinate of the left end point, b is the x-coordinate of the right end point, and $F(x)$ is the antiderivative of $f(x)$, the formula for speed. We have our first statement of the definite integral. It seems a bit premature to introduce the integral notation at this time since the integral sign is more meaningful as the sum of areas. It may be desireable to continue to use "antiderivative" until the summation of areas is considered.

Added experience with straight line functions is necessary before the generalized form just presented is discussed. Case by case, the idea is formed until the student is virtually able to state the general form himself. Once we have progressed to this stage, we may ask: Can we use this method for finding the area under any curve, not simply straight lines? In particular,

▶ Find the area under the curve $y = x^2$ between $x = 3$ and $x = 5$. (See Figure 9.19.) To state the question another way, if the speed of an object is described by $y = x^2$, find the distance it traveled in the 2 sec following the third second of its motion.

Figure 9.19

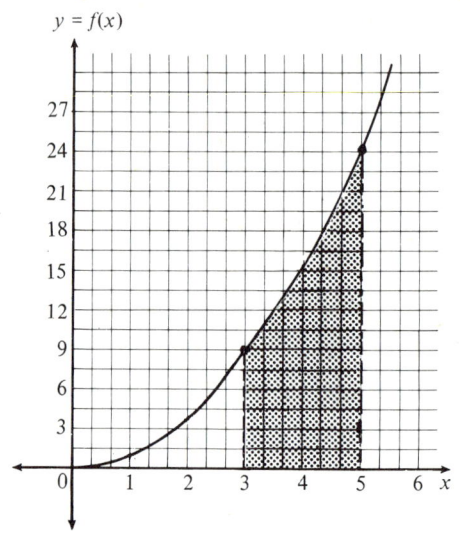

If we assume that the process will work,

$$f(x) = x^2$$

then $$F(x) = \frac{x^3}{3}$$

$a = 3 \quad b = 5$

$$A = F(5) - F(3) = \frac{(5)^3}{3} - \frac{(3)^3}{3} = \frac{125 - 27}{3} = \frac{98}{3} = 32\frac{2}{3}$$

The method indicates that the area is $32\frac{2}{3}$ square units, but is this correct? Once again the students must determine whether or not the answer is a good one. The methods used to ascertain this are as important as the particular processes we are focusing upon. The students may wish to draw straight lines approximating the curve; they may wish to subdivide the area. Whatever the method, their results will approximate $32\frac{2}{3}$. Can we ever be certain? Since rectangle areas are easily computed, let us explore an approximation of the area in question by subdividing it into rectangles. We may begin by thinking of the area as a single rectangle shown in Figure 9.20. We may use either end point to determine the height. Here we have selected the left end point. The area of the rectangle formed is base × height. The height is the function value for $x = 3$, or $f(3)$. The base is the difference between the x-values of the interval end points, Δx or $5 - 3$. The calculation is:

$$A = f(3) \, \Delta x = (9)(2) = 18$$

This approximation yields an area of 18 square units. This is not too close to $32\frac{2}{3}$. If you look at Figure 9.20, you will see that the rectangle is indeed a good

Figure 9.20

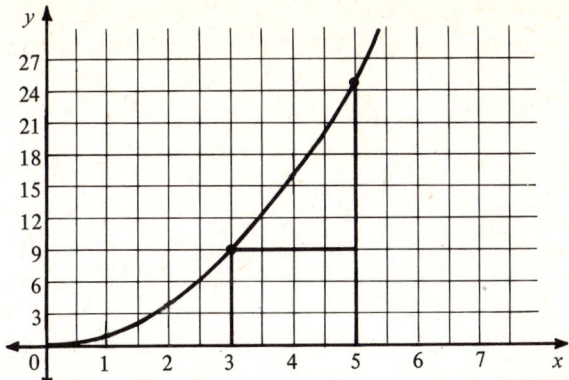

deal less in area than the region under the curve. However, if we subdivide the region into a greater number of rectangles, we get closer to the desired area. So we divide the area into two rectangles in the same manner as before, using the left end point (Figure 9.21). The sum of these rectangle areas forms our second approximation:

$$A = f(x_1)\,\Delta x + f(x_2)\,\Delta x = [f(x_1) + f(x_2)]\,\Delta x$$
$$= [f(3) + f(4)]\,(1) = 9 + 16 = 25$$

Figure 9.21

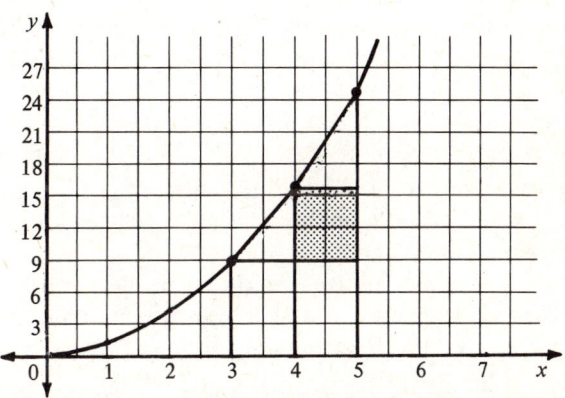

Now we see that we are moving closer to the expected area. A look at the curve shows just how much closer this second approximation has come. The shaded portion is included in this calculation and was not included in the earlier one. As you might expect at this point, if we continue to subdivide into more and more rectangles, gradually reducing the width of each (Δx), we get closer and closer to the actual area under the curve. Figure 9.22 (see page 146) shows the area subdivided into four rectangles. Once again the gap between the desired area and the area of the rectangles is narrowed:

$$\begin{aligned}
A &= f(x_1)\,\Delta x + f(x_2)\,\Delta x + f(x_3)\,\Delta x + f(x_4)\,\Delta x \\
&= [f(x_1) + f(x_2) + f(x_3) + f(x_4)]\,\Delta x \\
&= \left[f(3) + f\left(3\tfrac{1}{2}\right) + f(4) + f\left(4\tfrac{1}{2}\right)\right]\tfrac{1}{2} \\
&= 9 + \tfrac{49}{4} + 16 + \tfrac{81}{4}\ \ \tfrac{1}{2} \\
&= \left(57\tfrac{1}{2}\right)\left(\tfrac{1}{2}\right) = 28\tfrac{3}{4}
\end{aligned}$$

Figure 9.22

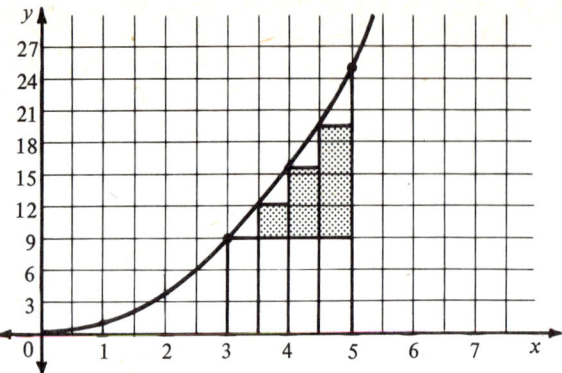

Breaking the region into 8 and 16 rectangles would serve to convince students that the area is indeed closing in on 32⅔. We seem to have another instance of the use of limits, and that is the case. As we reduce the width of the rectangles and construct more of them, we find that, in effect, we are doing the following:

$$\lim_{\Delta x \to 0} \sum_{i=3}^{5} f(x_i) \Delta x$$

where Σ indicates that we are taking the sum of all of the heights. The Greek letter sigma represents our letter S. Then it is only a short step to the integral notation

$$\lim_{\Delta x \to 0} \sum_{i=3}^{5} f(x_i) \Delta x = \int_{3}^{5} f(x) \, dx$$

which represents the limit of the sum of the areas of the rectangles as the width of each shrinks smaller and smaller. Since the end points are specified, this is known as the definite integral.

The method we found earlier does indeed work for all continuous functions, and we may state this in our new notation in several ways: The area under the curve $y = x^2$, from $x = 3$ to $x = 5$, is

$$A = \int_{3}^{5} x^2 \, dx$$

If $f(x) = x^2$, then $F(x) = \dfrac{x^3}{3}$ (antiderivative)

$$\int_{3}^{5} x^2 \, dx = F(5) - F(3)$$
$$= \frac{125}{3} - \frac{27}{3} = 32\frac{2}{3}$$

This may also be written in the following form:

$$\int_{3}^{5} x^2 \, dx = \frac{x^3}{3} \Big|_{3}^{5} = \frac{5^3}{3} - \frac{3^3}{3} = 32\frac{2}{3}$$

Practice with many problems will help to develop student confidence with the reverse of differentiation: integration. This practice should also include problems in which the constant is of consequence. For example, differentiate the following:

$3x^2 + 5$
$3x^2 + 105$
$3x^2 + 9000$

In each case the derivative is $6x$. If we reverse the process, how can we be sure which of these functions is the desired one? The indefinite integral then should actually be:

$$F(x) = \int x^2 \, dx = \frac{x^3}{3} + c$$

In the examples we have completed, we were in effect doing the following:

$$\int_3^5 x^2 \, dx = \frac{x^3}{3} \Big|_3^5 = F(5) - F(3) = \left(\frac{5^3}{3} + c\right) - \left(\frac{3^3}{3} + c\right)$$

Removing parentheses, we get

$$\frac{125}{3} + c - \frac{27}{3} - c = \frac{125 - 27}{3}$$

Each time $c = 0$. But this is not always the case. It is true here because the area at the left end point is zero. Other situations will result as the notion of integration is applied to a variety of problems going far beyond those employed here.

A genuine contribution to students' understanding of the power of mathematics is one outcome of the study of the calculus. Insight into the nature of the "queen" is virtually inevitable.

The Motion of Springs 9.6

The springs used earlier in experiments can now provide us with an excellent chance to study some additional functions, which demonstrate the critical role mathematics plays in the study of phenomena.

> If we were to hang a weight from a spring and pull the spring downward and release it, how shall we describe the motion of the spring?

It seems to move up and down, moving slower and slower until it eventually comes to a stop. In effect, the spring stretches out, contracts, stretches out again, and contracts somewhat less than before. Eventually, the movement ceases altogether. Think of the starting position of the spring and examine the different positions it takes. Any change from that at-rest position is a displacement of the spring. Since the displacements of the spring are dependent upon the time that has passed since the spring was set in motion, we may consider the change in position to be a function of time. If we do so, can we find a mathematical description of the function? To aid in this process, let us examine the situation, form a table of corresponding time and displacement values, and draw a graph of the function in order to see if it is recognizable.

Establishing equally spaced time intervals and making stop-action pictures of the motion of the spring results in Figure 9.23 (see page 148). The teacher can present such diagrams to the students so they can gather their own data about

Figure 9.23

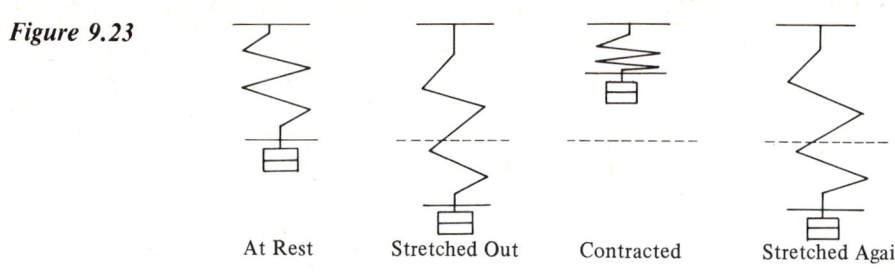

At Rest   Stretched Out   Contracted   Stretched Again

the behavior of the spring, in much the same fashion as was done earlier in algebra. The outcome is the table of values and the graph shown in Figure 9.24.

Figure 9.24

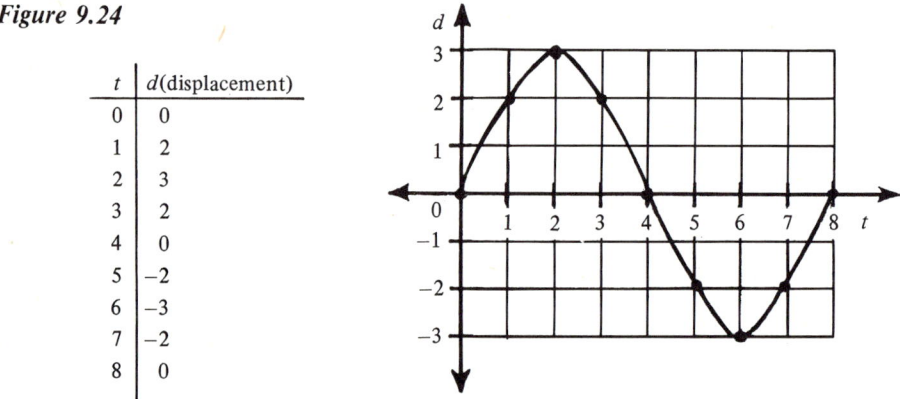

t	d(displacement)
0	0
1	2
2	3
3	2
4	0
5	−2
6	−3
7	−2
8	0

This is a function of a new kind. It is periodic in nature since it passes through a series of values and then repeats; thus far we have had no occasion to deal with such a function. It must be a new breed of function. Therefore, we shall have to find something new if we are to describe it properly. Perhaps trigonometry can help and, of course, it does.

These new functions called **periodic functions** are extremely interesting. E. T. Bell describes them as follows:

> Periodic phenomena in our daily lives are so common, we hardly notice them. At approximately equal spaced intervals of time we do the same things over and over again in approximately the same way. Our very breathing and heart beats are periodic. Even death is no escape. We shall rise again, we are assured, and the Hindus must submit to a yet more distressing periodicity.
>
> Nature too is a slave to periodicity. The seasons, the positions of the planets, the tides, the darkness and light, sunshine and moonlight, all these and scores of others are periodic or approximately so.[1]

How all pervasive! What better example can be found of the way mathematics has become a part of our lives?

When examining these trigonometric functions, it is noted that the variable x takes on a somewhat different role. Here the x is a placeholder for the measure of an angle. At this time the only possible replacements for x are contained in the set of angles from 0 to 90°. Let us explore how the functions derived from these descriptions would look on the graph. When we construct the table and draw the graph of $y = \sin x$ shown in Figure 9.25, we see it is a familiar one, as far as it goes. This graph appears to be a replica of the one showing the motion of the weight on a spring, although it is but a small portion of that graph. Is there some way we may extend the graph of the function described by $y = \sin x$? To accomplish this we will, in effect, have to define a new function.

Figure 9.25

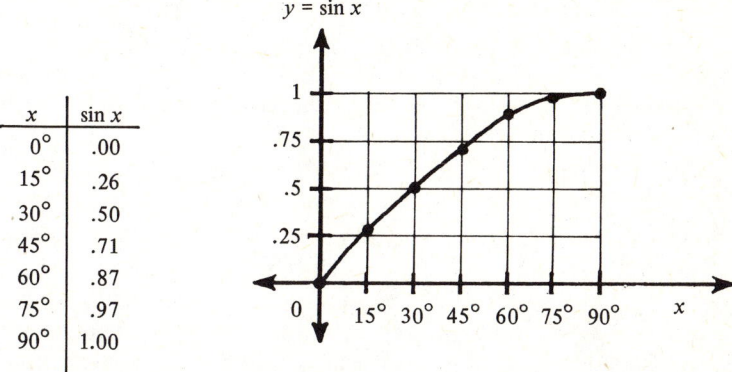

It may be well to look at some familiar ideas. The variable x in $y = \sin x$ is the measure of an angle. Usually, it is an angle of a right triangle. Therefore, it cannot possibly exceed 90°; indeed, it must be less than 90°. Let us take the equation $y = \sin x$ and think of the variable x simply as a real number. Each time we identify a new value for x, we find a corresponding one for y. The domain is now the set of real numbers. Of course, we do not know what the physical meaning of an x-value greater than 90° will be, but for now we are concerned only with the mathematical representations. Since we want the values for x to reflect the weight motion, they must repeat the displacement values of the weight in the same order. Thus, if we permit $x = 100$, the resulting y-value must match the value corresponding to $x = 80°$, or .9848. If we choose $x = 120$, the value of y must be the same as that of $x = 60°$; i.e., $y = .8660$. If any other values are chosen for y, the periodic nature of the function would be destroyed. Hence, we complete the table of extended x-values and their corresponding y-values, and we complete the graph as well. In general, we find that $\sin x = \sin(180 - x)$. It appears that selecting x-values up to and including 360 results in a construction that matches the graph in question rather well.

The trigonometric functions defined in this way are a perfect description of the periodic function of the oscillating spring. What an excellent development to show the interdependence of mathematics and science. Beginning with a physical experiment, we explored mathematical descriptions, resulting in a better understanding of the physical situation as well as the definition of a new function and an extension of our knowledge of mathematics.

Similar developments may extend our concepts of cosine and tangent. Indeed, once we have moved to the concept of x as a placeholder for a real number, we are free to extend the function to include negative x-values as well. In each instance we may stop and inquire as to the meaning of the expression before us in physical terms, in order to maintain our contact with the physical environment from whence these ideas came. Applications abound in any area concerned with the periodic nature of these functions. Musical sounds, electricity, and radio and television waves are some of these areas.[2] But there are still other ways in which we may look at the trigonometric functions.

9.7 Vectors in Trigonometry

Another recommendation of the Commission on Mathematics has been the reorganization of the trigonometry course because of new and vital applications in the fields of statics and dynamics and all kinds of vibration problems—to name but a few. In order to meet these needs, it is suggested that:

> computational emphasis should shift from triangles to vectors, and analytic emphasis from identities to functional properties. . . . The vital material of the reorganized trigonometry lies in the rectangular and polar descriptions of points, vectors, and complex numbers, and in the addition theorems and periodic character of the circular functions.[3]

Building on the definition of an angle as ". . . the configuration formed by two half-lines (rays) with a common end point," the Commission on Mathematics indicates how the concept of vectors is integrated into the study of trigonometry together with the notions of rectangular and polar coordinate systems.[4] A single diagram may serve to clarify the relationships (Figure 9.26). Once the standard position for the angle has been established, the trigonometric functions defined in terms of this newly defined angle may be determined. Thus, we are no longer concerned with the limitations imposed upon us by the fixed triangle approach used in the initial study of trigonometric ratios. While in this approach we have extended the domain of x to include values greater than 90°, we have developed this in a different manner from the previous discussion based upon an oscillating spring. Here, the x-values still represent angle measure, whereas the earlier discussion translated them into real numbers.

Figure 9.26

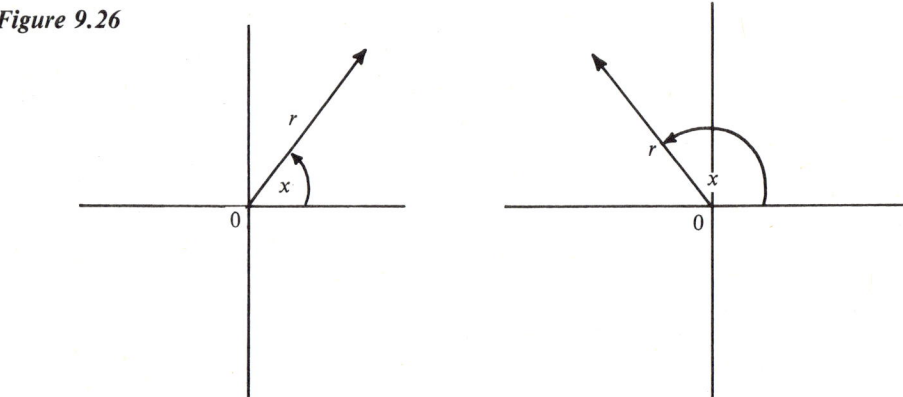

Exploration of the values of each of the functions in the four quadrants, graphs of the functions, operations with vectors, and the rectangular coordinate description of a vector as a complex number all result from the consideration of applications involving navigation and any other situation in which the physical quantities require a description of both magnitude and direction. For these, the concept of vector is uniquely suited. In order to demostrate the use of these ideas, two sample problems follow:

▶   *1.*   Find the velocity of a boat being rowed straight across a river with a 5 mi/hr current, if the boy in the boat can row at 4 mi/hr in still water.

2. A plane is flying on a course of 130° at a speed of 250 mi/hr. If a wind is blowing from the east with a speed of 50 mi/hr, what is the resulting speed and direction of the plane?

We have extended our earlier concept of trigonometry from ratio to function in two very different ways. One approach required a change in the domain from the set of angle measures to the real numbers. The other maintained the concept of angle. The Commission on Mathematics has indicated very clearly how the transition can be made from angle measures to real numbers by wrapping a line about a unit circle.[5] This is one way in which the circular functions may be introduced. However one decides to proceed, the way in which many diverse mathematical ideas run together should not be minimized. This is one of the great strengths of trigonometry.

Radian Measure

Perhaps emphasizing the nature of the variable x in the equation $y = \sin x$ as discussed previously will help to clarify the concept of radian measure. Somehow the description of angles in radians mystifies the student, despite the apparently simple concept of a radian as the measure of a central angle intercepting an arc equal to the radius (Figure 9.27). If we look at an angle of 180°, we see that we have intercepted a semicircle, or half the circumference: πr. Since the radian measure of any central angle is $\frac{s}{r}$, which is the ratio of its arc length to the length of the radius, we get $\frac{\pi r}{r}$ or

$$180° = \pi \text{ radians}$$

We may also conclude that there are 2π radians in the entire circle. This relationship will enable us to convert from degrees to radians and back again.

Figure 9.27

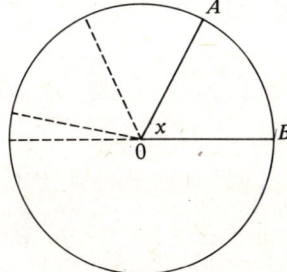

A beginning for the study of the vital ideas underlying the consideration of trigonometric relationships as functions has been presented. The trigonometric formulas, the area formula for a triangle, and the solution of triangles all follow these beginnings. If we keep our beginnings immersed in the physical and build abstractions slowly, even at this level, we offer the majority of our students the greatest opportunity for success. At the same time, a clear picture begins to emerge in the student's mind as to how important and how necessary mathematics is.

Footnotes

1. Eric T. Bell. *Mathematics: Queen and Servant of Science.* New York: McGraw-Hill, 1951, p. 360
2. Morris Kline. *Mathematics and the Physical World.* New York: Thomas Y. Crowell, 1959, pp. 274–315.
3. *Report of the Commission on Mathematics. Program for College Preparatory Mathematics.* New York: College Entrance Examination Board, 1959, p. 28.
4. *Report of the Commission on Mathematics. Appendices.* New York: College Entrance Examination Board, 1959, pp. 186–199.
5. *Report of the Commission on Mathematics. Appendices.* New York: College Entrance Examination Board, 1959, pp. 206–207.

For Investigation and Discussion

1. Describe how you would attempt to help students realize that the slope of the straight line of a linear distance-time graph will provide the speed of an object moving at a constant rate.
2. Develop a similar lesson to help students gain insight into the concept of instantaneous speed. Show how the slope of the tangent to the curve at a point is related to this.
3. Demonstrate how the area under a curve is related to finding rates of change.
4. List the steps you would prescribe to enable students to find out for themselves how they may sum the areas of an infinite number of rectangles and arrive at the area under a curved line.
5. Compare the introductions of the function-concept of trigonometry presented in this chapter, (i.e., through vectors, using oscillating springs). State which you would prefer and explain why.
6. Make a plan for a lesson that will encourage student exploration of periodic functions in addition to that derived from springs.

For Further Reading

Books

Bell, Eric T. *Mathematics: Queen and Servant of Science.* New York: McGraw-Hill, 1951.
Bitter, Francis. *Mathematical Aspects of Physics: An Introduction.* New York: Doubleday, 1963.
Engineering Concepts Curriculum Project, Polytechnic Institute of Brooklyn, *The Man Made World.* New York: McGraw-Hill, 1971.
Owen, George E. *Fundamentals of Scientific Mathematics.* New York: Harper and Row, 1961, pp. 165–270.
Sawyer, W. W. *What is Calculus About?* Vol. 2. New Mathematical Library. New York: Random House, 1961.

Periodicals

Amir-Moez, Ali R. "Teaching Trigonometry Through Vectors," *Mathematics Magazine.* Vol. 32 (September-October 1958), pp. 19–23.
Farrell, Margret. "An Intuitive Leap or an Unscholarly Lapse?" *The Mathematics Teacher.* Vol. 68 (February 1975), pp. 149–152.
Ferguson, W. Eugene. "Calculus in High School," *The Mathematics Teacher.* Vol. 58 (October 1960), pp. 451–453.

Harkin, J.B. "The Limit Concept on the Geoboard," *The Mathematics Teacher.* Vol. 65 (January 1972), pp. 13–17.

Hurley, James F. "An Application of Newton's Law of Cooling," *The Mathematics Teacher.* Vol. 67 (February 1974), pp. 141–142.

Mizrahi, Abe and Michael Sullivan. "Mathematical Models and Applications: Suggestions for the High School Curriculum," *The Mathematics Teacher.* Vol. 66 (May 1973), pp. 394–402.

Rodgers, John J. "Let's Use Trigonometry," *The Mathematics Teacher.* Vol. 68 (February 1975), pp. 157–160.

CHAPTER 10

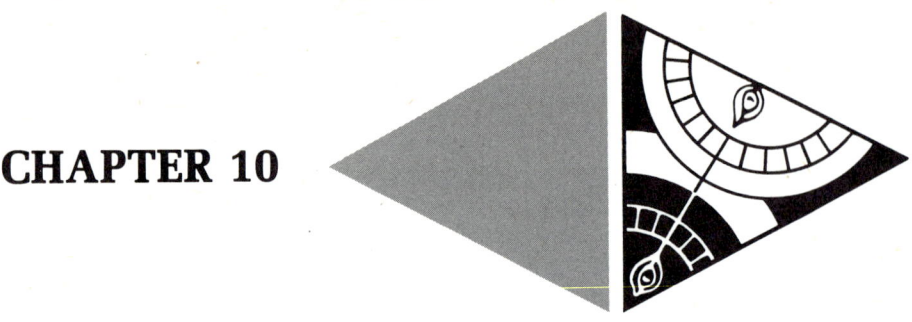

Light, Sound, and Mathematics

Mathematics is an indispensible tool in our quest to understand natural phenomena. It aids our knowledge of events and discloses similarities not readily apparent. Accurate prediction of eclipses, which has had some unexpected consequences, is a good example of this. Today the necessary mathematics is understood by high school students.

In addition, the number of everyday objects around us that make use of the reflection properties of light rays is surprising. What is perhaps more surprising is the fact that sound waves also share the very same properties. Through the use of mathematics, the similarities of such dissimilar phenomenon becomes clear.

10.1 Eclipses

You have probably read many stories about how strange and terrifying the sudden darkening of the sun was, and perhaps still is, to primitive peoples. Many were convinced that the end of the world was surely near! Eclipses are still major events that capture the attention of laymen and scientists all over the world, but the mystery is gone. The mathematics required to compute the time of its appearance as well as its duration and the position on the Earth from which it will become visible is known to high school mathematics students. With this brief introduction, let us consider the question: How is an eclipse caused?

As the planets and their moons travel through the plane of their orbits about the sun, they assume a variety of relative positions. There are times when the Earth is between the sun and the moon. There are also times when the moon passes between the Earth and the sun. These situations bring about eclipses. Figure 10.1 may help to clarify. If we think of the sun and the Earth as circles,

Figure 10.1

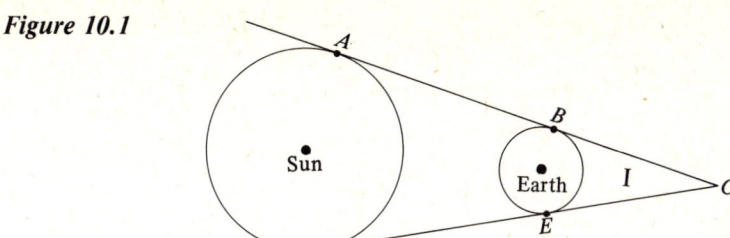

and also assume that each point on the sun is a light source sending out rays in all directions, we may investigate the shadow. The region to the right of the Earth, marked with Roman numeral I, is the region that is in shadow as the Earth blocks the sun's rays. We may think of ray AB emanating from A as the last ray illuminating space behind the Earth. Approaching from the other side, DE may be considered the last ray illuminating space behind the Earth. Both AB and DE are common external tangents. If they are extended beyond the Earth until they intersect, we complete region I, the region in shadow (bounded by these tangents and that portion of the circle, BE, included between them). All the while the moon is in this region, it will be eclipsed. Thus, many relationships can be investigated that will add to our knowledge of the physical phenomenon and of geometry. For example, we may consider the comparative sizes of tangents to a circle from a point outside, as well as the segments of the common external tangents.

The common internal tangents help us to identify other regions of interest (Figure 10.2). Rays coming from part of arc $AFHD$ pass through points such as point X in region III. In fact, as point X moves towards point W in region IV, more rays from the sun can reach it. Thus, point X is partially illuminated. These regions (II and III) of partial illumination are called **penumbra**.

Figure 10.2

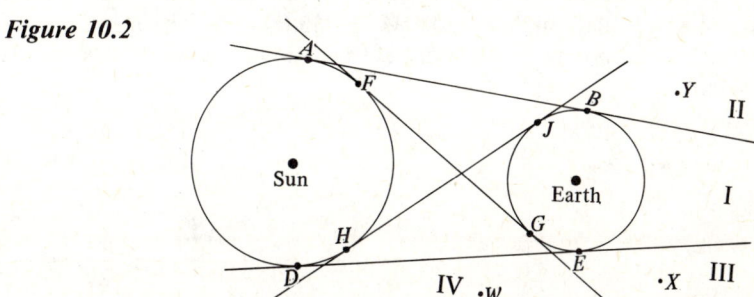

But it is the shadow region that is of greatest interest. Since the moon is in eclipse when it is in this region we may ask whether or not it does indeed pass through the region. It may well be that the moon is so far away from the Earth that when it is to the Earth's right, it is beyond the shadow region. How can we be sure? Here we have an interesting application of our knowledge of plane geometry, including similar triangles. How long is the shadow region? We know that the average distance of the moon from the Earth as it circles around is about 240,000 mi. Is the shadow region less than or greater than this distance? We solve the problem using Figure 10.3 (see page 156), and the following approximations:

BE, radius of Earth: 4000 mi
AS, radius of sun 432,000 mi
SE, average distance of Earth to sun: 93,000,000 mi

Figure 10.3

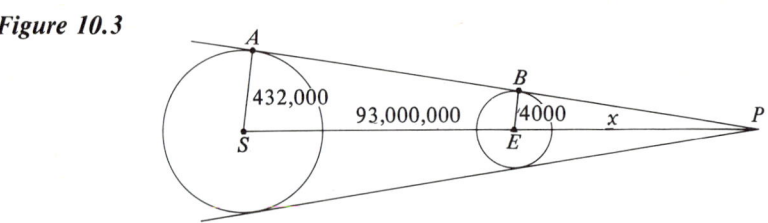

If we think of *PE* as the length of the shadow (less the length of the radius of the earth), it becomes the important distance to determine. We know enough mathematics to determine this length. The theorem about radii drawn to tangents and the similar triangle relationships yield

$$\frac{PE}{PS} = \frac{BE}{AS}$$

If we let $x = PE$,

$$\frac{x}{x + 93,000,000} = \frac{4000}{432,000}$$

Eventually we arrive at $x = 869,000$ (rounded off.) Since the average distance of the moon from the Earth is about 240,000 mi, we find that the moon is, indeed, going to pass through the shadow region; and we expect an eclipse to take place.

A similar investigation may be undertaken to determine the effects of the moon's passing between the Earth and the sun, as shown in Figure 10.4. The moon's shadow, in this instance, is darkening a small portion of the Earth's surface. If we determine the distance (*PM*) of the moon from the Earth, using a moon radius of 1080 mi, we find $PM = 233,000$ mi. The mean distance of the Earth from the moon is 238,857 mi but the distance varies from about 221,000 to 253,000 mi.

Figure 10.4

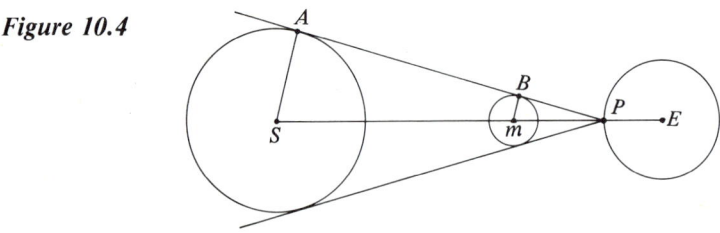

We may now indicate that if an observer on Earth is within the moon's shadow, he will observe things differently from one who is not so located. In the first instance, we have a total eclipse of the sun. In the second, the sun may be viewed in a variety of ways, depending upon position on the Earth's surface. Such a view would range from observation of an annular eclipse (i.e., a bright ring around the concealed central portion of the sun [Figure 10.5]) to a partial eclipse, in which a segment of the sun is covered (Figure 10.6). Of course, where it is night, there will be no visible sun at all.

Figure 10.5 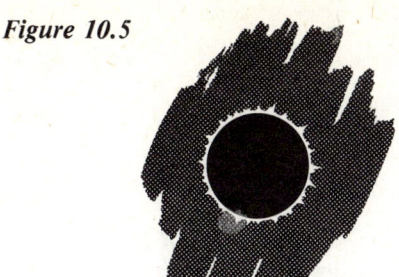 *Figure 10.6*

In this way, we can calculate when and where an eclipse will occur and how long it might last. This natural occurence of common internal and external tangents leads us to explore several important theorems about circles.

Circle Relationships 10.2

Before leaving tangency, we may explore tangent circles and extend this investigation to a purely mathematical consideration that asks: What are the possible relationships between two circles? If the circles are drawn on plastic sheets, they can actually be manuvered into a variety of positions and observations can be made (Figure 10.7). This is an excellent place to encourage student exploration of relationships and the generation of their own propositions which may or may not become theorems. The guiding force shall be the question: Can you find any relationships at all? The freedom to add lines should be made clear to the students so that, for example, they might explore lines connecting the centers and common chords. Often, the students' observations are too carefully directed. Here is an opportunity for nondirected explorations.

Figure 10.7

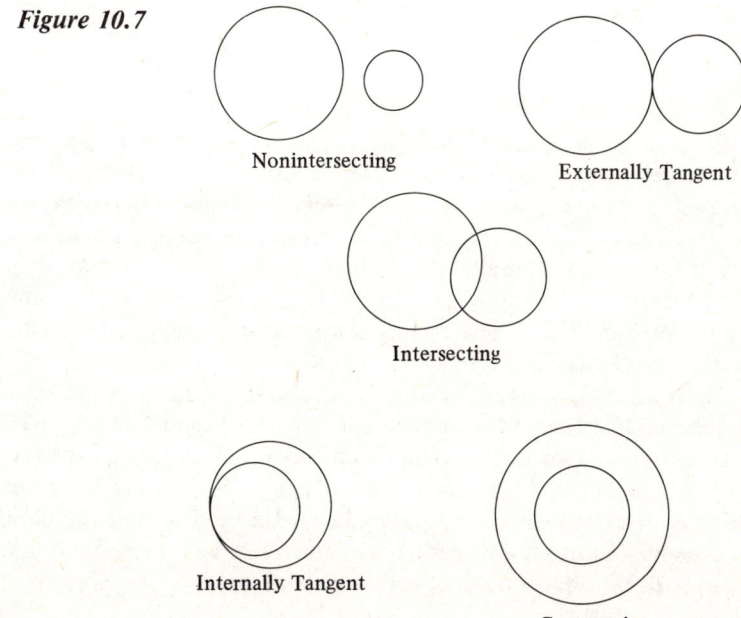

10.3 Reflections and Conic Sections

The Parabola

The headlight of a car and the major lens of a giant telescope share the same shape. What is this shape and why are these dissimilar objects using it?

To understand clearly what is going on, we will revisit the realm of light rays explored several times before. When an object is far away, its light rays reaching a small area of the Earth are practically parallel. If all these rays could be reflected by a mirror so that the reflected rays would go through a single point, there would be a strong image of the star at that point. This is exactly what happens when the shape of the mirror is parabolic. All the rays are focused upon a single point; therefore, we call that point the **focus** (Figure 10.8). In Latin, *focus* means hearth or burning place. It is no mere coincidence that a piece of paper placed at the focus of a parabolic mirror reflecting the sun's rays, will be set on fire. This focusing of light rays enables us to see images of objects far off in space; that is why the lens of a telescope is made in this parabolic shape. The shape enables us to concentrate the reflections of the entering light rays.

Figure 10.8

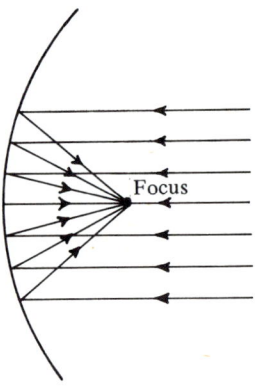

But what of an automobile headlight? Why is it made in the same shape? It does not receive light rays—rather, it sends them out. The reflecting property of a parabolic mirror can also be used in reverse. If we were to locate a light source at the focus (a light bulb), all its rays would be reflected by the parabolic mirror so as to travel out parallel to what we call the axis of the parabola shown in Figure 10.9. In this way all the reflected rays form a powerful beam of light traveling in one direction. These beams can be seem coming from flashlights as well as auto headlights.

The reflecting properties of the parabolic mirror are properties of a three-dimensional surface, while a parabola is a plane figure. Have we made use of the wrong figure? Not really. What we have done is to make use of a surface formed by rotating a parabola about its axis (Figure 10.10). Such a surface is called a **paraboloid**. The focus of the parabola is also the focus of the paraboloid. Since radio waves and sound waves behave much like light rays, we find this surface is also used in radar antennas and loudspeakers.

Figure 10.9

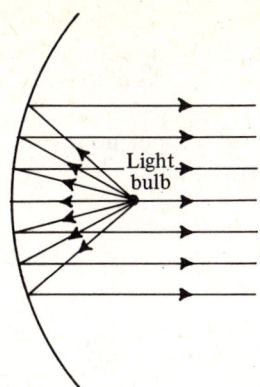

Figure 10.10

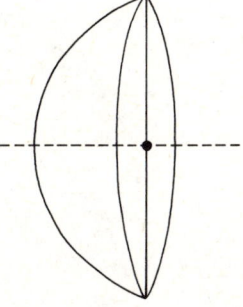

How shall we provide a careful description of the parabola? The concept of locus offers us the opportunity to describe a parabola as a set of points and also enables us to construct parabolas. We describe the circle as the set of points that are a given distance from a fixed point. The parabola has an analagous definition: It is the set of points equally distant from a fixed point and a fixed line. For example, if we are given line d and point F (Figure 10.11), each point of

Figure 10.11

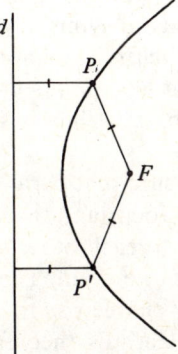

the parabola will be just as far from point F as it is from line d. The use of lined paper makes the construction of a parabola a simple task:

>Place point F and line d in any position as long as d is parallel to the lines of the paper. Draw the perpendicular AB to line d through point F as

shown in Figure 10.12. Using a compass, measure the distance along AB from d to any of the parallel lines on the paper, say line m. Mark off this same measure from F on line m, obtaining points X and Y. These are two points of the parabola. Repeating this process with other parallel lines will provide additional points on the parabola. The set of such points forms the parabola.

Figure 10.12

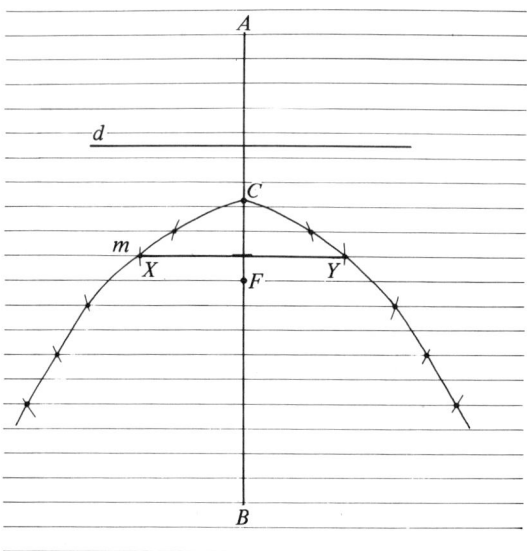

How does this process yield the parabola? How do we know where to locate point C, the turning point of the parabola? These are questions that may be discussed with students to help them see how the construction is built upon the locus definition.[1] After several parabolas are constructed placing F and d in a variety of positions, we can indicate that line d is called the directrix, F is the focus, and the axis of the parabola is the perpendicular to d through F. This is the line that we called the axis of symmetry in our study of algebra. Construction of the parabola not only helps to demonstrate the meaning of the locus which defines the parabola, but also points up the symmetry of the parabola about its axis. Each time a new parallel line is selected, two points are located—one on each side of the axis.

How can we be sure that parallel light rays entering the parabola will all be reflected through the focus and that light rays emanating from the focus will be reflected out parallel to each other and the axis of the parabola? Our knowledge of geometry comes to our aid. The complete proof is lengthy, but a brief indication of the plan may enable you to attempt to work it out for yourself. Once again we make use of Heron's theorem; this time we are concerned with the converse.

Look at Figure 10.13. If we can show that the distance from the focus (F) to a point on the parabola (P) to the fixed point V on a parallel to the axis from P is the shortest distance from F to the parabola to V, then we will have established that ∡1 = ∡2, the angles of incidence and reflection. Then according to Heron, we can conclude that PV must be the reflection of FP. The approach to a proof consists of selecting any other point on the tangent line Q and demonstrating that

$FP + PV < FQ + QV$. This is a challenging proof. You might like to refer back to the earlier work with Heron's theorems.

Figure 10.13

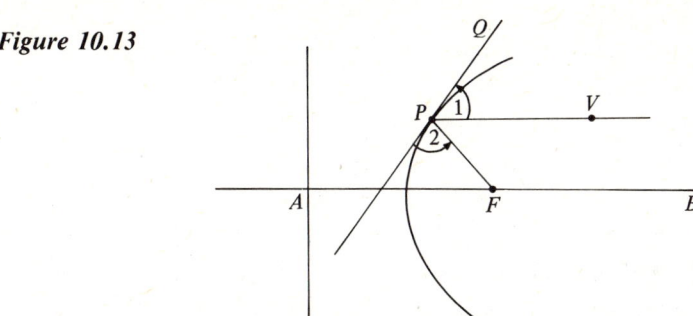

This unique property of the parabola helps us to understand how astronomers can manage to see the light reflected from stars so many light-years away. If the rays are feeble but are all concentrated at a single point, they become relatively brighter. The same is true of radio signals that may be faint when received but are comparatively strong at the focus of a paraboloid antenna. Finally, if you have ever wondered how a small light bulb in a flashlight could cast such a strong beam, you now have some insight into what is happening. It would seem that mathematics has again helped to explain what is going on about us. The ellipse has similar reflective properties.

The Ellipse

The paths of satellites moving around the Earth, of the planets of our solar system as they orbit the sun, and of comets are all described by the ellipse. The ellipse is a figure that has some surprising reflection properties. If you have ever made a tour of the Capitol in Washington, D.C., you may have been amazed by a simple demonstration carried out by the guide. After placing the tour group at a brass plate in the floor of the old House of Representatives, the guide walks some 100 ft away and whispers. Lo and behold, each syllable reaches you as clearly as if a microphone had been used. The same would be true of words spoken by the group to the guide. What makes the human voice travel so that whispers can be heard quite a distance away? As you might suspect by now, the ceiling of the room is elliptical and the sound waves are reflected so that they focus upon a single point. This phenomenon takes place in two directions because there are actually two foci present. But let us take a closer look at the ellipse.

Like the parabola, the ellipse may be defined as a set of points that satisfy a given condition. In this instance, the ellipse is the set of points whose combined distances from each of two fixed points is constant. For example:

> The fixed points are F and F' and we arbitrarily set the constant distance at 2 in. Then point A is a member of the set of points in question since it is ½ in. from F and 1½ in. from F' (Figure 10.14, see page 162). The same is true of B and any other point, the sum of whose distances from F and F' will be 2 in.

Figure 10.14

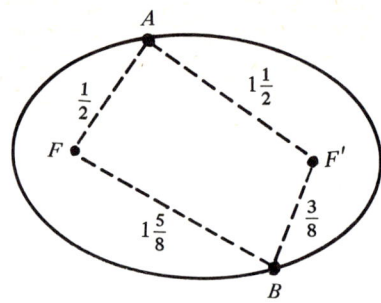

The ellipse may also be constructed using a compass and straightedge. Select any two points as the foci F and F' and choose any distance AB for the constant sum of the distances from the foci. Be sure that $AB > FF'$ or there will be no ellipse (Figure 10.15). Since $AB = PF + PF'$, use the compass to divide AB into two lengths of any size. This gives point C. Thus, $AC = PF$ and $CB = PF'$. Place the compass point at F and with opening AC draw an arc. Place the compass point at F' and draw a second arc intersecting the first with opening CB. You will have located two points of the ellipse P and Q. To find additional points, divide AB into two different lengths and repeat the procedures just described.

Figure 10.15

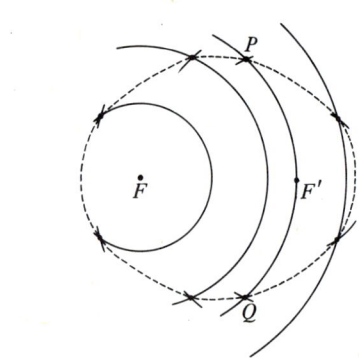

The magnification of the whispers on the Capitol tour was due to the remarkable reflection properties of the ellipse. All sound waves (or light waves) emanating from one focus reflect off the surface of the ellipse through the other focus. The very weak sound waves of the guide's voice, going out in all directions, were reflected through the other focus (both marked by brass plates) so that the tour group heard very clearly (Figure 10.16).

Figure 10.16

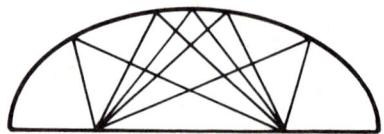

This unusual reflection property was also responsible for a remarkable demonstration of skill by a student. An elliptically shaped board had a 1-in. fence built around its edge. In one part of the board, there was a hole slightly larger than a nickel, a five-cent piece. On the other side of the board was a mark. The student would place a nickel on the mark and shoot it off the fence in a variety of directions, and every time it would bounce off the fence and into the hole! (See Figure 10.17). Amazing—but not really, because when I tried it, I too made the coin land in the hole. The mark and the hole were at the foci of the ellipse. The reflection property of the ellipse did the rest. This is an interesting project for a student to attempt because it provides a dramatic example of the reflection property. Let us explore the hyperbola to complete the study of the reflection properties of conic sections.

Figure 10.17

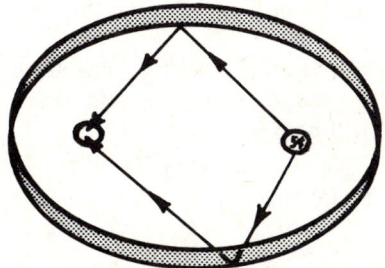

The Hyperbola and Sound Waves

A pilot in an airliner listens in on two radio stations and notes the difference in time between the two low frequency signals from these stations. He repeats this process with two other stations and is able to fix his location.

A hunter loses his way in the forest and fires his rifle to attract attention. Two forest rangers, a fixed distance apart, record the time they hear the shot and compare this with the time recorded at a third location. They now have a good approximation of the position of the lost hunter.

What do these two situations have to do with a hyperbola? In each case we were dealing with the distances from a given point to each of two other points—represented by the time of the two radio signals from two stations and the time the shot is heard at two different points. Thus far we seem to be in a situation calling for the ellipse locus. In this instance, however, we are working with the differences between the two distances rather than the sum. Whereas the ellipse was defined in terms of the sum of the distances from two fixed points, the hyperbola is concerned with the differences.

If we return to the second situation and look at it more carefully, we see that if the two rangers hear the shot 5 sec apart, since sound travels at the rate of about 1100 ft/sec, the rifle must be 5500 ft farther from one ranger than it is from the other. This is the difference between the distances from each ranger to the gun (Figure 10.18, see page 164). If we try to locate the hunter and ask where are all points whose distances differ by 5500 ft from the two rangers, we find the answer to be the hyperbola. For example, one such point might be 6000 ft from the first ranger and 500 ft from the second. The hunter's position is somewhere on the

Figure 10.18

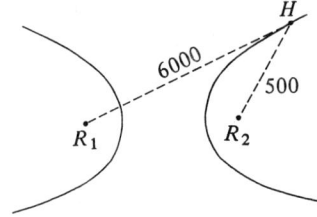

hyperbola. The time reading at the third location enables us to locate another hyperbola whose intersections with the first one provide possible locations for the missing hunter. The implications for the pilot of the first problem will be discussed later.

▶ How can we construct a hyperbola with a compass and straightedge as we did the other conic sections?

Choose two fixed points, F and F', that are 8 units apart as shown in Figure 10.19. Let us also assume that the constant difference between distances of points from F and F' will be 6 units.

Figure 10.19

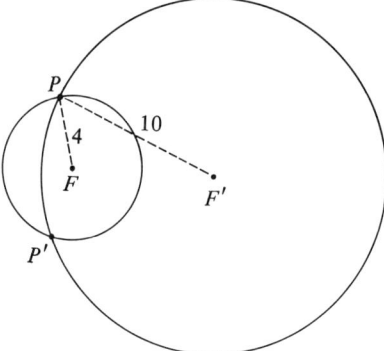

We begin by taking any length, for example, 10. If we describe a circular arc about F' with a radius of 10 units, we shall have points whose distance from F' is 10 units. We would like to have points whose distance from F' minus their distance from F is 6 units. So, let us take the difference $10 - 6$, or 4, and describe an arc with a radius of 4 units and F as the center. Suppose this arc cuts the former arc at P and P'. Now P is 10 units from F' and 4 units from F. Hence,

$$PF' - PF = 6$$

Then P must be a point on the hyperbola. For the same reason, so is P'. We note that for each point of intersection of the two arcs that lies above the line $F'F$ there will be a point below and these two points are symmetric with respect to FF'. Or we could say one point is the mirror image of the other in the "mirror" $F'F$.

If, instead of length 10, we had taken length 11 and then constructed circular arcs with radii 11 and $11 - 5$ or 6, about F' and F respectively, we would have gotten two more points which lie on the hyperbola. In fact, if we start with any given length greater than 6 and repeat the construction, we can get points on the hyperbola.

Let us reconsider the length 10 and this time describe an arc about F as center with radius 10 and another arc about F' as center with radius 4. Where these two arcs intersect at R and R', we have points such that

$RF - RF' = 6$ and $R'F - R'F' = 6$

Hence, R and R' also lie on the hyperbola as shown in Figure 10.20.

Figure 10.20

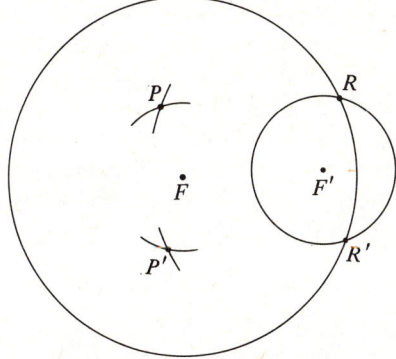

By constructing a number of points that meet the definition of the hyperbola, we find the curve shown in Figure 10.21. This curve is peculiar since it consists of two distinct parts or branches, which constitute a single hyperbola.

Figure 10.21

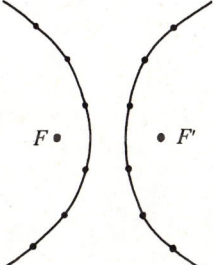

Of course, the numbers 8 and 6 used in the preceding discussion are just special cases. We can start with two points F and F', called **foci**, which are a fixed distance apart, $2c$. Choose a fixed quantity which we can denote by $2a$; and define a hyperbola generally as the set of all points whose distances from F and F' differ by the numerical value $2a$. ($|PF' - PF| = 2a$.)

We note that the quantity $2a$ must be less than $2c$ because the difference between any two sides of a triangle must be less than the third side (Figure 10.22.)

Figure 10.22

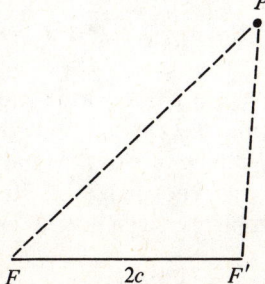

Other applications of the hyperbola using the same principle as locating a gun shot occur in navigation by ships and airplanes. An example of this is the pilot who listened in on two radio stations at F and F' and noted the time difference between two low frequency signals from these stations. Radio waves travel at the speed of light and this speed is known. Therefore, the difference in time multiplied by the speed of light is the difference in the distances between the airplane and the two stations. Hence, the pilot knows he is on a definite hyperbola (Figure 10.23). By listening in on signals from two other fixed stations, G and G', and again noting the difference in the time at which he receives these signals, the pilot determines another hyperbola on which he must be located. He must then be on the intersection (or intersections) of the two hyperbolas. If there is more than one intersection, he can generally tell from a knowledge of his approximate location which is the relevant one for him.

Figure 10.23

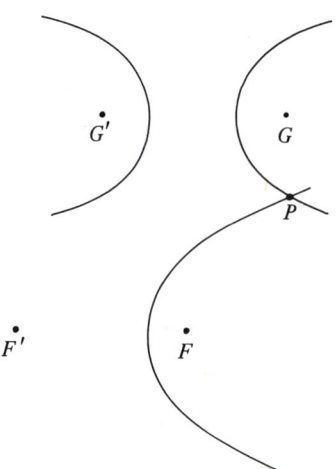

Since radio waves travel at such a high speed, the time difference must be measured accurately and this can be done with electronic equipment. The system known as Loran is useful within distances from the sending stations of about 1000 mi because the assumption is made that radio waves travel in straight lines or practically so; but this is not true over great distances. In practice, the pilot carries charts with all the possible hyperbolas mapped out. Then, by knowing the time differences, he can turn directly to his charts and determine the possible location immediately.

10.4 Mathematics and Science—In Conclusion

An attempt has been made to provide a wide selection of scientific applications of mathematics in this chapter. By carrying out the work here, students will solve real problems and will become aware of the vital contribution mathematics makes to the advancement of our knowledge. At the same time, mathematics also generates interesting problems, which will carry the state of mathematical development forward.

We have stressed two main roles for mathematics. It is the language of science, without which a scientist could not communicate his findings. Even more importantly, through mathematics the scientist can gain new insights and new understandings of the various phenomena under investigation. This symbiotic relationship of mathematics and science as well as the interrelation of the various branches of mathematics, adds to the growth of both disciplines.

By calling mathematics into play to resolve scientific problems, we can help make our subject matter come alive in the secondary school class.

Footnote

1. Ethel Saupe. "Simple Paper Models for the Conic Sections," *The Mathematics Teacher*. Vol. 48 (January 1955), pp. 42-44.

For Investigation and Discussion

1. Outline the steps you would develop to aid student discovery of the relationships inherent to two circles as they assume different positions in relation to each other, i.e., intersecting, tangent, concentric, etc.
2. Describe how the use of tangents to circles enables us to gain information resulting in the prediction of eclipses.
3. Heron's name has been used several times. Investigate the life of this man focusing on his contributions to mathematics.
4. Plan a lesson around a demonstration of the reflecting properties of a paraboloid using a flash light. Light the bulb without the reflector and then do the same with the reflector. Observe the light provided.
5. Briefly outline three lessons to help students to construct a parabola, an ellipse, and a hyperbola. Use any methods you prefer.
6. Select one article from the following list of periodicals. Read and discuss it in relation to the objective of student realization of the importance of mathematics, and its significance to continued progress in science.

For Further Reading

Books

Ahrendt, Myrl H. *The Mathematics of Space Exploration*. New York: Holt, Rinehart and Winston, 1965.

Greitzer, Samuel L. "Computing a Lunar Eclipse: An Exercise in Classical Mathematics," *Enrichment Mathematics for High School*, 28th Yearbook. Reston, Va.: National Council of Teachers of Mathematics, 1963, pp. 265-273.

Schiffer, Max M. *Applied Mathematics in the High School, Studies in Mathematics,* Vol. X. School Mathematics Study Group, Stanford University, Ca., 1963.

Periodicals

Byrne, Sister Maurice Marie, O.S.U. "A Geometric Approach to the Conic Sections," *The Mathematics Teacher*. Vol. 67 (April 1966), pp. 348-350.

Coxford, Arthur. "Classroom Inquiry into the Conic Sections," *The Mathematics Teacher*. Vol. 60 (April 1967), pp. 316-322.

Kline, Morris, "Geometry," *Scientific American*. Vol. 211 (Sepetember 1964), pp. 60-69.

Rose, Kenneth. "New Conic Graph Paper," *The Mathematics Teacher*. Vol. 67 (November 1974), pp. 604-606.

Sconyers, James M. "The Limits of Parabolas," *The Mathematics Teacher*. Vol. 67 (November 1974), pp. 652-653.

Von Baravalle, Hermann. "Conic Sections in Relation to Physics and Astronomy," *The Mathematics Teacher*. Vol. 63 (February 1970), pp. 101-109.

SECTION III

Mathematics and Society

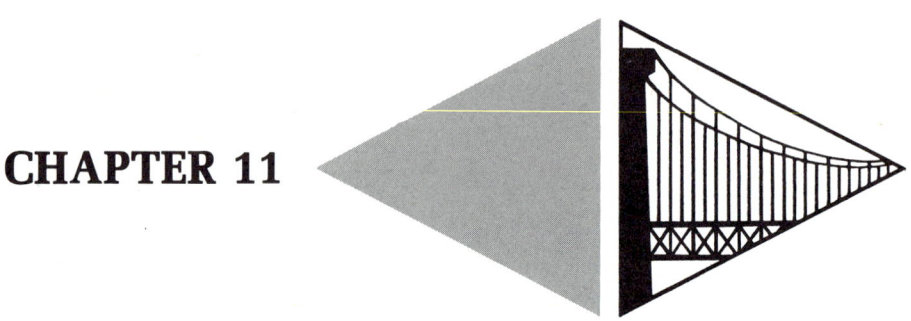

CHAPTER 11

Mathematics as a Model of Reality

We have seen how mathematics might be taught emphasizing the interaction between mathematics and science, and how mathematics helps us to learn more about our environment. We know that teaching mathematics without significant attachment to science, our lives, or society can leave students with a distorted view of mathematics. One of the chief criticisms often heard from youngsters is the lack of connection between mathematics and real life. In this section, we will attempt to exploit relationships between mathematics and society to enable students to comprehend the worth and the necessity for a highly developed mathematical system.

Carroll Newsom has written about this problem at length in several articles. He has expressed genuine concern not just for the student of mathematics but for the continued energetic existence of mathematics itself and its vital role in the life of our society. He sees the image of the mathematician deteriorating in American society. Speaking of John Von Neumann, Newsom remarks how Von Neumann,

> . . . could not separate mathematics from life; he saw mathematics wherever he looked. His feel for nature inspired him to be a better mathematician and his mathematics inspired him to better understand nature.[1]

Newsom then goes on to compare this attitude with current recipients of the Ph. D. in mathematics who,

> . . . look at their subject as merely a formal discipline without any relevance to nature; moreover, in general they possess no feel for mathematics as part of our culture or as a factor in the development of our culture.[2]

Newsom feels that the state of mathematics is in decline because of this attitude and is concerned that future demand for mathematicians will be accordingly depressed.

His concerns are shared by Robert E. Gaskell, Chairman of the Committee on Corporate Members of the Mathematical Association of America. In examination of the reasons for a sudden and sharp decline in the hiring of mathematicians, Gaskell and his committee sought out heads of government and industrial mathematics groups. The results of this study are rather surprising and frightening. It seems that most industrial mathematics is being done by engineering and physics graduates, "because of the weakness of mathematical education in America."[3] The general problem appears to be (in simple terms) that mathematicians are not trained as problem solvers. While they understand a good deal of mathematics, there seems to be relatively little that they can do with mathematics in order to formulate and solve problems outside of mathematics.

It appears that the approach being suggested in this text is more of a necessity than was at first believed. Not only is it vital for the mathematical well-being of the student who does not plan a career in mathematics or science, but it is also crucial for those who do. As a matter of fact, it seems that the survival of the prominent role that mathematics has played in the on-going development of our society is also endangered. Therefore, it is critical that all students of mathematics, particularly those planning careers in mathematics and science, study the subject in such a way as to enable them to understand and appreciate the relationships between mathematics, science, nature, and culture. In the words of A. B. Wilcox,

> If we lose contact with the essential ferment which is going on out there, then the world may simply walk away, not only from us but from mathematics.[4]

With the need for relevence clearly before us, let us approach the development of such experiences with our students.

Crossing Bridges and Mathematics 11.1

Here are three seemingly unrelated problems. Some may be familiar.

1. In the eighteenth century the city of Konigsberg in Germany had seven bridges that crossed the Pregel River. (Figure 11.1). Since the people of

Figure 11.1

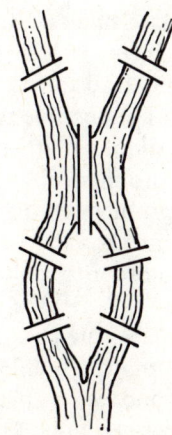

this area liked to take walks, they would try to see if they could walk so as to cross each bridge only once. They could start from any point in the city and end at any point. How could it be done?

2. A favorite puzzle of youngsters is to try to draw this figure without lifting the pencil or crossing over any line already drawn (Figure 11.2). How could this be done?

Figure 11.2

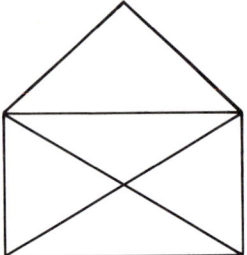

3. A town police precinct would like to figure out how to patrol all of its streets so that each block is covered in a minimum amount of time (Figure 11.3). More than one way to do it is important since it is not a good idea to be able to find the pattern the police cars are using in their patrols. How could they do it?[5]

Figure 11.3
The precinct is at point A (starting point).

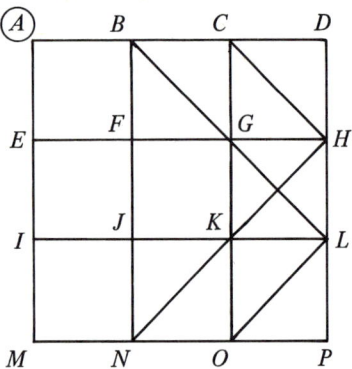

While these appear to be unrelated problems, from a mathematical point of view they are closely related. Ask students to attempt a solution.

The seven bridges problem is not as easy as it looks. Trial and error is an excellent starting point but may lead to frustration in this case. Leonhard Euler showed that there was no solution possible to this problem by changing it into an interesting and surprisingly simple mathematical network.[6] Figure 11.4 is a mathematical model for the problem of the bridges, which includes all of the necessary conditions of the problem in a stripped down, simple mathematical form. Present the model to students and ask if it enables them to find a solution.

Euler reasoned that in order to make a closed path either each vertex has an even number of lines joining it or there are exactly two vertices with an odd number of lines. In the latter case, the path must start at one of the odd number vertices and end at the other. An even number of lines is necessary in order to arrive at a vertex and then have another path upon which to leave (except for starting and end points). Once Euler had made the model and completed the analysis, the problem was virtually resolved. This is no small tribute to the power of mathematical models of reality.

Figure 11.4

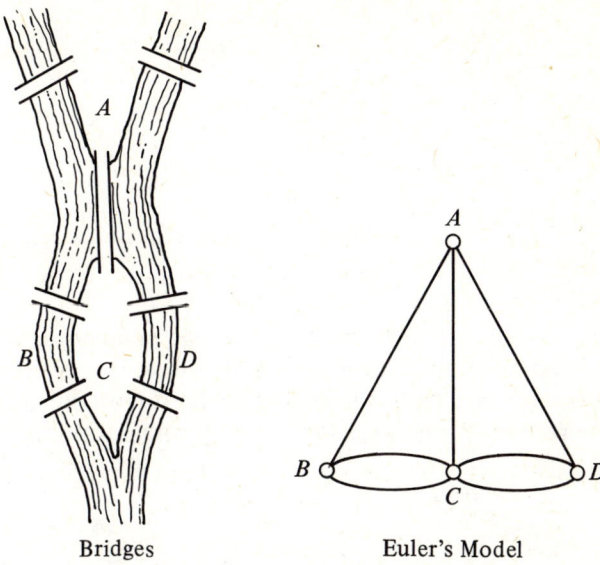

Bridges   Euler's Model

From Figure 11.4, you can see that the vertices have the following numbers of lines:

A: 3 lines   *B:* 3 lines   *C:* 5 lines   *D:* 3 lines

Since each vertex is odd, it is not possible to begin at one point and walk over each bridge once in a closed path. Hence the people of Konigsberg will never be able to achieve their goal. Euler's ingenious model makes the resolution of the problem obvious.

Through the construction of a mathematical model of a physical situation, students can begin to realize the power of mathematics in our society. We used geometry as the stuff from which the model came and reasoned through to a conclusion. In other cases, we may use other branches of mathematics.

This illustration shows how a mathematician becomes interested in some problem of his society and, as a consequence, develops the mathematics to deal with it. When the problem is resolved, the mathematician will often continue a purely mathematical investigation that goes beyond the needs of the original problem. Although this new mathematics may have no relationship at all to the physical world, it often becomes the basis for the future resolution of unforeseen problems. Euler's solution of the Konigsberg bridges puzzle is one of the building blocks of the study of topology.

What does the "bridges" problem have to do with the familiar puzzle shown in Figure 11.5 (see page 172)? Ask the students if they can make a connection.

This figure is thought of as a network like the one made by Euler. Does the application of Euler's reasoning help to work to a solution? Let us see. The vertices have the following numbers of lines:

A: 2 lines   *B:* 4   *C:* 3
D: 3   *E:* 4   *F:* 4

Figure 11.5

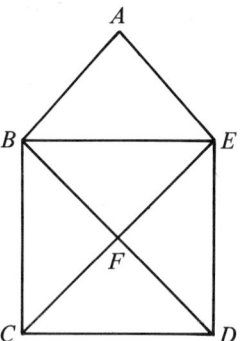

There are two vertices with odd numbers of lines. Each of the other vertices has an even number of lines. If we use the reasoning of Euler, it would seem that the closed path is indeed possible. It must either start at *C* and end at *D*, or the reverse. Figure 11.6 shows two possible ways to draw the path.

Figure 11.6

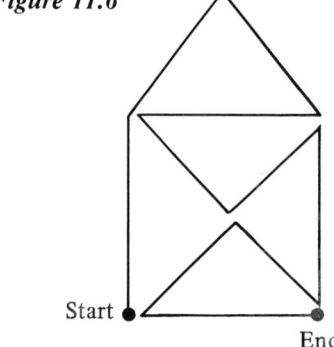 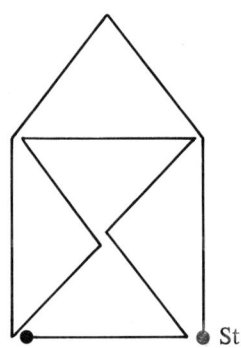

So we see that a common puzzle lends itself to a simple analysis through the use of mathematics. We do not know how the path shall be traced, but we have enough information to decide whether or not the closed path is possible. We can also decide where it shall begin and end. But Euler's work has implications beyond the puzzle. His work helps us resolve problems that he himself could not envision in the eighteenth century.

This brings us to the third problem involving the patrol route of a police car. In light of the discussion of the first two problems, we ask our students to try to resolve the network (problem 3 on page 170), beginning by listing vertices and their lines, or edges:

A:	2	B:	4	C:	4	D:	2
E:	3	F:	4	G:	6	H:	5
I:	3	J:	4	K:	6	L:	5
M:	2	N:	4	O:	4	P:	2

Ferreting out those vertices with odd numbers of edges gives:

E: 3   H: 5   I: 3   L: 5

We therefore know that a closed path starting from and ending up back at the station at *A* is impossible because of the odd numbered vertices. In order to find the desired minimum route, we must add edges to change these vertices into even numbered ones. This means that certain streets will have to be traversed more than once, but, nevertheless, the path will be minimum, which is what we are after. Which edges shall be added? How many? Since it is vertices *E, H, I, L* we are concerned about, we may add two lines changing all 4 vertices into even numbered vertices. Add *EI* and *HL* (Figure 11.7). We know that we can travel the desired path, retracing our steps in the two instances, *EI* and *HL*, and start and end at the police station at *A*. Finding the actual route, and indeed routes, that may be used for patrolling is left to the reader.

Figure 11.7

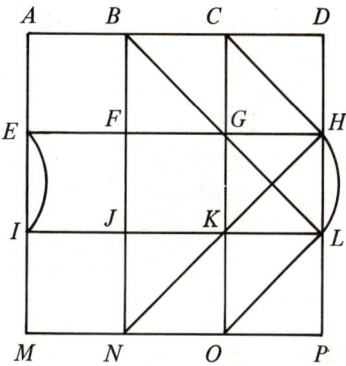

We began with a problem growing out of a supposed stroll of the people of Konigsberg. Thinking about the problem Euler constructed a model called a network. We then found that his description of the problem was applicable to many other situations since each involved the study of networks. Euler, in effect, provided us with an algorithm for solving problems, no less effective than any of the more familiar algorithms of multiplication or division. We also used this algorithm to determine the routes of patrol cars. As a result, from solving an immediately present problem, Euler provided the means for solving a host of problems totally unimaginable for him. We must somehow help our students begin to comprehend this interaction.

Of course it is possible to move in many directions at this point. If the students are interested, further study of networks would certainly be appropriate. Capitalizing on the interest value of the familiar puzzle, the work may be extended to include many other such puzzles and eventually into a more formal study of graph theory and topology.[7] More advanced work could lead into the study of matrices as well.[8] Still another possibility is to continue to work with models of physical situations. For our purposes, this seems to be most appropriate, and more about this will appear shortly.

Euclid and the "Real World" 11.2

An examination of the role played by Euclid in the development of mathematics during the "golden age" of the Greeks, 600–300 B.C., is pertinent here. To gain a sense of the impact these developments had upon society and mathematics, we examine the creation of the non-Euclidean geometries.

It must be remembered that Euclid's Elements were thought to be a description of the space in which we lived. His geometry was not seen as a mathematical system, or as a "model" of reality, but instead was considered the only true description of our world. Attempts to establish the fifth postulate as a theorem resulted in the startling notion that changing this postulate leads to other geometries. A change in the very basic conception of mathematics and of the world in which we live was a necessary consequence.

This was the beginning of an understanding of mathematics as the study of all structures that contained specified properties. In the society, a revised way of looking at reality was in order. For example, look at the Playfair derivative of Euclid's fifth postulate,

> Through a point, P, not on line m there is one and only one line that can be drawn through P parallel to m.

Examination of Figure 11.8 leaves one with the intuitive feeling that there can be no other possibility. How can there be more than one such line? Where would it be drawn? And if we assume that there are no such lines, how could there be any real life counterpart?

Figure 11.8

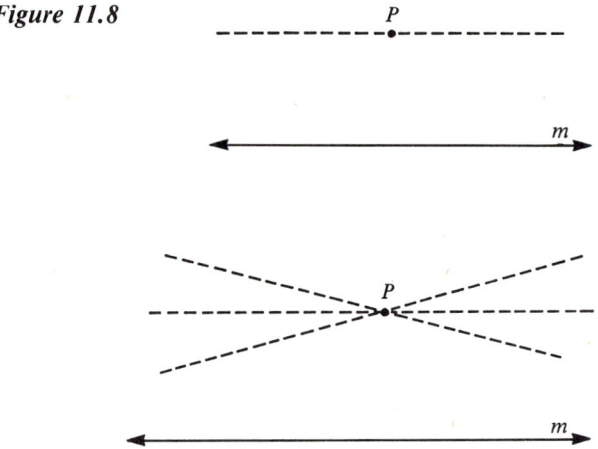

Clearly these alternatives geometries to Euclid's geometry do not reflect any part of reality. But as is often the case, our "common sense" only serves to reenforce our prejudices. We must fight off the intuitive urge if we are to progress. Indeed there are excellent illustrations to support the notions of more than one parallel, and no parallels (Figure 11.9).

A brief comparison of some properties of these geometries of different surfaces is listed in Table 11.1.[9]

Table 11.1 A Comparison of Different Geometries.

Geometry	Parallels	Sum of Angles of Triangle	Model
Euclidean (Euclid)	1	180°	Plane
Hyperbolic (Bolyai, Lobachevsky)	∞	Less than 180°	Pseudosphere
Elliptical (Reimann)	0	More than 180°	Sphere

To answer the question, "Which geometry is a true description of the space in which we live?" is to be both right and wrong no matter how you respond. Qualification is definitely in order.

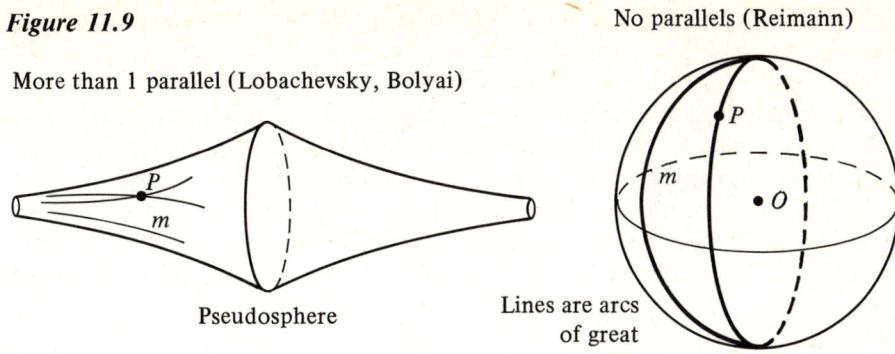

Figure 11.9

If we exclude the macrocosm of the universe and the microcosm of the insides of atoms, perhaps the Euclidean model is best since it is the simplest. If we consider the massive distances of outer space, then we find that the Reimannian model is perhaps best suited. Such was the case as Einstein developed his theory of relativity and found Euclidean geometry was simply not a good enough fit.

Thus the introduction of these other geometries had, and is having a profound effect upon how we conceive of the world in which we live as well as how we conceive of mathematics.

A similar situation evolved from the way in which the astronomers developed their model of our universe. As we move from the geocentric theory of Ptolemy, the earth at the center of the universe with the sun and the planets rotating about it, to the heliocentric theory of Copernicus with the sun at the center, we encounter two philosophically important different systems. The acceptance of the latter with its implications for the concept of man's role in the universe, was not an idea to go down easily. Man had to be the center of the universe for he was the reason that God created the Sun and the planets. As Kline so aptly states it,

> It made man appear to be one of a possible host of wanderers on many planets which, in turn, were drifting through a cold sky. It was unlikely therefore, that he was born to live gloriously and to attain paradise upon his death, or that he was the object of God's ministrations. The sacrifice of Christ for insignificant man appeared pointless. The sky as the seat of God, the destination of the saints and of a Deity ascended from the Earth, and the paradise to which good people could aspire, was shattered by the passage of a speeding Earth. In short, the undermining of the Ptolemaic order of the universe removed cornerstones of the Christian edifice and threatened to topple the whole structure.[10]

While the work of Copernicus was the opening wedge, a great deal of additional development was still to be done. The basic theory and resulting model of a planetary system with the Earth at the center was not to be denied.

Kepler's Laws of Motion 11.3

Early in the seventeenth century Johann Kepler, a German astronomer, working with the multitude of observations recorded by the Danish astronomer Tycho Brahe, developed three basic laws regarding the motion of the planets. The first of these laws stated that the path of each planet is an ellipse with the sun at one of the foci. The second law provides an estimate of the speed and distance of planets.

Kepler stated that in equal time periods, the planet sweeps out equal areas with the sun. For example, if it takes the planet an equal amount of time to move from *A* to *B* as it does to move from *C* to *D*, then area *ASB* is equal to area *DSC* (Figure 11.10). The derivation of this law was astounding since it was not easily inferred from observations. Finally, for his third law of motion, Kepler stated that the square of the time it takes a planet to complete an orbit is proportional to the cube of the major axis of the orbit. If the Earth's time to

Figure 11.10

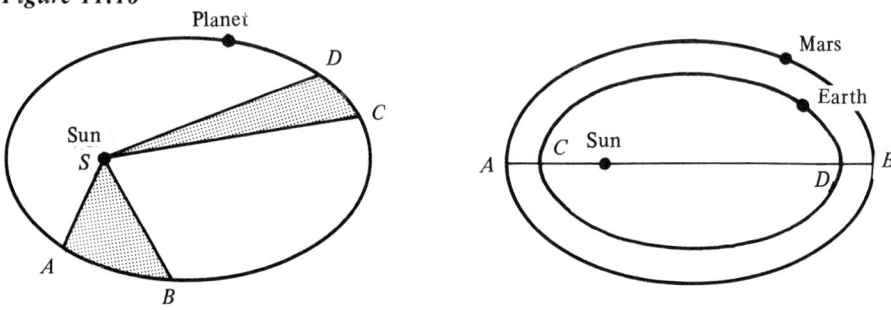

complete one orbit is T_1 and if the time for Mars is T_2 (see Figure 11.10), then the third law states that

$$\frac{T_1^2}{(CD)^3} = \frac{T_2^2}{(AB)^3}$$

Thus, Kepler formulated three laws that presented new insights into the motion of the planets, and he used mathematics to shed light upon the world in which we live.

There are many problems that can be studied here. The following are typical examples:

▶ *1.* Let $2a$ be the sum of the distances of any point on an ellipse to the foci. Show that the length of the major axis is $2a$. Let $2a$ be the length of the major axis of an ellipse. Show that the distance from one end of the minor axis *B* to either focus is a (Figure 11.11).

Figure 11.11 (a) *Given $FP + PF' = 2a$, prove $AA' = 2a$.*
(b) *Given $AA' = 2a$, prove $FB = F'B = a$.*

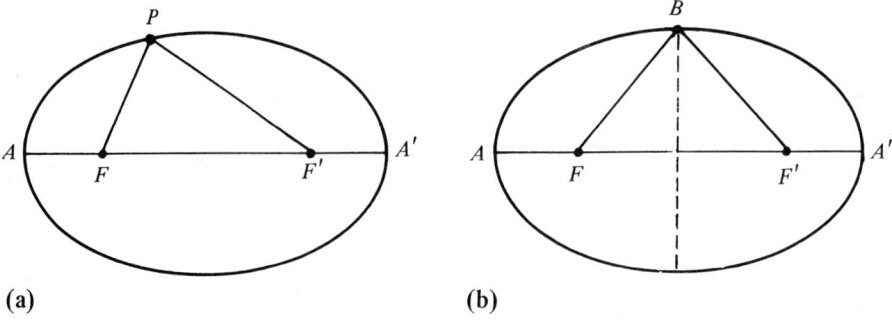

(a)   (b)

2. Let Q be any point outside of an ellipse. Prove that $QF' + QF$ is greater than a where a is the sum of the distances of any point P on the ellipse from the foci (Figure 11.12).

Figure 11.12

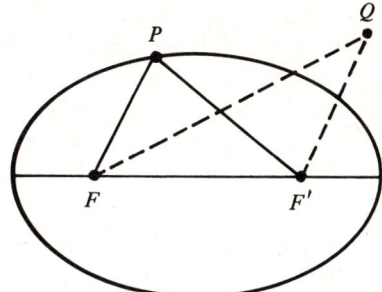

3. Let t be the tangent at any point P of an ellipse and let F' and F be the foci. Prove that PF' and PF make equal angles with the tangent at P (Figure 11.13).

Figure 11.13

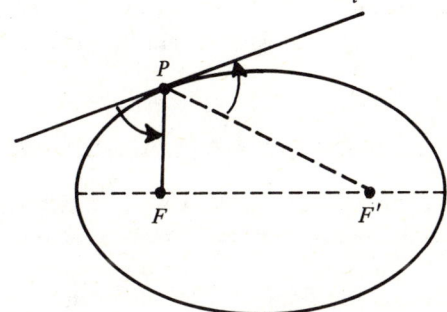

4. Suppose the foci F and F' coincide. Show that the ellipse becomes a circle.

5. The American artificial satellite Explorer followed an elliptical orbit around the Earth. At its closest point to the Earth (perigee) it was 230 miles away. Its farthest point (apogee) was 1700 miles away. If 4000 miles is the radius of the Earth and the center of the Earth is at one focus, find the major and minor axes of this orbit.

6. In its orbit around the sun, the closest the Earth comes to the sun (perihelion) is 91,5000,000 miles. Its farthest distance (aphelion) is 94,500,000 miles. If the sun is at one focus of the Earth's orbit, find the length of the major and minor axes of the Earth's orbit. (The diameter of the sun is about 850,000 miles, negligible in this case.)

The role of mathematics in this battle between theology and science was crucial. The struggle for the minds of men was not one to be easily resolved. Galileo was soon to enter the arena only to be persecuted himself for supporting the ideas of Kepler. Newton was to appear on the scene later to add a new dimension of unity to our worldly conceptions. But in the end it was mathematics that was instrumental in the acceptance and development of the heliocentric theory. So much so that Kline goes on to write,

The mathematical argument proved more compelling than the theological one and the battle for the freedom to think, speak, and write was finally won. The scientific Declaration of Independence is a collection of mathematical theorems.[11]

Interestingly enough either of the models can be used as a frame of reference for observing and describing motion, with a relative degree of suitability. The Sun at the center enables us to employ the relatively simple model of Kepler. But the model based on the Earth as a fixed planet at the center may also be used although it would be extremely difficult and even confusing. As stated in a high school textbook on physics,

> . . . geocentric and heliocentric descriptions of the planetary systems can be equivalent, as are the systems of Tycho Brahe and of Copernicus; and which we adopt is a matter of convenience.[12]

The book goes on to describe how in navigation an Earth-centered view is desirable since we are uninterested in how the motions seem on the Sun. Instead we want to know where we are when we see planets from the Earth.

The role of models in mathematics and science are quite comparable as can be seen by the discussions of the non-Euclidean geometries and the various theories about planetary motion. But most important of all is the vital role played by mathematics in helping man gain insight into the nature of his world.

11.4 *Linear Programming and Mathematical Models*

Perhaps one of the most fundamental ways in which mathematics has been instrumental in affecting our society is through the construction of mathematical models to deal with contemporary problems.

Achievement of optimum results, and ultimately higher profits, is a constant quest of industry in our society. When we deal with optimization, we turn to the methods of linear programming. Students might begin with this problem:

> You own a bike store and sell up to 60 bikes a year. The company you buy from insists that you must sell at least 3 times as many boys bikes as girls'. Your profit on a boy's bike is $10 and on a girl's bike is $12. Find the maximum possible profit you can make and how many of each kind of bike should be sold to make this profit.

Students need time to make their own attempt to solve any problems presented. The inherent difficulties encountered, point up the need to learn new techniques. We turn to one solution:

What must we find? How many of each type bike is sold.

Let x = number of boy's bikes sold
Let y = number of girl's bikes sold

What do we know about the numbers sold?

$x + y \leq 60$
$x \geq 3y$
$x \geq 0$ and $y \geq 0$.

These inequations are called the *constraints* because they state the limits placed on the use of the variables. Graphing the constraints gives a polygonal convex set

Figure 11.14

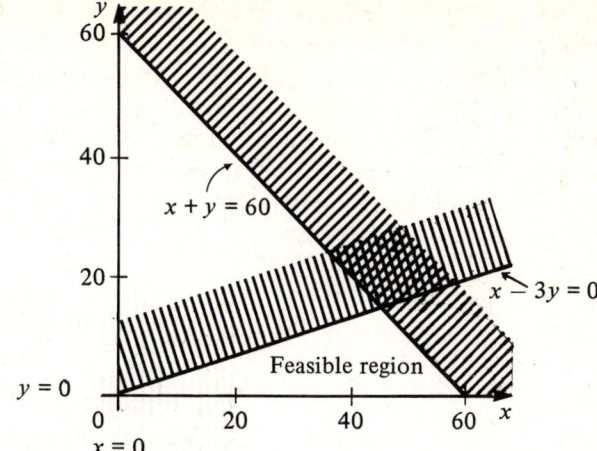

called the feasible region or domain shown in Figure 11.14. The polynomial we are attempting to maximize is:

$$10x + 12y$$

Which values of x and y will serve our purpose? Look at the graph. Set the polynomial equal to P, for profit.

$$10x + 12y = P$$

To get an idea of the graph, we solve for y:

$$12y = -10x + P$$
$$y = -\frac{10}{12}x + P$$

slope is $-\frac{10}{12}$ y-intercept is P

Since we are interested in the maximum value of P, we want that line with slope $-\frac{10}{12}$, which cuts the y-axis at the highest point, yet has a point in common with the domain. Look at Figure 11.15. We can achieve the highest intercept on the y-axis by drawing the line through the vertex (45, 15). For the points of the feasible region, the polynomial $10x + 12y$ will be at its maximum at (45, 15). Students should be encouraged to try other points to satisfy any doubts. They will soon

Figure 11.15

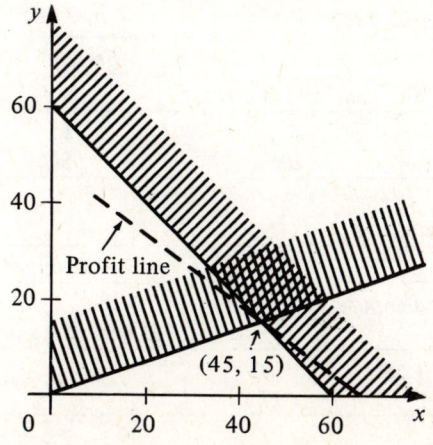

learn that only the verticies of the polygonal convex set need be considered. The solution becomes: to maximize profits sell 45 boys' bikes and 15 girls' bikes, which will yield a profit of (10 × 45) + (12 × 15) or $630.

In drawing the graph, you will notice that the shading of the included region was the reverse of the usual procedure. While this may be confusing to students, it makes it easier to deal with the included region, since crosshatching obscures the verticies (Figure 11.16). However, each teacher may certainly proceed as he or she thinks best.

Figure 11.16

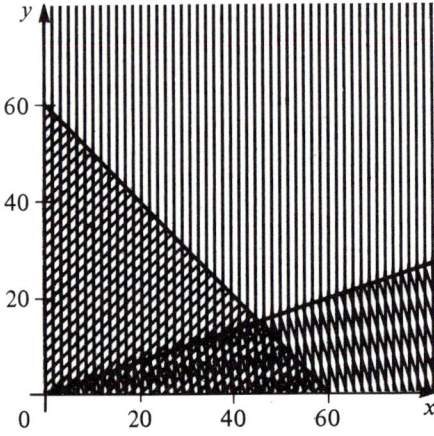

The simple problem presented highlights the procedures without creating too much difficulty and gives a good idea of the various branches of algebra that are considered. In addition, the inequalities of the constraints are the mathematical models the student constructs to deal with the situation. A more difficult problem may make this clearer:

▶ The Jones Tire Company has three stores, one in New York, one in Boston, and one in Philadelphia. Each store needs tires, and they are sent from two warehouses (A and B). Listed in Table 11.2 is the freight charge to each store from each warehouse. The amount stored in each warehouse and the number needed by each store is listed in Table 11.3. Determine the way to ship the tires at the lowest possible freight cost.

Table 11.2

Shipped from Warehouse	Freight Charges to Stores in:		
	NY	Boston	Philadelphia
A	$5	$3	$3
B	$4	$5	$4

Table 11.3

Warehouse	In Stock	Number Shipped to:		
		N.Y. (10 needed)	Boston (8 needed)	Philadelphia (12 needed)
A	13			
B	17			

How shall the student fill in the boxes so that the freight charges are minimum? To keep the number of variables manageable, we can:

Let x = number shipped from Warehouse A to New York
Let y = number shipped from Warehouse A to Boston

Table 11.4 can then be completed in terms of x and y. Each box offers a constraint on the variables and leads to the inequalities:

$$\begin{aligned} x &\geq 0 \\ y &\geq 0 \\ 10 - x &\geq 0 & x &\leq 10 \\ 8 - y &\geq 0 & y &\leq 8 \\ 13 - x - y &\geq 0 & y &\leq -x + 13 \\ -1 + x + y &\geq 0 & y &\geq -x + 1 \end{aligned}$$

The six inequalities above form the constraints of the model and are placed on the graph, with the *excluded* area shaded, as shown in Figure 11.17.

Figure 11.17

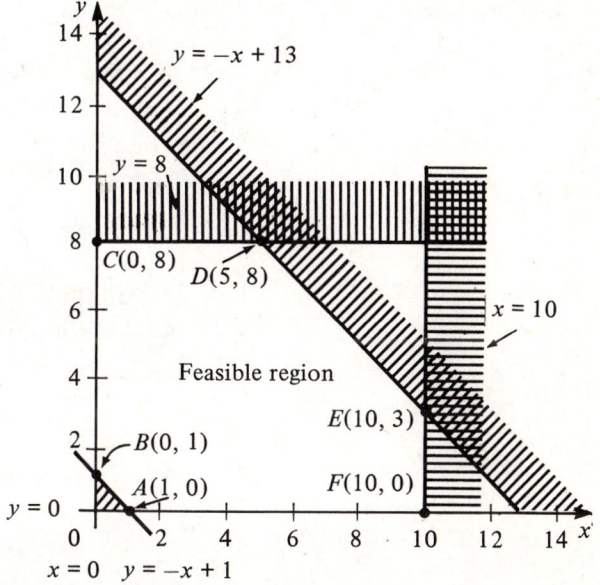

The vertices determined by graphing the polygonal convex set are lettered in Figure 11.17, and the feasible region is marked. What must we maximize or minimize? Minimum freight rates are required here. How can we describe these rates with a polynomial in x and y? Each cell of Table 11.4 yields a cost figure. All the student needs to do is multiply the number in each box by the cost of that shipment. The cost becomes:

$$C = 5x + 3y + 3(13 - x - y) + 4(10 - x) = 5(8 - y) + 4(-1 + x + y)$$

Table 11.4

Warehouse	In Stock	Number Shipped to:		
		N.Y. (10 needed)	Boston (8 needed)	Philadelphia (12 needed)
A	13	x	y	$13 - x - y$
B	17	$10 - x$	$8 - y$	$-1 + x + y$

Which simplifies to

$$C = 2x - y + 115.$$

Two things are necessary in order to determine the minimum freight cost. We need to find the values of x and y that:

1. are in the feasible region or on the boundary and
2. will minimize the polynomial $2x - y + 115$.

One way to proceed is to ask students to list each vertex and substitute its coordinates into the polynomial. Then select the pair of coordinates giving the smallest value. But first, try to find the proper vertex using the graph.

The cost is: $\quad C = 2x - y + 115$
Solving for y: $\quad y = 2x + (115 - C)$

In terms of the standard form, the slope of the line is $+2$, and the y-intercept is $(115 - C)$. If we think of the family of lines with slope $+2$ that will pass through points of the feasible region, we see they extend upward as they move to the right. From the y-intercept, $(115 - C)$, we can see that to minimize C we will maximize the y-intercept, $(115 - C)$. So we want the line with slope $+2$ that has the largest y-intercept in the domain. Figure 11.18 contains several such lines including the desired one. The largest y-intercept for any line through a point in the region with a slope of $+2$, is the line drawn through the vertex $C\,(0, 8)$.

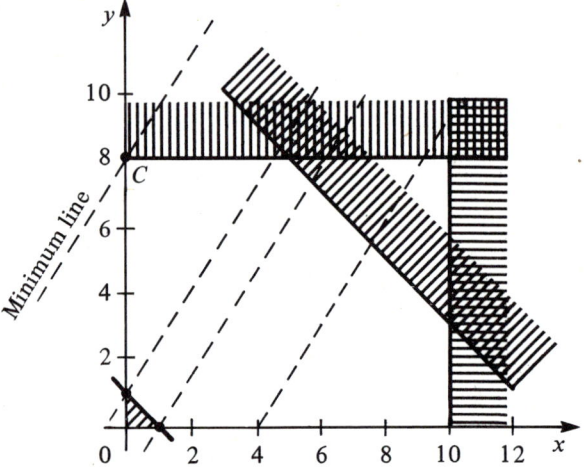

Figure 11.18

When C is minimized, $(115 - C)$ has its largest value, hence the point we seek must be point C or $(0, 8)$.

Students may now check this line of reasoning and the result, by finding the cost at each vertex and comparing. In this case, a reexamination of the criterion polynomial is more helpful:

$$2x - y + 115$$

Since values below zero are not permissable for either variable, to keep the polynomial at a minimum, $x = 0$. Since the y-value is subtracted, as y gets larger, the value of the polynomial becomes smaller. There are two points (vertices) with $x = 0$, point $C\,(0, 8)$ and point $B\,(0, 2)$. The larger y-value is 8 so the point desired is point $C\,(0, 8)$. Table 11.5 shows how the shipments are to be made. The minimum cost is:

$2(0) - (8) + 115 = 107$

All of the pieces fall neatly into place and the problem is solved.

Table 11.5

Warehouse	In Stock	Number Shipped to:		
		N.Y. (10 needed)	Boston (8 needed)	Philadelphia (12 needed)
A	13	0	8	5
B	17	10	0	7

In examining these problems, we come away with a rich harvest of relevant mathematics of the secondary school. These include:

Solution of linear inequalities and equations
Graphing of linear functions involving inequalities and equations
Operations with polynomials
Basic algebraic and arithmetic manipulative skills
Problem solving experience

Construction of mathematical models has provided us with extraordinary power to solve rather difficult problems in our society. Any problem of maximizing or minimizing profits, or costs, in a host of fields may be explored with the methods of linear programming. As the number of variables increases, linear programming becomes a technique to use together with high speed computers, dramatically reducing work time. Indeed, until recently, such problems were virtually impossible to do because of the time required for computation. We will briefly explore the revolutionary role of the computer in Chapter 16.

Here are some additional problems that may be done:

1. A go-cart maker constructs two models Alpha (A) and Beta (B). He can sell all that he can manufacture. Three machines are used to make the go-carts and are required as shown in Table 11.6. No machine may be used for more than 8 hours a day. The profit on an Alpha is \$4, and on a Beta is \$3. Determine how many of each model should be produced per day to maximize profits.

Table 11.6

Go-carts	Machine Hours		
	Machine 1	Machine 2	Machine 3
Alpha	1	2	8/5
Beta	2	1	8/5

2. Three stores A, B, C, draw on two warehouses, W_1 and W_2 for their supplies. Each warehouse has a stock of 12 cartons of an item. Each store wants 8 cartons. Shipping costs from the warehouse to the stores are presented in Table 11.7.

Table 11.7

Warehouse	Shipped to Stores:		
	A	B	C
W_1	2	2	3
W_2	4	3	4

Constructing mathematical models of the "real world" to solve "real world" problems is a vital role played by mathematics in today's society. A broad range of "real world" problems and a variety of approaches have been treated in many sections of this text besides linear programming. Probability problems, determination of patrol car routes, optimization, and physical experimentation all illustrate the vital use of mathematics in twentieth century society. The use of these applications may minimize the alienation from mathematics that too many students experience.

Footnotes

1. Carroll V. Newsom. "The Image of the Mathematician," *The American Mathematical Monthly.* Vol. 79 (October 1972), pp. 880–881.
2. Carroll V. Newsom. "The Image of the Mathematician," *The American Mathematical Monthly.* Vol. 79 (October 1972), pp. 880.
3. Robert E. Gaskell. "Some Realities for Mathematicians, Present and Future," *Newsletter.* Conference Board of the Mathematical Sciences. Vol. 8 (October 1973), p. 2.
4. A. B. Wilcox. "England was Lost on the Playing Fields of Eton: A Parable for Mathematics," *The American Mathematical Monthly.* Vol. 80 (January 1973), p. 40.
5. Engineering Concepts Curriculum Project, Polytechnical Institute of Brooklyn. *The Man-Made World.* New York: McGraw-Hill, 1971, p. 57.
6. Oystein Ore. *Graphs and Their Uses.* New Mathematical Library, No. 10 New York: Random House/Singer, 1963, pp. 23–27. (This can be ordered from the Mathematical Association of America, Washington, D.C.)
7. For an interesting discussion see "Patterns and Connections," Chapter 8 of *Some Lessons in Mathematics.* T. J. Fletcher, ed., New York: Cambridge University Press, 1965, pp. 223–248.
8. See "Matrices." Chapter 12 of *Some Lessons in Mathematics.* T. J. Fletcher, ed., New York: Cambridge University Press, 1965, pp. 324–355.
9. For additional information see: Richard Courant and Herbert Robbins. *What is Mathematics?* New York: Oxford University Press, 1941, pp. 214–227.

    Also see: Morris Kline. *Mathematics in Western Culture.* New York: Oxford University Press, 1953, pp. 410–431.
10. Morris Kline. *Mathematics in Western Culture.* New York: Oxford University Press, 1953, p. 117.
11. Morris Kline. *Mathematics in Western Culture.* New York: Oxford University Press, 1953, p. 125.
12. Physical Science Study Committee. *Physics.* Lexington, Mass: D. C. Heath, 1960, p. 353.

For Investigation and Discussion

1. Read the article by A. B. Wilcox listed in the references. Indicate what you agree and disagree with and explain your reasons.
2. Describe how you would develop a lesson to enable students to understand and solve the police patrol car problem on page 170.
3. Make up two additional problems for students studying networks.

4. Look up Leonhard Euler in a mathematics history text and collect information about the man that would make his work more interesting to students. (Try *Men of Mathematics* by E. T. Bell. New York: Simon and Schuster, 1937.)
5. List three theorems that illustrate the difference between Euclidean, elliptical and hyperbolic geometries.
6. Make an outline for a one-week unit designed to emphasize the role of mathematics in shaping man's view of the world around him. Choose a convenient grade level for the unit.
7. Plan a lesson designed to interest students in the solution of inequalities using linear programming techniques. The lesson should be based on problems from areas that are familiar to the students.
8. An eleventh grade student cannot understand why the solution to a problem requiring linear programming is found by examining the vertices of the polygonal convex set. Describe how you would assist this student.
9. Draw up a lesson plan that will enable students to write the constraints for the two problems listed on page 183.

For Further Reading

Books

Boehm, George A. W. and the editors of *Fortune*. *The New World of Math*. New York: Dial Press, 1959.

Courant, Richard and Herbert Robbins. *What is Mathematics?* New York: Oxford University Press, 1941.

Cundy, H. Martyn and A. P. Rollett. *Mathematical Models*. 2nd ed. New York: Oxford University Press, 1967.

Engineering Concepts Curriculum Project, Polytechnical Institute of Brooklyn. *The Man-Made World*. New York: McGraw-Hill, 1971.

Hooke, Robert and Douglas Shaffer. *Math and Aftermath*. New York: Walker, 1965.

Jacobs, Harold R. *Mathematics: A Human Endeavor*. San Francisco: W. H. Freeman and Co., 1970.

Konkle, Gail S. *Shapes and Perceptions*. Boston: Prindle, Weber & Schmidt, 1974, Chapter 5.

Kline, Morris. *Mathematics in Western Culture*. New York: Oxford University Press, 1953.

Ore, Oystein. *Graphs and Their Uses*. New Mathematical Library, No. 10. New York: Random House/Singer, 1963. (This can be obtained from the Mathematical Association of America, Washington, D.C.)

Pollack, H. O. "Applications of Mathematics," Part I in *Mathematics Education,* 69th Yearbook. National Society for the Study of Education, 1970, pp. 311-334 (distributed by University of Chicago Press).

Rosenberg, Herman. "The Art of Generating Interest," *The Teaching of Secondary School Mathematics,* 33rd Yearbook. Reston, Va.: National Council of Teachers of Mathematics, 1970, pp. 137-165.

Periodicals

Baker, J. E. "Traffic, A Vehicle for Functions," *Mathematics Teaching*. No. 56 (Autumn 1971), pp. 6-10.

Dunn, Samuel L. and Lawrence W. Wright. "Models of the U.S. Economy," *The Mathematics Teacher*. Vol. 70 (February 1977), pp. 102-110.

Fletcher, T. J. "What is the Use of Mathematics?" *Mathematics Teaching*. No. 48 (Autumn 1969), pp. 36-42.

Frank, Howard and Ivan T. Frisch. "Network Analysis," *Scientific American*. Vol. 223 (July 1970), pp. 94-103.

Hope, Cyril and Andrew Rothery. "Mathematical Modelling in the Classroom," *Mathematics Teaching.* No. 71 (June 1975), pp. 36–39.

Jacobson, Herbert R. "Ecology, Rapid Transit, and Graph Theory: An Intuitive Approach for Middle and Upper Elementary Grades," *The Arithmetic Teacher.* Vol. 21 (April 1974), pp. 291–293.

Lepowsky, William L. "Path Tracing and Vote Counting," *The Mathematics Teacher.* Vol. 69 (January 1976), pp. 22–26.

Lipsey, Sally I. "Adam Smith in the Mathematics Classroom," *The Mathematics Teacher* Vol. 68 (March 1975), pp. 189–194.

May, Kenneth O. "Mathematics and Art," *The Mathematics Teacher.* Vol. 60 (October 1967), pp. 568–572.

Mizrahi, Abe and Michael Sullivan. "Mathematical Models and Applications: Suggestions for the High School Classroom," *The Mathematics Teacher.* Vol. 66 (May 1973), pp. 394–402.

Papy, Frederique. "Nebuchadnezzar, Seller of Newspapers: An Introduction to Some Applied Mathematics," *The Arithmetic Teacher* Vol. 21 (April 1974), pp. 278–285.

Piele, Donald T. "Population Explosion: An Activity Lesson," *The Mathematics Teacher* Vol. 67 (October 1974), pp. 496–502.

Reeves, Charles A. "Network Theory—An Enrichment Topic," *The Mathematics Teacher.* Vol. 67 (February 1974), pp. 175–178.

Slawsky, Norman. "The Artist as Mathematician," *The Mathematics Teacher.* Vol. 70 (April 1977), pp. 298–308.

Sloyer, Clifford W. "A Quality Inequality," *The Mathematics Teacher.* Vol. 68 (February 1975), pp. 84–87.

Willcutt, Robert. "Paths on a Grid," *The Mathematics Teacher.* Vol. 66 (April 1973), pp. 303–307.

CHAPTER 12

Making Decisions: Statistics

One of the more important areas of mathematics utilized in modern day society is statistics. During labor-management disputes, both sides will try to influence each other, and the public, with the use of statistics. It is not uncommon for both sides to use the identical set of statistics and yet arrive at completely opposite conclusions. The same is true for a myriad of other problems that confront people each day in our society.

All forms of communication are quick to use statistical techniques in order to convey information clearly and effectively. Tables, charts, and graphs are common occurrences in most magazines, books and newspapers. The entire area of statistical sampling has had such a profound effect upon our lives that it is now possible for someone in a west coast city to be informed that a candidate has been elected in a national election almost before he has gone to the polls! This is not uncommon with the advent of high-speed computers for use by television networks.

The local weather forecasts indicate that "the probability of rain is 20%." A government bureau tells us the "the cost of living went up 0.3% last month." And the insurance company states that auto insurance for men under 25 will cost a lot more than it does for women of the same age. Everywhere we turn we find ourselves becoming involved one way or another with statistics. Our students need to understand statistical concepts if they are to become literate members of society.

There is still a more compelling reason for study in this area. The techniques of statistics provide us with a powerful tool for managing collections of numbers called **data**. The questions we ask about the data can lead to answers that may help us to make decisions. We also have the opportunity to introduce students to an important problem-solving method, which has implications for areas other than mathematics.

While students acquire skill and understanding with statistical techniques, they will also need to use all their basic arithmetic skills. Indeed, there is one text on statistics that attempts to teach a course in basic skills using statistics.[1] We can provide much needed instruction and practice in a setting of maximum utility.

In short, the area of statistics is most productive for vital, timely, and significant mathematical experiences, which point out how difficult it would be to resolve problems of our society without mathematics.

12.1 Collecting Data and Sketching Graphs

To be sure that the work done with statistics has meaning for students, organize situations so that the numbers that students collect are of some consequence. We can make class surveys of characteristics of the students. How many students have green eyes? gray? or brown? How is hair color distributed? How would these data appear if we broke the class group into two subgroups, boys and girls? Carrying out the survey and gathering the data are active classroom experiences for all.

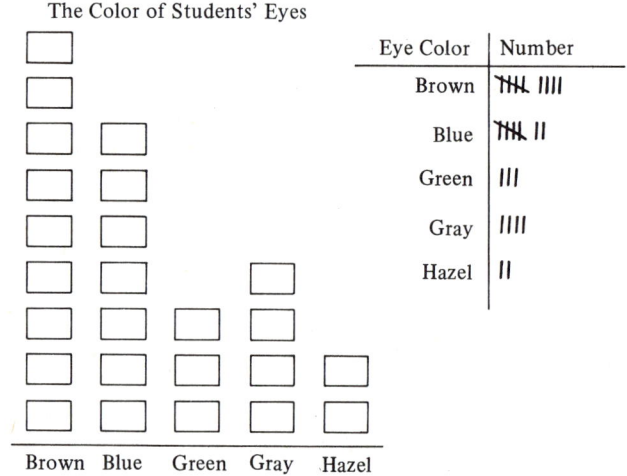

Figure 12.1
A column graph.

To examine our data, we arrange our information in tables and then sketch graphs to make pictures that are even easier to understand. For the beginning graph, students can use small discs or cardboard pieces to build what is sometimes called a column graph (Figure 12.1). This provides students with a wonderful physical introduction to bar graphing. When the column graph is made, everyone examines it in order to determine how the various columns compare. Specific questions such as

How many more students have brown eyes than green? and

What is the ratio of the number of students with gray eyes to the number of students with brown eyes?

are best answered by referring to the table, which contains an organized collection of the data. Questions that do not require exact numerical results but which refer to comparisons, such as:

> Which is there more of, green or brown eyes? and
>
> About how many times more students with brown than gray eyes are there?

are best answered by a quick look at the graph.

But these are not points to be dwelled upon by the students. Experiences will accumulate to help them realize the relative uses of different presentations of their data. If the students first survey eye color, they may then turn to hair color. Once again we have mathematical repetition: collect data, make tables, construct column graphs, and interpret, but we have a physically different situation. The only limit on the number of such investigations are those dictated by time and by the teacher's own power to identify a variety of circumstances. Family size, numbers of pets per family, shoe size, automobile makes, and even kind and number of books read (including comic books) are all possible sources for additional studies. The drawing of graphs may gradually shift from physical column graphs to paper and pencil column graphs drawn on graph paper. This enables the students to replace the physical block or disc with a shaded square. Eventually he is simply constructing a bar graph shown in Figure 12.2. The gradual movement from one to the other prevents thrusting too much upon students too soon.

Figure 12.2 **(a)** *"Filled-in squares."* **(b)** *Bar graph.*

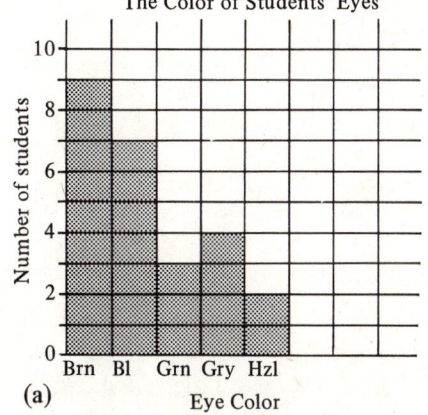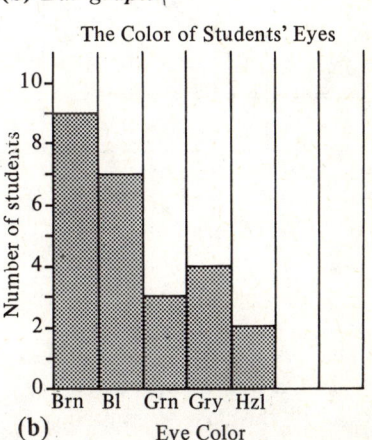

For extended studies, students might record the number of calories they consume each day over a period of, perhaps, a week. The data are tabulated, graphed, and discussed. The focus on calories, stressing what a good diet is, as well as the relationship of diet and good health, adds importance to the work. Simple calorie charts are inexpensive and available in five-and-dime stores, among others. Additional topics for extended study might include outside temperature readings at a given time each day, the height of a growing plant in the classroom measured daily, the daily attendance figures. In each case, the student finds mathematics at work in other areas, integrated into the study of other disciplines. Students may expand their knowledge of that discipline, as well as mathematics. The payoff is rather handsome.

12.2 Other Types of Graphs

Some of these collections of data may be better understood if we turn to graphs other than the bar graph. This will depend upon the nature of the data. If we were concerned with the various parts of the class that have a given hair color, we could well turn to a circle or rectangle graph (Figure 12.3). Our purpose is served more effectively. In addition, the use of ratios and percents comes into play, as well as the introduction of geometric concepts, when students face the problems of subdividing the geometric figure used, circle or rectangle.

Figure 12.3 Illustrating data by **(a)** *a circle graph and* **(b)** *a rectangle graph.*

The Color of Students' Hair

Color	No.	Part of Class	Percent of Class	No. of Degrees
Black	5	$\frac{5}{25}$	20%	72°
Brown	8	$\frac{8}{25}$	32%	115°
Brunette	6	$\frac{6}{25}$	24%	86°
Blonde	4	$\frac{4}{25}$	16%	58°
Red	2	$\frac{2}{25}$	8%	29°
Total	25	1	100%	360°

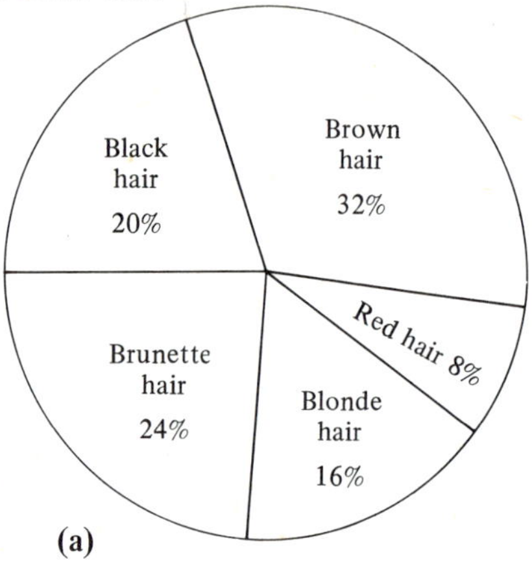

(a) Circle graph showing: Black hair 20%, Brown hair 32%, Brunette hair 24%, Blonde hair 16%, Red hair 8%.

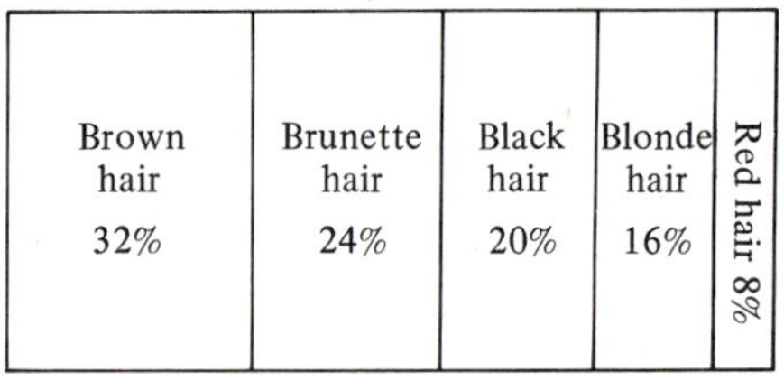

(b) Rectangle graph showing: Brown hair 32%, Brunette hair 24%, Black hair 20%, Blonde hair 16%, Red hair 8%.

A student once inquired as to whether or not he could make a square graph or a triangle graph. This was an example of some fine thinking. In pursuing his ideas, the class attempted construction with these geometric figures, shown in Figure 12.4. It was startling to observe the ingenuity of students attempting to subdivide triangles. We may use what best serves our purpose, of course. There is nothing sacred about the circle or the rectangle, although their use may result in more dramatic pictures of how an entity is subdivided.

As for line graphs, one teacher demonstrated the construction of a line graph by using an overhead projector. Projected upon the chalkboard was a bar graph made by a student on a piece of acetate. The teacher projected the graph onto the board, then had the students draw with chalk right over the projection, the scales of the graph, and the midpoints of each bar. The projector was turned off, leaving the points of a line graph, which the teacher then connected (Figure 12.5, see page 192).

The data will determine whether or not in-between points will be meaningful. But the relationship between bar and line graphs was made dramatically

Figure 12.4 **(a)** *A square graph.* **(b)** *A triangle graph.*

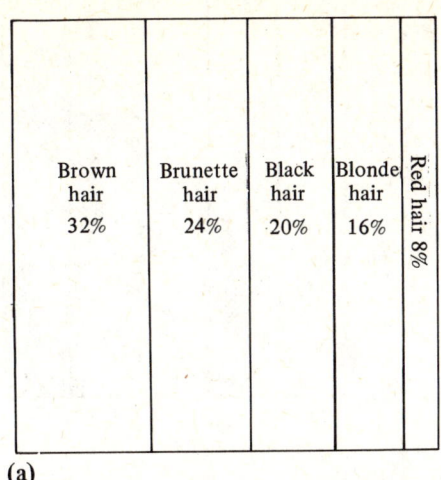
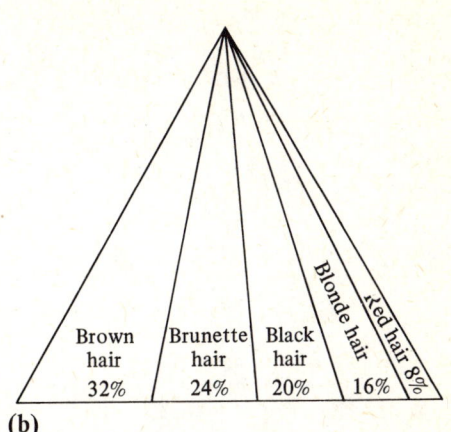

(a) (b)

apparent to the students. It is important for them to understand that the type of graph to use is not a function of one's personal taste, but of the data and the uses to which the data will be put:

Comparing individual readings:	bar graph
Demonstrating how some entity is broken up into parts:	circle or rectangle graph
Determining rise or fall:	line graphs

Of course there are many varieties of each of these standard types.

It is also important to discuss the graphs made and to interpret some of the conclusions apparently reached. This is particularly necessary if students are permitted to fumble and draw graphs based upon misleading practices (such as starting a bar graph at some number other than zero). Questioning these conclusions will help students to appreciate the need for care in the construction of all their graphs.[2]

The teacher might tell the students to look at the graph (Figure 12.6, see page 193) and then ask such questions as:

> How did the number of boxes of cookies sold by Amie and Carol compare?
>
> The bar showing Ellen's sales is how many times higher than that showing Amie's sales?
>
> Did Ellen sell five times as much?
>
> Why does the graph indicate that she did?
>
> The same data are made into another bar graph (Figure 12.7, see page 193). How do the bars compare now?
>
> How is it that the graphs appear to be so different?

As they see bar graphs distorted, as they see the curves of line graphs smoothed out or exaggerated because the scales have been tampered with, students will soon come to realize that graphs can easily be misused.

Figure 12.5
Method of illustrating the relationship between the bar graph and the line graph. (See text for discussion.)

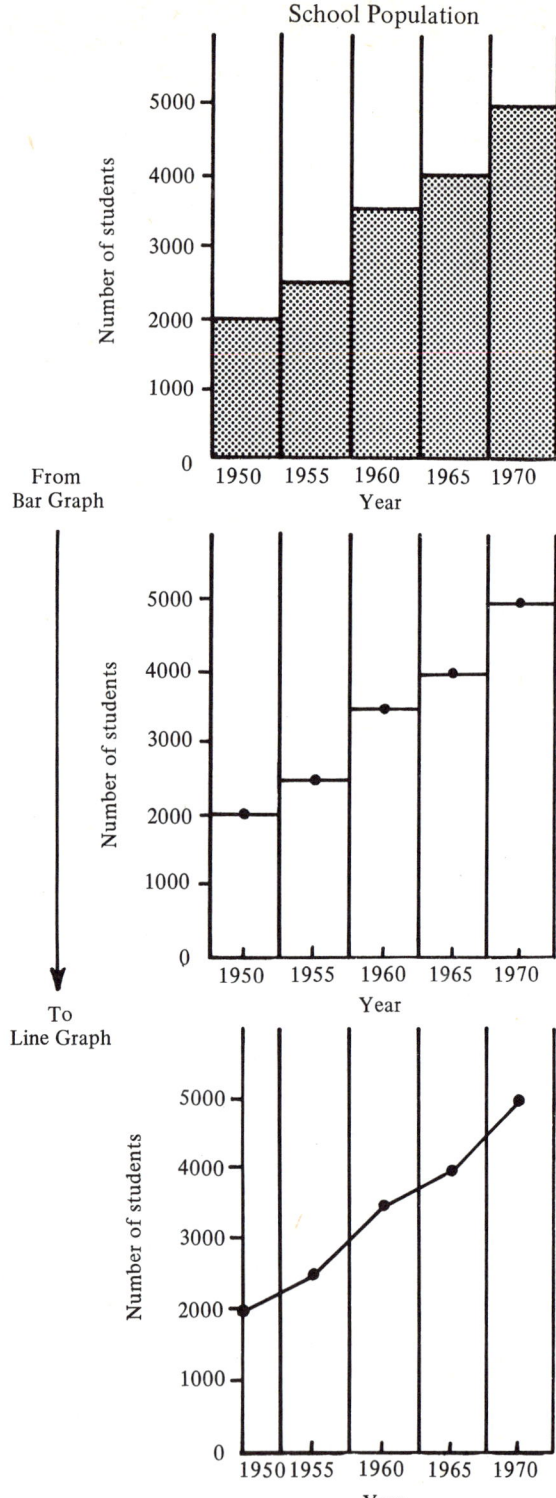

Figure 12.6

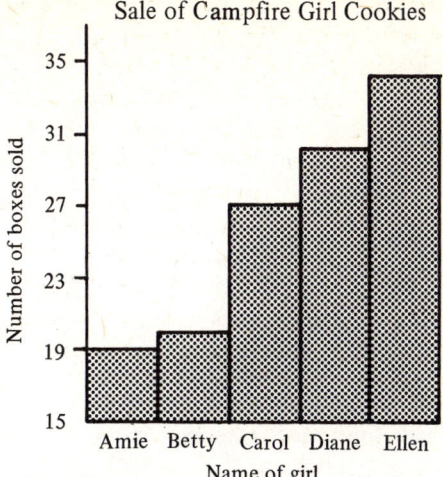

Figure 12.7

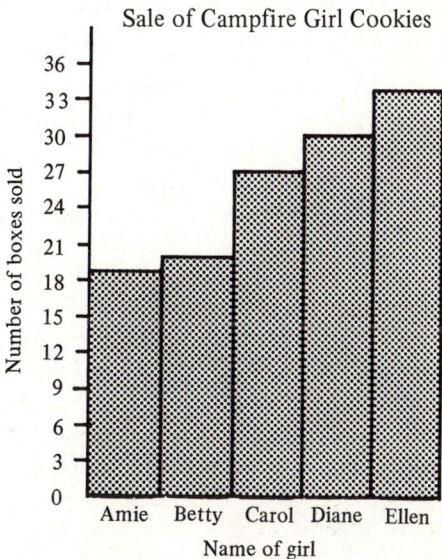

Sampling and Decision Making 12.3

The techniques we have just considered also enable us to make the best decision in certain instances. An appropriate next step in statistical analysis would be to involve our students in decision-making experiences.

    Which TV shows are popular in our school? ◀
    Who will win the school election?
    How many cars pass the school during school hours?
    How many children in our class will be absent next week?

All these questions and many more may best be answered by applying the ideas learned earlier. For example, if we were to pursue the question of how many cars pass the school in a day, we could arrange our data in table form, draw graphs, and examine these carefully in an attempt to provide an answer.

Of course, there is one slight complication: How shall we go about collecting our data? It would not be possible to stand in front of the school all day and simply count. What can we do? At this point, we may introduce the notion of **sampling**. Since we cannot find the total for the 6-hr period (9 A.M. to 3 P.M.), why not take a count for 1 hr and multiply by 6? Perhaps we can take the count for only a quarter hour and multiply 6×4 or 24. Class discussion could serve to highlight many of the important considerations of sampling:

▶
How can we tell that this quarter hour is typical of all quarter hours in the 6-hr period?

Don't fewer cars pass the school at certain times than at other times?

Which are the busy and quiet hours of the day?

Does the day of the week influence the traffic?

What effect does the weather have?

Selecting time periods at random and taking counts would serve to provide some information. Comparing results would indicate whether or not we could use any particular number as an average per quarter hour. And so we find ourselves involved not only with the notion of sampling but also with an introduction to the concept of average. At this point, the arithmetic mean could be quickly computed and the work carried out without interruption. However, should the data so warrant, it may be better to make use of the median or mode. Whatever the case, it would seem to be wise to complete the task at hand, rather than to take time for extended discussions about averages. Later, as more and more of these situations are met, the problem of deciding upon the proper average to use can be given careful attention.

When the traffic volume investigation has been completed, students could undertake a number of similar investigations. One particularly convenient question that may be explored is the total number of words in a composition or story they have recently written. The number of words in a particular section or article of a familiar book or magazine may also be used. It is a rather tiresome task to count each and every word particularly if a selection runs more than just a few pages. Choosing a line of printing at random, the students can count the number of words in a single line. Then, as before, they select the typical number to represent each line (the concept of average again) and simply multiply by the number of lines on a page and the total number of pages. In this instance, the students may check their accuracy by making an actual count of every word. If the pages are divided among the youngsters in the class, the total can be found without any undue waste of time and effort.

As we have already noted, the popularity of various television shows and the prediction of sucess in election campaigns at the school, local, or national level, as well as student opinion on any given topic of the day, all form excellent areas for statistical investigation. Each situation enables the student to gain needed practice but always seems to introduce some new wrinkle that was not encountered before. Practice and continued learning are traveling companions. Let us briefly examine how each of these explorations might be carried out.

TV Ratings

First, we turn to the popularity of television programs. All students have heard about the TV "ratings." Some youngsters keep track of these in much the same manner as they do the batting averages of their favorite baseball stars. What do the numbers of a rating mean and how are they arrived at? Since it is impossible for any company to check every home and find out exactly what each family watches, how do companies get figures on how many people watch a given program? Once more the idea of sampling comes into focus. A discussion of how the sample might be selected helps students identify the important characteristics of the sample if it is going to be truly representative of the population at large:

Are the people surveyed young or old?

What is their income bracket?

What is their level of education?

Where are they located?

Are they male or female?

These questions are some of the notions that would probably arise in the class discussion.

We can readily see that a good deal more than statistical concepts will be considered in this work. Social aspects are of great importance to our students. Once the sample characteristics have been considered, a decision must be made about how these people will be reached and what questions shall be asked of them. All these problems must be settled before any information gathering can even begin. A good parallel may be developed and actually carried out in class.

Select a particular time period and try to determine how many people in the class watched each show. Instead of simply polling all the students, select a random sample containing about one quarter of the class. (Use the telephone book to select numbers that correspond to class members; use a table of random numbers that may be found in most statistics books; or simply put the name of each student into a hat and draw out a few.) Poll these students. Each student should tabulate the results and convert them into percents of the sample, as shown in Table 12.1).

Table 12.1   TV Poll.

Program	Number Watching	Part of Class	Percent of Class
Western hour	7	7/25	28%
Cartoon hour	5	5/25	20%
Comedy hour	8	8/25	32%
Mystery hour	4	4/25	16%
Did not watch	1	1/25	4%
Total	25	25/25 = 1	100%

The students can now predict how the entire class will respond by taking the given percents of the entire class. When everyone has made predictions, poll the entire class and compare the tabulated results with the predicted results.

Graphs may be drawn of the data to illustrate these comparisons. In this way we immediately verify the accuracy of our predictions. We can then consider why our sample did or did not provide us with enough information to make predictions with reasonable accuracy. What is more important is that an activity such as this eliminates the need for explanations about what is going on and why specific things happen. The students will have experienced it for themselves. The drill work with percent and proportion, as well as the construction and use of graphs, are inherent parts of this activity.

Class discussion could conclude with an examination of actual rating figures and some explanation of what they represent. Comparisons can be made between class preference and large audience preference. This gives a measure of how much like the larger group the class has been in its responses.

▶ A follow-up activity could be predicting how the entire grade level or school as a whole might respond to the same questions, using the class at hand as a sample itself. Polling could take place throughout the school if it is considered worthwhile.

In any event, the work is real, immediate, and of consequence to the student. Mathematics becomes vital when it provides the student with the tools to study questions of interest. It also offers an opportunity to do something that might otherwise be very difficult, or almost impossible. In addition, the student uses ideas previously learned and extends his knowledge by encountering new ideas. This all adds up to a collection of rather productive experiences.

Opinions and Attitudes

In exploring student opinions and attitudes, we have another extremely fertile field for investigation. By carrying out almost all the activities just described, we may seek out student attitudes in many socially important areas. For instance:

▶ How old should a youngster be before he or she is permitted to start dating?

Should parents hit their children when they misbehave?

Should boys be allowed in school with long hair?

Are jeans appropriate dress for school?

There is an endless stream of important questions to place before students and investigate. Of course, the opportunity for lively discussion of the issues themselves must not be missed. This is indeed one of the significant reasons for traveling this path in the first place. Although our goals are mathematical, we must not lose sight of the human goals. Again, applying mathematical techniques to issues of importance to youngsters builds the concept of the importance of mathematics.

The prediction of successful election candidates is another area ripe for use of these same techniques since the "poll" has become so well integrated into our daily lives. Reports of polls in the newspapers may be used as a guide for classwork. Computers have had a great influence on these practices—so much so that we find newscasters on TV predicting winners before polling places are closed.

Undertaking a poll of the student body in a school election offers students an excellent chance to gain real insight into the entire process. The next time they see polls in a newspaper or on TV, they will have a much better understanding of the strengths and limitations of the results. Knowing some good questions to ask about such data is, in itself, a major learning goal.

Using "Stored" Data

Looking at the experiences described, we notice that in each case the data was gathered by some kind of sampling procedure. These same analytical techniques—gathering data, making tables, constructing graphs, and interpreting the results— can also be applied to situations in which the data collection process involves digging up figures that have already been organized into tables, "**stored data.**" If the class undertakes an exploration of which drivers appear to be the safest, they could find statistics about accidents in their local area and see if the driver's age and sex are indicated. The statistics would already have been collected by official government agencies. It would then be up to the students to organize the data and follow through with the other techniques described. Some typical questions that may follow under this kind of study are:

Why are auto insurance rates higher for boys under 25 than for girls?
Why do older men pay higher life insurance premiums for the same policy as younger men?
Does having more education result in greater earning power?

A word is in order about another type of investigative research, which is carried out by industry—market research studies. These studies involve attempts to assess public reaction to unknown products or particular kinds of packages for familiar ones. Students could carry out their simplified sampling procedures by attempting to determine whether or not most students would be interested in a make-believe new product, such as a flying belt or a single-seater spaceship. Of course, the product must not be too remote from reality or else the responses would be meaningless.

The failure of some well-known, reliable corporations to sucessfully make use of new product research studies is fascinating to students. They are amazed, for example, to find out how much money the Ford Motor Company lost on its famous Edsel. The perils of statistical sampling must be considered carefully.

Mean, Median, and Mode 12.4

Students meet averages long before they undertake the study of averages in mathematics. School marks and test marks lead to continuous comparison with friends and corresponding judgements about how well a student is doing. In sports, virtually all participants, whatever the sport, are constantly aware of their "averages." The new context in which the student encounters the idea of **average** in mathematics results in a new perspective about this important statistic.

Earlier we mentioned the use of various averages. Let us explore this further. For one thing, if we study traffic flow as an example, we may be better off using a number that seems to occur repeatedly, rather than adding and dividing. If our quarter-hour traffic counts have been like those shown in Table 12.2, it would seem that 14 might be a better number to use, rather than the arithmetic mean—the familiar "average," which in this case would be 11. The 14 seems to be more "typical" of what is happening. This typical average, which we find by looking for the most frequently appearing number, is a newcomer to most students. It is the **mode**.

Table 12.2 Traffic Volume Survey.

Time Period	Tally	Number
9:00–9:15	++++ ++++ ////	14
9:15–9:30	++++ ++++ ////	14
9:30–9:45	++++ /	6
9:45–10:00	////	4
12:00–12:15	++++ ++++ ++++	15
12:15–12:30	++++ ++++ ////	14
12:30–12:45	++++ ++++	10
3:00–3:15	++++ ++++ ////	14

The idea that there is more than one kind of average is somewhat surprising to students. For the most part, they have used only one and have had little inkling that any others exist.

The **median** or middle number of a collection of figures that have been arranged from smaller to larger, is the third average to be encountered by students. While there are additional averages that may well be computed, it is usually not necessary for students to become involved any further.

How shall we know when to use which average? It is rather important to help students understand that two factors influence such a decision. First, we have the nature of the numbers themselves. If we sought to determine the average salary of workers in a paper mill, we might find the salaries listed in Table 12.3. The *mean* would be $24,000; yet we would find that out of 12 people on the payroll, nine are earning far less than $24,000. The reason for this is that the few high salaries are distorting the data. It would seem that this number is not really representative of the numbers in the set making up the payroll. What would be better? If the numbers are arranged from smallest to highest, we might find the *median*, or middle number, to be useful; or perhaps we might use the *mode*, the number that appears most often. In this case both of these averages are identical: $14,000. This number does seem more representative of the data. So we must scrutinize the data carefully before deciding which average will be most appropriate.

Another factor to be considered is the use to which you intend to put the average. If it is typicality that is sought, then the mode seems to be the best choice. If, on the other hand, we simply do not wish to permit our average to be distorted by extremely high or low values, then we should employ the median. The freedom of choice left with the individual computing the averages should serve to help students become a bit more discriminating in dealing with averages in any case. Certainly we should want to ask which average is being referred to.

Table 12.3 Annual Salaries—Jones Paper Mill.

Name	Salary
R. Jones	$ 70,000
T. Jones	70,000
Mr. A	41,000
Mr. B	14,000
Mr. C	14,000
Mr. D	14,000
Mr. E	14,000
Mr. F	14,000
Mr. G	14,000
Mr. H	8,000
Mr. I	8,000
Mr. J	7,000
Total Salaries	$288,000
Mean	24,000
Median	14,000
Mode	14,000

The Bureau of Labor Statistics of the United States Government computes all kinds of indexes about our society. When they say that the average family earned $14,000, what are they referring to? Do they use the mean, median or mode? Which do you think they should use? Why? Should more than one average be used?

The entire concept of average, as generally employed in society, bears close examination. For example, we say in school that a youngster is an "average" student. What does that tell you about him? Here are some other common averages that could lead to interesting discussions: He is an average American man; his batting average is .300; an average family has 2.4 children; she's an average teenager. You can add many more. This is another bit of evidence that some words common to both society and mathematics have rather different meanings in each place. But even more important, we are emphasizing the need for students to seek out the idea behind the words and to determine exactly what is being portrayed when certain words are used.

An interesting activity to aid student understanding of these three basic averages was provided for us earlier when we had students making physical column graphs prior to the paper-pencil bar graph. If you recall, the students piled up discs or cardboard pieces or perhaps made use of a pegboard. If we return to one of the situations described earlier but employ different data, we can represent the data with the physical column graph and quickly demonstrate the influence of the three different averages (Figure 12.8, see page 200). The column graph shows how many boxes of cookies each girl sold. To find the mean, simply move the pieces (i.e., pegs and discs) until all the columns are the same height (Figure 12.9, see page 200). The height of each column is the arithmetic mean. When a student carries out the physical movement of pieces and observes how all the values are spread evenly over each column, he will have a better notion of the mean than you can ever supply with words. Restoring the columns to their original heights, we now seek the median average number of boxes sold. To do this we simply rearrange the columns so that they are in order from lowest to highest. The one in the

Figure 12.8

Sale of Campfire Girl Cookies

Name of Girl	Number of Boxes Sold
Amie	6
Betty	6
Carol	10
Diane	11
Ellen	12

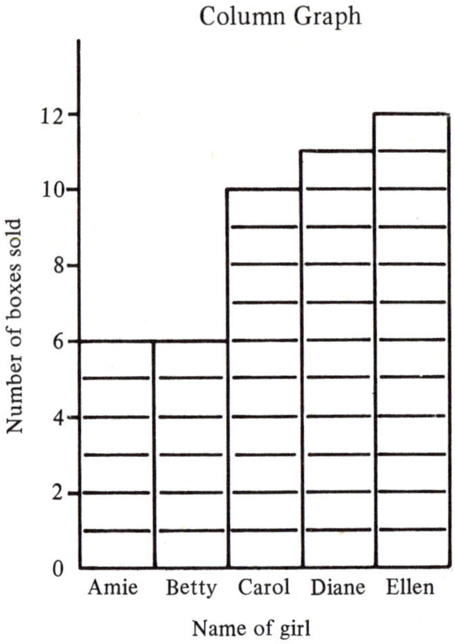

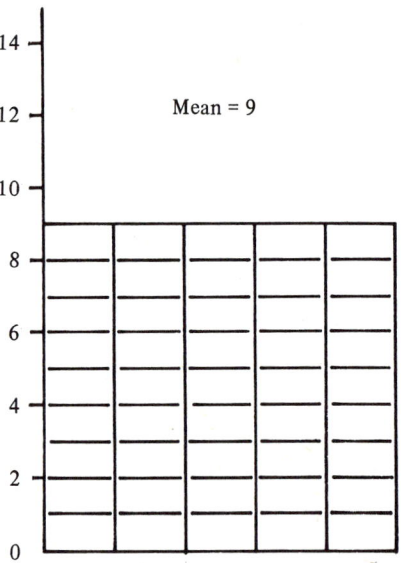

Column Graph

Figure 12.9
Mean—Rearrange so that all bars have equal height.

middle is the median (Figure 12.10). If any one column height is repeated most often, you will have found the mode (Figure 12.11). Of course, more than a single experience is necessary for students to grasp what is happening; but as they move the pieces, it is expected that any mystery that surrounds a given average will gradually be dispelled.

Figure 12.10
Median—Average in order from lowest to highest. The middle value is the indicator.

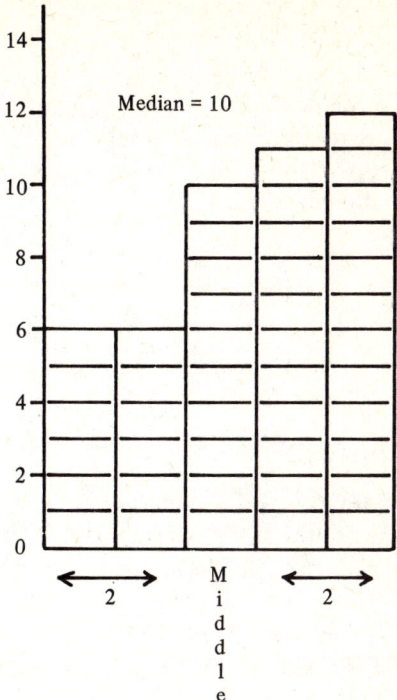

Figure 12.11
Mode—Are any bars of equal height?

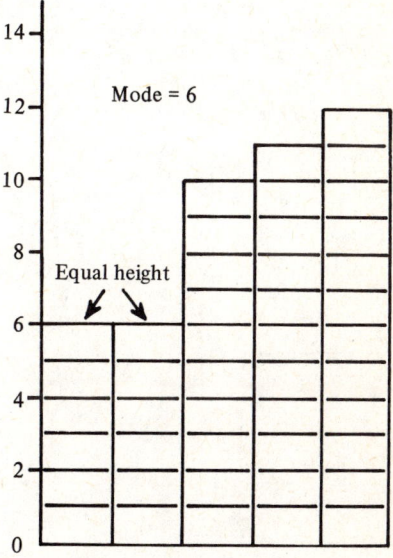

Finally, in order to help students remain clear about which average is which, they may concentrate on these words to aid the memory:

Mean   = the old friend always used
Median = middle
Mode   = most

12.5 Using Spinners

Students can generate many sets of data that may be used to calulate averages through the use of student-made spinners. These spinners may be cut from cardboard and easily assembled using cardboard arrows or arrows made from paper clips. The making of the spinner is as important to the learning process as is the data generated from its use.

For example:

▶
> Students may construct a spinner designed to enable them to bowl against each other. Instead of rolling a bowling ball, they spin the spinner to get their scores.

This is one of the units in the Dyna-Math system.[3] The spinner is made from a circle, divided into 8 equal parts (Figure 12.12). Each student "bowls" five games. Then the scores are totaled and the mean is computed. Students then compare averages to determine the "better bowler." An examination of the scores shows that they are unusually high when compared to the scores students get in real life. Why? Discussion reveals that it is the makeup of the spinner.

The problem of making a new spinner to yield more realistic results is considered with the conclusion leading to the construction of varying size, rather than equal, angles for the different spinner parts. (Figure 12.13). Through this activity, students can derive many sets of data for interesting practice in computation of averages. More than that, they are gaining a better "feel" for the idea of "average" as well as an informal, intuitive understanding of the concept of probability. A question such as, How likely is it for a score to be 300 as compared to 100? can aid in understanding probability.

Figure 12.12

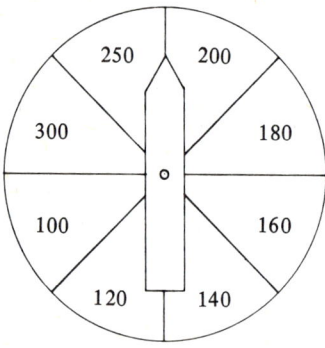

Figure 12.13

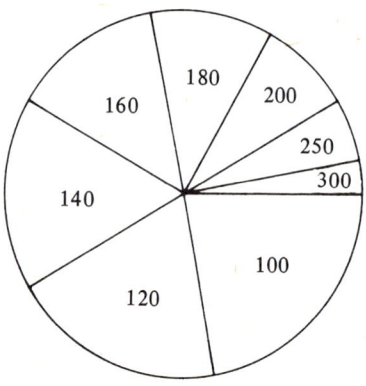

An infinite variety of spinners may be made, which would yield sets of data that are meaningful to students. All sports, baseball, football, auto racing, plus any other form of race that holds students' interest may be used. In addition, you may construct a variety of games. More work with spinners can be found in the section on probability.

Measures of Dispersion   12.6

To increase appreciation for the importance of statistics and the collection of data, we may extend the work to include measures of dispersion and correlation. After a study of probability, work with the normal distribution would also be of interest.

Where the mean was a representative statistic for the set of data, the variance and standard deviation give an idea of the spread of the scores in a set of data. To help students see the meaning and importance of these statistics, ask them to examine sets of scores with equal means but very different distributions. For example:

Two students have the following test scores:

Louis		*Judy*	
80		90	
70		60	
75	Mean 76	75	Mean 76
85		65	
70		90	

Both students have an average test score of 76 but their scores are quite different. The variance will inform us of how the scores are scattered about the mean.

Find the deviations from the mean:

Louis	*Judy*
80 − 76 = 4	90 − 76 = 14
70 − 76 = −6	60 − 76 = −16
75 − 76 = −1	75 − 76 = − 1
85 − 76 = 9	65 − 76 = −11
70 − 76 = −6	90 − 76 = 14

We now see how each score differs from the mean. If we try to find a typical deviation and add the deviations, what do we get? The sum will always be zero since this is the definition of the mean score. Absolute values can help, but such a score causes problems if you extend your analysis of these figures. Instead we take a different tack. If the deviation shows how a score differs from the mean, then squaring the deviation will magnify the difference greatly and thereby make it easier to deal with. In addition, we get around the zero sum.

Squaring the deviations:

Louis			Judy		
80 − 76 =	4	16	90 − 76 =	14	196
70 − 76 =	−6	36	60 − 76 =	−16	256
75 − 76 =	−1	1	75 − 76 =	−1	1
85 − 76 =	9	81	65 − 76 =	−11	121
70 − 76 =	−6	36	90 − 76 =	14	196

Now find the mean of the squared deviations:

Louis: 16 + 36 + 1 + 81 + 36 = 170
                    170 ÷ 5 = 34

Judy: 196 + 256 + 1 + 121 + 196 = 770
                    770 ÷ 5 = 154

We have found the average squared deviations, and we see that the difference between these two sets of data with equal means is great. Judy's scores vary much more than the scores of Louis do. One conclusion is that even though the two students test scores have equal means, Louis is more consistent on his test scores than Judy is. Her scores vary greatly from test to test. Her test results are less predictable.

While we have a good measure of the spread of the scores, the variance is not in the same units as the scores. How would you interpret the figure of 34 for Louis? This score is not in test score units, but in test score units squared. (Remember the squaring process.) To get back into test units, let's take the square root of the variance:

Louis: $\sqrt{34}$ = 5.8   *Judy:* $\sqrt{154}$ = 12.4

This score is called the standard deviation, and is shown in test units. Louis has a standard deviation of 5.8 test points. Judy has 12.4 test points. We have a rather powerful statistic which is often used in statistical analyses to deal with scientific, industrial, and technological problems, as well as human behavior problems.[4]

It may be helpful to briefly summarize what has been done and to make use of mathematical symbols.

We found the deviations from the mean ($\bar{x}$): $(x - \bar{x})$

Squared them: $(x - \bar{x})^2$

Found the mean of the squares, which is the variance (s^2): $s^2 = \dfrac{\Sigma (x - \bar{x})^2}{N}$

Took the square root to get the standard deviation (s): $s = \sqrt{\dfrac{\Sigma (x - \bar{x})^2}{N}}$

To add significance to the standard deviation, we can point out that if the distribution is close to symmetrical about its mean and approximates the normal curve then there is little error in assuming that two-thirds of the distribution will fall within one standard deviation of the mean. Furthermore, moving out two standard deviations from the mean will take in 95% of the scores as shown in

Figure 12.14

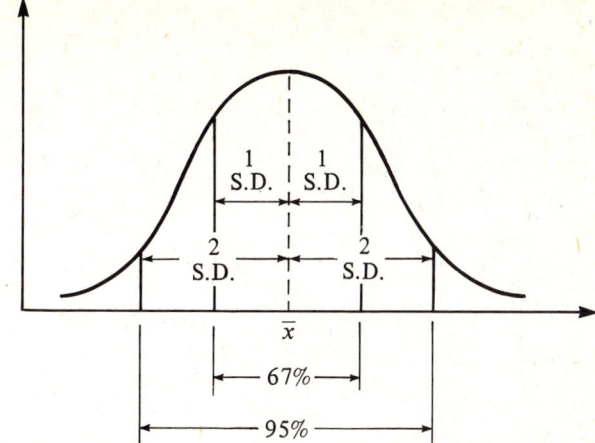

Figure 12.12. Assuming that Louis' and Judy's test scores satisfy this condition, then to include 67% of Louis scores about the mean, you would go from 70.2 to 81.8, which is a spread about the mean of 11.6 points. (Remember the standard deviation was 5.8.) To do the same for Judy, the spread would run from 63.6 to 88.4, a spread of 24.8 points. (The standard deviation here was 12.4.) Once again we see the dramatic spread of the scores. It might be helpful to mention Chebyshev's Theorem. Stated briefly:

> **Theorem:** For any set of numbers at the least the fraction $1 - \frac{1}{h^2}$ of the numbers fall within h standard deviations of the mean. To find the least fraction of scores falling within two standard deviations yields:
>
> $1 - \frac{1}{2^2} = 1 - \frac{1}{4}$ or $\frac{3}{4}$
>
> At least 75% of the scores fall within two standard deviations.

For additional information about this see Willoughby's interesting text.[5]

There are alternative methods of computation for these statistics. We present the following formula, which is another and quicker way to compute the standard deviation (s):

$$s = \sqrt{\frac{\Sigma x^2}{N} - (\bar{x})^2}$$

It may be an interesting exercise for students to show algebraically that this formula is equivalent to the one used earlier. This new formula has the distinct advantage of enabling the students to work with the actual scores rather than differences.

Additional sets of data may be derived from a number of situations of interest to students including:

> Comparing scores of students on spinner games.
> Comparing variability of two distributions involving heights or weights.
> Comparing variability of bowling scores of students.
> Comparing variability of hours spent watching television.

There is a ready link with probability that may be exploited here. In addition, more advanced statistical topics may result from an exploration of the normal distribution, from comparing means of two or more groups for significant differences to the study of the concept of correlation. Throughout, the work in statistics is experience-based and requires making good use of the mathematical skills learned earlier. The role of mathematics in adding to our power to solve difficult problems is reenforced.

Footnotes

1. Louis Auslander, Frank J. Avenoso, et. al. *Mathematics Through Statistics.* Baltimore: Williams and Wilkins, 1973.
2. Darrell Huff and Irving Gels. *How To Lie With Statistics.* New York: W. W. Norton, 1964.
3. Herbert Fremont and William Blossfield. *Dyna-Math.* New York: MacMillan, 1975.
4. For interesting examples, see: M. J. Moroney. *Facts From Figures.* New York: Penguin Books, 1951.

    Also see: Horace C. Levinson. *Chance, Luck and Statistics.* New York: Dover Publications, 1963.
5. Stephen C. Willoughby. *Probability and Statistics.* Morristown, N. J.: Silver Burdette, 1968, pp. 94–98.

For Investigation and Discussion

1. List topics suitable for making graphs at the junior high school level that include the comparison of meaningful factors in students' lives.
2. Construct a plan for the development of a study that requires students to make use of random sampling in an area of some consequence to them.
3. Establish criteria for students to carry out and evaluate the sampling procedure used in the previous problem.
4. Collect sets of data that will help students to understand and use the mean, median, and mode.
5. Plan a two-week unit built around some problem that requires students to collect their own data, organize the data, present the data, and draw conclusions to solve the original problem.
6. Outline a plan that emphasizes the importance and use of the variance and the standard deviation. Choose a topic that is familiar to the students.

For Further Reading

Books

Auslander, Louis; Frank J. Avenoso; et al. *Mathematics Through Statistics.* Baltimore: Williams and Wilkins, 1973.

Johnson, Donovan and William H. Glenn. *The World of Statistics.* Exploring Mathematics on Your Own Series. New York: McGraw-Hill, 1961.

Moroney, M. J. *Facts From Figures.* New York: Penguin Books, 1951.

Pieters, Richard S. and John J. Kinsella. "Statistics," *The Growth of Mathematical Ideas, K–12.* 24th Yearbook. Reston, Va.: National Council of Teachers of Mathematics, 1959.

Tanur, Judith M.; Fredrick Mosteller; et al, eds. *Statistics: A Guide to the Unknown.* San Francisco: Holden-Day, 1972.

Periodicals

Booth, Ada. "Two-Thirds of the Most Sucessful . . ." *The Mathematics Teacher.* Vol. 66 (November 1973), pp. 593–597.

Huck, Schuyler W. "A Procedure for Generating Data for which the Correlation is Exactly .50," *The Mathematics Teacher.* Vol. 68 (March 1975), pp. 200–202.

Joiner, Brian L. and Cathy Campbell. "Some Interesting Examples for Teaching Statistics," *The Mathematics Teacher.* Vol. 68 (May 1975), pp. 364–369.

Mosteller, Frederick. "Progress Report of the Joint Committee of the American Statistical Association and the National Council of Teachers of Mathematics," *The Mathematics Teacher.* Vol. 63 (March 1970), pp. 199–208.

Noether, Gottfried E. "The Nonparametric Approach in Elementary Statistics," *The Mathematics Teacher.* Vol. 67 (February 1974), pp. 123–126.

Stevens, S. S. "Measurement, Statistics and the Schemapiric View, *Science.* Vol. 181 (August 30, 1968), pp. 849–856.

CHAPTER 13

Probability

Probability is a topic that is relatively new to the secondary school curriculum. It's importance can easily be verified by simply listing the number of places the idea occurs in our daily lives. The local weatherman reports the chances of rain in terms of probability, and often our plans for the day are a consequence of these probability statements. People talk about taking a chance in a variety of circumstances from the ancient practice of wagering, to making a blind date, to deciding how to invest money. Each activity involved with risk-taking is a proper sphere for the use of probability.

Many experiments may easily be carried out by students in this area. A list would include:

    Coin tossing
    Dice tossing
    Drawing cards from a deck
    Tossing a thumb tack
    Drawing colored balls (marbles) from urns

What is more, a variety of spinners may be used just as we used spinners to generate sets of data in the study of averages. Computers can also help us predict the probability of events, making otherwise very difficult computations relatively easy.

13.1 *Expecting the Unexpected*

We begin with a discussion of what one would expect to happen. This is followed by the construction of a plan for testing hypotheses or guesses. The experiments are completed, the results are tabulated and charted, and conclusions are drawn as the hypotheses are reexamined in light of experimental evidence. Each student is able to conduct his own experiment or is part of a small group carrying out an experiment. In this manner each student becomes personally involved. For example:

> If the students were testing the hypothesis that half the time a tossed coin should turn up heads ($P = 50\%$), each student could toss and tally or the students could work in small teams.

Large numbers of trials may be accumulated by adding all the separate experiments—assuming that the coins are enough alike, of course. Whereas it might be tiresome for a single student to carry out 1000 tosses, with a class of 30 only some 35 tosses each is necessary. The same approach could be applied to tossing dice, tacks, and other such items in similar experiments.

Spinners offer many interesting possibilities, as was indicated in a British curriculum improvement program, the Midlands Mathematical Experiment.[1] The students cut out two kinds of octagonal cards and stick short pencil stubs through the center of each to make spinning tops. One card is a regular octagon, but the second one is made with two different central angles, causing it to be somewhat distorted (Figure 13.1). The resulting effect should form an interesting experiment for students.

Figure 13.1

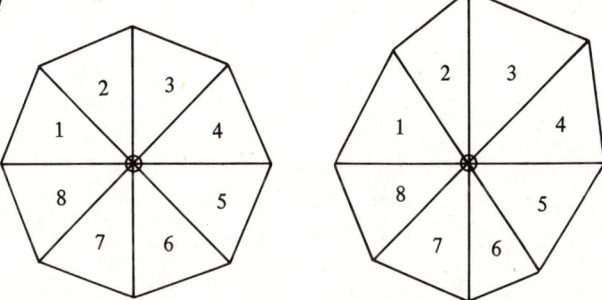

The students begin by spinning the regular octagon. They gather data about the number of times each number occurs, and consider the probabilities of each. They then turn to the unusual "off-center" card. We ask students to consider these questions:

> John chose number 4. Which number do you think will turn up more often?
>
> Which number will turn up the least number of times?
>
> Which numbers do you think have the same chance of turning up?
>
> How can we find out what the chances are of each number turning up?

The students could work in pairs or individually and spin the top a predetermined number of times. In this way, they can gather data to help formulate responses to the above questions *after* they have first guessed at the outcome. Checking their intuitive feelings by experiment heightens interest in doing the experiment. While the original spinner with equal sectors may give predictable results, the "off-center" spinner is full of surprises. The unpredictability of the spinner arouses student curiosity.

Numerous additional possibilities for developing interesting and challenging experiments are available. For example, instead of just tallying numbers, the whole process can be converted into a game of auto or bicycle races. Making the spinners requires mathematical knowledge and offers a good intuitive base for the important idea of equally likely events. If no student is to have an advantage over the other, the spinner must be divided into equal parts. This poses an interesting problem. What does "equal parts" mean?

In the previous section, where averages were discussed, the same idea was encountered. Were the arrow spinners used there the same as the spinners described here? Now the entire card is rotated (rather than just the arrow) by pushing a small pencil through the center. What do the probabilities depend on? In the case of the arrow spinner, the probability depends upon the portion of the circle that is swept out by the spinner. To form the probability, students take the ratio of the measure of the central angle of the sector to the measure of the entire circle:

$$\frac{x°}{360°}$$

If you change the angle, you change the probability. When the pencil is pushed through the center and the entire card rotated, the ratio of the *area* of the section to the *area* of the entire card gives the probability:

$$\frac{A_s}{A_c}$$

If you can change the area, you change the probability. The geometry of construction of spinners whose sections are a function of their area is good practice for students. As students make and use the spinners, they come to grips with the important ideas underlying the study of probability in an intuitive fashion. They may play games with cards equally divided, to offer equally likely situations as well as with cards that are not equally divided (Figure 13.2). Determining beforehand a desired probability, constructing the card to reflect that, playing spinning games with the card to verify conjectures, are all activities that involve students in lively, challenging experiences. This important and difficult topic begins to make sense to students. Discussions involving betting odds are also a possibility. Since probability began with wagering, it is a valid area for investigation if treated carefully.

Figure 13.2

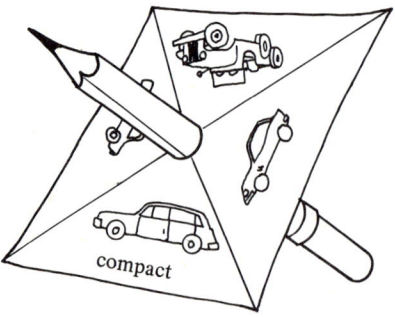
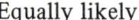
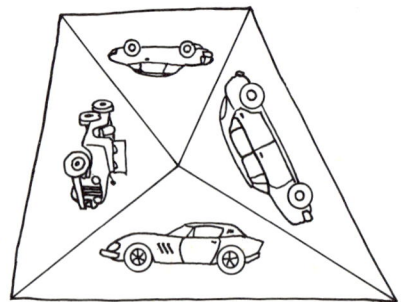

Equally likely　　　　　　　　　　Not equally likely

Redrawn from Herbert Fremont and William Blossfield. "Guess the Spinner," *DynaMath*. New York: Macmillan, 1975.

Probability: Theory vs. Practice 13.2

After introductory work on an intuitive level, attention should be turned to probability theory. Dealing with areas that yield definitive results gives us less difficulty than when we operate in a probabilistic area. We talk in terms of the likelihood of an event and misunderstandings abound on the part of students and teachers alike. When we toss a coin, for example, we expect a probability (given a fair coin) of ½ for either heads of tails. When students toss the coin, say 50 times, and record results, there is a tendency to recognize results close to or at 25-25 as "better" results. In one situation, students were going to add together all of their trials to determine the number of heads and tails that resulted. As students called out their results, everyone, students and teacher alike, would react to outcomes by saying that's good, that's better, etc. One result happened to be 34 heads, 16 tails. Everyone quickly labeled it a "bad" result or even a "wrong" result. Be clear about what is happening. In any given trial, results may be quite divergent from the expected. That is the nature of probability. Outcomes are not *bad* or *good*. They are descriptions of what has happened.

Similar caution is necessary when doing experiments and implying that with increasing numbers of trials students will get closer and closer to theoretical probabilities. How could you explain the following situation:

> Students are tossing coins and tallying. At the end of 20 trials, one student tallies 10 heads and 10 tails. Yet, when the entire class results are added, they turn out to be 285 heads and 315 tails out of 600 trials.

You tell the student that the more trials, the closer you approximate $P(h) = P(t) = ½$. Yet, the student sees the probability go from .5, which he found after 20 trials, to $P(h) = .475$ and $P(t) = .525$.

There are two things that must be kept clearly in mind. The first is that the nature of probability theory is such that application to individual outcomes is very risky. Indeed, anything can happen. That is exactly why a theory has developed to enable us to determine just what the chances are. But anything can, and over a period of time, probably will, happen. Such results are as valid as any other. Help students to realize this.

The other and more important idea to clarify is the difference between **empirical probabilities** and **theoretical probabilities**. Warren Weaver likens these two probability definitions to real world and model respectively. He then goes on to point out:

> What one does in probability theory is invent a mathematical model, which can be calculated in a completely clear and tidy way, and then hope that this model will correspond in a useful way to some real phenomena. If, conversely, one faces a real problem, then through increasing experience one learns how to invent a model which is very likely to be useful for the real problem in question.[2]

We can think of and emphasize the idea of "model construction" in our work with probability. Then we may more easily differentiate between empirical probabilities, resulting from actual conduct of a number of trials, and theoretical probabilities, the result of a model that we have constructed.

Look at a die, assume equally likely chances for any face to appear, and theorize that the probability of getting a given number is 1/6. You are using theoretical probability. The die is tossed 30 times. A particular number appears 7 times. The empirical probability of this number appearing is 7/30. The model proves to be a good one since doing the experiment roughly approximates the results of the model. Exact agreement is not expected when you test the model. In fact, if each number on a die appeared exactly 1/6 of the time, no matter how many trials, the results would be suspect.

Imagine a coin tossed 1000 times with the result of 500 heads and 500 tails. This would be hard to believe: possible, but not probable. That is where the difference between the model and the real-life event come into play. We often glibly slide over the difference between the two, and perhaps that is as it should be. Do not allow misunderstandings, however, to be a result of the interchangeability of model and reality. The construction of mathematical models of reality is a central idea in the study of mathematics. It is important here to see probability theory with mathematical models in mind.

13.3 The Normal Curve

The study of probability must go beyond games of chance. If we stop at this point, we tell only a small part of the story. In our society today, we use the concept of probability to make predictions about demand for products, establish the reliability of rockets in the space program, determine birth and death rates, test the effectiveness of medical discoveries such as the polio vaccine. And this is far from the whole story! Probability theory touches more areas of twentieth century society than students are even briefly aware of. Additional food for thought is presented here.

Although the **normal curve** is familiar to most students, they generally have little understanding of the concept. What student has not been "graded on the curve?" Yet what does this mean? Short of the knowledge that the test scores will all be raised or lowered, how does it work? A specific case, which is an excellent exercise for a statistics class, follows.

▶ A math class of 10 students has the following results on a test:

76   66   62   53   50
48   45   38   35   22

The teacher decides to "curve" the grades. What happens?

One way to proceed is to convert each score to a standard score, z, which is a score given in terms of the standard deviation. In this way, we can then fit each score into one of five categories, which correspond to the grade intervals A, B, C, D, and F shown in Figure 13.3. When completed, this adjustment will convert each number score to a letter grade. The procedures are:

Figure 13.3

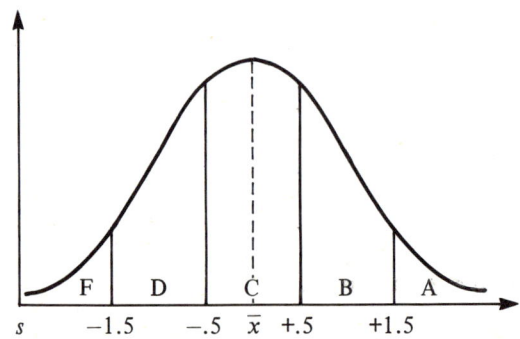

1. Compute the mean, $\bar{x}$.

```
 76
 66
 62
 53        49.5
 50   10 )495.0
 48
 45   Mean, x̄ = 49.5
 38
 35
 22
---
495
```

2. Compute the standard deviations, s.

$76 - 49.5 =26.5 \qquad (26.5)^2 =702.25$
$66 - 49.5 =16.5 \qquad (16.5)^2 =272.25$
$62 - 49.5 =12.5 \qquad (12.5)^2 =156.25$
$53 - 49.5 =3.5 \qquad (3.5)^2 =12.25$
$50 - 49.5 =0.5 \qquad (0.5)^2 =0.25$
$48 - 49.5 =-1.5 \qquad (-1.5)^2 =2.25$
$45 - 49.5 =-4.5 \qquad (-4.5)^2 =20.25$
$38 - 49.5 = -11.5 \qquad (-11.5)^2 =132.25$
$35 - 49.5 = -14.5 \qquad (-14.5)^2 =210.25$
$22 - 49.5 = -27.5 \qquad (-27.5)^2 =756.25$

$$ 2264.50$$

```
     226.45
10 )2264.50              √226.45 = 15.05
```

3. Convert to standard scores, z.

```
76:     26.5 ÷ 15.05 =    1.76
66:     16.5 ÷ 15.05 =    1.10
62:     12.5 ÷ 15.05 =    0.83
53:      3.5 ÷ 15.05 =    0.23
50:       .5 ÷ 15.05 =    0.03
48:    - 1.5 ÷ 15.05 =  - 0.10
45:    - 4.5 ÷ 15.05 =  - 0.30
38:   - 11.5 ÷ 15.05 =  - 0.76
35:   - 14.5 ÷ 15.05 =  - 0.96
22:   - 27.5 ÷ 15.05 =  - 1.83
```

4. Locate letter grade interval for each score (Figure 13.4, see page 214).

5. Resulting conversion:

```
76  A      53  C      45  C      22  F
66  B      50  C      38  D
62  B      48  C      35  D
```

Figure 13.4

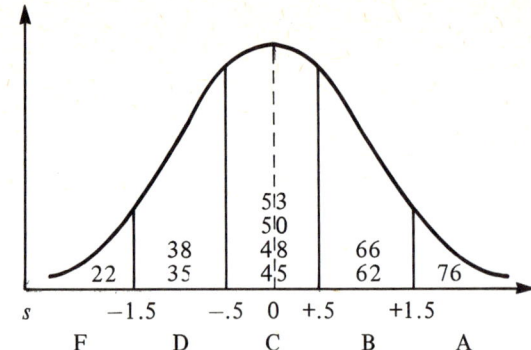

The teacher has "curved" the scores, and has established a letter grade for each score, arranging these scores to fit a normal curve. A quick look at Figure 13.4 shows the symmetical nature of the distribution as the scores are dropped into their slots and measured in standard deviations. This is only one of the ways that grading "on the curve" can be done.

The entire procedure is highly questionable on many counts. An assumption is made that the data are normally distributed. This is seldom the case with the relatively small sample involved in classroom tests. In addition, if a test is too easy, the procedure assures the failure of some student. Conversely, if the test is too hard, someone must still manage to be graded A. This may happen despite the fact that relatively little knowledge has been demonstrated on the test. In the above example, two students received "C" grades (an average score) despite the fact that they knew less than half of the test material. Our concern here, however, is the normal probability curve rather than sound grading techniques. (In Chapter 20 we will discuss grading itself.)

The normal distribution is a powerful statistical tool with many applications. Let's explore this further.

▶   A fair coin is tossed 3 times. What are the expected outcomes? What are the possibilities? Making a tree diagram yields Figure 13.5.

Figure 13.5

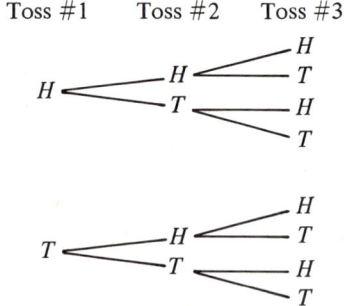

Looking at the last row and following back along the diagram, we find that there are 8 possibilities in our sample space. They are:

```
HHH     HTH     THH     TTH
HHT     HTT     THT     TTT
```

Tallying we get:

3 heads: 1 $P(3) = \frac{1}{8}$

2 heads: 3 $P(2) = \frac{3}{8}$

1 head: 3 $P(1) = \frac{3}{8}$

0 head: 1 $P(0) = \frac{1}{8}$

Do these numbers look familiar? We have seen them in the binomial distribution and in Pascal's triangle. Is it an accident? Let us explore further.

A fair coin in tossed 4 times. What are the expected outcomes? What are the probabilities of tossing heads?

As you expected, there are now 16 events in the sample space, with the probabilities for heads being:

4 heads: 1 $P(4) = \frac{1}{16}$

3 heads: 4 $P(3) = \frac{4}{16}$

2 heads: 6 $P(2) = \frac{6}{16}$

1 head: 4 $P(1) = \frac{4}{16}$

0 head: 1 $P(0) = \frac{1}{16}$

Once again we see the binomial coefficients and another line of the Pascal triangle. Our suspicion is becoming confirmed. Students should be encouraged to try as many additional examples as they wish, to satisfy themselves.

When we graph these events and construct probability histograms, we begin to see why we use the words: normal probability curve (Figure 13.6).

Figure 13.6

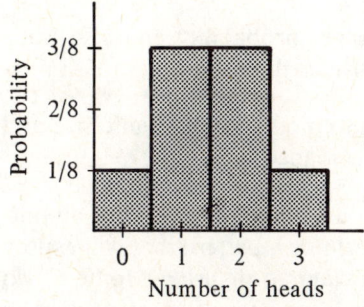
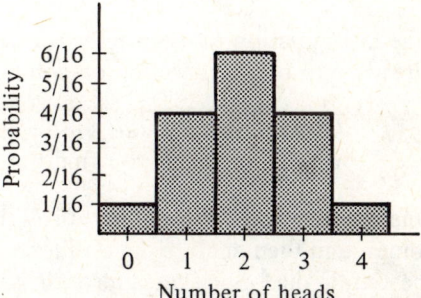

The distribution has a decided "normal" look being symmetrical about the mean. Increasing the number of tosses or even thinking in terms of multiple coin tosssing (i.e., toss ten coins, how many heads?) will continue the pattern briefly illustrated here.

This beginning link between the normal curve and probability may be extended to include a study of:

▶ I.Q. test results, where $\bar{x} = 100$ and $s = 13$. The probability, for example, that an individual drawn at random has a score in a given interval is given by the area under the curve for that interval.

SAT test results, where $\bar{x} = 500$ and $s = 100$.

Hypothesis testing to consider such questions as: Candidate A claims that he will get 65% of the vote in the race for the Senate. If 100 voters are chosen at random and polled, how many must vote for A to test this hypothesis at the 90% level?

The field is unlimited in terms of finding areas of meaningful applications for youngsters. While it is not true that all sets of data related to human beings result in normal distributions, many do. Some of these include the distribution of the heights of men homogenous in racial origin and living under similar conditions, but not women; and an unselected group of children of a certain age taking intelligence tests.

Probability theory plays a larger role in our daily lives than ever before, and it will play an even larger role in the future. Excellent examples of a broad variety of situations in our society that are analyzed and better understood because of probability theory appear in the fine publication edited by Judith M. Tanur and Frederick Mosteller.[3] These cases in point range from predicting the course of disease epidemics, to evaluating a new product, to determining the probability of rain. An unusual supply of applications are available for class use.

The variety and complexity of mathematical skills and ideas that are involved in probability and normal distribution concepts are handsome extra dividends of work in this area. In addition to the basic skills, this work offers practice in the use of signed numbers (positive and negative z-scores), squaring and finding square roots, and elementary concepts of integral calculus as the student seeks the area under the normal curve in a given integral. The opportunities for significant use of mathematical ideas abounds.

13.4 Monte Carlo Methods

One last situation to be briefly considered involves probability and also leads directly into the next section on computers. Consider the following question:

▶ Given four dice, one unfair, of different colors, but the same size and weight, how can you find the one that is loaded?

One way to proceed would be to roll the dice a number of times, record all outcomes, and then analyze the results to try to determine a pattern that will expose the unfair die.[4] Such an approach is a simple example of using Monte Carlo methods. This method was devised to enable mathematicians and scientists who are studying very complex phenomena to represent that phenomena with a game of chance. Playing the game many times (using computers), information is gathered and analyzed. These data offer insights and knowledge about the original phenomenon. The loaded die problem is one such example. The dice need not be physically thrown since directions for "throwing" the dice by computer can be written and results of thousands of "tosses" recorded in a matter of minutes.

Monte Carlo methods illustrate the application of probabilistic empirical methods to gain solutions to nonprobabilistic problems. Thus the range of applications to which probability theory may be applied is enhanced markedly. For our purpose here, suffice it to say that mathematical models are created and programmed into computers. We can then gain information about problems that may otherwise be too complex to do. In this case the field of probability theory becomes the tool for establishing and analyzing the model. A good example of this is presented by George A. W. Boehm.[5] He gives a brief account of how nuclear physicists used Monte Carlo methods to determine what proportion of subatomic particles would be screened out by a new shielding material, what proportion would be absorbed, and what proportion would be allowed to pass through. Since the experiment involved radioactive particles, a good deal of danger as well as complex and lengthy work was avoided by simulating the problem using probability theory. The computer comes into play when it is necessary to examine repeated trials. The saving in time is inestimable.

Computers 13.5

Hardly a facet of modern (and sometimes ancient) life has not been reviewed and possibly altered by the capability provided man through the use of the computer. The roles that computers take seem to be limited only by man's ability to write the necessary program. Whether it is in industry, in education, in government, or in retail sales, the computer has been responsible for vast reorganizations.

In education, the part being played by the computer is truly a ubiquitous one. We find the computer involved in construction and reconstruction of curriculum as well as in attempts to develop methods more responsive to students. We have seen the computer used to provide individualized practice of skills previously learned, a form of CAI (Computer Assisted Instruction); it is also used to provide initial instruction itself, a form of CII (Computer Initiated Instruction), in addition to any number of mixtures in between. The legacy of the computer is a lively subject for debate between mathematics teachers and other educators. Almost an entire issue of *The Mathematics Teacher* was recently devoted to an examination of the role of the computer.[6]

All of our students have heard about computers. Indeed many of them are now using electronic hand calculators, many bills are calculated and printed by computers, from credit cards to book clubs, and, in many instances, paychecks are also printed out by them. In short, we live in a society computerized to such a degree that we are often concerned about being dehumanized in our headlong rush to improve the quality of life. Many of these seemingly esoteric concerns have direct application to our mathematics classrooms, which each person must consider.

We have already seen part of the role computers can play in the discussion of probability, especially Monte Carlo methods, and in the previous section on mathematical model construction. Let us look briefly at the computer itself to determine how it may assist teachers and students of mathematics.

Numeration Systems and Computers

Computer use has a role to play in elementary work and in advanced work. Here is a case in point. One of the "new" topics highlighted by recent curriculum changes has been the study of numeration systems with bases other than 10. Why shall we bother students with these numeration systems when all their lives students will probably only compute with decimal numbers? The question is not as easily answered as it may appear. A great deal will depend upon the way concepts are developed in class. The reasons for wanting to introduce these concepts at all relate to the important characteristics of our decimal system: It is a place-value system utilizing only nine figures and zero. The base, of course, is 10. Can we help our students appreciate the place-value system when they work with it without thinking?

In order to sharpen their awareness, let us thrust them into a strange, new system, but one that has all the important qualities of the decimal system. To find such a parallel system, all we have to do is change the base. Everything will operate like the decimal system except that the base will be different. Correspondingly, the number of figures used will diminish or increase; i.e., if we decide upon base 5, we shall only need the numerals 1, 2, 3, 4, and zero. One rationale for including the concepts in the school program is to aid understanding of our decimal system. There is also the concomitant aim of helping students learn a bit about the numeration system used in many computers, the binary system. Howard Fehr considered this goal and concluded that ". . . to educate elementary school children as though everyone would become a computer programmer is nonsense."[7] This condition would not seem to have suddenly changed at the secondary school level.

Does this mean that we are better off forgetting about introducing such concepts? Not entirely. Earlier it was mentioned that much would depend upon the way in which the concepts are taught to students. This is the crucial point. Z. P. Dienes, the English mathematician and psychologist, has developed what he refers to as "multibase blocks."[8] These are wooden blocks made up in a variety of bases. They consist of cubes that are scored in accord with the base: A base cube 9 would be scored so that it demonstrates nine squares on every face. Smaller pieces complete the set for each base and are constructed so that students may build up the larger cube with the pieces. The point of it all is that the students have concrete representations of the different numeration systems. These together with the games devised by Dienes provide the student with experiences that are important to understanding the significant ideas of the base system. He has children begin using these different systems early enough and in a way that helps them to naturally learn about each of them. Later they turn their attention to the one system that is used thoughout society. From this point on, they concentrate on becoming proficient with the decimal system.

This kind of experience seems to make a good deal of sense. It involves the sorely needed concrete experiences and works gradually toward the abstractions. Shall we teach different base numeration systems? If it is taught in this manner and at the early elementary grades the answer is yes. Otherwise, it would be advisable to limit the work to some simple translations from one base to another and let it go at that, with the possible inclusion of some simple addition and multiplication examples. The chief purpose would be to clarify the decimal system.

The binary numbers hold a special appeal in light of the role of computers in society today. The reason for using binary numbers in digital computers (i.e., computers used for counting like your fingers—as opposed to analogue computers used for measuring, like a slide rule) is the use of electrical current. Either there is a current or there is not; the light is either on or off. To represent numbers with these lights and currents we must use but two figures to match the two states of the computers. We could use a large number of bulbs to set up as many different columns as we feel we may need, but each light can be either on or off; hence, it can represent only two possible figures. Our familiar decimal system is a place-value system, and that is good. But the base is 10, which requires the use of nine figures and zero, and that is bad. Is there a system that is a place-value system that requires the use of only two symbols? The binary system fills the bill perfectly. It is a place-value system employing only the numerals 1 and 0 to write all possible numbers (Figure 13.7). This is the key to the high-speed electronic

Figure 13.7

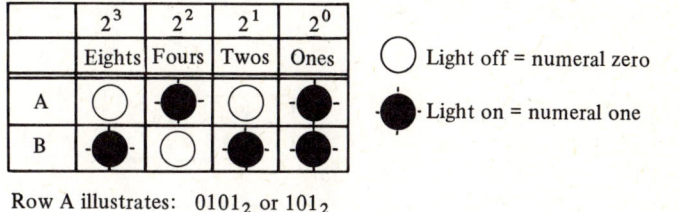

Row A illustrates: 0101_2 or 101_2
$(0 \times 8) + (1 \times 4) + (0 \times 2) + (1 \times 1) = 4 + 1 = 5_{10}$

Row B illustrates: 1011_2
$(1 \times 8) + (0 \times 4) + (1 \times 2) + (1 \times 1) = 8 + 2 + 1 = 11_{10}$

computer. It is possible for students to send word messages through the binary computer by assigning numbers to the letters and then translating these numbers into binary notation. When the computer responses are recorded and translated into binary numbers, the students must then decipher the number code back into letters (Figure 13.8). In this way a good deal of interesting practice is painlessly carried out at the same time that the students gain insight into the role played by the binary system in computer operation. If interest warrants, the instructions given to a computer, "the program," can also be attempted in some simple

Figure 13.8 *The binary numeration system.*

Code:

Base 10 Numeral	1	2	3	4	5	6	7	8	9	10	11	12	13	...
Letter	A	B	C	D	E	F	G	H	I	J	K	L	M	...

● Light on = 1
○ Light off = 0 } in base 2

					Base 2 Numeral	Equivalent Base 10 Numeral	Corresponding Letter
○	●	○	○	○	1st Letter →	1000	8	H
○	○	●	○	●	2nd Letter →	101	5	
○	●	●	○		3rd Letter →	1100		
●	○	○	○		4th Letter →	10000		

situations. The sharply detailed instructions required by a program offer the student an excellent opportunity to test his understanding of basic processes (Figure 13.9). As he attempts to write a program for the addition of whole numbers, or perhaps the division of two decimal fractions, he must call upon all his understandings of the particular process. There is no stigma attached to this work no matter what the level, since it is the instructions for a computer. In fact, it may well be of value to pair a student with a lower-grade student who is attempting to learn the very process for which the upper grader has constructed a program. One way to learn is to teach.

Figure 13.9 A program for addition.

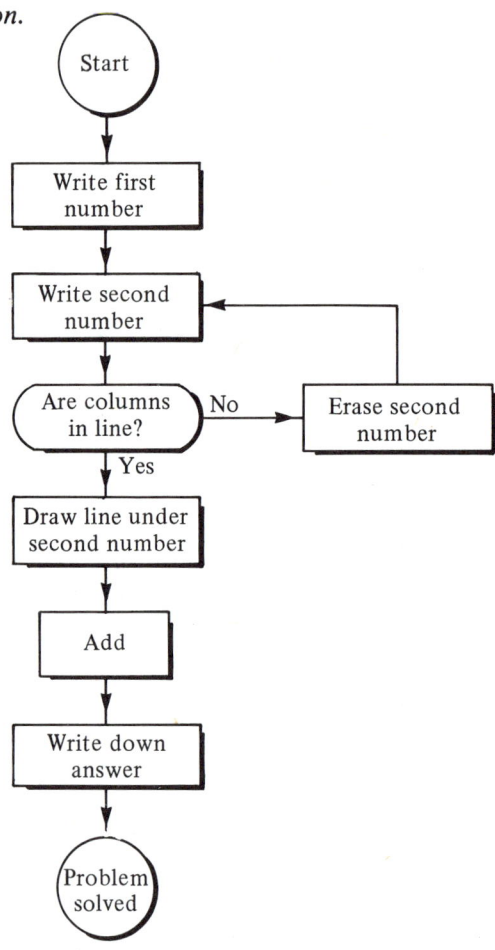

While the basic problem presented offers one end of the mathematical scale for computer application, there are many others. The approximation of values through repetitive processes, which would quickly tire out the human mind and hand, is accomplished quickly by the computer.[9] Approximations of areas under a curve (the integral calculus) are easily accomplished using probability theory (as mentioned earlier); also easily done are physical problems involving rates of change of velocity, time, and distance; and growth rates of populations, to mention a few.

Many schools have computer terminals which are used in a variety of ways. If programming techniques are taught to a few students, they may easily become responsible for teaching other students how to "talk" to the computer. The burden of requiring a teachers' time at the terminal is minimized and the entire experience creates confidence and interest in mathematics. It is not unusual to find students with little previous success in mathematics becoming teachers of programming as they suddenly "find" themselves on the computer. This could have some implications for helping the underachiever. Many school problems such as teacher and class scheduling are consigned to the school computer, offering students real and interesting problems. The positive feelings that develop about mathematics is handsome payoff indeed.

Finally, these activities help give students an awareness of the real nature of computers. A computer can only do what we program it to do. Used in a positive fashion, we accrue positive results from the computer. Not the least important of these results is additional insight into the role of mathematics in our society.

Footnotes

1. *The Midlands Mathematics Experiment.* "O" Level, Book II. London: George G. Harrap & Co., 1964, p. 152.
2. Warren Weaver. *Lady Luck: The Theory of Probability.* New York: Doubleday, 1963, p. 60.
3. Judith M. Tanur, Frederick Mosteller, et al., eds. *Statistics: A Guide to the Unknown.* San Francisco: Holden-Day, 1972.
4. Herbert Fremont and William Blossfield. "Roll the Dice," *Dyna-Math.* New York: MacMillan, 1975.
5. George A. W. Boehm and the Editors of *Fortune. The New World of Math.* New York: Dial Press, 1959, pp. 80-81.
6. *The Mathematics Teacher.* Vol. 66 (January 1973).
7. Howard Fehr. "Sense and Nonsense in a Modern School Mathematics Program," *The Arithmetic Teacher.* Vol. 13 (February 1966), p. 84.
8. Z. P. Dienes. *Building Up Mathematics.* Atalntic Highlands, N.J.: Humanities Press, 1960, pp. 55-74.
9. For interesting examples of this, see:

    Richard Johnsonbaugh. "Application of Calculators and Computers to Limits," *The Mathematics Teacher.* Vol. 69 (January 1976), pp. 60-65.

    Joseph Cieply and J. Kevin McCoy. "Reel-Eee . . ." *The Mathematics Teacher.* Vol. 69 (April 1976), pp. 268-270.

    Thomas W. Smithson. "An Eulerian Development for π: A Research Project for High School Students," *The Mathematics Teacher.* Vol. 63 (November 1970), pp. 597-608.

For Investigation and Discussion

1. Compile a list of common uses of probability found in today's society. You may draw examples from a variety of sources such as professional journals, television, radio, and newspapers.

2. Devise a plan for the experimental determination of the probabilities of the tossing of a thumb tack. Compare the position of tack point upward with tack point facing downward.

3. A coin is tossed 8 times, turning up heads each time. Some students say "The next toss must be tails. It's the law of averages." Explain how you would respond to this statement. Consider questions or activities you could present to students to enable them to better understand the nature of probability.

4. Explain how you would make use of student constructed spinners to begin a unit on probability. Select three possible topics as the subject of the spinner.

5. Construct an outline of a series of lessons, which show students how to discover the ways in which coin-tossing, the binomial theorem, and Pascal's triangle are related.

6. Monte Carlo methods are employed in the section on probability. What are these methods; how did they get their name? Name one specific problem in which Monte Carlo methods may be used other than the one given in this text.

7. Our students will need to compute only with a base 10 system when they leave school. Why should or shouldn't we teach systems with bases other than 10?

8. Plan a lesson whose objective is to clarify why a binary system is important to electronic computers.

9. Select one topic from the secondary school curriculum and show how flowcharting may help develop student mastery of the topic you have selected.

10. Read one of the articles listed under footnote 9 and demonstrate in specific terms how the computer has enlarged our problem solving ability.

11. Read the two articles in the references by William F. Atcheson and E. Glenadine Gibb respectively, that appear in the January 1973 issue of *The Mathematics Teacher*. Compare the points of view presented. State which you agree with and give your reasons.

For Further Reading

Books

Johnson, Donovan. *Probability and Chance.* Exploring Mathematics on Your Own Series. New York: McGraw-Hill, 1963.

Kac, Mark. "Probability," *The Mathematical Sciences.* Committee on Support of Research in the Mathematical Sciences (COSRIMS) and George A. W. Boehm, ed. Cambridge: M.I.T. Press, 1969, pp. 232–251.

Levinson, Horace C. *Chance, Luck and Statistics.* New York: Dover Publications, 1963.

Weaver, Warren. *Lady Luck: The Theory of Probability.* New York: Doubleday, 1963.

Periodicals

Archer, J. Andrew. "The Odds Meet the Great Martingale," *The Mathematics Teacher.* Vol. 69 (March 1976), pp. 234–240.

Buxton, R. "Probability and Its Measurement," *Mathematics Teaching.* No. 49 (Winter 1969), pp. 4–12.

Loase, John Frederick. "Extrasensory Probability," *The Mathematics Teacher.* Vol. 69 (February 1976), pp. 116–118.

Litwhiller, Bonnie H. and David R. Duncan. "Poker Probabilities: A New SettiPg," *The Mathematics Teache 116*–118.

Litwhiller, Bonnie H. and David R. Duncan. "Poker Probabilities: A New Setting," *The Mathematics Teacher.* Vol. 70 (December 1977), pp. 766–771.

Ogborn, Jon. "How the Normal Distribution Got Its Hump," *Mathematics Teaching.* Vol. 66 (March 1974), pp. 53–55.

Polya, George. "Probabilities in Proof Reading," *The American Mathematical Monthly.* Vol. 83 (January 1976) p. 42.

Sherlock, Alan. "New Techniques in Logic and Probability," *Mathematics Teaching.* Vol. 67 (June 1974), pp. 52–56.

Simon, Julian and Allen Holmes. "A Really New Way to Teach Probability-Statistics," *The Mathematics Teacher.* Vol. 62 (April 1969), pp. 283–291.

Tanis, Elliot A. "A Statistical Hypothesis Test for the Classroom," *The Mathematics Teacher.* Vol. 66 (November 1973), pp. 657–658.

For Further Reading on Computers

Books

Albrecht, Robert L.; William F. Atchison; et al. "The Role of Electronic Computers and Calculators," *Instructional Aids in Mathematics.* 34th Yearbook. Reston, Va.: National Council of Teachers of Mathematics, 1973, pp. 153–201.

Conference Board of the Mathematical Sciences. Committee on Computer Education. *Recommendations Regarding Computers in High School Education.* April 1972.

Heimer, R. T. ed. *Computer Assisted Instruction and the Teaching of Mathematics.* Reston, Va.: National Council of Teachers of Mathematics, 1969.

Periodicals

Atchison, William F. "The Impact of Computer Science Education on the Curriculum," *The Mathematics Teacher.* Vol. 66 (January 1973), pp. 7 and ff.

Gibb, E. Glenadine. "The Computer—A Facilitator in Management and Instruction," *The Mathematics Teacher.* Vol. 66 (January 1973), pp. 6 and ff.

LaFrenz, Dale E. and Thomas E. Kieren. "Computers for All Students: A New Philosophy of Computer Use," *School Science and Mathematics.* Vol. 69 (January 1969), pp. 39–41.

Hughes, Helen S. "Gauss, Computer Assisted," *The Mathematics Teacher.* Vol. 64 (February 1971), pp. 155–166.

Morrow, Lorna J. "Flow Charts for Equation Solving and Maintenance of Skills," *The Mathematics Teacher.* Vol. 66 (October 1973), pp. 499–506.

"This is How Computers Work," *Changing Times.* The Kiplinger Magazine. (November, 1968), pp. 41–45.

SECTION IV

Mathematics: An Abstract System

CHAPTER 14

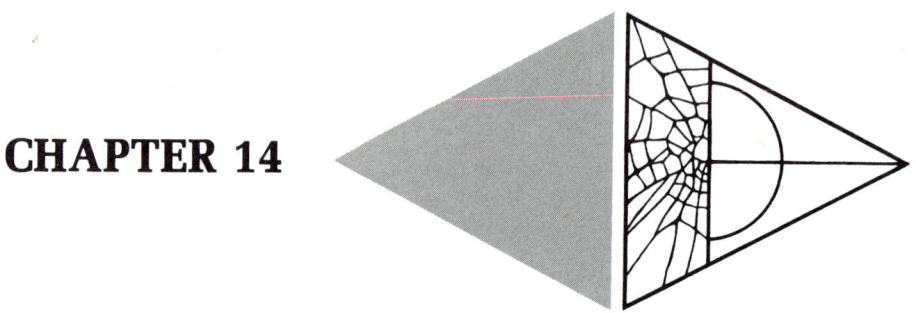

Abstraction is Power

Although this text emphasizes the vital role of mathematics in science and society, we will not neglect the abstract nature of mathematics. If students are to gain facility with mathematics, they must learn to master abstract concepts and skills. The confusion of students who try to compensate for lack of understanding through memorization of ideas is well known to most teachers. But what alternative do most students have? Abstractions are often thrust upon them without collections of experiences that encourage the development of mental images for the ideas. Students then attempt to memorize mathematics in self defense; survival becomes an overriding issue.

Mathematics is one grand abstraction. It is this quality that results in tremendous power to deal with problems from a multitude of physical and conceptual situations. This point was emphasized repeatedly in the previous chapter as we considered the nature and use of mathematical models. Let us look at some specific examples.

14.1 Flips to Groups

Here is an interesting activity for students:

▶ Take a blank index card. Place it on an empty sheet of paper and trace around it. Make a little square in the upper right-hand corner of both the index card and the rectangle you just traced and shade it in. On the back of the index card, make another little square on the very same corner. But this time do not shade it in so that you will know that this is the back of the card. (See Figure 14.1.) How many different ways can you move the card so that it fits exactly into its outline on the paper? Try it.

Figure 14.1

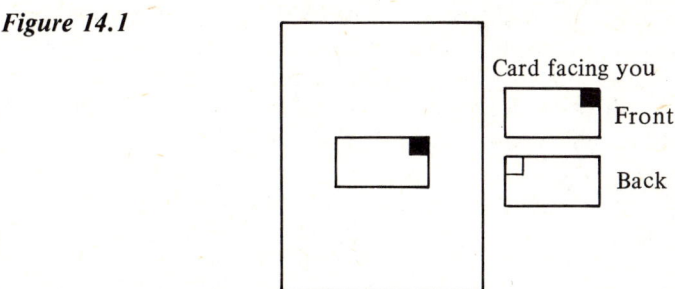

This simple problem in its own way demonstrates the complete abstractness of mathematics. It shows the way in which working with abstractions enables you to blend together many mathematical concepts to form a unified whole. Let us take it one step at a time.

Did you figure out the moves? It seems that there are three moves and one significant failure to move which gives four moves in all. They are:

1. Flip the card over about a horizontal axis (Figure 14.2). Call this move X.

    Figure 14.2

    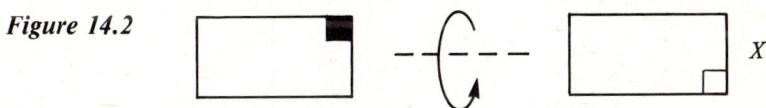

2. Flip the card over about a vertical axis (Figure 14.3). Call this move Y.

    Figure 14.3

3. Rotate the card around a point in the center, 180° (Figure 14.4). Call this move R.

    Figure 14.4

    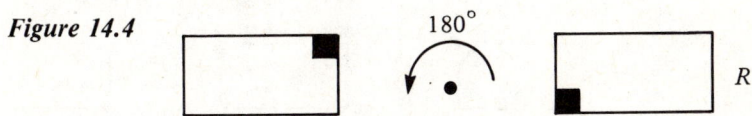

4. Leave it alone (Figure 14.5). Call this "move" I.

    Figure 14.5

Each of these moves leaves the card in a position to "fit" into the original tracing. There are no other moves that will do so except for these four or some combination of them. Let students take as much time as they need to verify this before going on. It is a difficult idea for students to see.

When the four moves or flips have been clarified, we may then consider what might happen if we carried out two of the transformations consecutively. Will we find new resulting positions not found earlier, or do we have them all? Will some results of two flips be equivalent to single moves? To keep track of what happens, write your results in tabular form. The first transformation is at the top and the second listed down the side. The results of the individual transformations and the table are shown in Figure 14.6.

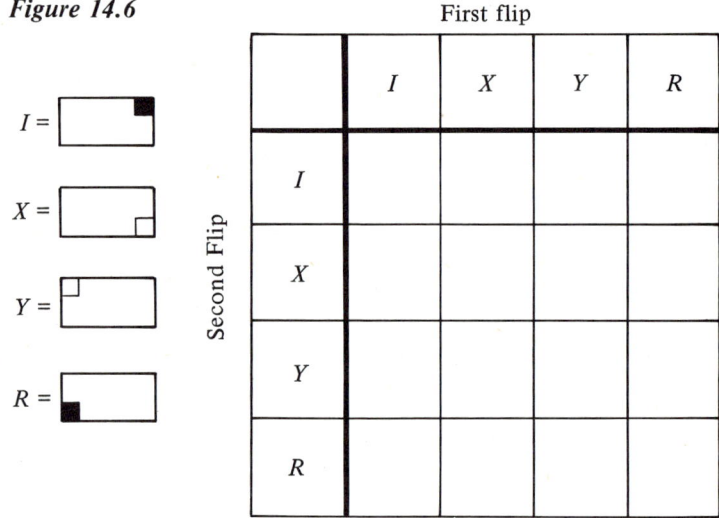

Figure 14.6

You may want to apply the transformations and record the results in your table. There are several operations illustrated in Figure 14.7. The completed table is presented in Figure 14.8.

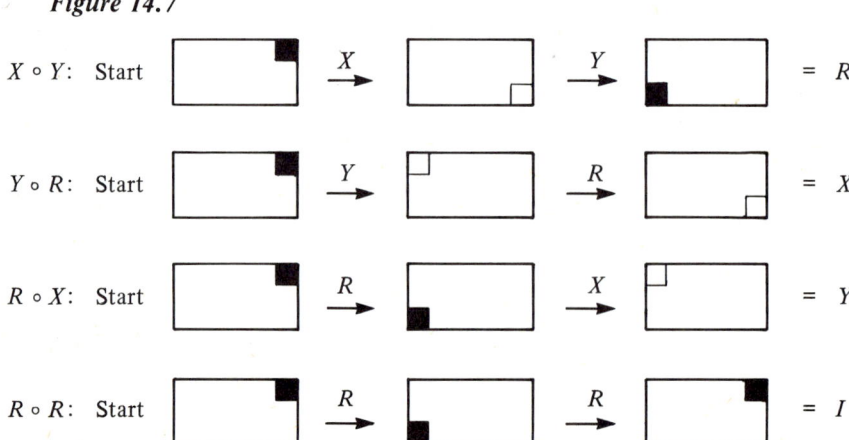

Figure 14.7

Figure 14.8

∘	I	X	Y	R
I	I	X	Y	R
X	X	I	R	Y
Y	Y	R	I	X
R	R	Y	X	I

Not only does every combination of two transformations yield one of the original transformations, but any combination of two of the three flips X, Y, R gives the third. Looking at Figure 14.8, students may find all sorts of relationships:

The system is commutative.

It has an identity element.

Each element has a unique inverse, itself.

These are some of the ideas that are noticed. More importantly, the properties of a group are satisfied, which enables us to point out an important mathematical structure. The properties in question that define a group are:

A group is a set of elements $a, b, \ldots$ which can be combined by an operation ∘ such that:

1. The result $a \circ b$ is a number of the set: closure property.
2. $(a \circ b) \circ c = a \circ (b \circ c)$ for any elements of the set: associative property.
3. $I \circ a = a \circ I = a$ for every element a in the group: identity property.
4. $a \circ \bar{a} = \bar{a} \circ a = I$ for every element a, there is a unique inverse $\bar{a}$.

It would be of value to ask students to verify the associative property of this operation.

The identification of a group is done intentionally. Whatever your priorities, the importance of the work done so far is to offer a concrete action (flipping index cards). From this, students gain an appreciation of an abstract mathematical structure, a group.

If student interest is high, add experiences by asking students to construct the group resulting from other figures: an equilateral triangle or a square would be interesting alternatives. Upon completion of this work, point out that the transformations are called linear transformations since each of them can be described with linear equations. There were only two kinds of transformations in finding the group of the rectangle:

Reflection, which was done about an axis, operations *X* and *Y*.

Rotation, which was done for 180° around a fixed point, operation *R*.

The transformations of translation, expansion, and shearing, also linear transformations, were not a part of the example used.

To illustrate the connection between the reflections, rotations and linear equations, think of a point in the Cartesian plane, *P*. If we apply the transformation *X*, reflection about the horizontal *x*-axis, *P* becomes *P'* as shown in Figure 14.9. Looking at the change in coordinates, we see that the *x*-coordinate has remained the same but the *y*-coordinate has become the negative of what it was at *P*. We can describe these changes as

$$X \begin{cases} x' = x \\ y' = -y \end{cases}$$

which are two linear equations. The equations describing the transformation, shown in Figure 14.10, about the vertical axis are

$$Y \begin{cases} x' = -x \\ y' = y \end{cases}$$

Figure 14.9

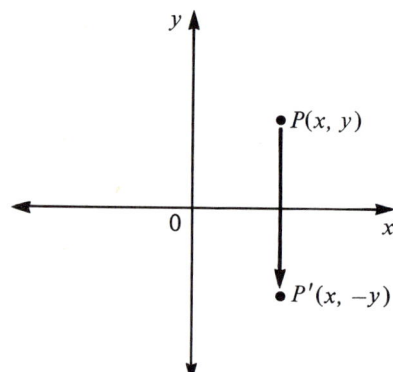

Figure 14.10

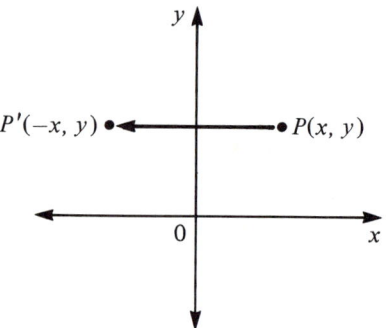

As for the transformation of a rotation about the origin of 180°, the equations for this operation are

$$R \begin{cases} x' = -x \\ y' = -y \end{cases}$$

This is illustrated in Figure 14.11.

Figure 14.11

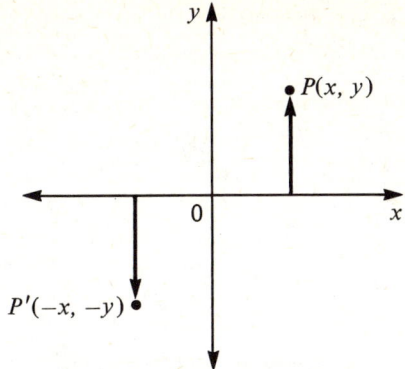

We have taken reflection and rotation and converted them into algebraic equations. Geometry and algebra are brought together. Our simple problem of fitting a rectangle into a slot is becoming more interesting as we go.

Matrices

Once we have expressed the operations as linear equations, we may represent them as a matrix. The standard form of the linear equation:

$$x' = ax + by$$
$$y' = cx + dy$$

may be used for the transformation equations. In this form, we can easily convert the equations to the matrix notation using coefficients a, b, c, d. They are usually written in the matrix in the same positions they had in the equations. The two equations above become

$$\begin{matrix} a & b \\ c & d \end{matrix}$$

The matrix is a kind of code or shorthand notation for the equations. To translate the equations of transformation into a matrix be sure to account for any terms that might be missing in the standard form. Here is how these equations would look:

$$X \begin{cases} x' = x \\ y' = -y \end{cases} \text{ or } \begin{matrix} x' = & 1 \cdot x + 0 \cdot y \\ y' = & 0 \cdot x - 1 \cdot y \end{matrix} \quad X = \begin{bmatrix} 1 & 0 \\ 0 & -1 \end{bmatrix}$$

$$Y \begin{cases} x' = -x \\ y' = y \end{cases} \text{ or } \begin{matrix} x' = & -1 \cdot x + 0 \cdot y \\ y' = & 0 \cdot x + 1 \cdot y \end{matrix} \quad Y = \begin{bmatrix} -1 & 0 \\ 0 & 1 \end{bmatrix}$$

$$R \begin{cases} x' = -x \\ y' = -y \end{cases} \text{ or } \begin{matrix} x' = & -1 \cdot x + 0 \cdot y \\ y' = & 0 \cdot x - 1 \cdot y \end{matrix} \quad R = \begin{bmatrix} -1 & 0 \\ 0 & -1 \end{bmatrix}$$

Each of the transformations has thus been expressed in matrix notation, a short, more compact way to express the same mathematical information. Of course, the equations that were used apply to the specific situation under consideration. For example, if we were to attempt to find a general equation for rotations of the angle θ, the matrix would look rather different since the equation of transformation would also change. This might be an interesting exercise for students:

▶ Determine the equation for a rotation about the origin of an angle β in the coordinate plane. Then express this equation as a matrix.

In our journey through abstractions, we have flipped an index card, determined the group of the rectangle, expressed the equations of transformation, and arrived at the equivalent matrix notation. Quite a journey! It is typical of the nature of mathematics that the importance lies more in the journey than in the individual signposts or the final destination. We hope that students will gain a feel for and an appreciation of how working with abstractions enables ideas to grow. Our concern at this point is not to emphasize the structural properties of the group, the ideas of transformational geometry, or the study of matrix algebra. Instead our emphasis is on the interrelatedness of mathematical ideas and the power we gain through dealing with abstractions. A return to the real world may be made by pointing out some of the many applications of matrix algebra, which includes stress and strain in building construction, electrical and magnetic forces, and aerodynamics.[1]

14.2 Transformations and Living Things

The role of transformational geometry in the study of the shapes of living things may also be pursued. There is some fascinating material in this area in the excellent book by Sir D'Arcy Thompson.[2] The transformation of living forms also helps connect mathematics and reality in the classroom. For example, consider the following:

▶ Using only the first quadrant of the Cartesian plane, draw the picture resulting from plotting these points and connecting them up in order.
1. (0, 3) *2.* (1, 6) *3.* (3, 6) *4.* (4, 4)
5. (6, 5) *6.* (6, 1) *7.* (4, 2) *8.* (3, 0)
9. (1, 0) *10.* (0, 3)

This is a favorite exercise of many teachers, which offers interesting practice plotting points in the plane. The resulting figure is a fish (species unknown and an eye added for realism) shown in Figure 14.12. Now what would happen to the fish if we plot the same points but alter the angle between the x and y-axes so that the angles formed a 45° angle rather than the usual 90° angle?

Figure 14.12

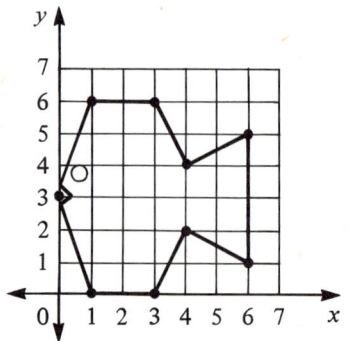

Ask the students to guess and then draw these new axes and plot the points a second time. The easiest way to draw the axes is to use graph paper. Leave the *x*-axis as it is but draw diagonals through the squares on the graph paper to establish the *y*-axis. The finished product is Figure 14.13.

Figure 14.13

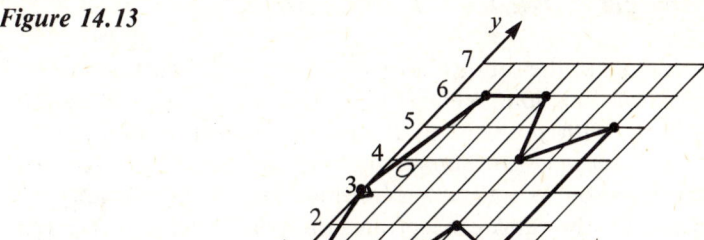

The result is another fish, similar to the first but different because of the transformation that has taken place. This transformation is called shearing and is another of the linear transformations mentioned earlier.

Students may try to find the equation of transformation. The real surprise in all of this is that nature has carried out these very same transformations, providing different members of the same species. Nature must have been a geometer! We seem to be harking back to the Greeks. Whatever path we take we so often find that we are back in some familiar place. This cyclical nature of the ideas and abstractions of mathematics add to its wonder and its power. We open up the world of mathematics to our youngsters by sharing these ideas with them.

The simple exercise in graphing above unites algebra and geometry. At the same time, it offers students the opportunity to plot points, to carry out transformations, and to use algebra to describe the operation. Although the work was highly abstract, it closely related to a fascinating part of the real world since the process of transformation added to our knowledge of living things. Here are some additional problems.

1. Show how the fish in Figure 14.12 would change if the axes formed a 60° angle.

2. Using Figure 14.12 as the original, keep the axes the same. Then find the new coordinates and draw the fish resulting from the following transformation: Describe the effect in each case.

Translation: $(x, y) \rightarrow (x + 5, y + 5)$
Reflection: $(x, y) \rightarrow (-x, y)$
Dilation: $(x, y) \rightarrow (2x, y)$

3. Make your own drawing on the coordinate axes of a simple figure. List the coordinates of each point and perform the transformations listed in the previous exercise.

We have focused on the purely abstract side of mathematics in order to round out the picture of mathematics being presented to the students. In doing this, we have come full circle and seen how the abstractions can add to our understanding of the real world.

14.3 Trigonometry: Ratios or Functions?

Another example of the subtle nature of mathematical abstraction is the concept of trigonometric function. When students are introduced to trigonometry, they generally begin with problems that involve indirect measures of inaccessible heights or distances in elementary algebra classes. This approach offers practice in equation solution as well as an introduction to trigonometry. The work is usually based on the ratio concept and the relationships of the right triangle. Generally, the work is grounded in physical problems and is of a concrete nature.

When students encounter trigonometry again, on the tenth or eleventh grade level, suddenly the familiar ratios are applied to all triangles not just right triangles. Even more startling, the ratios are described as trigonometric functions and not as ratios at all. So where the student was comparing the lengths of sides of a right triangle, now he is transported into a total abstraction as he is confronted with another kind of mathematical function. The transition from ratio to function takes place abruptly; the student is thrust into a virtually new area with a minimum of preparation.

To help students understand what is taking place and to reenforce earlier understandings, we ask them to carry out the following exercise:

▶

> Instead of ratio, let us think of the trigonometric relationships in terms of coordinates. To accomplish this, work on millimeter paper, using a scale that will allow for accuracy to the hundredths place.
>
> First, draw the unit circle on an appropriate set of axes in the *xy*-plane with the center O at the origin.
>
> Then, draw an angle less than 90° with a vertex at the center of the circle, and a perpendicular dropped to the *x*-axis from the point of intersection of the terminal side of the angle and the circle.

We have formed a right triangle, $\triangle OAB$ with a right angle at B (Figure 14.14). The angle at the circle center (the origin) will be the reference angle, θ. Using the ratio idea of elementary algebra, describe the trigonometric ratios of $\triangle OAB$.

What have you accomplished? The sides of this triangle may be expressed in terms of their distances from the coordinate axes, so that $OA = 1$, $OB = x$, $AB = y$. The trigonometric ratios become:

$$\sin \theta = \frac{y}{1} \quad \text{or} \quad y = \sin \theta$$

$$\cos \theta = \frac{x}{1} \quad \text{or} \quad x = \cos \theta$$

$$\tan \theta = \frac{y}{x}$$

Many different relationships may be derived by the students from this rather simple beginning. Most important for our purposes here is that the sin θ

Figure 14.14

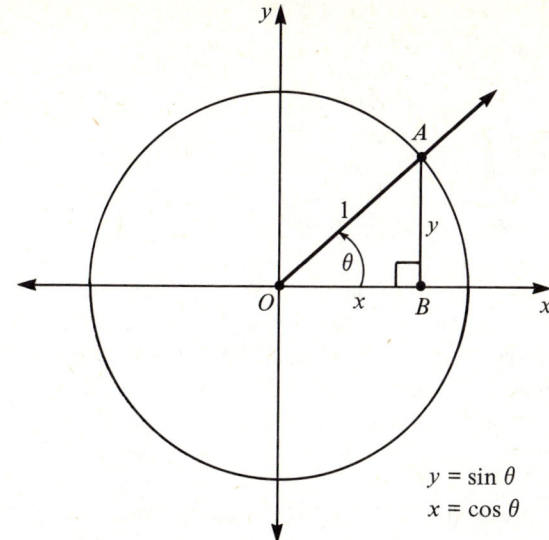

$y = \sin \theta$
$x = \cos \theta$

and cos θ are expressed in terms of coordinates, y and x respectively. This enables us to read the values of these functions directly from the graph with remarkable accuracy simply by measuring line lengths. For example, the graph that shows θ = 30° is pictured in Figure 14.15. Looking at △OAB and the coordinates of point A, we find that A has coordinates estimated to be (.86, .51). This gives:

$y = .51$ or $\sin \theta = .51$
$x = .86$ or $\cos \theta = .86$

Figure 14.15

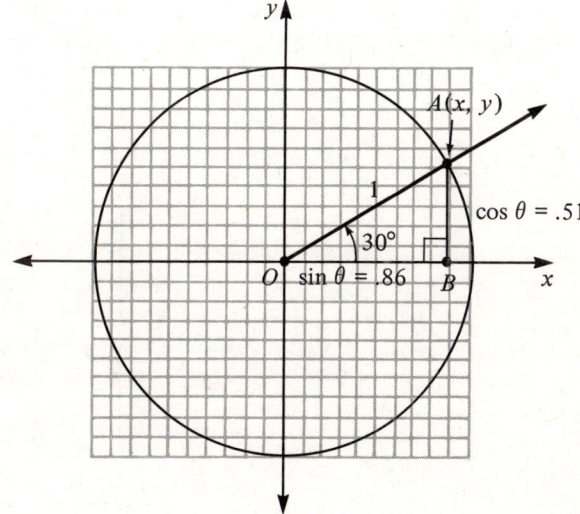

We have found the sine and cosine by simply looking at the coordinates of point A. As the angle gets larger or smaller, we will continue to focus on the intersection of the terminal angle side and the unit circle, which indicates the values of the trigonometric ratios. You may try other angles and check the results using a trigonometry table. The accuracy will surprise you. At the start, limit the values of the angle to $0° \leq \theta \leq 90°$.

Many things have been accomplished. For one, we enable students to build their own trigonometry tables. Their understanding of the values found in printed trigonometry tables is enhanced considerably. These tables do not contain mysterious numbers but give changing line lengths, which vary as the angle varies. This, in itself, is a good intuitive idea that connects ratios with the concept of function. For every θ, we find one and only one cosine and sine value. Hence we reenforce students' concept of function, and the transition from ratio to function begins in an intuitive way based on a picture of the coordinate plane.

But that is not all. We also lay the ground work for the transition from the angles of right triangles to the angles of any triangle. In this way, we extend our concepts into greater abstraction and into greater utility. (An increase in abstraction is not necessarily equated with getting further from reality.) Before we look at angles greater than $90°$ or less than $0°$, let us consider the tangent function.

We have found the sine and cosine by examining the coordinates of point A. Where is the tangent? Can we find some line length that will represent this value? We know we can determine the tangent value from the basic relationship:

$$\tan \theta = \frac{\sin \theta}{\cos \theta} \quad \text{or} \quad \tan \theta = \frac{y}{x}$$

The tangent is therefore found by dividing, but can we find it directly from the graph? The name itself is a clue. Perhaps we can find the tangent using the intersection of the terminal side of the angle and a line that is *tangent* to the unit circle. It's worth a try.

▶ We ask the students to draw tangents to the unit circle in two interesting places on the right side of our graph: through the intersection point of the unit circle and *x*-axis parallel to the *y*-axis, or through the intersection with the *y*-axis parallel to the *x*-axis (Figure 14.16).

Figure 14.16

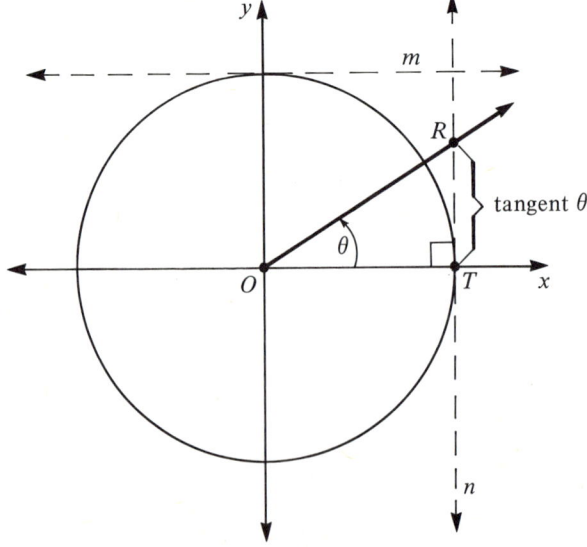

Of course, there are any number of tangent lines that may be drawn, but let us look at these for a start. The tangent lines are designated lines n and m. Since line n is parallel to the y-axis, all points on it have an x-coordinate of unit size 1. Take an angle in the first quadrant, θ, and extend its terminal side until it intersects line n, which is the tangent. We find that the tangent ratio will be described by

$$\tan \theta = \frac{RT}{OT} \quad \text{or} \quad \tan \theta = \frac{RT}{1} = RT$$

The length of the segment of the tangent cut off by the terminal side of the angle gives the tangent ratio. We now have a line segment for the tangent.

The geometric idea of tangent blends with the trigonometric idea as students complete the identification of the sine, cosine, and tangent with line segments in the coordinate plane. Following the earlier discussion, the students move easily from tangent ratio to tangent function. They proceed to identify several values of the tangent function from the graph, using familiar and unfamiliar angles, and checking the results against the table values (Figure 14.17). We can readily extend the work to include angles greater than 90°. We also minimize problems determining the correct sign of values in each quadrant when this approach is utilized. Figure 14.18, on page 236, illustrates how different values and their signs are determined in the other three quadrants.

Figure 14.17

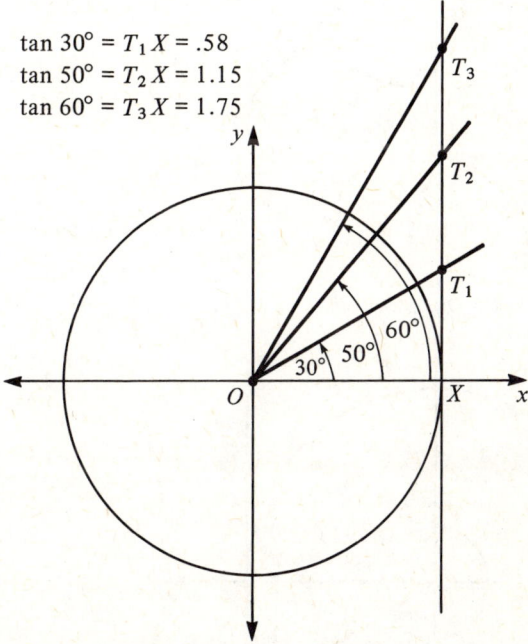

$\tan 30° = T_1 X = .58$
$\tan 50° = T_2 X = 1.15$
$\tan 60° = T_3 X = 1.75$

The work is compact. From a minimum of sketches, we shed light upon a host of mathematical concepts including:

Transition from trigonometric ratios to functions
Deriving the trigonometric tables
Finding the functions of angles greater than 90°

Finding the signs of these function-values
Determining the reference angles for large angles
Determining the trigonometric relationships.

With a bit of thought, we can find additional concepts inherent in this work.

The excursion into abstractness has given us the ability to deal with a multitude of otherwise difficult problems. Such problems include navigation,

Figure 14.18

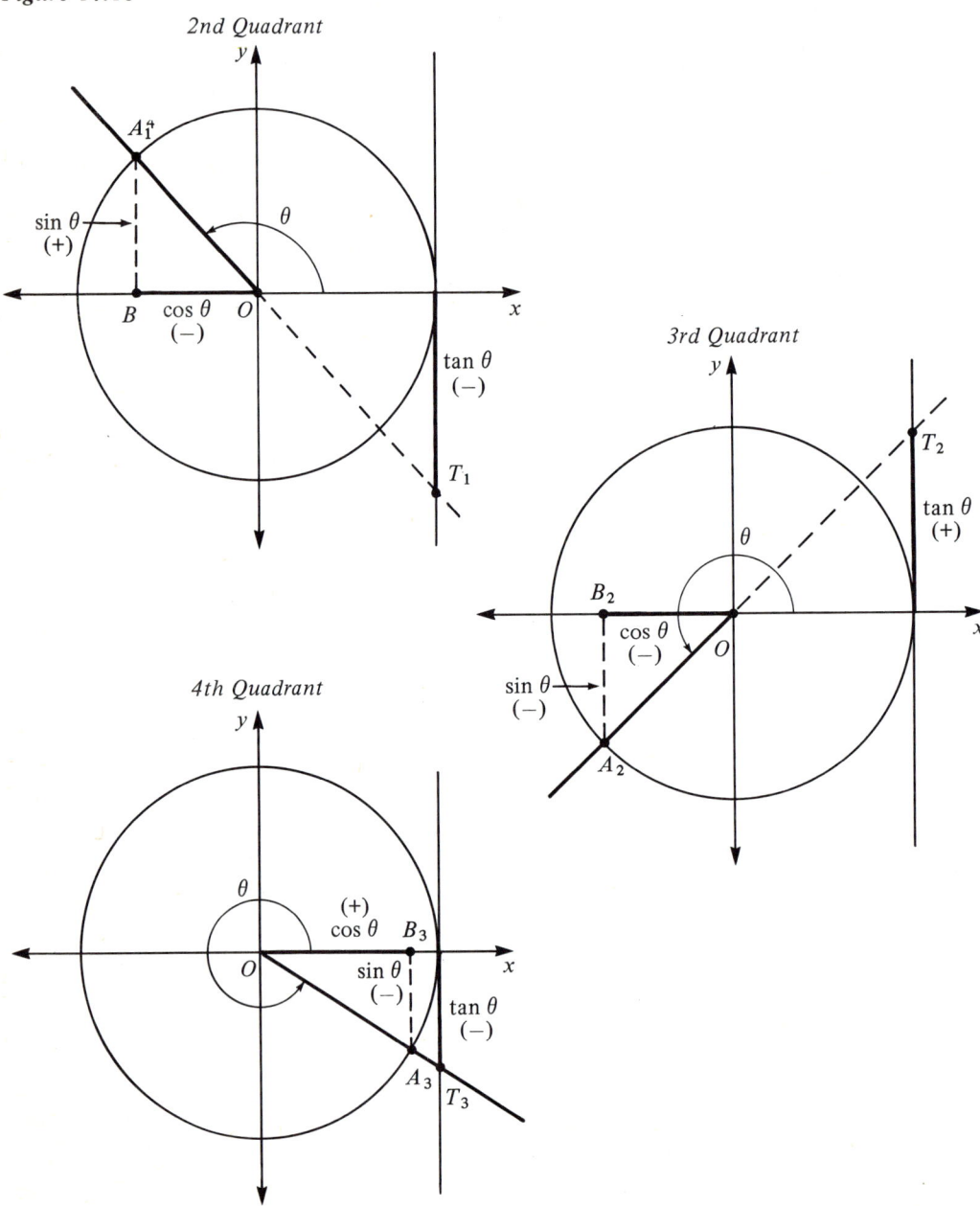

surveying, parallelograms of forces, and any periodic phenomena. The latter point is of such consequence that E. T. Bell was prompted to write,

> It is because the sine and cosine are periodic functions of their variables that they are of importance in modern science and technology. These functions are the natural alphabet of all periodic change.[3]

Therefore, we have developed power to deal with a broad variety of natural phenomena including sound waves, radio waves, light waves, pendula, and springs. Some problems were presented in Chapter 9. The pathway taken here is a familiar one in mathematics. Students can experience the movement from problems in the real world to mathematical abstraction and back into an expanded view of the physical world.

Footnotes

1. W. W. Sawyer. *Prelude to Mathematics.* New York: Penguin Books, 1955, pp. 103–124.
2. Sir D'Arcy Thompson. *On Growth and Form.* J. T. Bonner, ed. New York: Cambridge University Press, 1961, pp. 268–325.
3. Eric T. Bell. *Mathematics: Queen and Servant of Science.* New York: McGraw-Hill, 1951, p. 362.

For Investigation and Discussion

1. What is the difference between thinking of the sine, cosine, and tangent as ratios and as functions?
2. Plan a lesson in which students construct their own trigonometry tables. Use the angles 0°, 15°, 30°, 45°, 60°, 75°, 90°.
3. Select a topic from trigonometry and devise a detailed plan to emphasize the way in which trigonometry unifies the earlier work of arithmetic, algebra, and geometry.
4. Use the "flips" of the equilateral triangle in a manner similar to that of the rectangle used in this chapter. Clarify the implications of such an activity for teaching groups and matrices.
5. Make up a simple picture in the Cartesian plane, and list the coordinates that students need to reproduce it. Use this graph as the basis for a lesson, and develop the entire lesson to introduce students to geometric transformations.
6. Discuss the place of transformational geometry in the secondary school mathematics curriculum. Present arguments for and against its inclusion.
7. All students of mathematics need to learn to deal with abstractions. Explain some of the dangers and some of the necessities for such a statement.

For Further Reading

Books

Fletcher, T. J. ed. *Some Lessons in Mathematics.* New York: Cambridge University Press, 1965.

Insights Into Modern Mathematics. 23rd Yearbook. Reston, Va.: National Council of Teachers of Mathematics, 1957, pp. 100–144.

Mathematical Reflections, edited by Members of the Association of Teachers of Mathematics. New York: Cambridge University Press, 1970.

Sawyer, W. W. *A Concrete Approach to Abstract Algebra.* San Francisco: W. H. Freeman, 1959, pp. 208–222.

Thompson, Sir D'Arcy. *On Growth and Form.* J. T. Bonner, ed. New York: Cambridge University Press, 1961.

Periodicals

Bell, A. W. "Proof in Transformation Geometry (III)," *Mathematics Teaching.* No. 61 (December 1972), pp. 52–56.

Branfield, John R. "Teaching Matrices Via Networks," *The Mathematics Teacher.* Vol. 65 (October 1972), pp. 561–566.

Collins, Peter. "Introducing Trigonometry," *Mathematics Teaching.* No. 63 (June 1973), pp. 44–48.

Faulkner, J. Earl. "Paper Folding as a Technique in Visualizing a Certain Class of Transformations," *The Mathematics Teacher.* Vol. 68 (May 1975), pp. 376–377.

Swadener, Marc. "Pictures, Graphs, and Transformations: A Distorted View of Plane Figures for Middle Grades," *The Arithmetic Teacher.* Vol. 21 (May 1974), pp. 383–389.

Troccolo, Joseph A. "A Strip of Wallpaper," *The Mathemtics Teacher.* Vol. 70 (January 1977), pp. 55–58.

CHAPTER 15

Mathematical Thinking, Problem Solving, and Proof

We cannot focus upon abstraction without giving proper attention to mathematical thinking, problem solving, and proof. Problem solving here refers to the general approach applied to any mathematical question from equation solution, to the construction of proofs, to the development of new mathematics.

The familiar word problems of mathematics, verbal problems, are also included but are only a small part of the total area of problem solving. Let us first explore learning to solve word problems.

Solving Verbal Problems 15.1

Should there be a distinct topic called "solving word problems"?

Perhaps the solution of verbal problems should be meshed with all of our teaching. When we approach new concepts or techniques, we should work within the context of some problem. The aim of previous sections of this text has been to provide a wealth of ideas for this purpose. Assuming that we always try to give students challenging problems that stir their curiosity, there are still particular things to do to increase the ability of students to solve verbal problems.

The work of George Polya and Z. P. Dienes, among others, provides us with some guidelines, however this is still a difficult faculty to develop.[1] Let us briefly explore some of the difficulties.

Reading the Problem

One possible cause for student troubles is their inability to read the problem. Can the student read the words, and is he able to make sense of what is being read? It is not unusual for a student to comprehend every word of a given problem without any basic understanding of what is happening. Does the student understand the action described? Is the situation something from experience or is it totally new?

An elementary school youngster, when asked how big a cow was, held up two fingers about 3 inches apart! The only cows this child had ever seen were those in the pictures in her reader. Perhaps a brief discussion of what is taking place without the use of numbers will help each student be aware of the problem's story and get a clear picture of what is needed.

Translation to Mathematical Symbols

Can the student translate the information of the problem into mathematical symbols? If so, then the student can use all the available techniques and skills with symbols to work to a solution. The movement from words to symbols, however, seems to be a most difficult step. Many teachers have bravely tried to list the problem words and their corresponding symbols one below the other. This may be helpful to some students. For example, if we emphasize algebra as a language as indicated in Chapter 7, students should be able to deal with translation more easily. However, this is a creative process; there is no one way that will enable all students to be sucessful.

Alternate Solutions

Alternate solutions should be presented to students without any evaluative comments other than the fact that the mathematics is sound. Methods need not be compared to see which involves fewer steps or takes less time. If students have the freedom to select methods for themselves, they may feel encouraged to do more thinking and less rote memorizing.

Analysis

To provide some starting point for the solution of word problems, techniques of analysis may be employed. At times it may be helpful to answer such questions as

1. What does the problem tell us?
2. What are we to find?
3. What information is given to us?
4. Can I express the relationships in equation form?
5. Can I solve the particular equation?
6. Does the answer satisfy the conditions of the problem?

We must also face the fact that students may be able to answer the first three questions and still be at a loss as to what to do. Forming equations and deciding upon the operations to carry out are creative acts that require the freedom to think without fear of ridicule or failure. Indeed the ingenuity of students often astounds teachers who have encouraged such behavior! Contributions of this kind do not always depend upon previous sucess or ability with mathematics. This is another indication that we have only begun to scratch the surface in uncovering the mathematical abilities of our students.

Flashes of Insight 15.2

Many students have the uncanny ability to suddenly experience a flash of insight that lays the innermost secret of a problem bare to them, despite the fact that they may be unable to explain what has transpired! This is a treasured skill often mentioned in histories of great mathematicians. While we are unable to cause such insights to occur, we seem to be able to prevent them from ever taking place. What generally happens is that the student offers his sudden inspriation, and the teacher asks for an explanation and justification of what has been presented. Unable to comply, the student flounders and often withdraws, convinced that he does not know after all. A student, who presents evidence of some excellent thinking may feel that he has failed because his verbal power or awareness does not match the quickness of his ability to think. Perhaps the flashes of insight that occur would be a natural experience for most students if we did not demand careful, verbal explanations for every thought presented in our classrooms. Who can tell? Let us honor ideas at all times. We should give lavish praise to good thinking, to the extent of entertaining all the interesting ideas behind student statements, even those that are not paragons of clarity.

A specific example of an incident that actually happened may help. During a lesson on solving consecutive number problems, the teacher wrote the following on the chalkboard:

The sum of 3 consecutive integers is 39.
Find the 3 consecutive integers.

Before the teacher could return to his desk, Johnny had raised his hand. He had a solution. The surprised teacher, after asking if Johnny had done any work, had him write his solution on the board. He wrote:

$$3 \overline{)39}^{\,13} \qquad \text{The integers are 12, 13, 14.}$$

Check: $12 + 13 + 14 = 39$

How would you respond? The teacher remarked that Johnny had not used algebra. Johnny quickly responded that he didn't but managed to solve the problem. The teacher tried to impress Johnny with the need for algebra by telling him, in a derisive fashion, that his method was good this time but would certainly fail when the *difficult* problems came.

Do we build mathematical minds by encouraging students to bow to our superior knowledge of the curriculum? Is this how we hope to encourage mathematical thinking? "Take my word for it . . ."

This time Johnny was not to be put off. He claimed his method would solve any consecutive integer problem. The teacher accepted the challenge:

*The sum of 3 consecutive even numbers is 24.
Find the numbers.*

Johnny wrote,

$$3\overline{)24}^{8}$$ The numbers are 6, 8, 10.

Check: $6 + 8 + 10 = 24$

*The sum of 4 consecutive odd numbers is 48.
Find them.*

$$4\overline{)48}^{12}$$ The numbers are 9, 11, 13, 15.

Check: $9 + 11 + 13 + 15 = 48$

The teacher realized Johnny had sucessfully met the challenge and, in frustration, put Johnny down by warning him that such solutions would get no test credit.

How does Johnny feel after such treatment? It is no mystery that his brilliant flash of insight met with no encouragement. His excellent mathematics became a negative experience for him. In this case, the teacher then went on to explain the algebraic solution so that the class had two solutions before them:

Johnny	Teacher
$$3\overline{)39}^{13}$$ The integers are 12, 13, 14.	Let x = first consecutive integer $x + 1$ = next consecutive integer $x + 2$ = third consecutive integer $x + x + 1 + x + 2 = 39$ $3x + 3 = 39$ $3x = 36$ $x = 12$ $x + 1 = 13$ $x + 2 = 14$ The integers are 12, 13, 14.

Looking at the two solutions, what impression do you get of algebra? It must be a way to make simple problems difficult. What also happens is that most students begin to distrust their own ability to think; the teacher's work becomes a meaningless model that must be duplicated to pass the test. What we generally call problem solving becomes, in many cases, a memory task. With memorization and repetition as the hidden aim, we make it difficult for students to grow mathematically. While the case of Johnny is extreme, it is certainly not an isolated one.

What is a teacher to do in this situation? Johnny has done some fine creative thinking, but how will he learn to use algebraic methods? If Johnny had been praised for his effort rather than faulted, the teacher could have then gone on to explain that there are many methods to use, one of which is an algebraic approach. In this way, alternatives are offered to everyone's advantage, and the important idea that there are many ways to get to a correct mathematical solution is emphasized. In praising Johnny, the teacher would find the ripple effect encouraging every member of the class to use his or her imagination in solving problems. The message from teacher to students becomes "Think!" instead of "Think like me!"

Within Johnny's solution lies an interesting algebraic problem. Will the method always work? Once again an opportunity is present to explore the concept of proof, which we will examine a bit further on.

Trial and Error   15.3

When we move into mathematical thinking applied to general problem solving, we find that one abused but respected mathematical technique is trial and error. A simple problem serves as an example:

> I am thinking of two numbers. I will not tell you what they are, but I will give you their sum and their difference. Their sum is 54 and their difference is 16. See if you can find my two numbers. ◄

Many students immediately try different number pairs until they find the ones that satisfy the conditions of the problem. Do not discourage this kind of solution. A very real part of creative work involves the use of trial and error. While this may not be an economical approach, it frequently provides insights into what is happening, with the net result that unsuccessful trials offer enough information to help us work toward a solution. Students often are discouraged by teachers from using any but formal algebraic techniques and, just as often, find themselves at the complete mercy of these techniques. As a consequence, they bring this rigid approach to all mathematical problems. Instead of looking for relationships in problems, they put complete faith in the power of algebra. Sometimes algebra works for them, but frequently it does not. In either case, students lose the adventurous spirit that is a prerequisite for mathematical thinking.

To get students to move from trial and error to a more logical approach, introduce problems that simply overwhelm a trial and error technique. Rather than insist upon a particular solution now because difficulties will be encountered later, select problems that cause students to need the concepts you have in mind. For example, if you wish to discourage trial and error in the solution of number puzzles, make them more complex:

> This time I am thinking of two numbers, one number is three less than twice the other, and the difference between the numbers is six. What numbers am I thinking of now? ◄

Some die-hard students may still preservere with hit-and-miss attempts at solution, but in general a genuine need develops to use the best techniques available. In this case, the most powerful technique is the solution of systems of two equations and two unknowns. The teaching of mathematical techniques is enhanced when students experience the need for such methods.

Finding a Simple Equivalent   15.4

Another technique of problem solving, which is typical of mathematical thinking, is the process of resolving a difficult problem by first solving an equivalent but simpler one. Students frequently do this in algebra classes unknowingly when instead of solving

$$3x + 8 = 26$$

they simplify it to

$$3x = 18$$

and finally

$$x = 6$$

The initial difficult equation yields to the equivalent but obvious one of $x = 6$. What students see as the statement of the solution is actually an equivalent equation, one which is so simple that the root jumps out at you. This same approach is made throughout the study of mathematics and is of special interest in discussing problem solving. Let us take a specific case:

> A gardener wanted to plant 176 flowers in a rectangular garden 20 ft by 30 ft. How far apart should the flowers be planted?

This problem seems difficult so we ask students to look at a similar but simpler situation:

> If we put the flowers 1 ft apart in a garden 8 ft by 4 ft, how many flowers could be planted? (See Figure 15.1.) How many could we plant if we placed them 2 ft apart? 4 ft apart?

Figure 15.1   The Garden: 4 Feet by 8 Feet

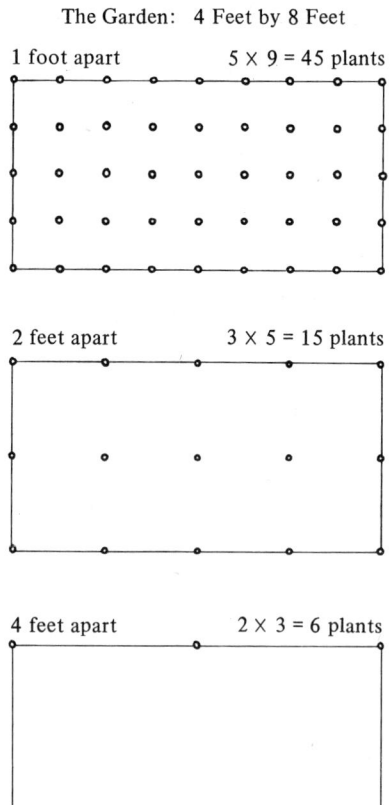

Let us examine the results carefully: If we can find a pattern we may have a solution. We arrange the information as shown in Table 15.1.

Table 15.1

Length	Width	Distance Apart	Number of Plants
8	4	1 ft	9 × 5 = 45
8	4	2 ft	5 × 3 = 15
8	4	4 ft	3 × 2 = 6

The numbers to be multiplied appear to be one more than the length or width divided by the distance apart as shown in Table 15.2.

Table 15.2

Distance Apart	Length	Width	Multiply
1 ft	8 ÷ 1 = 8	4 ÷ 1 = 4	9 × 5
2 ft	8 ÷ 2 = 4	4 ÷ 2 = 2	5 × 3
4 ft	8 ÷ 4 = 2	4 ÷ 4 = 1	3 × 2

A formula for the number of plants is

$$N = \left(\frac{L}{d} + 1\right)\left(\frac{W}{d} + 1\right)$$

In this case, we are looking for d; hence,

$$176 = \left(\frac{20}{d} + 1\right)\left(\frac{30}{d} + 1\right)$$

[handwritten: $\frac{600}{d^2} + \frac{50}{d} + 1 = 176$; $600 + 50d + d^2 = 176d^2$]

This problem is particularly fruitful since it introduces a multitude of new ideas. The students may proceed in a variety of ways; using the multiplication axiom, combining and then multiplying, and possibly others.

The simpler problem yielded a solution using a general approach that can apply to all such problems. It showed us what we had to do and how to do it. This technique helps develop the problem solving skills of our students.

15.5 Mathematical Thinking and Drawing Generalizations

Closely allied with problem solving is the process of generalization. In dealing with abstractions, it is necessary to consider how patterns are discerned from observation of a multitude of cases. The previous problem illustrated this. Generalizing is difficult for students. Time constraints and other pressures often compel teachers to move students into conclusions before they are ready. To be able to generalize, students must become involved with enough cases, to take in enough information, so that they may begin to see patterns. Then they can formulate their own generalizations. We turn to a specific example.

A rancher has 100 ft of fencing and wishes to fence off a rectangularly shaped corral that will provide him with the greatest possible area. What dimensions should the corral be?

After permitting a good deal of free experimentation in attempting a solution, we try to organize the students' thinking in a mathematical way. Discussion will result in the recognition of the fact that the perimeter is fixed. If x and y are used to represent the length and width of the rectangle in question, we may write a formula for all possible rectangles whose perimeter is 100:

$$2x + 2y = 100$$

Substituting arbitrary values for the length (x) would result in fixing values for the width (y). The students could tabulate these results (Table 15.3) and then add a third column with the heading *Area* to their table:

Table 15.3

x	y	Area
5	45	225
10	40	400
15	35	525
20	30	600
25	25	625
30	20	600
35	15	525
40	10	400

The information demonstrates that the peak area seems to result when about 25 feet is taken for both length and width. This is the shape of the square. Computations of areas when the sides are close to 25 ft are in order. Perhaps a length of 24.9 and width of 25.1 will yield a greater area. The students compute the area and find it is 624.99, still less than 625. They may try numbers to 3 or 4 decimal places, but it seems that the square is the figure of greatest area.

We have resolved the problem, but there is a gnawing thought lurking in the background. Is this example a fluke, or will the square always give maximum area under these conditions? Can we make a generalization about this? The students try additional problems:

▶ Given a fixed perimeter, find the maximum enclosed rectangular area. Try perimeters of 48, 60, 200 (Table 15.4).

Table 15.4

$P = 48$			$P = 60$			$P = 200$		
x	y	Area	x	y	Area	x	y	Area
4	20	80	5	25	125	30	70	2100
8	16	98	10	20	200	40	60	2400
12	12	144	15	15	225	50	50	2500
16	8	98	20	10	200	60	40	2400
20	4	80	25	5	125	70	30	2100

Each trial adds confirmation and the generalization grows stronger. It appears the square (under certain conditions) will always be of maximum area. Let's see.

Try a very small perimeter, say 6. Does the square result from this? Now try a large number, say, 5000. Does this give a square? Let us try one with fractions. What is the result this time?

Somewhere in this chain, it becomes clear we can try cases all day and never be sure. We need a different method; we need to try to prove the result is always a square. At this point, we clarify what we have, what we are trying to establish, and proceed to use a deductive argument to get to an ending we were gradually beginning to accept anyway. The proof itself may be an interesting exercise for the reader, as would the effect of dropping the restriction that the figure be a rectangle.[2]

Mathematical Thinking and Proof 15.6

The free development of ideas through the use of intuition based upon geometrical perceptions must also be mentioned. This is one of the major reasons for the study of geometry in the first place. In a most unusual work probing into the very heart of the invention of mathematical ideas, Hadamard has pointed out that most mathematicans think in terms of geometrical representations of the ideas under consideration. Visual images in the mind serve as the stuff from which mathematical inventions are realized. The importance of this for teachers of mathematics is plainly stated by Hadamard.

> Between the work of the student who tries to solve a problem in geometry or algebra and a work of invention, one can say that there is only a difference of degree, a difference of level, both works being of similar nature.[3]

Indeed, the entire process of invention growing out of the intuitive consideration of mental, visual images is considered to be so vital by Hadamard that he leaves little room for question as he concludes that this process

> ... gives the leading thread, without which one would be like the blind man who can walk but would never know in what direction to go.

How interesting a parallel for describing the behavior of many of our students in problem solving and geometry today.

The Role of Diagrams 15.7

The use of diagrams in developing the deductive argument has often come under fire. The figures we draw are not the concepts of geometry but merely a representation of these concepts. As such, it is quite possible to be mislead by a diagram since we may be unaware of using many unstated assumptions about the ideas under consideration. To highlight this danger, the proof of the fact that all triangles are isosceles is generally offered together with the caution that pure logic must persist rather than the intuitive notions contained in or derived from any representative pictures.[4] Allendoerfer discusses just this point and states that

> ... the student is taught that figures are only a crutch to his insight, but that his reasoning is supposed to be independent of the figures which he has drawn.[5]

This same matter is considered by Sitomer, who recommends that students should or should not be admonished for drawing conclusions from the diagrams instead of by pure logic, according to their mathematical ability.[6] Do not permit the top mathematics students to use conclusions based upon observation, says Sitomer, but do accept this as valid from those less able. These are interesting arguments.

Consider the importance of visualization in the act of creating mathematics, as discussed. Also consider our goals of maximum appeal to the intuition and deemphasis of the strictly logical form. It would then seem that, despite some shortcomings, the use of diagrams to gain both sight and insight into what is happening are a virtual necessity. Make the necessary cautions if you are so inclined, but encourage the use and construction of diagrams by the students. Often we have a splendid visual representation for the mathematical ideas under consideration. Let us take advantage of it and indeed encourage reliance upon figures, rather than turn away from them in order to serve the needs of logic.

Evidently, seeing and reasoning are integral parts of a single process for the majority of our students. In a sense, aren't we trying to help our students "see" mathematics? Felix Klein sums it up rather pointedly,

> To follow a geometrical argument purely logically without having the figure on which the argument bears constantly before me is for me impossible.[7]

So it is for virtually all of our students. Let us now turn to the important notion of proof.

15.8 Proof, Logic, and Rigor

Why is the concept of proof so distressing to our students?

Why do they grope in the dark attempting to complete proofs and leave the unmistaken impression that they have absolutely no "feel" for what is being asked of them? Perhaps the closest thing to the number of students who have little or no conception of proof would be the number of students who have an erroneous impression of proof.

Role of Proof

For the most part, mathematical relationships should be fully known and accepted by our students before they undertake to prove them. A report of the British Mathematical Association goes so far as to state that

> until this has been to some extent acquired, attempts to reason on the facts are constantly hampered. The paradox may also be ventured that in many cases until a fact is obvious, argument will be of little avail.[8]

The report later goes on to say that

> ... a boy ought to feel fully convinced by mere intuition ... conviction should be reached without formal proof and by his own activity.

The report flatly states that the purpose of proof is neither the discovery nor the realization of the fact. Rather, the role of proof is seen as an aid to understanding why things are what they are, as well as to confirm a fact and to settle doubt about it. Thus, intuition is the creator and logic is the vehicle for confirmation; or, in the words of the same report, ". . . the path is blazed by the one, consolidated by the other." What a far cry from the notion that deduction will enable us to uncover hitherto unseen facts! The maximum area rectangle problem followed this suggested pattern.

Many educators have expressed concern over the fact that students are attempting to prove relationships that are obvious. Hence, geometry, for example, is seen as a form of nonsense task. Why bother to "prove" something you know is true? The role of proof as just discussed is verification. Proof also adds to our understanding of why things are what they are. The proof confirms that a given proposition is indeed a theorem, that a statement will always hold (or fail to hold, as the case may be). It is a means of convincing others that, unfortunately, is not available to us in other fields, such as politics and international relations.

Rigor and the Forms of Proof

We are seldom as rigorous as we would like to be in teaching mathematics, but is this necessarily a weakness? The central question would seem to be: Are we as rigorous as necessary at the moment? Probably each of us has been a student in a class in which the teacher's standard of rigor for his students far exceeded that which he demanded of himself. Frustration and resentment grow in each student as one man's rigor becomes another man's excuses. But the instructor is not solely at fault. It is the very nature of mathematics that makes such occurences commonplace. Willoughby, in considering rigor, has put the problem into an interesting perspective by indicating that he was:

> . . . willing to agree that rigor may be central to mathematics. However, when it is simply memorized, without an understanding and appreciation of its need, it is central in the same sense that the hole is central in the doughnut. Sterile rigor is neither more appetizing nor more nutritious to the young mind than the hole in the doughnut is to the young body.[9]

It is the custom in courses in geometry to use the famous T-bar proof, the statement-reason format. This rigid form and the attempts at logical perfection, which may be desirable at advanced levels, are at best questionable in the secondary school. Demanding each step in a proof to be carefully justified may create results that are opposite from what was intended. A Canadian publication explains this situation in an elegant manner:

> In school, the avoidance of certain logical subtleties is not a serious offence and may even be a virtue. What is a serious offence is to give the student the impression that mathematics is just a waste of time . . . The majority of students who write out proofs of such results with the authority for each step carefully cited, do so to oblige the teacher or to keep out of trouble. Very few do it because they feel in their hearts that such a result needs careful proof. They are not thinking, nor are they learning to think; they are carrying out a prescribed ritual. When students feel their time is being wasted, they are being driven away from mathematics and logical thinking.[10]

The report goes on to suggest that geometry be taught as an exercise in "informal reasoning."

There is no doubt that deductive proof is seen to be an important part of the development of mathematics. In order to keep the important ideas in focus, however, we must try not to become victims of rigid formulations for the proofs that are considered.

The Report of the Commission on Mathematics, in considering the case for a "logically unimpeachable treatment of Euclidean geometry suitable for use in secondary schools," arrived at the conclusion that no such treatment exists. What is more, the report cautioned against "boring students with logical subtleties." It goes on to recommend that "textbook writers and teachers should feel free to modify the Euclidean development to attain a more incisive and interesting program.[11] This seems to make good sense.

Since the reasoning is primary and not the form in which it is cast, the key ideas in the development of proofs should be brought out, with reasons stated whenever they may not be obvious. Perhaps the presentation of one such proof will make the intent clear.

We encounter the idea that a pair of vertical angles, angles formed by two intersecting lines in the plane, are equal. After observing the phenomenon, we investigate by trying another pair of lines to determine if this relationship will hold. The students may examine several different pairs of intersecting lines and by measurement determine that the vertical angles always appear to be equal. Can we try all such possible pairs of lines? Unless we approach the problem in some other way we may never be certain. We present a proof of this relationship to establish certainty and to illustrate the point of the earlier discussion regarding form and degree of rigor.

Prove: ∡1 = ∡2
We Know: AB and CD are straight lines intersecting at E (Figure 15.2).

Figure 15.2

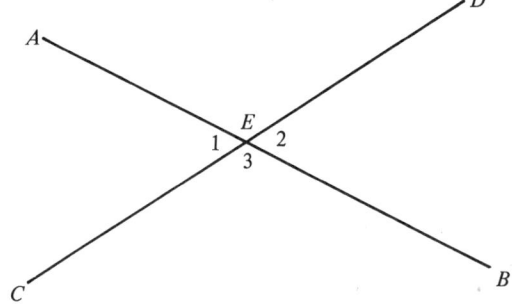

∡1 is a supplement of ∡3
∡2 is a supplement of ∡3
Therefore: ∡1 + ∡3 = 180°
            ∡2 + ∡3 = 180°

∡1 + ∡3 = ∡2 + ∡3   Since both sums are 180°, they are equal.
    ∡1 = ∡2   Subtract ∡3 from each side.

Now that we have completed our deductive demonstration, we have changed the proposition regarding vertical angles into a theorem. We have established the fact that whenever any two straight lines intersect, vertical angles formed will always be equal angles. We need not try any more specific cases: We now know this property holds in all cases. There is no other way in which this fact could have been established (aside from different proofs) since we could not possibly have examined every situation.

The form of the preceding proof is much like that generally employed when one works with algebraic ideas. It does not follow the strict statement-reason form so often found in geometry textbooks. It does, however, present just about everything that is necessary to make the argument clear to the reader. It would seem helpful to students to refrain from writing the obvious but to be specifically clear about questionable statements. For example, instead of stating "things equal to the same or equal quantities are equal to each other," it may be more beneficial to students if they present the specific parts under discussion. In the proof we just completed, the simple statement that both sums are 180° tells more, in fewer words, than does the equality axiom. The same is true of the final statement. Rather than use the general statement of the subtraction axiom, let us state specifically what *is* being subtracted. Thus, there need be little mystery in the mind of the student about what is or is not being added or subtracted, as the case may be. At the same time that we seek to eliminate unnecessary formalism, we also wish to add to the clarity of ideas.

Analysis of Proof

Finally, the use of analysis may also provide students with a tool for the discovery of proofs. The familiar process of working backward frequently helps students identify the missing links and guides and directs their thinking. For example, if we wanted to prove that two lines are parallel, we might analyze the situation as follows:

> How can I show lines are parallel? I can do this if I show (1) that a pair of alternate-interior angles are equal or (2) that a pair of corresponding angles are equal.

> How can I show equal angles? I can do this if I can show (1) that the angles are corresponding parts of congruent triangles or (2) that the angles are equal to the same angle.

> How can I show the triangles are congruent? I can do this if I can show . . .

By following this chain of reasoning, we may begin with what we seek to prove and work backward until we arrive at the given information, or some link with it. This method will not always aid our thinking, but it does provide us with a starting point as we begin to think about a theorem. It also offers a plan for working with the relationships we have already mastered as a probe for a proof.

Footnotes

1. George Polya. *How to Solve It.* 2nd ed. New York: Doubleday, 1951.

   Z. P. Dienes. *Building Up Mathematics.* New York: Humanities, 1960.

2. See: Gail S. Kronkle. *Shapes and Perceptions.* Boston: Prindle, Weber & Schmidt, 1974, pp. 162–176.

Also see: George Polya. *Mathematics and Plausible Reasoning.* Vol. 1, Princeton, N.J.: Princeton University Press, 1954, pp. 168–189.

3. Jacques Hadamard. *The Psychology of Invention in the Mathematical Field.* New York: Dover, 1954, p. 104.
4. Aubrey J. Kempner. *Paradoxes and Common Sense.* New York: Van Nostrand, 1959, pp. 4–6.
5. Carl B. Allendoerfer. *"Deductive Methods in Mathematics." Insights Into Modern Mathematics.* 23rd Yearbook. Reston, Va.: National Council of Teachers of Mathematics, 1957, p. 95.
6. Harry Sitomer. "Sight Versus Insight," *The Mathematics Teacher.* Vol. 60 (May 1967), pp. 474–478.
7. Felix Klein. Zur Nicht-Euklidsche Geometrie, *Math. Ann.* 37 (1890) 571, Ges. Math Abh. 1, 381. As described by Morris Kline in "Logic Verus Pedagogy," *The American Mathematical Monthly.* Vol. 77 (March 1970), p. 276.
8. *A Second Report on the Teaching of Geometry in Schools.* Mathematical Association (England). London: G. Bell and Sons, 1951, p. 5.
9. Stephen S. Willoughby. "Revolution, Rigor, and Rigor Mortis," *The Mathematics Teacher.* Vol. 60 (February 1967), p. 108.
10. *Geometry, Kindergarten to Grade 13.* Report of K–13 Geometry Committee, The Ontario Institute for Studies in Education, 1967, pp. 19–20.
11. *Report of the Commission on Mathematics. Appendices.* New York: College Entrance Examination Board, 1959, p. 24.

For Investigation and Discussion

1. Describe three possible causes for difficulty with solving verbal problems. Indicate specific things you might do to enable students to overcome each of these difficulties.
2. Select three mathematical problems and illustrate how students may be taught to apply the method of analysis presented in this chapter.
3. Read *How to Solve It* by George Polya and devise a lesson(s) for students based upon Polya's approach to problem solving.
4. Describe the role of proof in mathematics. Then select a specific topic in plane geometry to illustrate how the role of proof will influence the manner in which the topic may be taught.
5. Discuss whether the concept of proof is better taught in geometry or algebra classes.
6. Read the articles in the references by Morris Kline and Judith V. Grabiner. Then discuss this statement: "A mathematical proof establishes the certainty of a proposition for all time."
7. Explain reasons for and against student reliance upon diagrams when attempting proofs in geometry.
8. Select a concept from algebra or geometry. Outline how you would teach a lesson designed to provide many experiences with this concept for students so they may abstract their own generalizations about using the particular concept.

For Further Reading

Books

Cooney, Thomas J.; Edward J. Davis; K. B. Henderson. *Dynamics of Teaching Secondary School Mathematics,* Boston: Houghton Mifflin, 1975, pp. 240–324.

Fawcett, Harold P. *The Nature of Proof.* 13th Yearbook. Reston, Va.: National Council of Teachers of Mathematics. AMS Reprint Co., 1966.

Getzels, J. W. "Creative Thinking, Problem Solving, and Instruction," *Theories of Learning and Instruction.* 63rd Yearbook. National Society for the Study of Education, 1964, pp. 240-267 (distributed by University of Chicago Press).

Johnson, Donovan and Gerald Rising. *Guidelines for Teaching Mathematics.* 2nd ed. Belmont, Ca.: Wadsworth, 1972, pp. 234-258.

Kinsella, John J. "Problem Solving," *The Teaching of Secondary School Mathematics.* 33rd Yearbook. Reston, Va.: National Council of Teachers of Mathematics, 1970, pp. 241-266.

Polya, George. *How to Solve It.* 2nd ed. Princeton, N.J.: Princeton University Press, 1957.

Simon, Herbert, *Learning with Understanding.* Based on a presentation made March 31, 1975 at A.E.R.A. meeting, Washington, D.C. Eric Information Analysis Center for Science, Mathematics and Environmental Education. Ohio State University. June 1975.

Willis, Herbert. "Generalizations," *The Teaching of Secondary School Mathematics.* 33rd Yearbook. Reston, Va.: National Council of Teachers of Mathematics, 1970, pp. 267-290.

Periodicals

Arnold, William R. "Students Can Pose and Solve Original Problems," *The Mathematics Teacher.* Vol. 64 (April 1971), pp. 325-327.

Bellman, Richard. "On the Concepts of a Problem and Problem Solving," *The American Mathematical Monthly.* Vol. 67 (February 1960), pp. 119-134.

Cartwright, M. L. "Mathematics and Thinking Mathematically," *The American Mathematical Monthly.* Vol. 77 (January 1970), pp. 20-28.

Francis, Richard L. "Word Problems: Abundant and Deficient Data," *The Mathematics Teacher.* Vol. 71 (January 1978), pp. 6-11.

Grabiner, Judith V. "Is Mathematical Truth Time-Dependent?" *The American Mathematical Monthly.* Vol. 81 (April 1974), pp. 354-365.

Kane, Robert B. "On the Proof-Making Task," *The Mathematics Teacher.* Vol. 68 (February 1975), pp. 89-94.

Kline, Morris. "Logic Versus Pedagogy," *The American Mathematical Monthly.* Vol. 77 (March 1970), pp. 264-281.

Morley, Arthur. "Mathematics as Process," *The Mathematics Teacher.* Vol. 66 (January 1973), pp. 39-45.

Snyder, Henry D. "Problem Solutions that Ask Questions," *School Science and Mathematics.* Vol. 66 (April 1966), pp. 373-376.

Van Engen, Henry. "Strategies of Proof in Secondary Mathematics," *The Mathematics Teacher.* Vol. 63 (December 1970), pp. 637-645.

Walter, Marion I. and Stephen I. Brown. "Problem Posing and Problem Solving: An Illustration of their Independence," *The Mathematics Teacher.* Vol. 70 (January 1977), pp. 4-13.

SECTION V

Mathematics and Finding Patterns

CHAPTER 16

Patterns in Numbers

Mathematics is the study of all possible patterns. We cannot hope to give a complete view of mathematics without involving students in the process of looking for patterns. This search is fundamental to methods of inquiry in science as well as mathematics and requires proper recognition.

We hear a good deal about "discovery" learning, perhaps more than we see in action. A collection of experiences that will enable students to see certain regularities for themselves, to find their own patterns, is prerequisite for discovery learning. We can expect that self-discovered patterns are easily remembered, thereby reducing the need for drill and rendering the entire process of learning more efficient and more lasting. Paradoxically, most teachers are reluctant to employ discovery approaches because they think they are too time consuming. Can an approach require more time and still be more efficient? If we look at the whole learning picture, rather than just the introductory period, we may well find that time spent exploring and trying to find patterns is offset by the time saved by eliminating unnecessary repetition. When we "tell" students instead of helping them find out, they require much more practice. Whatever the case, at the heart of most discovery experiences is the search for regularity, the pattern that ties all of the individual pieces together. We shall now give our attention to this process.

Odd and Even 16.1

Do you know that numbers have shapes? The early work of the Greeks referred to the way in which the Pythagoreans studied number properties using pebbles. These pebbles would be arranged in a variety of patterns and the properties of the numbers sought out. While it may not be worthwhile to give students a stack of pebbles, you can duplicate the work of the Greeks using geoboards or pegboards. The geoboards are used with rubber bands, and the pegboards can employ a variety of pegs or even golf tees. Geopaper requires no loose parts at all. (See Figure 16.1.) Whatever is used, these devices can offer excellent action experiences for students. Some questions that students might consider:

How do odd numbers differ from even numbers in shape?
How do the shapes of prime and composite numbers compare?
Are there numbers shaped like a triangle? List them.
Are there numbers shaped like a square? List them.

Figure 16.1

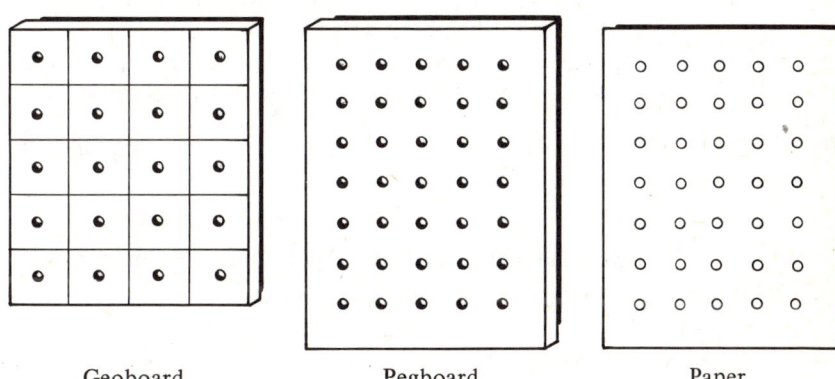

Geoboard   Pegboard   Paper

This apparently innocent and simple work is surprisingly fruitful. For example, in the case of odd and even numbers, representing the numbers from one to eight points up an interesting difference shown in Figure 16.2. No matter how you arrange the pegs or rubber bands, the even numbers are arranged in groups of two, while the odd numbers always have a peg left over. This can be verified by trying all sorts of numbers as long as they fit on the board or paper. In addition, by placing arrangements of pegs on the board, students can determine whether the number represented is odd or even without knowing the number itself.

Figure 16.2

Odd Numbers:

1   3   5   7

Even Numbers:

2   4   6   8

Figure 16.3
● ● ● ● ● ● ●
● ● ● ● ● ● ○

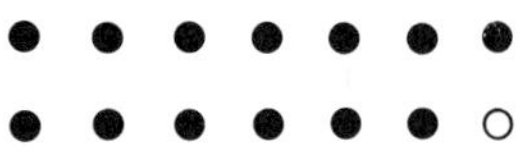

For example, a quick look at Figure 16.3 indicates that the number shown is odd; there is a peg left over. While this difference is rather obvious, the use of the device has accomplished several things. For one, the student has a visual image, which hopefully will remain in his mind, of the nature of odd and even numbers. Secondly, the picture image, groups of two, or groups of two with one left over, also illustrates the algebraic representation of odd and even numbers:

Even:	groups of two	$2n$
Odd:	groups of two, one left over	$2n + 1$

Thirdly, we are laying the groundwork for visualization of multiplication that will be helpful when considering algebraic multiplication and factoring, as well as the addition and subtraction of polynomials. Our simple beginning has opened the door to a number of important mathematical ideas. You may be able to add substantially to what has been offered here.

We now have the ability to turn to the algebraic representations of even-odd numbers, and explore additional questions including:

▶ Is the sum of two even numbers always an even number, an odd number, or does it change?

What happens to the sum of two odd numbers?

What happens when an even and an odd number are added?

What happens in multipication?

We are moving into somewhat more sophisticated areas, including an interesting beginning on the concept of proof. For example, look at the question of the sum of two odd numbers. Students may first guess an answer after some brief thought. Guessing gives the students a stake in finding the answer. Have they guessed correctly? How can we find out what happens? Try some numbers, observe the results.

▶ Students try any two odd numbers:

$9 + 5 = ?$ $13 + 17 = ?$ $7 + 21 = ?$

Each time the sum is an even number. Try some more, maybe it was an accident. The result is still even.

Will it always be even?

How do you know?

Can we try all possible sums?

What shall we do?

At this point, the process of proof can take on some genuine importance for youngsters. We need something to resolve the situation. We are prepared to accept that the result is even, but how can we convince the skeptic who still doubts?

The experience reflects the realities of mathematics. We have not dropped a diagram with "given"; we have not asked for a proof of a relationship, which the student has not had an opportunity to explore, as is so often done in plane geometry classes. We also have not implied in any way that the proof will help us to find out a relationship that we did not previously know. Instead, like mathematicians, the students are attempting to verify a result they are already aware of, but would like to make certain.

Working out the proof is actually visualized with the pegboard, so that the end product holds little mystery for students. Let us examine the specifics.

How do we proceed? Look at the pegboard. What is the form of an odd number? Put one on the board.

$2n + 1$ (Figure 16.4)

Figure 16.4

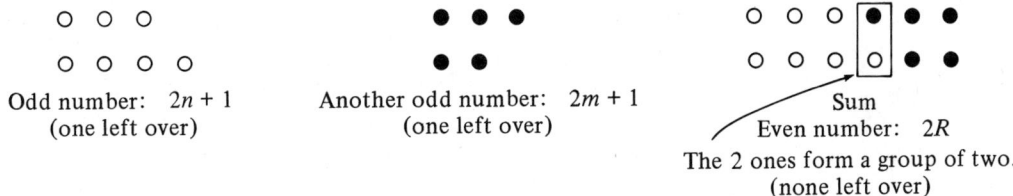

Odd number: $2n + 1$ (one left over)   Another odd number: $2m + 1$ (one left over)   Sum
Even number: $2R$
The 2 ones form a group of two.
(none left over)

Add another odd number to it. What is its form?

$2m + 1$.

What happens to the sum? It is an even number. The two "ones" left over become another group of two and the sum is even. This will be true no matter what the odd numbers that we add are!

To write out what happened using algebraic symbols:

$2n + 1$ first odd number
$2m + 1$ different odd number
$2n + 2m + 2$ all groups of two, therefore an even number.

We have as much formality as necessary at this point. The concept of proof enabled the students to do something that would not otherwise be possible. Perhaps using powers of reason to achieve certain ends is becoming an important activity for students. Students check the original guess and find out how accurate their guesses were. At this point, it would seem that questions such as those on page 256 could be considered to add experience with proofs and to increase understanding of the nature of number. Do not push for more rigorous developments at this point. The work is introductory; moving too far too fast may neutralize any good feelings of confidence about proof that are being built within students. (Chapter 15 considered proof in more detail.)

Prime and Composite 16.2

In representing numbers with pegs, we may also look for shape patterns different than the odd-even one.

Represent the number 6 with pegs and leave no spaces, empty holes, between pegs. Represent 9. Now make 7. What do you notice about these numbers? Try more numbers to see if you get any new information. How do these numbers compare?

With this innocent start, we may find that some numbers can be represented by pegs in the shape of a rectangle:

6, 9, 12, 15, 20, . . .

Others cannot be made into a rectangle, no matter how you try:

7, 11, 13, 17, 19, . . .

In this way, the students encounter the ideas of prime numbers and composite numbers. We may then pose all sorts of questions to continue this experience and to offer students opportunities to search out any inherent patterns. Leave their search as open as described above since, at this point, we are not really concerned with particular ideas.

As students discover and check patterns, the notion of prime and composite numbers will become familiar. In addition, you may be surprised to find properties of these numbers that you never thought about; students given an open field run in unpredictable directions and often amaze teachers with their findings. Some questions that may be asked:

▶
How do prime and composite numbers differ?

What properties of prime numbers can you find?

How do prime and composite numbers relate to odd and even numbers?

What becomes of the sum of two primes? Two composites?

What happens when you add a prime number and a composite?

What happens in multiplication?

Can you find the next prime number if you know the preceding ones?

The Sieve of Eratosthenes may be explored, leading students to consider number representations of additional shapes such as squares and triangles. The "square" numbers are particularly interesting in terms of patterns since they have much to offer in addition to their shape.

16.3 Perfect Squares

In forming squares with pegs on a board or on geopaper, students will find many curious patterns. For example:

▶
What do you notice about the squares in Figure 16.5?

Is there any pattern to the movement from one square number to another?

There are many patterns that students may find, including:

▶
The addition of an L-shaped row and a column of pegs changes a square into the next perfect square (Figure 16.6).

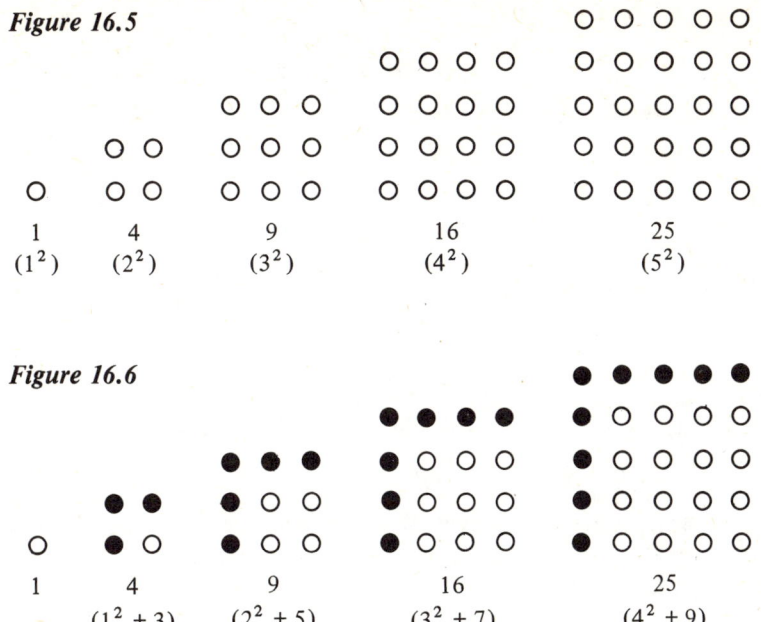

Figure 16.5

Figure 16.6

These added pegs can be described in a variety of ways that involve a host of concepts from arithmetic and algebra as a greater understanding of perfect squares is developed.

A given perfect square leads to the next square by successive addition of numbers: the familiar odd numbers. Moving from one to four, we add 3; from 4 to 7, we add 5; and so on. We know from the pegs that the increment added on, the L-shaped set of pegs, must be odd since it is always made up of two equal sets of pegs plus the one in the corner. This gives us once again the familiar form $2n + 1$, the odd number. Using pegs, or diagrams representing pegs, enables us to find patterns, to see and confirm our conjectures. While the discussion of square numbers may sound rather elementary, the payoff in terms of mathematical thinking and concepts is significant. In addition, we bring many diverse ideas together, adding to the understanding and familiarity of each. The pattern of adding two equal numbers of pegs, plus one, may be considered further.

What is the makeup of each square number? ◀

After the number one, we find that each perfect square is the sum of the pegs forming a square, two equal sets of pegs, plus one. For example:

Look at the number 16. It is made up of a square of 3 pegs on a side, plus two times that number of pegs, plus one. (Figure 16.7, see page 260). The next square, $25 = 4^2 + 2 \times 4 + 1$, and so on. ◀

This takes us a step further in our search for patterns and enables the student to write down a general form for the perfect squares:

Figure 16.7

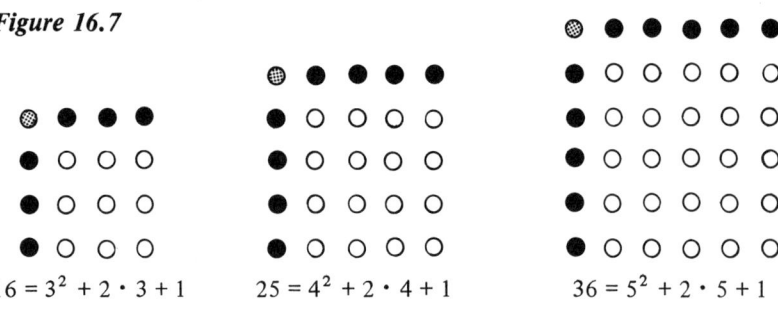

$$n^2 + 2n + 1$$

where the side of the square is $n + 1$ as shown in Figure 16.8. Our investigation has, in effect, carried out the multiplication of binomials

$$(n + 1)(n + 1) = n^2 + 2n + 1$$

which, in turn, can lead into general methods for multiplication. The blend of algebra, geometry, and arithmetic is a natural one. In fact, isolation of each subject is unnatural.

Figure 16.8

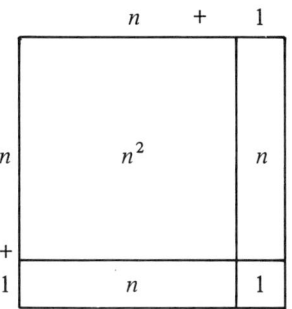

With a limited number of patterns considered, we have offered students a picture of perfect squares, a clear visual representation. By representing these numbers both visually and algebraically, we have found and described patterns that lead into a rich collection of concepts to explore. We have established both present and future gains, a good example of efficient teaching. In addition, we have reinforced the notion that mathematics is the study of patterns. Other patterns to consider include:

▶   1.   Is the sum of two square numbers a square number?

   $4^2 + 3^2 = ?$ $2^2 + 5^2 = ?$

2.   Is the product of two square numbers a square number?

   $4^2 \times 3^2 = ?$ $2^2 \times 5^2 = ?$

3.   If you know a square number, can you find the next highest square number?

Introduction to the operations of squaring, cubing, and, in general, raising numbers to a power and finding square roots has also been accomplished. While the work is neither formal or comprehensive at this time, it is a concrete beginning.

Basic Number Facts 16.4

There are many number patterns around us that we seldom notice because we seem to take simple ideas for granted. One good example of this inability to see the forest for the trees is the familiar multiplication table. Using half-inch graph paper, students can make 10 × 10 blocks of 100 squares and enter the numbers from 1 to 100 as shown in Figure 16.9. Just looking at the 100 squares can lead to students finding patterns on their own. The infinite number of patterns that are possible virtually assures each student of at least one successful experience. Examining diagonals, vertical or horizontal rows, or any other paths will lead to some sort of pattern.[1] Our discussion here will focus on the patterns that result from the multiplication tables.

Figure 16.9

1	2	3	4	5	6	7	8	9	10
11	12	13	14	15	16	17	18	19	20
21	22	23	24	25	26	27	28	29	30
31	32	33	34	35	36	37	38	39	40
41	42	43	44	45	46	47	48	49	50
51	52	53	54	55	56	57	58	59	60
61	62	63	64	65	66	67	68	69	70
71	72	73	74	75	76	77	78	79	80
81	82	83	84	85	86	87	88	89	90
91	92	93	94	95	96	97	98	99	100

After constructing several drawings of 100 squares, first ask students to circle each number that is a product of the two-times table. This means drawing circles around 2, 4, 6, 8, . . . (Figure 16.10, see page 262). Then students can do the same on another 100 square for the three-table and so on up to 9.

Many varied geometrical patterns arise that aid student awareness (Figure 16.11, see page 262). Some of the patterns created by moving from number to number are similar to the moves of a chess piece. Besides the interesting patterns that emerge, the student can also observe whether or not he has circled the correct number. If a mistake is made, the pattern will be distorted. The work is almost self-checking. In addition, if the table is incomplete, the student can complete it,

Figure 16.10

Figure 16.11

without necessarily writing down every number. Determining patterns of the multiplication tables, therefore, offers students the opportunity to learn the tables, to check their own responses, and offers practice keeping the facts permanently in mind. Another use for the 100-squares drawings follows:

▶ The squares should be made on half-inch graph paper or larger. Have students cut out the boxes with circled numbers in them. This would result in 100 squares that look like those in Figure 16.12, provided for the 3-table and the 4-table. Besides making the pattern of the products more vivid, we have made an interesting tool to assist students with computations, particularly with fractions. The collection of tables for the numbers 1 through 9 now becomes a "common-denominator finder," a process that always seems to bedevil youngsters. For example,

Figure 16.12

3-Table

1	2		4	5		7	8		10
11		13	14		16	17		19	20
	22	23		25	26		28	29	
31	32		34	35		37	38		40
41		43	44		46	47		49	50
	52	53		55	56		58	59	
61	62		64	65		67	68		70
71		73	74		76	77		79	80
	82	83		85	86		88	89	
91	92		94	95		97	98		100

4-Table

1	2	3		5	6	7		9	10
11		13	14	15		17	18	19	
21	22	23		25	26	27		29	30
31		33	34	35		37	38	39	
40	41	42		45	46	47		49	50
51		53	54	55		57	58	59	
61	62	63		65	66	67		69	70
71		73	74	75		77	78	79	
81	82	83		85	86	87		89	90
91		93	94	95		97	98	99	

$$\frac{1}{3} + \frac{1}{4} = ?$$

The student can be encouraged to do the example in the best way possible. Once the work is finished, or the student is stuck, the cut-out tables are used for checking or helping the student out.

What is the lowest common denominator (LCD) of 3 and 4?

First take either the 3- or the 4-table and place it before you. Then take the other table and place it directly over the first so that each number is over its matching number. When the tables are lined up, the cutouts will also line up with an interesting result illustrated by Figure 16.13.

Figure 16.13

3-Table Over 4-Table

1	2	3	4	5	6	7	8	9	10
11		13	14	15	16	17	18	19	20
21	22	23		25	26	27	28	29	30
31	32	33	34	35		37	38	39	40
41	42	43	44	45	46	47		49	50
51	52	53	54	55	56	57	58	59	
61	62	63	64	65	66	67	68	69	70
71		73	74	75	76	77	78	79	80
81	82	83		85	86	87	88	89	90
91	92	93	94	95		97	98	99	100

The holes match in the spaces for the numbers 12, 24, 36, 48, . . . The student sees at an instant all of the common denominators up to and including 96. The LCD is also apparent. When students use these cutout tables, the mystery goes out of finding the LCD.

Of course, the same procedures will also yield the least common multiple (LCM), depending on the purpose in mind when the tables are used. The intersection of the two patterns points up vividly exactly what the student is trying to find. After a time, the student should be able to carry out the work without the use of the tables. This is generally best determined by the student, although, in some instances, teachers find it necessary to encourage students to relinquish the aids.

16.5 Graphing Multiplication Tables

The patterns of the multiplication tables can lead to other activities. Students with a knowledge of graphing techniques can place the multiplication relationship on the rectangular coordinate plane. Sketching the graph of the 3-times table, $y = 3x$, on the same set of axes as the 4-times table, $y = 4x$, gives another view of these patterns (Figure 16.14). We do not often think about graphs in this way, but the lines drawn clearly show patterns of relationship and pictures of functions.

Figure 16.14

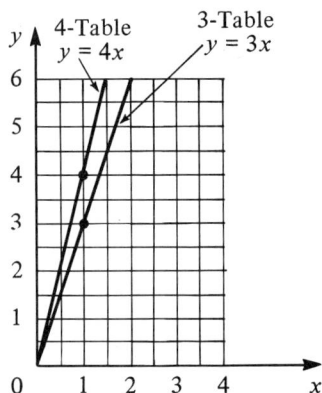

Drawing these graphs is not merely an exercise in seeing patterns. A British publication has given some idea of the possibilities that emerge.[2] The elusive number π comes into play rather nicely. If we collect several round objects of varying sizes such as jar tops, coins, and chips, the students could wind masking tape about the edge just long enough to cover the circumference. Have the students place the diameter along the x-axis with one end point at the origin and the other along the x-axis and mark its length to locate one diameter along the x-axis. Peeling off the tape and sticking it to the graph extending upward vertically from the diameter end point will give a length for the y-coordinate. Connect this point to the origin with a straight line, and you obtain an interesting result.

▶ What has been drawn in Figure 16.15?

What is the relationship of the diameter of a circle to the circumference?

Figure 16.15

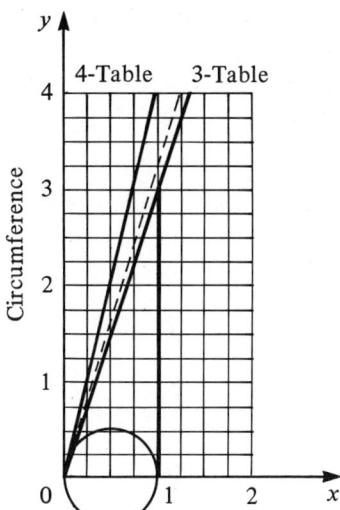

With little knowledge about the nature of π, students can quickly see that π lies somewhere between the 3-line and the 4-line, closer to the 3. That value, which we call π, is a bit more than 3. Of course, this general pattern would emerge after taping several different size objects and comparing circumference and diameter with several strips on the graph. Students are surprised that the edges of the strips seem to lie along a straight line. If this activity is done on large (half-inch or bigger) graph paper, students can work with little difficulty.

There are many paths to follow after such experiences. We are certainly in the area of slope, which in itself involves an interesting pattern-finding exercise. The entire process offers practice with sketching graphs. We also lay the foundation for a good deal of algebra. The search for patterns in the familiar multiplication tables generates varied results. Like much pattern-finding, we know where we are headed, but we are seldom sure of what we will encounter along the way. The work is open-ended and dependent to no small degree on the students' ability to see. The resulting work is a constant source of surprise and pleasure to both students and teachers. Open up your challenge to the students. Be prepared to deal with whatever arises as it happens, and your class will become a more interesting and exciting place. The danger lies in the time pressures usually felt by teachers. Avoid the tendency to discourage student ideas that may diverge from ours. In helping students look for patterns, we must be ready to honor their ideas with only one necessary criteria: *Is the pattern consistent with the data?* This is the only legitimate question. There is no *one* pattern; there is no *best* pattern; there are only patterns. Some work, and some don't. When the minds of the students are free to explore, they begin to develop a feeling for mathematics.

Directed Numbers 16.6

Pattern-finding can be carried out at many levels. Finding regularity in a collection of numbers, and exploring physical patterns of number representations are one level. We move to a more advanced level when we ask that students find patterns to deal with mathematical operations. A good example of this is the work with integers. How do you add, subtract, multiply or divide these integers? Do they behave like the natural numbers or are they different? If so, how and where? These questions may all be approached through pattern-finding. An introduction to this topic may be made with problems from familiar situations, such as the use of the temperature scale:

▶
Consider the scientist doing an experiment in the laboratory, carefully controlling the temperature of, and examining the change in, a particular metal. Table 16.1 gives the temperature readings for the experiment for each hour:

Table 16.1

After h hours	Temperature T is
0	10
1	8
2	6
3	4

The students examine the table, look for a pattern, write a formula, and draw the graph.

In a discussion of the situation, it is brought out that at the start of the experiment the temperature was 10°; thus we see that $T = 10$ when $h = 0$. The temperature is decreasing at a steady rate of 2° per hour. When the formula $T = 10 - 2h$ is checked against the table, all the ordered pairs seem to fit. We begin to discuss predictions:

What would the temperature be after 4 hours? 5 hours? Substitutions are made and the desired values of T are computed and then checked by alternate methods, i.e., from the graph and by extending the table. We arrive at the question, What will the temperature be after 6 hours? Substitution yields:

$$T = 10 - 2h$$
$$T = 10 - 2 \times 6$$
$$T = 10 - 12$$

This is an interesting problem since it requires that we subtract 12 from 10. How can we take away 12 from 10? It is apparent that there will be some temperature reading in the room after 6 hours have elapsed. Therefore, if our mathematics is to work, there must be an answer to the 10 minus 12 question, and by reasoning we also know what this answer should be! If the temperature is at zero and falls two degrees, it will be at $-2°$. To keep our mathematical ideas "working" we find that if

$$T = 10 - 2h \text{ and } h = 6, \text{ then}$$
$$T = 10 - 2 \times 6$$
$$T = 10 - 12$$
$$T = -2$$

which in this case translates to a temperature of $-2°$.

We extend our work by exploring the T-values corresponding to h-values of 7, 8, 9, and higher; and we encounter additional examples similar to the one just discussed. Each time an answer is determined, students should be encouraged to use the temperature scale either as a check or as a means for finding the correct response. In this way we build up a reservoir of acceptable answers to the examples.

Additional experiences with these "new" numbers may be provided by examining the changing height above sea level as we descend a mountain side into Death Valley, the lowest point in the United States. If we start recording these heights when we are 250 ft above sea level and if we are descending at the rate of 50 ft/hr, then our height will be described by the formula

$$H = 250 - 50t$$

In this case, since we are able to reason what the formula should be and can begin with the formula, students can construct the table of values by substituting values for t and calculating the corresponding values of H. Of course after 5 hrs we begin to reach land levels below sea level and once again encounter negative numbers.

Additional examples can be introduced by examining the profit and loss record of a business that made $20,000 but has since been declining in profits steadily at the rate of $5,000 per year. After 4 years, a loss is encountered and once again negative numbers appear ($P = 20,000 - 5,000y$).

We have begun to extend our number system. The introduction of negative numbers through the use of familiar relationships not only places these numbers in a meaningful context, but also parallels the introduction of such numbers historically—recording profits and losses in commerce. While the context is somewhat different, the basic process is mathematically the same, or as students frequently describe it, "We're taking away more than we have." Although the mathematical elegance of this statement leaves much to be desired, the idea of subtraction as "take away" is a sound notion to build upon. Later, we may emphasize that subtraction is the inverse operation of addition and that "take-away" is meaningless with numbers. But for now, it provides a sharp visual image of what is happening, somewhat all too often lacking when one considers mathematical operations. It is also a notion we shall build upon to develop skill in calculating with directed numbers. And so we have introduced directed numbers with the process of subtraction, rather than with the familiar procedure of using addition as a starting point. After additional examples that lead to the need to operate with such numbers, we may turn our attention to mastery of the process.

Operations with Integers

We assume that students have had many different experiences related to signed numbers in much the same manner as the initial ones described here. (Chapter 7 makes use of the motion formula for this purpose.) Since students know what a signed number is, we now confront them with problems calling for operations with these numbers. We turn away from the physical situation and look at a purely mathematical exploration.

The number line is an old standby but in this instance it is used to point up an important relationship, the additive inverse, $x + (-x) = 0$ (Figure 16.16, see page 268).

Perhaps the most difficult of all operations with directed numbers is the process of subtraction. For the most part, the student has been accustomed to

Figure 16.16

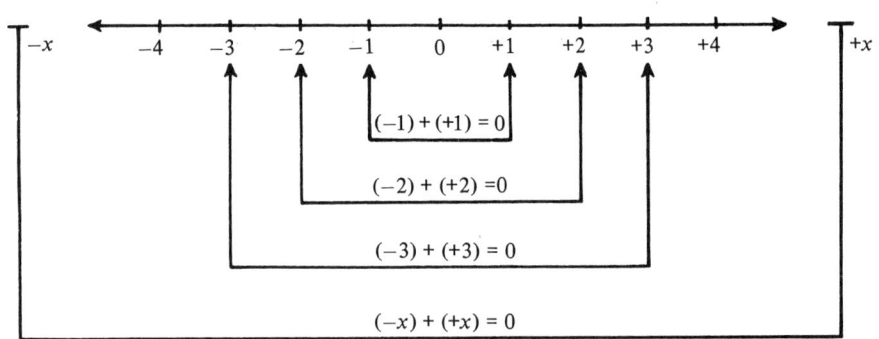

think of subtraction in terms of "take away." Now he comes upon negative numbers and the "take away" procedure is no longer applicable. We present one way to take advantage of the physical idea of "take away" and to help students visualize what is happening when adding and subtracting integers.[3] To enable students to represent examples visually, the following scheme has been devised: We shall use the letter "P" for positive, with one "P" standing for one positive unit. However, in the interest of brevity, we shall write only the upper portion of the "P," just ⊃. Thus, +3 will be represented by ⊃⊃⊃ and other positive numbers may be visualized as shown:

+ 4   ⊃⊃⊃⊃
+ 2   ⊃⊃
+ 6   ⊃⊃⊃⊃⊃⊃

Since the negative numbers are the opposites of the positives, we can illustrate negative numbers by reversing the symbol:

− 2   ⊂⊂
− 3   ⊂⊂⊂
− 4   ⊂⊂⊂⊂

If we keep in mind the notion of the additive inverse, $x + (-x) = 0$, we are ready to operate with these numbers. We begin with addition. Problems involving only the positive integers are not in need of discussion. The students should complete the problems as they have been doing for years in arithmetic. These should not be treated as new examples and the use of aids is unwarranted. However, we demonstrate one here simply to illustrate the use of symbols.

▶

  (+5)   We represent this as   ⊃⊃⊃⊃⊃
+ (+3)   We represent this as   ⊃⊃⊃
          Thus we have in all   ⊃⊃⊃⊃⊃⊃⊃⊃   or +8.

We turn to an addition involving negative numbers, $(+4) + (-3)$, and use the loops.

▶

  (+4)   ⊃⊃⊃⊃
+ (−3)   ⊂⊂⊂

Since we are adding, we combine sets and, in so doing, we come upon an interesting occurrence: If the loops are placed alongside each other, they appear like this:

```
  (+4)  ⊃ ⊃ ⊃ ⊃
+ (−3)  ⊂ ⊂ ⊂
─────────────────
        ⊖ ⊖ ⊖ ⊃
```

A positive loop joined with a negative loop forms a figure that looks remarkably like a zero, ⊖ , and in fact we consider it to be a zero for we have already established that $(+1) - (-1) = 0$. Thus, the result of the example just given is the single positive loop , or +1. Other examples follow this pattern:

```
  (+2)  ⊃ ⊃                    (−4)  ⊂ ⊂ ⊂ ⊂
+ (−3)  ⊂ ⊂ ⊂                + (−1)  ⊂
──────────────                 ─────────────────
        ⊖ ⊖ ⊂   or −1                ⊂ ⊂ ⊂ ⊂ ⊂   or −5
```

The students now have a way of determining the correct answer to all addition problems. These same loops may be made from the common variety of pipe cleaners. They are easily shaped and just as easily joined and separated again. In this way the students can do these problems physcially on their desks to find the correct answer.

As for subtraction, the approach is exactly the same except for the fact that we think of subtraction as "taking away" part of a single set and determining how many are left, rather than combining two sets to form a new third set, as in addition. With the loops or pipe cleaners, we are now physically able to employ the concept of "take away." Those examples involving only the positive integers with the larger magnitude at the top do not need the use of loops. We turn to the following example as a demonstration of the method:

```
  (+4)  ⊃ ⊃ ⊃ ⊃
− (+2)
──────────────
```

We may now physically take away two positive units:

```
  (+4)  ⊅ ⊅ ⊃ ⊃
− (+2)
──────────────
```

and thus we are left with +2, the correct result.

The problem of a larger subtrahend is most interesting. Let us reverse the position of the numbers and work with the newly formulated example:

```
  (+2)  ⊃ ⊃
− (+4)
──────────────
```

Here at most we can take away only two positive units; yet our example requires that we remove four such units. But we have a way out. We make use of the additive-identity property of zero. Since adding zero does not alter the example, we do so twice:

```
  (+2)  ⊃ ⊃ ⊖ ⊖
− (+4)
──────────────
```

Now we find that we *are* able to take away four positive units. Doing just this results in the following:

(+2) ⌒̸ ⌒̸ ⌣̸ ⌣̸
− (+4)
───────────────────────
leaving   ⊂ ⊂   or −2, the correct answer.

This work can now be applied to any subtraction example, simply adding zeros wherever it is necessary to do so in order that we may be able to "take away." Some additional examples follow:

▶

(−3) ⊄ ⊄ ⊄ ⌒̸   (−2) ⊂ ⊂ ⌣̸
− (−4)   − (+1)
─────────────   ──────────────
     ⊃   or +1   ⊂ ⊂ ⊂   or −3

The loops or pipe cleaners, whichever are used, may then be employed by the students in doing a wide variety of addition and subtraction examples. Larger numbers will discourage the use of this device and move students to examine the results of their work with an eye toward creating their own methods.

This is the key to the development of pattern-finding skills. Some device or other means is necessary to generate correct responses to a situation. The student uses the device and is able to get answers. When we introduce an example for which the device is too tedious or not helpful at all, how shall the student proceed? Observe what has happened in all previous cases and make up some method to successfully find results without the device. Initially it is important to try examples without the device, but use the device to verify the student constructed method. Later, the device is dropped altogether.

This is a prototype exercise in one kind of discovery. Finding patterns in an attempt to construct methods of solution is difficult at first, but like most things in mathematics, the experience itself eases future constructions. Although this is a higher order of pattern-finding, (there is more to do than find simple number relationships), it is always surprising how students are able to succeed. Giving students room to think can become as easy a habit as "tell and drill."

When discussing multiplication and division of integers, there is always disbelief on the part of students that $(-1)(-1) = +1$, as many teachers know only too well. While some rather elaborate schemes have been devised to make this result more palatable, a simple pattern can be surprisingly eloquent:

▶

$(-3)(+3) = -9$
$(-3)(+2) = -6$
$(-3)(+1) = -3$
$(-3)(+0) = 0$
$(-3)(-1) = ?$

If the pattern is maintained, the result $+3$ is a necessity.

Searching for the pattern can also lead students to accept otherwise rejected results. Of course, in both cases described here, lots of practice with many situations helps to reinforce ideas that have been found through the hunt for patterns.

Number Patterns—In Conclusion 16.7

There are endless situations to use for a pattern search that involve the idea of number. In the work presented here, we have found the pattern of a collection of numbers, of a method for operating on numbers, as well as for the physical shapes of number representations. In each case, the consequences of finding the pattern went far beyond the initial problem. Once students begin to master mathematics with the emphasis upon their own thinking, they are frequently surprised with the additional ideas encountered, other than those originally sought. The nature of mathematics makes this possible, and the nature of the way in which people learn makes the process so effective. Below are some samples of additional pattern-finding exercises.

1. Find the next number:

    1, 4, 9, 16, 25, 36, ___   1, 1, 2, 3, 5, 8, 11, ___
    1, 3, 7, 15, 31, 63, ___   (Fibonacci Sequence)

2. Do the work shown:

    $2 \times 2 - 1 \times 3 =$ $3 \times 3 - 2 \times 4 =$
    $4 \times 4 - 3 \times 5 =$ $5 \times 5 - 4 \times 5 =$

    What do you think $11 \times 11 - 10 \times 12$ will be? ___
    Work it out and check.
    What will be $9{,}873 \times 9{,}873 - 9{,}872 \times 9{,}874$? ___
    Make up your own exercises like this one.

3. Do this work:

    $3 \times 6 - 1 \times 8 =$ $4 \times 7 - 2 \times 9 =$ $5 \times 8 - 3 \times 10 =$

    What will be the answer to $73 \times 76 - 71 \times 77$? ___

4. Complete Tables 16.2 and 16.3.

    Table 16.2 Addition table.

+	0	1	2	3
0		1	2	3
1	1	2		0
2	2	3	0	1
3	3	0		1

    Table 16.3 Multiplication Table.

×	0	1	2	3
0	0		0	0
1	0	1	2	
2		2	0	2
3	0	3		1

5. Answer these questions using the above tables:

    $3 \times 3 =$ $2 \times 1 =$ $2 \times 3 =$
    $2 + 2 =$ $3 + 1 =$ $1 + 3 =$

    Is the order important in addition? $3 + 2 =$ ___ $2 + 3 =$ ___
    Is the order important in multiplication?
        $3 \times 1 =$ ___ $1 \times 3 =$ ___
    Is $(2 + 1) + 3$ the same as $2 + (1 + 3)$?
    Is $(2 \times 1) \times 3$ the same as $2 \times (1 \times 3)$?
    Make up your own tables for $+$ and $\times$ using 0, 1, 2, 3, 4.

Footnotes

1. For more information, see: *Mathematics in Primary Schools.* Curriculum Bulletin No. 1. 3rd. ed. Her Majesty's Stationery Office, London, England, 1969, pp. 25-31.
2. *Mathematics in Primary Schools.* Curriculum Bulletin No. 1. 3rd ed. Her Majesty's Stationery Office, London, England, 1969, pp. 73-80.
3. Herbert Fremont. "Pipe Cleaners and Loops—Discovering How to Add and Subtract Directed Numbers," *The Arithmetic Teacher.* Vol. 13. (November 1966), pp. 568-572.

For Investigation and Discussion

1. Collect information about the Fibonacci sequence and the diverse areas in which it occurs. Plan a lesson for students to enable them to share your findings.
2. Construct a detailed lesson to establish the importance of proof centered about the proposition that the product of an even number with any number (odd or even) is an even number.
3. Explore cube numbers to determine any interesting patterns. How could you use your findings in a lesson whose objective is to develop student's abilities to find and describe patterns?
4. Look at the multiplication table of Figure 16.9. Write down at least three patterns that are not described in the text.
5. What are the advantages and disadvantages of combining a study of the patterns of the various times tables with making graphs?
6. Demonstrate two different ways to introduce the addition and subtraction of signed numbers. Compare one with the other.
7. Describe and compare two methods for building acceptance of the fact that $(-1)(-1) = +1$.

For Further Reading

Books

Honsberger, Ross. *Ingenuity in Mathematics.* New Mathematical Library, New York: Random House/Singer, 1970, p. 73. (This can be ordered from the Mathematical Association of America, Washington, D.C.)

Sawyer, W. W. *The Search for Pattern.* New York: Penguin Books, 1970.

Shoemaker, Richard W. *Perfect Numbers.* Reston, Va.: National Council of Teachers of Mathematics, 1973.

Zippin, Leo. *Uses of Infinity.* New Mathematical Library, No. 7. New York: Random House/Singer, 1962. (This can be ordered from the Mathematical Association of America, Washington, D.C.)

Periodicals

Ainsworth, Nathan. "An Introduction to Sequence: Elementary School Mathematics and Science Enrichment," *The Arithmetic Teacher.* Vol. 17 (February 1970), pp. 143-145.

Arcidiacono, Michael J. "The Magic of Manhattan," *The Mathematics Teacher.* Vol. 68 (January 1975), pp. 59-60.

Ashlock, Robert B. and Tommie A. West. "Physical Representations for Signed-Number Operations," *The Arithmetic Teacher.* Vol. 14 (November 1967), pp. 549-554.

Botts, Truman. "More on the Mathematics of Musical Scales," *The Mathematics Teacher.* Vol. 67 (January 1974), pp. 75-84.

Branfield, J. R. "Find the Mathematician," *Mathematics Teaching*. No. 47 (Summer 1969), pp. 4-6.
Brown, Stephen I. "From the Golden Rectangle and Fibonacci to Pedagogy and Problem Posing," *The Mathematics Teacher*. Vol. 69 (March 1976), pp. 180-188.
Duncan, David R. and Bonnie H. Litwiller. "Patterns: Digits, Squares, and Bases," *The Mathematics Teacher*. Vol. 69 (March 1976), pp. 190-192.
Edmonds, George F. "An Intuitive Approach to Square Numbers," *The Mathematics Teacher*. Vol. 63 (February 1970), pp. 113-117.
Locke, Phil. "Residue Designs," *The Mathematics Teacher*. Vol. 65 (March 1972), pp. 260-263.
Weaver, Cloman. "Figurate Numbers," *The Mathematics Teacher*. Vol. 67 (November 1974), pp. 661-666.
Smith, Lyle R. "Discovery in One, Two and Three Dimensions," *The Mathematics Teacher*. Vol. 70 (December 1977), pp. 733-738.

CHAPTER 17

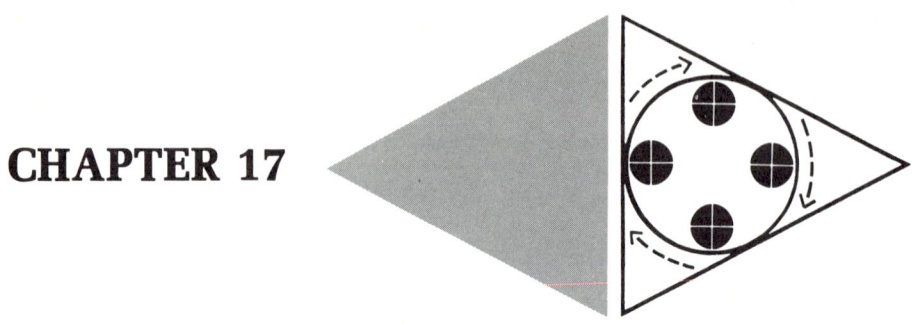

Patterns in Algebra

In section 16.6, there was a problem about a scientist doing experiments, in which the temperature of a metal was lowered and the changes were observed. A formula was written describing the pattern of the relation between time, in hours elapsed, and in temperature. The process of observing collected data from an experiment, then looking for and describing patterns in the data is a vital role that mathematics plays in science. Algebra, in particular, is of significance as the language of science. This use of algebra was exploited in Chapter 7. Here we will focus on the pattern-search aspect of the process.

17.1 Patterns from Experiments

We present the student with a typical experiment:

▶
> A baseball is dropped from a height on the moon. The speeds (v) recorded at each second (t) that it falls are given. Write a formula for the pattern of the relation.
>
> | t | 0 | 1 | 2 | 3 | 4 |
> |---|---|---|---|---|---|
> | v | 0 | 5 | 10 | 15 | 20 |

After a time, students generally find that the relationship is described by a simple

$$v = 5t$$

They then attempt predictions and verify their findings. This is a simple "find the number-pattern" kind of problem.

As the experiment becomes more complex, so does the task of finding a pattern. After observing a variety of patterns of the form $y = ax$, the students may consider other linear functions. Here is a typical one.

> An object is thrown upward on the surface of the moon with an initial speed of 15 ft/sec. Here is the velocity at each second. Find a pattern describing the speed-time relationship.
>
> | t | 0 | 1 | 2 | 3 | 4 | 5 |
> |---|---|---|---|---|---|---|
> | v | 15 | 10 | 5 | 0 | -5 | -10 |

Students have many different ways of trying to find some regularity in the numbers if they are allowed to do so. One response is usually:

> "v goes down by 5 as t goes up by one."

Another may be:

> "multiply the t by 5 and take away 15."

After some experience with these experiments, there are many students who use still different approaches. One student went to the chalkboard and wrote the following.

	1	1	1	1	1	
t	0	1	2	3	4	5
v	15	10	5	0	-5	-10
	5	5	5	5	5	

"One goes up by 1, the other down by 5. Its start was 15 ft/sec so the $5t$ is subtracted from it."

Then the formula was written,

$$v = 15 - 5t$$

This last solution is not as unusual as you might think when students are encouraged to search for patterns. It is also a step up in complexity in the finding of patterns.

Finally, we look at an example from a beginning algebra lesson in an average general mathematics class, average in terms of the usual general mathematics class problems. The students had moved beyond the experiments and were finding patterns in abstract collections of data and doing rather well. The teacher presented a table that was not completed in consecutive order and did not have a zero value. This is what students saw and how they dealt with the problem of finding the pattern:

Find the pattern:

x	1	3	5	7
y	1	7	13	19

Students write:

	2	2	2	
x	1	3	5	7
y	1	7	13	19
	6	6	6	

"x goes up by 2, y goes up by 6. So one part is $y = 3x$.
To find the other part, you need zero for x.
x goes down 2, y goes down 6.
So when x goes down 1, y goes down 3.
3 down from 1 is -2."

The table now is

x	0	1	2	3	4	5	6	7
y	-2	1	4	7	10	13	16	19

The pattern formula is

$y = 3x - 2$

In this case, students demonstrated that they not only were able to observe and describe patterns in the relationship between numbers, but that they were also able to generalize a method for working with all such collections of numbers (provided the function was linear, of course). This is rather mature thinking for students, especially general mathematics students. We now see how general mathematics students may think as mathematicians do under the proper circumstance.

17.2 Rolling Circles

A wide variety of interesting and challenging mathematical experiments may be undertaken outside the realm of the physical sciences. One such experiment is related to an old paradox, and can provide a challenge for students.

▶   Take two quarters and place them face side up. Hold one and rotate the other around it counterclockwise, keeping the edges in contact. Be careful not to let the rolling quarter slip (Figure 17.1).

Figure 17.1

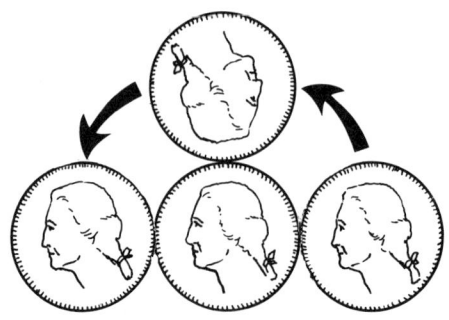

An odd thing seems to happen. The rolling quarter has apparently made a complete revolution around only half of itself! Is it possible that half of the circumference is equal to the whole circumference? Not likely. How do you explain the result? This little paradox holds greater interest than is apparent. We ask students to take a more general look at rolling circles about circles.

You may be wondering why these rolling circles are in a section on algebra. We shall soon see. To gain some sense of what is happening and to emphasize the experimental aspect of this investigation, ask students to begin by rolling a 1-in. diameter circle about circles of varying diameters in turn, 1-in., 2-in., and 3-in. The rolling process can be made a good deal easier if caulk cutouts are used for the circles. Students can carry out the rolling freehand with enough accuracy to observe and draw conclusions from the results. We begin with the 1-in. circle. The question to be answered is:

> How many turns will a rolling circle make around the outside of a fixed circle?

A turn is defined to be a complete rotation. Mark arrows on both the circle that will move and on the fixed circle. Begin by positioning the circles so that the arrows point at each other as illustrated by Figure 17.2. Now roll the circle and count the number of times the arrow returns to its original position. Partial rotations are also counted. In short, how many times does the arrow return to its original position as the circle is rolled about another circle?

Figure 17.2 One inch diameter: rolling circle. One inch diameter: fixed circle.

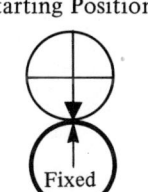

With our objectives clear, we set up groups of students to experiment; or we can use a large model for demonstration before the entire class. Students take a 1-in. diameter rolling circle and rotate it about a 1-in. diameter fixed circle (Figure 17.3).

Figure 17.3

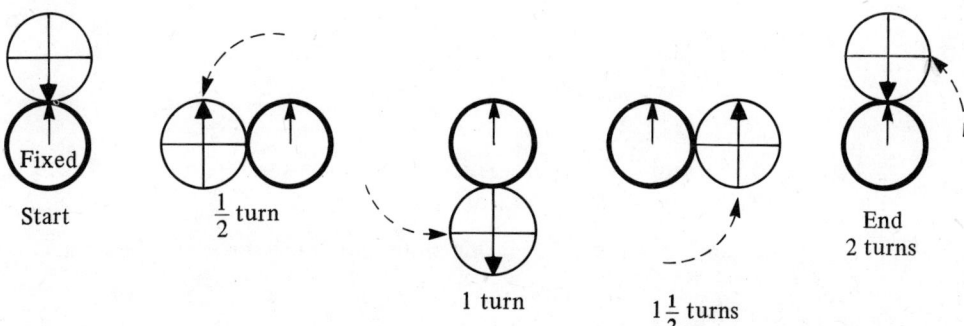

At the start, the arrows point towards each other. The number of times the arrow of the rolling circle comes back to the down position is counted, and the answer is 2. This matches the result of the quarter paradox above. To keep track of results, students make a table and record what happens:

Rolling a 1-in. diameter circle

F(diameter of a fixed circle)	1	2	3	4
T(number of turns)	2			

Now they try rolling the circle with a 1-in. diameter around a fixed circle of 2-in. diameter. Before doing so, a guess at what will happen is in order. How many turns will it make? Students do it, as shown in Figure 17.4, and find out how close their guess is. When finished, students record the new results in the table. We continue to do the same for a fixed circle with a 3-in. diameter and a 4-in. diameter. Each time, we encourage guessing at the answer before doing the rolling. When these results are recorded, the table should look like this:

Rolling a 1-in. diameter circle

F	1	2	3	4
T	2	3	4	5

Figure 17.4
One inch diameter: rolling circle. Two inch diameter: fixed circle.

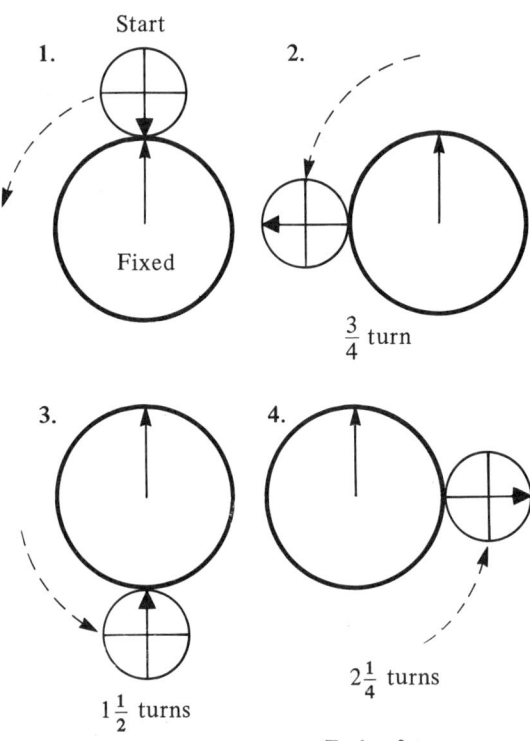

End: 3 turns

When the experiment is complete, students look for some pattern. In this case, the pattern is readily apparent and turns out to be:

The number of turns (T) is one more than the diameter of the fixed circle (F),

or $T = F + 1$

Always compare experimental results with the guesses, and then look at the pattern to make sure it "fits" the table values. We may now pursue other useful mathematical experiences. We can make a graph of the relation, or we can simply extend the relation to different size circles:

How many turns will the 1-in. rolling circle make around a fixed 5-in. circle? A fixed 6-in. circle?

How large should the diameter of the fixed circle be to give 9 turns? 15 turns? 20 turns?

These additional examples should be done mathematically without rolling circles until students figure the answers. Then rolling circles can act as a check. Of course, eventually the circles used become too large for rolling and algebra takes over.

This entire experience dramatizes how experimentation and pattern-finding give information about relationships. It also illustrates how mathematics enables us to do things that are otherwise too difficult. The possibilities in this work, which at first seem limited, expand surprisingly to provide a vehicle for teaching a good deal of algebra.

Roll a 2-in. diameter circle and repeat the experiment. Before doing it, what do you think will happen? Do it and see. The results of rolling the 2-in. circle are presented in the table:

Rolling 2-in. diameter circle

F	1	2	3	4
T	$1\frac{1}{2}$	2	$2\frac{1}{2}$	3

This pattern offers a greater challenge to the students. It may help if they make the graph before trying to find any regularity. When the pattern is found, it can be described algebraically with a formula:

$$T = \frac{1}{2}F + 1 \quad \text{or} \quad T = \frac{F}{2} + 1.$$

The result here is interesting for many reasons, not the least of which is the opportunity to involve students with fractions. Equation solution may then be extended to include equations with fractions.

Our pattern also becomes increasingly interesting, as we find some regularity in the outcomes of each of the experiments. Is there any pattern to all of these formulas? Before students attempt to answer that question, they should explore at least one additional rolling circle, a 3-in. circle. Again after guessing what will happen, students perform the experiment and record the results.

Rolling a 3-in. diameter circle

F	1	2	3	4
T	$1\frac{1}{3}$	$1\frac{2}{3}$	2	$2\frac{1}{3}$

The pattern this time is:

$$T = \frac{1}{3}F + 1 \quad \text{or} \quad T = \frac{F}{3} + 1.$$

To search for a pattern of all the formulas, we list them for easier comparison.

Rolling a 1-in. diameter circle: $T = F + 1$

Rolling a 2-in. diameter circle: $T = \frac{F}{2} + 1$

Rolling a 3-in. diameter circle: $T = \frac{F}{3} + 1$

Lined up in this fashion, the formulas seem to have a good deal in common. Eventually a general pattern is found for rolling circles of any size about a fixed circle:

$$T = \frac{F}{R} + 1$$

Students have moved from finding a pattern that describes a single case to finding a pattern for all cases. This is a giant leap forward, not only because students now can predict results of these circle experiments, but also because of the insight into thinking that is typical of mathematics. We always seem to be reaching for the next level of generalization. Perhaps these circles will give students more than just a brief glimpse of these extended searches for patterns. The work described involves many mathematical skills and concepts that should be exploited, but we are not yet through.

Rolling Inside

What about rolling a circle *inside* another circle? Will the results match those of rolling outside or will they differ? Will there be any regularity at all? Some simple experiments can follow preliminary discussion of what might happen. As before, the work can be done more easily if caulk circle cutouts are used. If students also glue the fixed circle on oaktag, they can roll the moving circle without the need to hold on to the other. As before, we must be clear about how to count turns. One turn is counted as the arrow returns to its original position, in this case, facing upward (Figure 17.5).

Figure 17.5

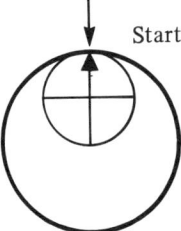

Begin by rolling the 1-in. circle along the inside of various diameter fixed circles. The procedures are much the same as before. Guess *first*; do it; then check. Figure 17.6 illustrates rolling a 1-in. circle inside a fixed circle with a diameter of 4 in. Rolling the 1-in. circle inside several fixed circles, yields the following results:

1-in. circle rolling inside

F	1	2	3	4	5
T	0	1	2	3	4

The result of rolling a 1-in. circle inside a 1-in. circle gives the zero value meaning and offers another step away from the "zero is nothing" misconception of many students. Zero becomes as important as any other number as it describes a physical as well as a mathematical condition. In this case, the zero means that we cannot roll the 1-in. circle inside a circle of equal size.

Figure 17.6

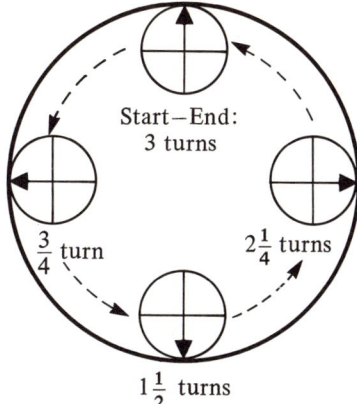

With the results on hand, a graph is a possibility. When the pattern is examined, it may be described with a formula:

$$T = F - 1$$

The general formula for rolling along the outside of a circle doesn't seem to apply here and so we have a new formula. We can move on to experiment with a 2-in. circle in a similar manner: guess, roll, record. The results recorded are:

2-in. circle rolling inside

F	2	3	4	5
T	0	½	1	1½

Once again we find fractional results, which have physical and mathematical meaning. A formula for this pattern:

$$T = \tfrac{1}{2}F - 1 \quad \text{or} \quad T = \tfrac{F}{2} - 1.$$

Many questions may be asked at this point, each leading to interesting investigations in trying to observe patterns:

> What would the mathematical result be for T if $F = 1$ and $R = 2$? ◀
>
> What would the result mean in terms of the rolling circles?
>
> How does rolling a 1-in. circle outside compare with the same circle being rolled on the inside?
>
> Is there any overall relationship between the formulas for rolling circles inside?

If we focus on the last question and add experiments rolling 3-in. and 4-in. circles, we get two additional formulas giving the following collection:

> 1-in. circle rolling inside: $T = F - 1$
>
> 2-in. circle rolling inside: $T = \dfrac{F}{2} - 1$
>
> 3-in. circle rolling inside: $T = \dfrac{F}{3} - 1$

As we did before with the formulas for rolling along the outside of circles, we now find a general formula for rolling inside:

$$T = \frac{F}{R} - 1.$$

Comparing with the outside formula:

$$T = \frac{F}{R} + 1$$

is fascinating; the patterns abound.

Our simple little paradox about rolling a quarter about another quarter has yielded a surprising collection of algebraic ideas and skills. We have only explored the more obvious ones here, but the ground is extremely fertile. If you are interested, you may wish to give some thought the the following related notions:

▶ What would happen if we used fractional diameters for either the rolling or the fixed circles? (2½, 3¼, . . .)

How do we interpret the negative numbers that result from the formula when rolling a circle inside a smaller one?

Is there some pattern to be learned about the tangent circles?

How do the properties of circles that are tangent internally compare with those of circles tangent externally?

What is the locus of all the centers of the rolling circles outside the circle? (This may help with the coin paradox.)

What is the locus of all the centers of circles rolling on the inside?

What other loci are of interest?

These questions offer some starting points for launching into a multitude of areas of additional interest; some involve algebra, and some involve geometry. The more we look into the circles, the more there is to know. All this is in addition to excellent opportunities for finding patterns on different levels. Going around in circles does not seem so bad after all.

17.3 *Discovery and Factoring*

Another activity designed to encourage student invention of methods, similar to that described for signed numbers, can be carried out for operations on the polynomials and factoring. We make use of devices or manipulatives to enable students to arrive at correct answers. By observing some pattern in the results, students can construct their own techniques. The device, initially used to provide answers, later is used to check the results of the students' own conjectures. We present a problem that was introduced earlier:

▶ A rancher has 100 ft of fencing and wishes to fence off a rectangularly shaped corral that will provide him with the greatest possible area. What are the dimensions of the corral?

While the solution of this problem is explored in Chapter 15 our concern here is with an introduction to the study of polynomials. If x and y represent the length and width of the rectangle, a formula for all rectangles of perimeter 100 is:

$$2x + 2y = 100.$$

This algebraic expression contains two terms, one in x and the other in y. Since the area of a rectangle is found by multiplying its length and width, any multiplication involving two factors can be represented as an area. In this way we are able to make a picture of an abstract mathematical expression. For example, we can make a visual counterpart of the expression $2x + 2y$. We can achieve an area of $2x$ if we have a rectangle of length 2 and width x. In like fashion we can represent an area $2y$ (Figure 17.7). Since we are adding these two terms, all we need do is place the rectangles alongside each other to have an illustration of the expression $2x + 2y$ (Figure 17.8). A close examination of the picture points up an item of interest. If we look at the large rectangle, which is the sum of the two smaller ones, it appears that $2x + 2y = 2(x + y)$. This is a fact worthy of further investigation. After the students draw the visual representation of many expressions of the form $a(x + y)$, it may be indicated that this relationship is a basic one in mathematics called the distributive, or do-it-to-each, law. We have a method for the elimination of parentheses and, what is more, a way of picturing polynomials. *Polynomial* is introduced as the name we apply to a collection of terms. We use *monomial* for a single-term expression and *binomial* for an expression containing two terms (such as $2x + 2y$), but all such expressions have the general name of polynomial.

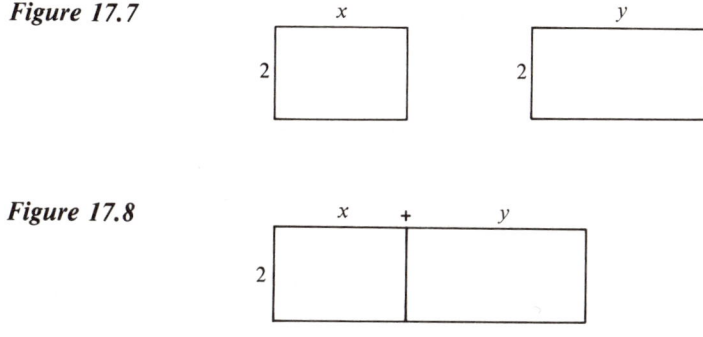

Figure 17.7

Figure 17.8

Operations on Polynomials *17.4*

Students know that we can carry out certain operations with numbers and the same may be done with polynomials. They may be added, subtracted, multiplied, and divided. Consistent use of the geometrical representations of polynomials helps to prevent the usual students confusion in carrying out these operations, as well as in attempting to combine like terms. For example, we made use of rectangles to demonstrate how $2x + 2y = 2(x + y)$. The pictures vividly illustrate why the sum cannot be $4xy$ or some other curious statement we frequently find students assigning to this example. This process seems more to the point than the explanation of adding apples and oranges. Some sample problems have been illustrated in Figure 17.9.

Another approach to the problem of visualizing operations with polynomials is most effectively presented by W. W. Sawyer in his excellent book *Vi-*

Figure 17.9

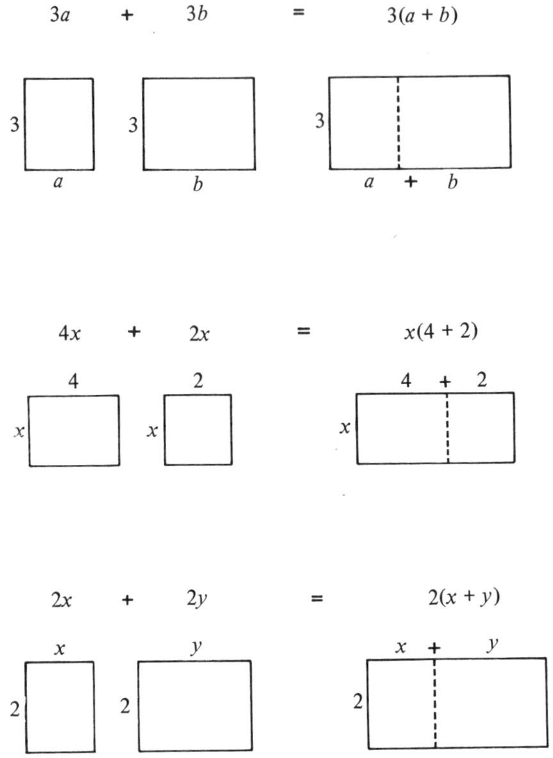
3a + 3b = 3(a + b)
3
a
3
b
3
a + b
4x + 2x = x(4 + 2)
4
x
2
x
4 + 2
x
2x + 2y = 2(x + y)
x
2
y
2
x + y
2

sion in Elementary Mathematics.[1] Sawyer represents the variables as unknown numbers of objects, and he demonstrates this visually through the use of little clouds over the array. For example, $5a$ is five equal rows of objects while $3b$ represents three equal rows of objects with a different number of objects in each row that is indicated by b. We see the first and last object of each row (circles) but the cloud covers the amount in between (Figure 17.10). The sum of $5a$ and $3b$ is then pictured in Figure 17.11. Sawyer is trying to present a clear demonstration of the fact that $5a + b$ cannot be written in any shorter way. He is attempting to eliminate the tendency of some students to add $5a$ and $3b$ and arrive at some incorrect response such as $8ab$. The visual representation seems to be most effective.

Figure 17.10

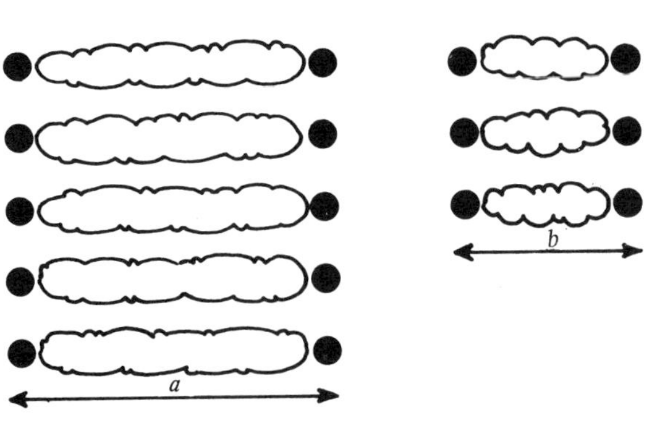
b
a

Figure 17.11

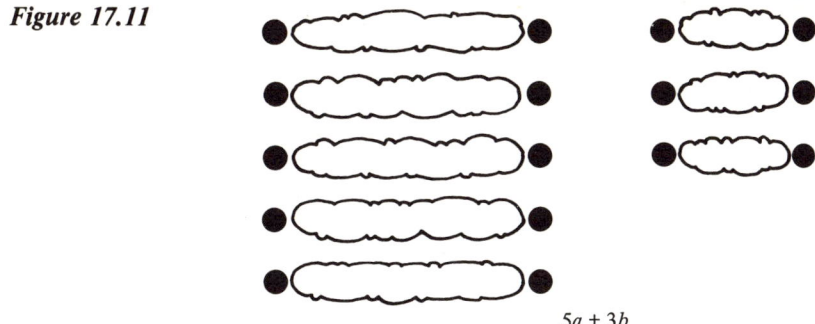

$5a + 3b$

Addition of like terms—in fact, the general process of addition of polynomials—may be neatly developed using Sawyer's illustration technique. The sum of $(2x + 3y)$ and $(4x + 2y)$ is shown in Figure 17.12. Subtraction may be

Figure 17.12

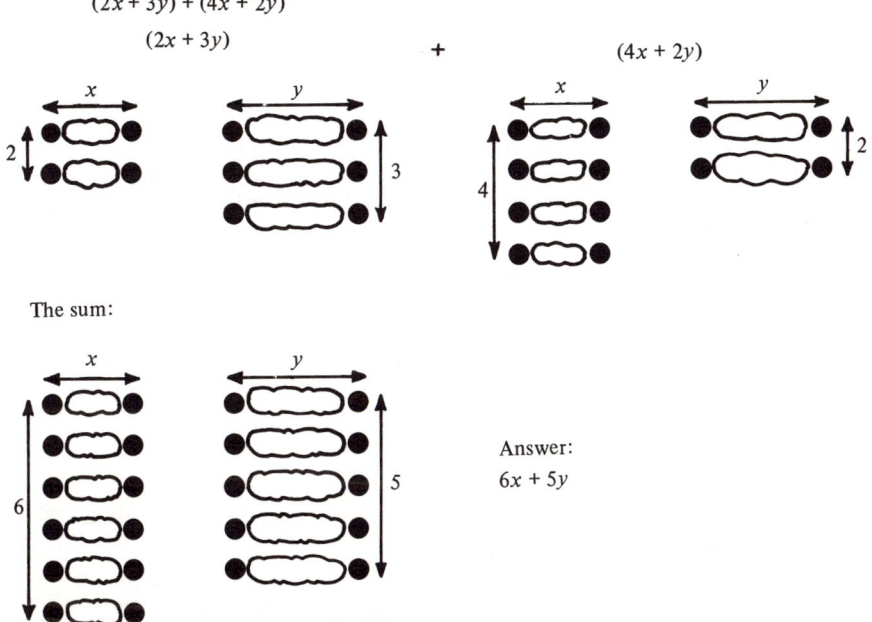

demonstrated with equal effectiveness, as the "take-away" idea is once more employed. Figure 17.13 (see page 286) shows how the example $(5x + 4y) - (3x + 2y)$ would appear using these visuals. The implications for removal of parentheses in carrying out subtraction are clear. A variety of examples completed using these visualizations would enable most students to formulate their own rules for such techniques. At the least, the student has a picture in his mind upon which to hang the mathematical abstraction. Similar "pictures" may aid the consideration of multiplication and division.

Representative materials enable students to find the sought-after answers. As they work, they keep track of their results and begin to formulate their own ideas for finding the answers without aids. Evenutally patterns are observed and tested with the aids being used as a check rather than as an initial

Figure 17.13

$(5x + 4y) - (3x + 2y)$

$(5x + 4y)$

With $3x + 2y$ taken away:

Answer: $2x + 2y$

response vehicle. The more devices we have for the variety of skills and concepts to be learned, the greater the probability of fostering student discovery.

Factoring Trinomials

In considering multiplication and factoring, we follow a similar pattern. As an example, we look at factoring trinomials in the manner of the work shown in Chapter 8. We represent each term of a trinomial by an area using pieces of cardboard or diagrams (Figure 17.14). In this way $x^2 + 4x - 5$ is represented by

Figure 17.14 x^2 may be shown as the area of a square with side x.

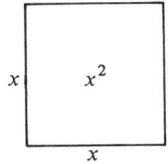

$4x$ is made up of four rectangles, 1 by x.

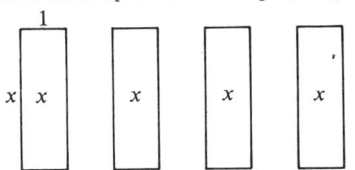

5 is represented by five 1 by 1 squares.

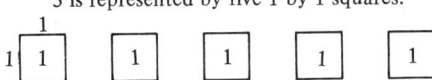

adding the first two terms and subtracting the third. The sum of the first two terms is easy enough to show (Figure 17.15). We simply place the pieces alongside each other to form a single figure. But how shall we subtract the last term? Since this term is represented by the five 1-in. by 1-in. squares, we take these pieces and place them on top of the figure formed by the first two terms, as illustrated in Figure 17.16. Four of the little squares are easily placed. But what of the fifth? In order to be able to remove it without destroying the rectangular shape, we must make some adjustments. Let us add on another rectangle, 1 by x, at the right end of the figure. In order to maintain the same amount of area, however, we now subtract a rectangle, 1 by x, at the left end of the figure (Figure 17.17).

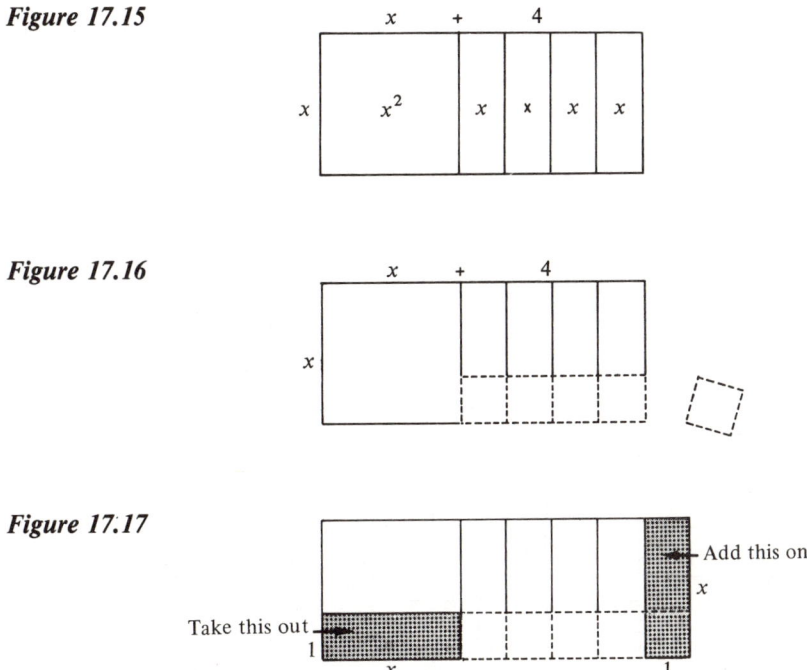

Figure 17.15

Figure 17.16

Figure 17.17

Now we may place the fifth little square that must be subtracted alongside the other four, on top of the pieces already there. If diagrams are used, the little square areas may be effectively erased. If cardboard pieces are being employed, we focus now upon the area remaining after the five little square areas have been eliminated (Figure 17.18).

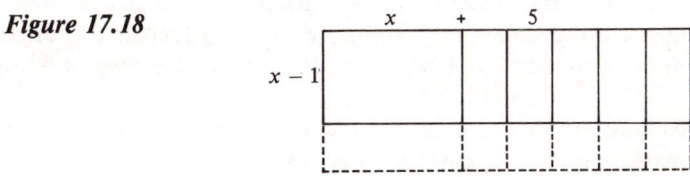

Figure 17.18

Examination of the results of this process discloses that the final rectangle is indeed equal in area to the desired $x^2 + 4x - 5$. If we read off the length and width of the result, in effect, we will have factored a trinomial:

$x^2 + 4x - 5 = (x + 5)(x - 1)$

The rectangular cardboard pieces or diagrams enable students to find the factors. Two examples are completed in Figure 17.19. These are but two of a wide variety of examples that may be done by students. As the pieces or diagrams become burdensome, students are encouraged to seeks ways of finding factors without aids by looking for patterns in neatly arranged lists of completed examples. They are encouraged to guess and then use the representative materials to check themselves. As the work progresses, the trinomials to be factored are made more and more difficult. Negative signs appear as in the previous example, and the coefficient of the x^2 term becomes some value other than 1. Figure 17.20 demonstrates how one such example might be completed using the materials.

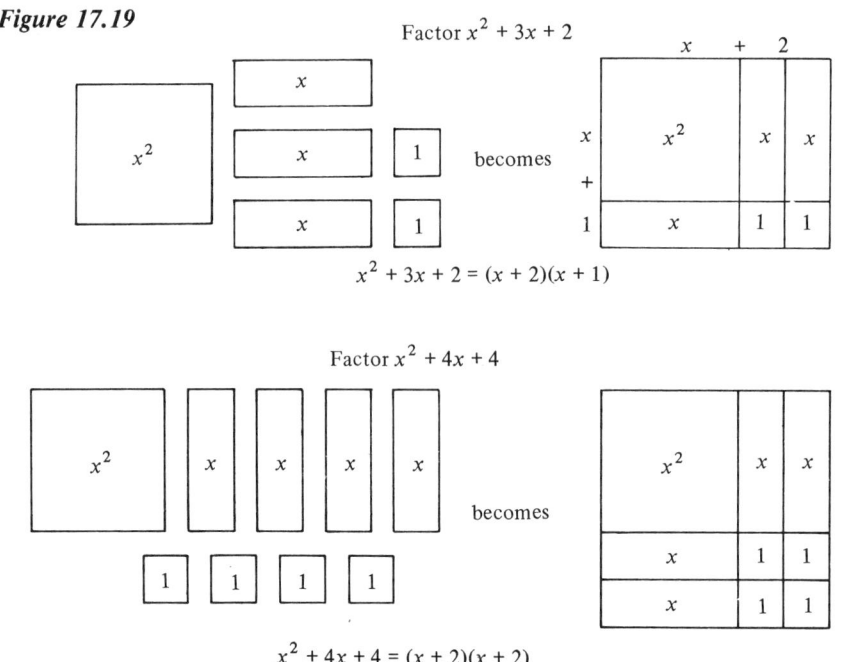

Figure 17.19

$x^2 + 3x + 2 = (x + 2)(x + 1)$

$x^2 + 4x + 4 = (x + 2)(x + 2)$

The use of these aids not only encourages the students to build their own methods but also provides evidence for the unique factorization theorem. No matter how the pieces may be arranged (there are many alternative arrangements), the factors are always the same. For example, in finding the factors of x^2 ⁵ $3x + 2$, the pieces might have been arranged as indicated in Figure 17.21. While the arrangement may vary, the resulting factors do not. In this interesting, intuitive fashion, we begin to build an understanding of an important theorem.

Most importantly, students are free to proceed to find their own ways of doing the mathematics. The patterns they find provide them with a means for constructing methods of solution, not just for a given exercise, but for the general collection of such exercises. The use of rectangles and squares is readily adapted to completing the square. We take words literally and proceed to finish off an incomplete square. As the student finds a pattern, he finds a solution original to

Figure 17.20

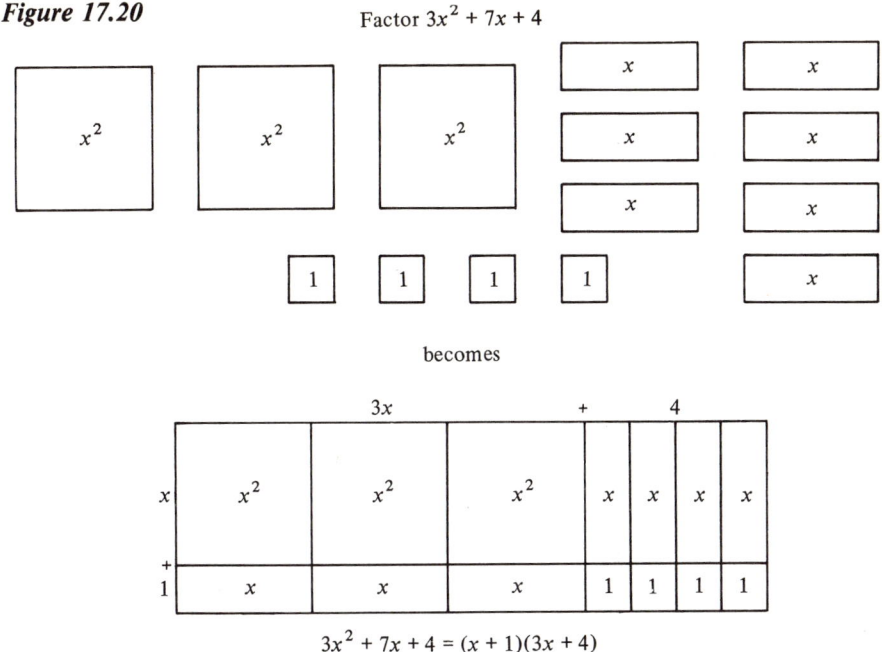

Factor $3x^2 + 7x + 4$

becomes

$3x^2 + 7x + 4 = (x + 1)(3x + 4)$

Figure 17.21

$x^2 + 3x + 2$ may be arranged as follows:

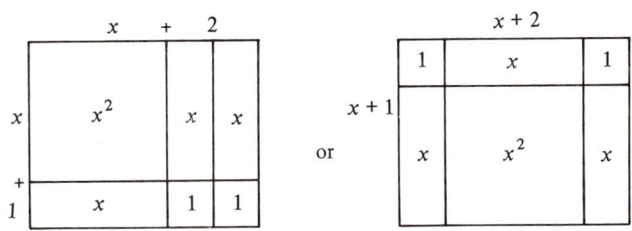

In either case the factors are $(x + 1)(x + 2)$.

him. With use of this approach, retention of original methods is more likely than those committed to memory.

Variation 17.5

One way in which functions can be classified is to focus upon how one variable changes with another. While the classification *linear function* is a general category that includes an infinite number of relationships, mathematically, when you consider this in terms of variation, still broader classifications can be seen. For example, the area-distance relationship for a picture projected upon a wall is an example of a quadratic function. It involves a specific case—the use of a particular projector. If we were to describe this situation using the language of variation, we would say that the area of the picture varies directly with the square of the distance. We would then symbolically describe this function with $A = kx^2$. It is true that this formula describes a quadratic relationship, but it does more than that: It describes how the area of a projected picture will change as the distance from the screen is changed, and it does so for *all projectors,* not merely the case in which 1/9 was the value of k. Thus, working with variation makes the dependency of a relationship more apparent, emphasizes the meaning of functional relationship in its essence, and classifies various kinds of relationships.

One interesting situation can introduce students to many types of variation in a single stroke: the amount of weight that can be supported by a wooden plank. To test the strength of the plank, it is set up as a bridge, resting upon two supports (Figure 17.22). The formula that relates the weight with the dimensions of the board is

$$N = \frac{3}{4}\left(\frac{Wd^2}{L}\right)$$

where

N = weight in 100-lb units
W = width of board in in.
L = length of board in ft.
d = thickness of board in in.

Figure 17.22

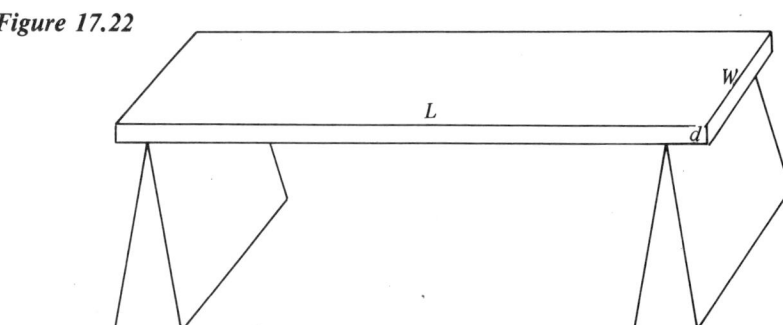

In order to simplify our work, we may drop the ¾ factor in the formula, since this is close to one, without distorting the results too much for our purposes. This would provide us with a simpler formula:

$$N = \frac{Wd^2}{L}$$

What kind of variation is this? Since there are several variables (W, d and L) that determine the weight to be supported (N), this is an example of *joint variation.* But let us examine the effect upon the weight if we hold all things constant with the exception of a single variable, taking each variable in turn.

▶ *The width (W) varies:* If the plank is 10 ft long and 1 in. thick, for the sake of this discussion, how does the weight supported (N) change as we alter the width (W)? (See Figure 17.23.) The students can calculate the effect of changing W by using the formula and then setting up a table of results. They might follow up by drawing the graph. This general procedure would apply to each case demonstrated here. Thus, students readily see the changes taking place.

Figure 17.23

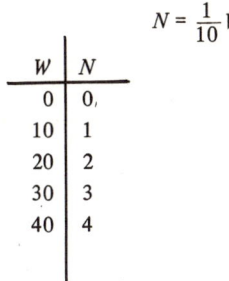
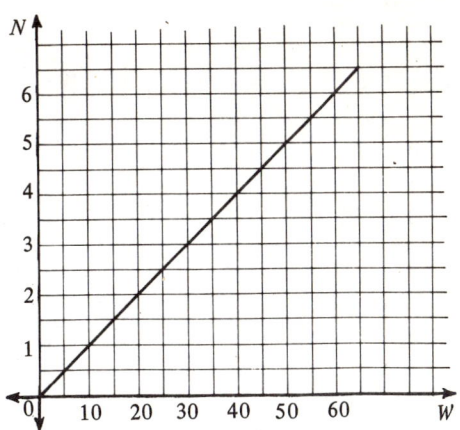

The thickness (d) varies: If we fix the width at 10 in. and maintain the length at 10 ft, what happens to the weight (N) as we alter the thickness (d)? (See Figure 17.24.)

Figure 17.24

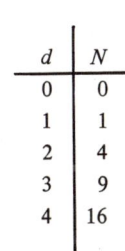
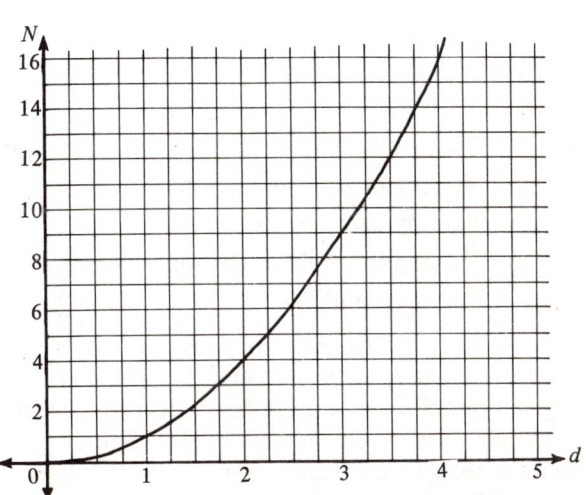

The length (L) varies: If we fix the width at 10 in. and the thickness at 1 in., how does the weight (N) change as the length (L) is changed? (See Figure 17.25, page 292)

A summary of the results of this investigation should be made by the students as shown in Table 17.1.

Table 17.1

Formula	Graph	Kind of Variation
$N = \frac{1}{10} W$	Straight line	Direct
$N = d^2$	Curved line	Direct
$N = \frac{10}{L}$	Curved line	Inverse

Figure 17.25

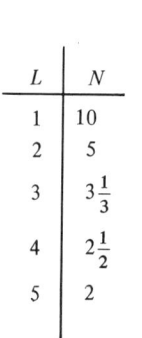 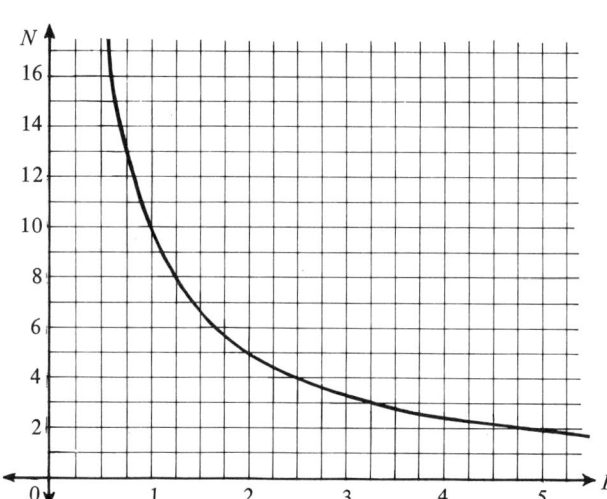

Students should examine the three situations carefully and satisfy themselves about the different relationships involved, as well as the apparent effects upon the graphs. Additional experiences will enable the students to compute the constant of variation as needed and to begin to see clearly the differences between each of the following:

Varying directly as . . .

Varying directly as the square of . . .

Varying inversely as . . .

Varying inversely as the square of . . .

Varying jointly as . . .

In every instance the graph adds to our understanding of the relationship. As a matter of fact, recognition of the general type of variation involved in a given situation will enable the student to describe tabulated data by a formula, if the data have been gathered by direct observation. Thus, the entire process of pattern recognition receives some powerful assistance. For example, if physical experiments had led to the collection of the data in Table 17.2 could we fit a formula?

Table 17.2

Time of fall (t)	Distance Fallen (d)
0	0
1	16
2	64
3	144
4	256

If students draw a graph of this information, something more interesting takes place (Figure 17.26). From previous work with variation and functions, we can see that this seems to be a case of "varying directly as the square of . . .," which indicates the formula is of the form $d = kt^2$. If we can compute k, we will

Figure 17.26

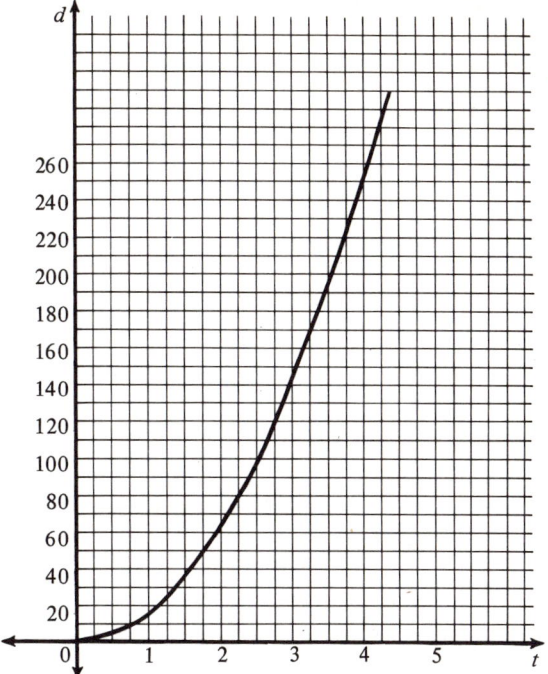

have found the desired formula. This is an interesting problem for students, who should be encouraged to check the table for possible help. At any rate, substitution of any of the ordered pairs of the table will yield an equation with only k unknown. If we choose (1, 16), we get

$$d = kt^2$$
$$16 = k(1)$$
$$k = 16$$

Thus, we may conclude that the data are described by the formula $d = 16t^2$. Of course, once we have found k, we may calculate any set of values for t and d. Many examples should follow this work; each time the student should be presented with another table of data.

Finally, a whole host of problems involving ratio and proportion may be attacked as variation problems. In the general equation of variation, k becomes the constant of proportionality. As indicated before, it can be computed, if necessary, thereby providing access to any desired values of either variable. The approach through variation becomes a most powerful ally in curve fitting, equation solution, and solution of proportions, as well as in helping students with their intuitive understanding of the nature of functional relationships. The following list is a collection of situations involving variation that would prove fruitful in trying to select interesting, meaningful situations for student study with the emphasis on finding patterns.

Direct Variation ($y = kx$)

Spring-stretch-weight:	$s = kw$
Velocity-time for dropped objects:	$v = kt$
Weight of stone block is proportional to length:	$w = kL$

Shadow length varies with height of object: $\quad L = kh$

Pressure of a liquid varies with the depth in feet: $\quad P = kd$

Food required (in pounds) to maintain body temperature depends upon weight: $\quad F = kw$

Volume of water in tank depends on depth: $\quad V = kd$

Direct Variation ($y = kx^2$)

Distance fallen by a dropped object depends upon time: $\quad d = kt^2$

Value of a silver coin (same thickness) varies with diameter: $\quad V = kd^2$

Strength of steel girder depends upon cross section: $\quad s = kx^2$

Area of a picture projection depends upon distance: $\quad A = kx^2$

Air resistance to a locomotive depends upon speed: $\quad A = kv^2$

Other Direct Variation

Estimate of weight-height relationship for elephants: $\quad W = kh^3$

Velocity (ft/sec) of water escaping through a hole in a dam h feet below surface: $\quad v = k\sqrt{h}$

Volume of a sphere depends upon its radius: $\quad V = kr^3$

Distance to horizon (miles) depends upon height above sea level (feet): $\quad d = k\sqrt{H}$

Value of blue whales depends upon length: $\quad V = kL^3$

Inverse Variation

Weight needed to balance a lever depends upon distance from fulcrum: $\quad w = \dfrac{k}{d}$

Number of ball bearings to a pound depends upon diameter: $\quad N = \dfrac{k}{d^3}$

Weight of a body depends upon distance from center of earth: $\quad w = \dfrac{k}{r^2}$

Number of plants to an acre depends upon distance apart: $\quad N = \dfrac{k}{d^2}$

Joint Variation

Volume of wood in a tree depends on height and girth: $\quad V = khg^2$

Time for a procession to pass a point depends on its length and speed: $\quad T = \dfrac{kL}{r}$

Altitude of a triangle varies directly as its area and inversely as its base: $\quad h = \dfrac{kA}{b}$

Footnote

1. W. W. Sawyer. *Vision in Elementary Mathematics.* New York: Penguin Books, 1964.

For Investigation and Discussion

1. Devise a lesson plan for the learning of multiplication of polynomials using geometric representations.
2. Select an example of direct variation from the list provided and make a plan for an introductory lesson in this area.
3. Do the same for inverse variation.
4. Using the activity of one circle rolling around the outside of another, outline a lesson whose objective is the solution of simple linear equations. (Make a physical model for students to use.)
5. Do the same for circles rolling inside other circles.
6. Show how the circle rolling problem can be used as a means of motivation for a lesson on locus.
7. Select an example(s) of direct variation from the list provided and make a plan for an introductory lesson in this area.
8. Do the same as above for inverse variation.

For Further Reading

Books

Sawyer, W. W., ed. *Mathematics in Theory and Practice.* London: Odhams Press Ltd., pp. 180–187.

Steinhaus, Hugo. *Mathematical Snapshots.* 2nd ed. New York: Oxford University Press, 1960.

Periodicals

Aman, George. "Discovery on a Geoboard," *The Arithmetic Teacher.* Vol. 21 (April 1974), pp. 267–272.

Gardner, Martin. "Mathematical Games," *Scientific American.* Vol. 233 (September 1970), pp. 210–218.

Malcolm, Paul S. "The Math of Musical Scales," *The Mathematics Teacher.* Vol. 65 (November 1972), pp. 611–615.

Norris, Theodore R. "An Inverse Square Relationship in Science," *The Arithmetic Teacher.* Vol. 15 (December 1968), pp. 707–712.

Troccolo, Joseph A. "The Algebra and Geometry of Polyhedra," *The Mathematics Teacher.* Vol. 69 (March 1976), pp. 220–224.

CHAPTER 18

Patterns in Geometry

We now turn our attention to geometric ideas that emphasize the search for patterns. The separation of branches of mathematics is frequently artificial, and in our explorations we will encounter work with number, algebra, and trigonometry, as well as the geometric ideas we seek.

18.1 *Pythagorean Patterns*

The Pythagorean Theorem is a mathematical milestone that has contributed much to the study of patterns.

Some history books on mathematics state that the first recognition of this theorem probably came about when someone noticed the design in a regular patterned tile floor.[1] If one looks at the tile floor in a certain way a pattern emerges that virtually demonstrates the theorem. (Figure 18.1) This picture is said

Figure 18.1

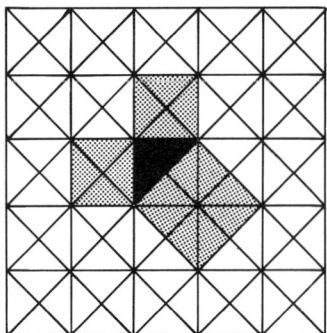

to have been found in the Chinese manuscripts of Chou Pei Souan Ching dating from 202 B.C.–220 A.D., the Han period.[2] Look at the picture of the tiles and see if you have the pattern "sense" to find the hidden proof. This is an interesting challenge for our students. There are many different ways to look at things, and Figure 18.2 is shaded to illustrate one way to see it. We have here a lively way to begin a study of the Pythagorean Theorem in either informal or formal geometry classes.

Figure 18.2

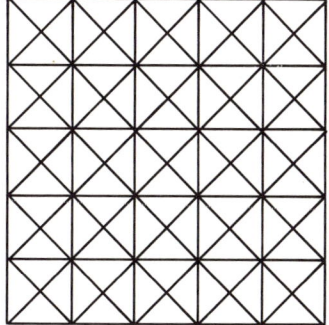

After the beginning puzzle, we continue our pattern "hunt" and extend student experiences with the Pythagorean Theorem. It may be of interest to know that probably more proofs for this one theorem have been recorded than for any other theorem in mathematics. There are 370 different demonstrations included in a book originally done in 1940.[3] The approach used here is perhaps the most familiar of all cases of the theorem, the 3–4–5 triangle. We ask our students to focus on this case as follows:

> Using graph paper, draw two 3 by 4 rectangles as shown in Figure 18.3. Bisect each rectangle with a diagonal, dividing each into two right triangles (Figure 18.4).

Figure 18.3

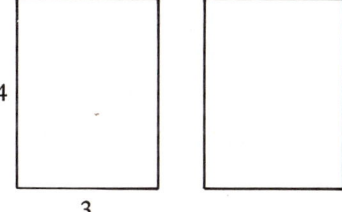

Figure 18.4

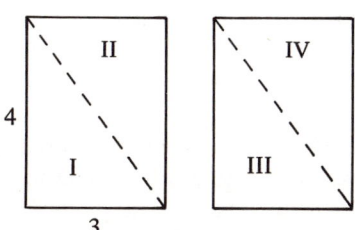

Each student has four right triangles. We pose the following challenge:

▶ Arrange these right triangles in such a way, to form such a pattern, so you can establish that each triangle has a hypotenuse of 5 units, and is therefore a 3-4-5 triangle, a right triangle.

It is much easier for students if the triangles are cut out of cardboard or paper and then manipulated. Index cards may be used for the cut-outs. You might try it for yourself.

An arrangement that offers some assistance is shown in Figure 18.5. Place triangles I and II as shown, and then add III and IV to complete the picture shown in Figure 18.6. The pattern is an interesting one because we have formed a square with each triangle-hypotenuse as a side (they were equal at the start), with another smaller square in the center completing the larger one.

Figure 18.5

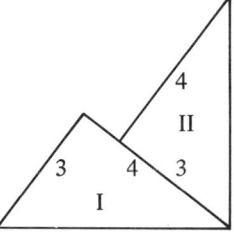

Figure 18.6

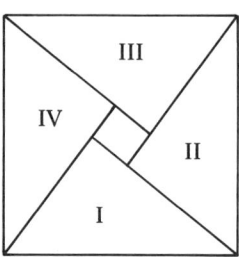

▶ What is the area of each right triangle?
What is the total area of the four triangles?
What is the area of the smaller square?
What is the total area of the larger square?
What is the length of a side?

The pattern we used resulted in a large square with an area of 24 + 1 or 25 square units. The side of the larger square must be $\sqrt{25}$ or 5. The triangle is a 3-4-5 right triangle. How shall we generalize to all right triangles? The students must be aware that we have only established a special case. The same pattern, however, can be used by students to generalize to all right triangles as follows:

▶ Cut out four right triangles from index cards that are congruent to each other. Label the sides a, b, c. Be sure that $a \neq b \neq c$. The challenge this time: Think about how we did the previous puzzle, and try to arrange these triangles to demonstrate the fact that $a^2 + b^2 = c^2$.

The triangles are fitted together small side to longer side with the hypotenuse out (Figure 18.7). The completed pattern is seen in Figure 18.8. Concentrating on the areas, the students answer the questions listed above once again. Their work may proceed like this:

The triangle area is ½ab. Four triangles give $2ab$. The small square has side $b - a$, and area $(b - a)^2$ or $b^2 - 2ab + a^2$. Adding we get:

$$2ab + b^2 - 2ab + a^2,$$

which is the area of the larger square, c^2. All this resolves to:

$$c^2 = a^2 + b^2$$

Figure 18.7

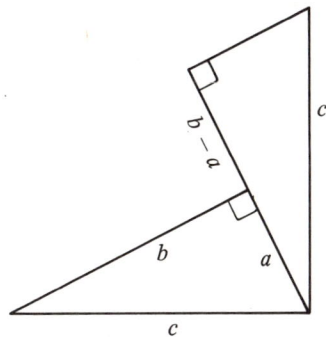

Figure 18.8

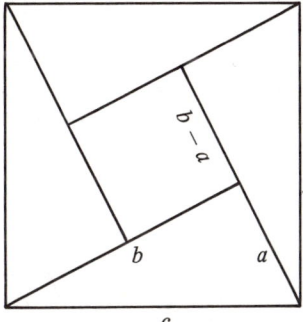

Using the patterns, students have established the theorem for any right triangle. This is not the only way in which patterns of triangles and other figures may be used. One other will be presented here that also offers a curious puzzle of rearranging geometric figures.

If we look once again at the first arrangement of floor tiles (Figure 18.1), we find that we have literally shown that the square on the hypotenuse is equal to the sums of the squares on the two legs. Using a similar approach:

Students can lay out a right triangle and construct the three squares (one on each side) with a compass on contruction or graph paper. They may then cut out the squares on the legs and try to fit them to cover the surface of the square on the hypotenuse (Figure 18.9, see page 300). While a^2 fits over part of c^2 easily enough, how can they get the rest of c^2

covered by b^2? The idea is for students to use their compasses and construct a division of b^2 into parts that will, together with a^2, completely cover c^2. Try it.

Figure 18.9

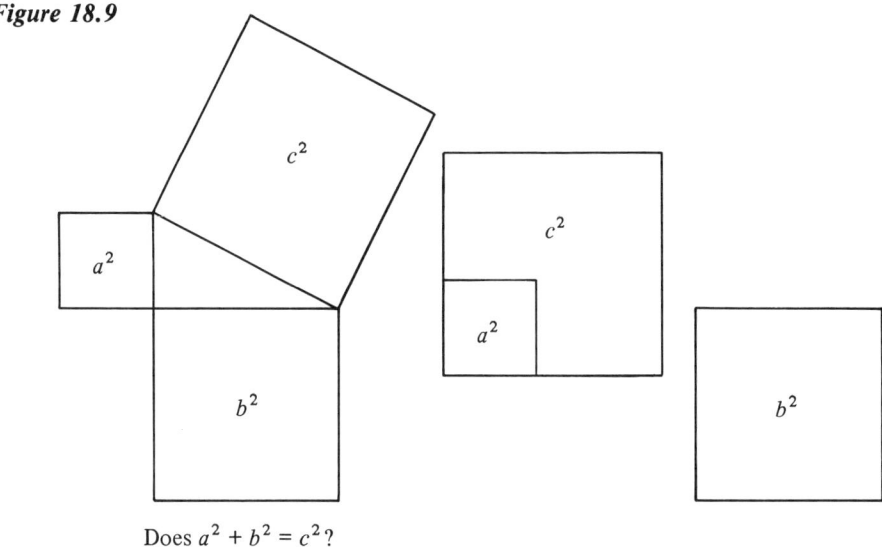

Does $a^2 + b^2 = c^2$?

If students were suitably impressed with the pattern of the earlier proof, you might try the same approach here. The idea is to cut the square on b into four congruent pieces (Figure 18.10), in this case, quadrilaterals. Then, with a^2 in the center, the four pieces can be fit around a^2 to give c^2. The arrangement of pieces in Figure 18.11 shows that the two squares do have an area sum equal to the area of c^2. You might want to try to determine for yourself why this does work.

Figure 18.10

Figure 18.11

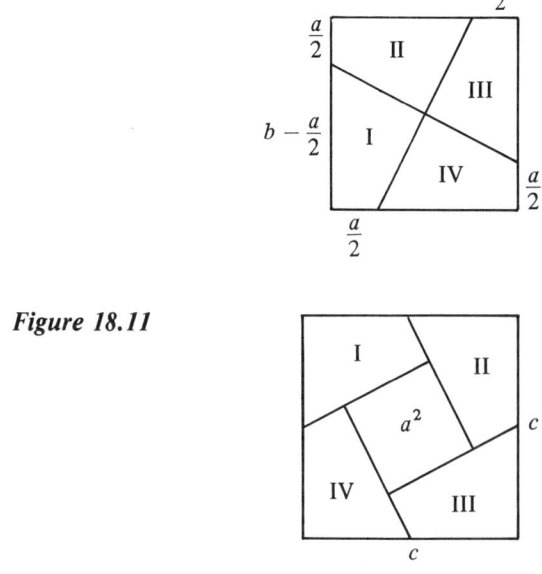

Patterns and Indirect Proof 18.2

The use of compasses for constructions, rulers for measuring, trying to determine the patterns that are needed, the use of algebra to analyze what is happening, and the use of geometric properties all combine to make the pattern-emphasis in relation to the Pythagorean theorem a fruitful set of activities.

There are patterns in all areas of mathematics and proof is no exception. Most students of formal geometry have a difficult time with proof, especially indirect proofs. Perhaps if we clarify and emphasize the pattern of an indirect proof, some of the difficulties might diminish. We will first examine a direct proof and then compare it with an indirect proof to emphasize the differences.

We try to prove the proposition: If two angles of a triangle are unequal, the sides opposite them are unequal in the same order (Figure 18.12).

Figure 18.12

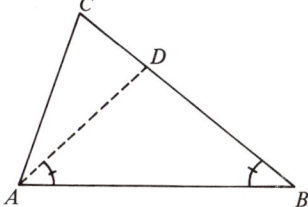

Prove: $CB > CA$
We Know: $\triangle ABC$ with $\angle A > \angle B$

We begin by constructing $\angle BAD = \angle B$. Therefore, $\triangle ADB$ is isosceles and $DA = DB$.

$CD + DA > CA$	Sum of two sides of a triangle is greater than the third.
$CD + DB > CA$	Substitution of DB for DA
$CB > CA$	$CB = CD + DB$

Thus, the direct proof is complete. Once we may use the fact that the sum of two sides of a triangle is greater than the third, the proof becomes a rather simple matter.

The indirect proof is a bit more involved but it does not require the "two sides greater than the third" theorem. The method of indirect reasoning is our focal point. We state the proposition: If two angles of a triangle are unequal, the sides opposite them are unequal in the same order (Figure 18.13)

Figure 18.13

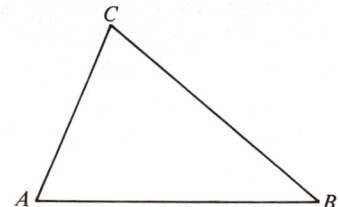

▶ *Prove:* $CB > CA$
Given: $\triangle ABC$ with $\angle A > \angle B$

There are three possiblities in comparing the lengths of the sides:

1. $CB < CA$
2. $CB = CA$
3. $CB > CA$

If the first possibility were true, then $\angle A$, which is opposite CB, would be less than $\angle B$, which is opposite CA, because of the theorem about unequal sides of a triangle. This is impossible, since we were given that $\angle A > \angle B$.

If the second possibility were true, then $\triangle ABC$ would be isosceles and $\angle A = \angle B$. But this contradicts the given information that $\angle A > \angle B$.

The only remaining possibility is the third.

Look at the pattern of indirect proof. Most reasoning outside the geometry classroom would proceed in a similar manner. For example, if a car simply stopped running, the mechanic, in trying to make the necessary repairs, would proceed in the manner of the indirect proof. Here is the proof of the theorem placed side by side with the thinking of the mechanic:

Proof	*Mechanic*
1. List all possibilities: $CB < CA$ $CB = CA$ $CB > CA$	1. List all possibilites: No gas Clogged gas line Broken fuel pump
2. Test the consequences of each: If $CB < CA$, then $\angle A < \angle B$, which is impossible since it was given that $\angle A > \angle B$. If $CB = CA$, then $\angle A = \angle B$, which is impossible since it was given that $\angle A > \angle B$.	2. Test the consequences of each: Put gas in car. It still does not start. Take apart all gas lines; clean and replace them. The car still does not start.
3. $CB > CA$ must be true since it is the only remaining possibility.	3. The trouble must be with the fuel pump. Replace it and the car works!

Of course, there may well be many other possibilities for the auto trouble that were not listed. A few causes were chosen to emphasize the comparison presented. This is, after all, the key idea when using the indirect method of proof: Have you considered all possibilities? At times it may not be easy to answer, but when you can definitely list all the possibilities, the method is a powerful tool for proof. Not only is this pattern of reasoning employed by car mechanics but it is also used by many other members of our society. Doctors do exactly what the mechanic has done when they ask you for the symptoms you have with regard to an illness. They then make a tentative diagnosis and prescribe medicine. If you feel better, that is the end of it. If not, their assumption is contradicted, and another possibility is explored.

The method of indirect proof is a natural thought process. If our students find it difficult, perhaps it is because few of the patterns of thought we attempt to develop in mathematics classes have been emphasized as patterns and realted to things outside the mathematics class.

Tessellations 18.3

In completing the Pythagorean proofs, we were concerned with the areas of figures. Area is a confusing concept to many students who somehow cannot seem to organize a mental picture of covering surface. The general patterns that result from covering surfaces are becoming part of school curriculum in both formal and informal geometry. Greater understanding of the notion of area is a consequence of thinking of area as a special case of tessellations, that of the square. Few students see any figure in use for tiling other than the square. Perhaps this is one reason for student difficulties.[4] When we look into other patterns, perhaps the way the square is used will take on some added significance.

> *What figures can be used to cover plane surfaces?*
> *Can we form patterns that will cover surfaces completely without overlap using any plane figure?*

As you might guess, the regular polygons and the rectangle seem the most likely candidates. To guide our work, we ask students to concentrate on a single point and attempt to fit figures completely around the point. (We limit our discussion to regular polygons unless otherwise indicated.)

> Will squares work? Students know that squares will work from familiar area problems.
> Will the equilateral triangle be suitable for tiling a floor?
> What about the rectangle?
> What about the pentagon? hexagon? . . .

To add a sense of reality, ask students to think of covering a bathroom floor with tiles. What shapes could these tiles be? Begin by exploring tessellations of one regular polygon. Figure 18.14 (see page 304) presents the outcomes of experimenting with various regular polygons. The work may be made easier for students if quantities of these polygons are constructed and cut out. Making the cut-outs can be a fruitful learning experience, and also enable students to physically try to tile a surface.

Only the rectangle (of which the square is a special case), the equilateral triangle, and the hexagon, cover the "floor" without leaving any spaces. The others do not work.

To make things more interesting, we can allow combinations of cut-out polygons to be used. What happens to the tiling possibilities now? How many of these figures will "fit" around a point? Two possibilities are shown in Figure 18.15 (see page 304).

After experimentation, students can look for patterns in their work without using cut-outs. Since a complete circle contains 360°, the figures built

Figure 18.14

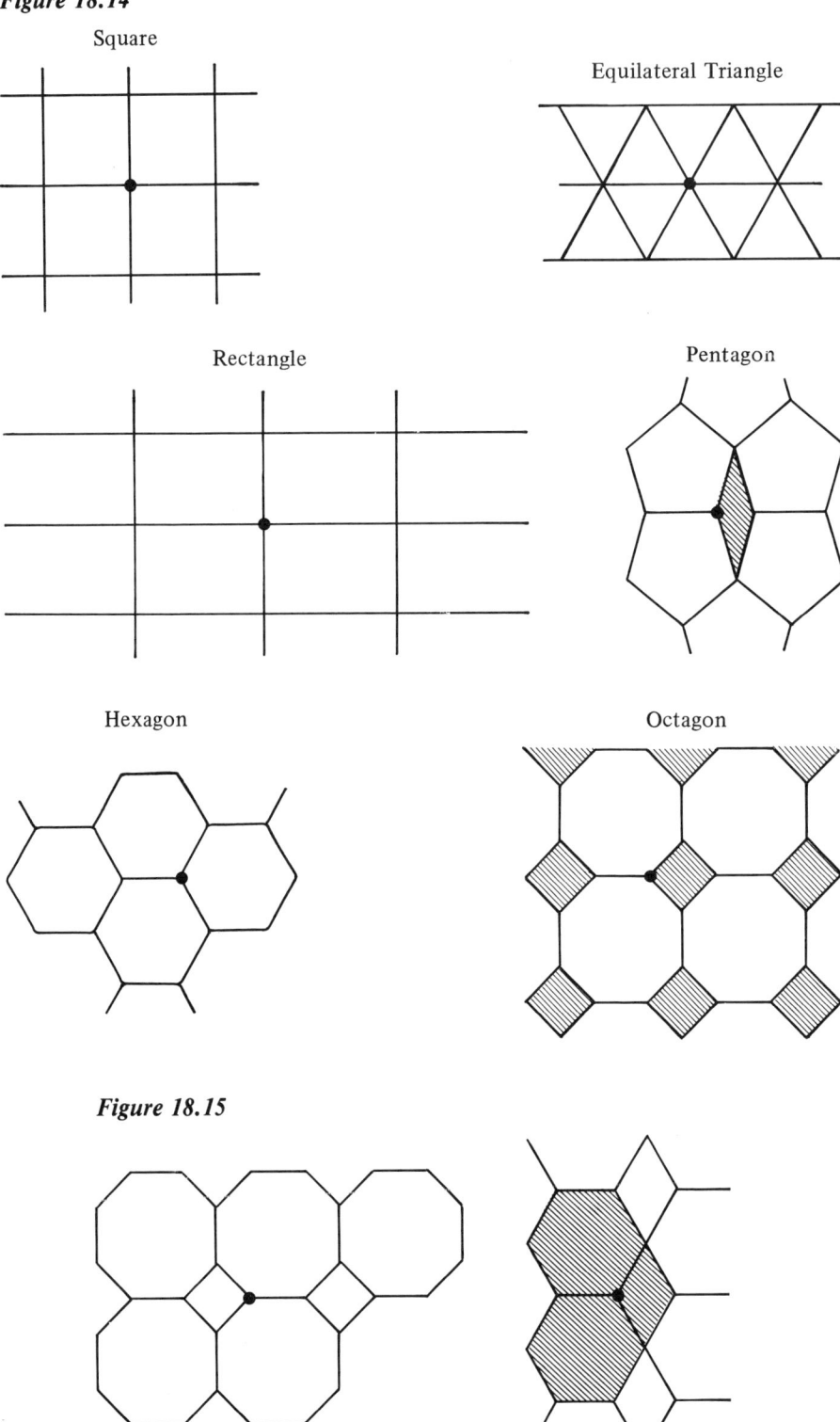

Figure 18.15

around a point must also have angles at that point that will sum to 360°. Using regular figures simplifies the work since all of the angles are equal in measure. Two important facts for making tessellations emerge:

The angles with a common vertex must sum to 360°.

The interior angle of a regular polygon must have a measure that is a factor of 360°.

Students can list the measures of interior angles, as shown in Table 18.1, in order to facilitate drawing conclusions.

Table 18.1

Figure	Measure of Interior Angle
Rectangle	90°
Triangle	60°
Pentagon	108°
Hexagon	120°
Septagon	128°
Octagon	135°
Nonagon	140°
Decagon	144°

Many different concepts arise at this point. Some prominent ones are:

Formulas for the measures of the interior and exterior angles of regular polygons.

Algebraic equations

Geometric constructions

Congruence and similarity

Tranformational geometry concepts

Number factors

This discussion is still at an elementary stage. Students could explore tessellations with polygons that are not regular, including any oddly shaped figure.

For our purposes here, the hunt for patterns has provided introductions into a myriad of mathematical ideas. There are references at the chapter's end for those who would like to explore tessellations still further. Some specific questions that may be considered include:

What is the relationship between the number of sides of a regular polygon and the measure of an interior angle, or of an exterior angle?

In the tessellation of a single regular polygon on a plane, what transformations are made to that polygon?

In the tessellations of two regular octagons and a square what transformations are carried out?

Look at the tessellations of an equilateral triangle. See if you can find and justify examples of congruent triangles and similar triangles.

We have seen a cross-section of pattern-finding ideas from geometry. As indicated before, it is virtually impossible to work in isolation with a single branch of mathematics, and so there will be additional geometric ideas that involve pattern-finding in Chapter 19.

Footnotes

1. Constance Reid. *A Long Way From Euclid.* New York: Thomas Y. Crowell, 1963, p. 4.
2. Harriet D. Hirschy. "The Pythagorean Theorem," *Historical Topics for the Mathematics Classroom.* 31st Yearbook. Reston, Va.: National Council of Teachers of Mathematics, 1969, pp. 215-218.
3. Elisha S. Loomis. *The Pythagorean Proposition.* Reston, Va.: National Council of Teachers of Mathematics, 1968.
4. For an interesting alternative see: Margaret Farrell. "Area from a Triangular Point of View," *The Mathematics Teacher.* Vol. 63 (January 1970), pp. 18-21.

For Investigation and Discussion

1. Demonstrate three proofs of the Pythagorean theorem that are not mentioned in this chapter.
2. Compare the advantages and disadvantages of showing students more than one proof of the Pythagorean theorem.
3. An example of indirect proof is presented in the text and compared with the problem-solving pattern of an auto mechanic. Select another example of indirect proof from the students' backgrounds, and plan a lesson to help students do indirect proofs based on the example.
4. Discuss the advantages of direct vs. indirect proofs. Give specific examples.
5. Show how looking for patterns can result in establishing a proof of the Pythagorean theorem.
6. Construct a lesson whose objective is an understanding of area based upon tiling a surface with squares and other regular polygons.
7. Select one case of tiling and describe how it may be used to emphasize the "pattern-finding" process.
8. Develop a lesson plan to teach students how to tessellate a figure other than a regular polygon or a rectangle.

For Further Reading

Books

Association of Teacher of Mathematics. *Notes on Mathematics in Primary Schools.* New York: Cambridge University Press. 1967, pp. 131-160.

Friedrichs, K. O. *From Pythagoras to Einstein.* New Mathematical Library, No. 16. New York: Random House, 1965, pp. 5-12. (This can be ordered from the Mathematical Association of America, Washington, D.C.).

Glenn, William H. and Donovan A. Johnson. *The Pythagorean Theorem.* Exploring Mathematics on Your Own Series. New York: McGraw-Hill, 1960.

Walter, Marion I. *Boxes, Squares, and Other Things: A Teacher's Guide for a Unit in Informal Geometry.* Reston, Va.: National Council of Teachers of Mathematics, 1970.

Periodicals

Eagle, J. Edwin. "Helping Students to See the Patterns," *The Mathematics Teacher.* Vol. 64 (April 1971), pp. 315-322.

Forseth, Sonia and Andria Price Troutman. "Using Mathematical Structures to Generate Designs," *The Mathematics Teacher.* Vol. 67 (May 1974), pp. 393-398.

Giles, Geoff and David Fielker. "Tessellations by Overlays," *Mathematics Teaching.* No. 71 (June 1975), pp. 30-35.

Graening, Jay. "Induction: Fallible but Valuable," *The Mathematics Teacher.* Vol. 64 (February 1971), pp. 127-131.

Lehnert, Reinhard. "Layered Surface Design, Its Pictures and Games," *Mathematics Teaching.* No. 55 (Summer 1971), p. 36-43.

Ranucci, Ernest R. "Space Filling in Two Dimensions," *The Mathematics Teacher.* Vol. 64 (Novemeber 1971), pp. 587-593.

Ranucci, Ernest R. "Master of Tessellations: M. C. Escher, 1898-1972," *The Mathematics Teacher.* Vol. 67 (April 1974), pp. 299-306.

Teeters, Joseph L. "How to Draw Tessellations of the Escher Type," *The Mathematics Teacher.* Vol. 67 (April 1974), pp. 307-310.

Thomas, F. H. "The Pythagorean Proposition," *Mathematics Teaching.* No. 74 (March 1976), pp. 52-55.

CHAPTER 19

Paradoxes, Puzzles, and Patterns

Recreation in mathematics can be a serious business. What begins as a pastime has often led to the development of new and important branches of mathematics, as well as greater insight into the nature of the subject. Paradoxes and puzzles have played an important role throughout the history of mathematics and have greatly influenced its development. Let us see where the following provocative problems will lead us in our study of patterns.

19.1 Sum the Series

Here is an interesting but baffling puzzle.

▶   Evaluate: $S = 1 - 1 + 1 - 1 + \ldots$

How you look at a pattern makes a difference, especially in this case. Students can get an idea of the importance of the concepts of convergence and divergence by attempting to sum this series. Mathematicians were able to find a variety of results. Two possibilities are:

$S = (1 - 1) + (1 - 1) + (1 - 1) + \ldots = 0$

or $S = 1 - (1 - 1) - (1 - 1) - (1 - 1) - \ldots = 1$

Did you find another? Don't be surprised because this series occupied the time of men like Leibniz and Euler and eventually led to the development of the theory of convergence and, later, the theory of divergence.[1] Most students offer a third result:

$$\frac{a}{1-r} = \frac{1}{1-(-1)} = \frac{1}{2}$$

At least this last response has the virtue of being a compromise between the first two sums. Here's a new method of solution: If you can't decide which of two answers is correct, simply take their average!

It is important to be clear about definitions and assumptions; students must not simply apply formulas without first making sure that the situation warrants and permits it. What is the correct answer? In this case, the series is a divergent one, and its sum will depend upon your definitions. There is a general agreement, however, that this series has no limit.

Here are some other infinite series problems to examine:

1. Consider: $1 - 2 + 4 - 8 + 16 - \ldots$

    It may be

    $= 1 + (-2 + 4) + (-8 + 16) + \ldots$
    $= 1 + 2 + 8 + 16 + \ldots \to +\infty$

    But it may also be

    $= (1 - 2) + (4 - 8) + (16 - 32) + \ldots$
    $= -1 - 4 - 16 - \ldots \to -\infty$

    How could the same series tend towards both positive and negative infinity?

2. $1 - \frac{1}{2} + \frac{1}{3} - \frac{1}{4} + \ldots$

    $\neq \left(1 + \frac{1}{3} + \frac{1}{5} + \ldots\right) - \left(\frac{1}{2} + \frac{1}{4} + \frac{1}{6} + \ldots\right)$

    Why not?

The assumptions made by students about the commutative and associative laws are called into question. Perhaps our students will develop a new found respect for these structure properties. Most importantly, this study of divergent series encourages our students to be a bit more prudent before jumping at seemingly obvious mathematical patterns. Things aren't always quite what they seem to be.

Fill the Jug 19.2

There is a very popular collection of problems, particularly attractive to high school students of algebra, that involves filling jugs of stated sizes. For example:

> You have a 5- and 3-gal jug. How can you measure off 4 gal of water from a jug of 8 gal?

Students generally will use trial and error in trying to solve such problems. They may also attempt an algebraic representation. A few students begin to notice patterns that offer guidance to a solution. After students have attempted the problem, you might want to compare their method of solution with the following fascinating process that was included in a Martin Gardner book of mathematical games.[2]

We have a rather ingenious "computer" for finding solutions to jug problems, which is in the shape of a grid made up of equilateral triangles. The grid represents rhomboidal tables upon which an imaginary game of pool or billiards can be played. In this case, the grid will measure 5 units on the vertical scale (for the larger jug), and 3 units on the horizontal axis (for the smaller jug). We imagine a ball starting at the origin (0,0). The ball proceeds along one axis until it strikes a cushion and then bounces off (following the reflection laws of light rays) along a new path, until it again strikes a cushion and rebounds in still another direction. Each point of contact has coordinates that, miraculously enough, represent one step in the jug filling problem! The bouncing ball continues (this time) until it strikes the number 4 on the vertical axis. The path followed gives the desired solution.

To gain a better understanding look at Figure 19.1. The graph contains the path traced by the ball. It leaves the origin and moves along the vertical axis, at (0, 5). This fills the large jug. The ball rebounds across the table downward and to the right until it hits again at (3, 2). This move represents that act of pouring from the large jug to fill the smaller one. The result is that the coordinates of the latter point give the contents of each jug:

(3, 2)   3 gal in the smaller jug, 2 in the larger.

As we follow the ball around, the additional steps are spelled out. The table in Figure 19.1 lists the coordinates of each point and the corresponding meaning. In this case, six steps were required. Begin along the horizontal axis, and you will find another solution. This is a powerful tool indeed.

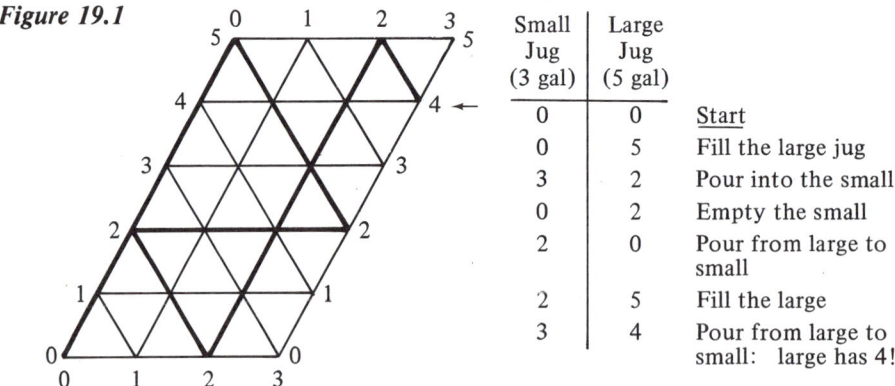

Figure 19.1

Small Jug (3 gal)	Large Jug (5 gal)	
0	0	Start
0	5	Fill the large jug
3	2	Pour into the small
0	2	Empty the small
2	0	Pour from large to small
2	5	Fill the large
3	4	Pour from large to small: large has 4!

Try another problem to test students' understanding of the "computer."

▶ You have a 7- and a 4-gal jug. How can you divide the contents of another full 10-gal jug so that there are 5 gal measured off?

This time we require a 7 by 4 grid. Figure 19.2 shows the path of the billiard ball that rebounds eventually to a position of 5.

This triangular coordinate system has proved to be a veritable gold mine of high school mathematical ideas.

A new set of coordinates were introduced based on equilateral triangles offering new meaning to coordinate planes.

We have made a mathematical model of a physical situation that works to our satisfaction.

We have made use of physical laws of reflection to resolve a mathematical puzzle.

We have put into use the geometric transformation of reflection in resolving our problem.

Figure 19.2

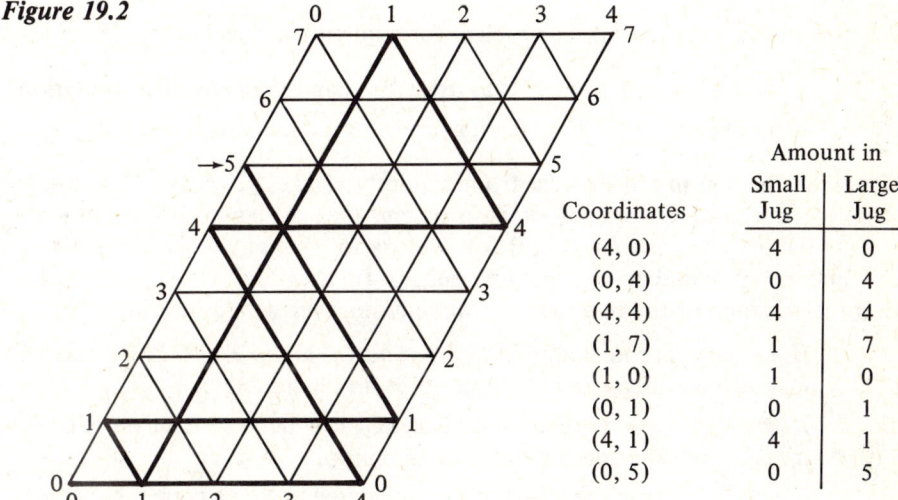

Coordinates	Amount in Small Jug	Amount in Large Jug
(4, 0)	4	0
(0, 4)	0	4
(4, 4)	4	4
(1, 7)	1	7
(1, 0)	1	0
(0, 1)	0	1
(4, 1)	4	1
(0, 5)	0	5

We may now place stronger emphasis upon patterns and ask students what happens if we allow the ball to keep rebounding beyond the desired answer? Is there any pattern to the results? The students go back and observe all of the coordinates of the initial problem of the 5- and 3-gal jugs. In order to arrive at a solution, the ball bounded through the following points:

(0, 0) (0, 5) (3, 2) (0, 2) (2, 0) (2, 5) (3, 4)

The last point contained a coordinate of 4, the desired amount to solve the problem. Let the ball continue, however, and it passes through these additional points:

(0, 4) (3, 1) (0, 1) (1, 0) (1, 5) (3, 3) (0, 3) (3, 0)

We see that every number from 1 through 5 has been recorded. In effect, we could have poured any number of gallons from 1–5. Will this always be true? Students may check the second problem involving the 7- and 4-gal jugs. Could we have poured out any number from 1 to 7 gal?

It works again, but will it always work? Try another problem and see what happens.

▶ From a jug of 10 gal pour out 5 gal using a 6- and a 4-gal jug.

Something rather unusual took place. The coordinates traversed this time include:

(4, 0) (0, 4) (4, 4) (2, 6) (2, 0) (0, 2) (4, 2) (0, 6)

The students do not seem to be able to land on a point with a coordinate of 5! As a matter of fact, there isn't a single odd number in the bunch. Pouring any odd number of gallons under these conditions is impossible. Our "computer" not only finds the solution, but makes clear when there is no solution at all.

Generalizing the Jugs

We now pose a very important problem for student consideration:

▶ Is there some way to be able to tell beforehand if there will be a solution?

Is there some pattern to the jug sizes in relation to each other?

If we label the jugs in order of size from smallest to largest, a, b, and c, we can try to write some general laws describing problems that can and cannot be done.

To arrive at conclusions, it is necessary to try many other combinations of numbers. We can then observe the results to find regularities where they exist. Eventually, some of the relationships we may uncover would include:

If a and b have no common divisor ($b > a$) and $c \geq a + b$, then we can measure out any whole number up to and including b.

If a and b have a common divisor and $c \geq a + b$, then we can only measure out the common divisor or multiples of it.

If $c < a + b$, then the graph must be changed so that a corner is sliced off since the sum of the coordinates of any point must be less than or equal to c.

Following a path that leads from the pouring of jugs, to the triangular coordinates, to the algebraic descriptions of patterns, is not an atypical mathematical experience. What is atypical is to find such experiences in school mathematics classrooms. These graphs have been around for quite a while with little impact upon the way mathematics is learned. Perhaps the use of such ideas will offer students experiences to help mathematics come to life for them.

19.3 Magic Squares

An apparently simple and yet challenging problem to students is the familiar magic square:

▶ Using the consecutive integers from 1 through 9, fit them into a 3 by 3 square so that the sum is the same for all rows, columns, and diagonals.

Students generally use trial and error (and a good eraser) and usually arrive at a solution (Figure 19.3). It is a pleasant and interesting activity, which provides practice in addition and may be extended by varying the integers used to fill the squares. For example, any multiple of each number will give another magic square whose row-sum will be that multiple of the original sum. Multiply each number by 4. The resulting magic square (Figure 19.4) has a column-sum of 15×4 or 60. Students can also gain much practice in multiplication by choosing a multiple of the original and forming their own magic squares.

Figure 19.3

6	1	8
7	5	3
2	9	4

Figure 19.4

24	4	32
28	20	12
8	36	16

We can extend this work to algebra by placing algebraic statements in the boxes instead of integers as shown in Figure 19.5. In this way, we offer a good deal of practice in the addition of polynomials. Here too, students can design their own squares, and the construction process offers still more practice with algebraic skills. There are numerous possibilities.

Figure 19.5

$x+1$	$x+6$	$x+5$
$x+8$	$x+4$	x
$x+3$	$x+2$	$x+7$

But the basic 3 by 3, or third-order square, and the exclusive use of consecutive integers will open new directions for us. When students find magic squares by trial and error, they come up with a variety of solutions, not simply the one shown in Figure 19.3. Some of these are shown in Figure 19.6. Look at these squares and compare them with the original in Figure 19.3. Although the integers are in different positions, the relationships between the numbers have not been touched. We have an excellent example of the geometric transformations of rotation (squares *A* and *B*) and reflection (square *C*) with regard to the original square. Subjecting the square to these transformations does not alter its status as a magic square. We now have an opportunity to involve students in transformations by posing questions such as:

▶
Which transformations do not affect the magic square property?

Which transformations destroy this property?

In this way, we add transformational geometry to the mathematics of the magic square.

Figure 19.6

8	3	4
1	5	9
6	7	2

A

4	9	2
3	5	7
8	1	6

B

8	1	6
3	5	7
4	9	2

C

A central question in this work, and an important one particularly when we emphasize pattern-finding, is how to build a magic square without resorting to trial and error. At this point, the squares can be extended to include higher-order squares.

The complexity of the work grows rapidly as the order of the squares increases, although there are comparatively simple methods for generating some magic squares of odd-numbered orders. After a new period of trial and error, you might ask students if they see any pattern that would show how a fifth-order square is to be filled in from scratch. If they need help, you might ask them to focus upon the path traced by the consecutive numbers and the diagonals of the square. The key to the pattern lies in recognition of the diagonals, used here in an unfamilar sense. Figure 19.7 shows the upward diagonals, each of which must be completed before moving to another. It is this path that enables the student to complete the square. The main diagonal is easy to see, but the others take a bit of care. Here is one way to work:

▶
Start by placing the number 1 in the middle column at the top. The number 1 is part of diagonal *C*. Complete this diagonal before anything else. Thus 2 goes to column 4 row 5. (Rows run horizontally.)

Continue the diagonal: 3 goes to column 5 row 4. The diagonal is not yet complete.

Figure 19.7   The Upward Diagonals

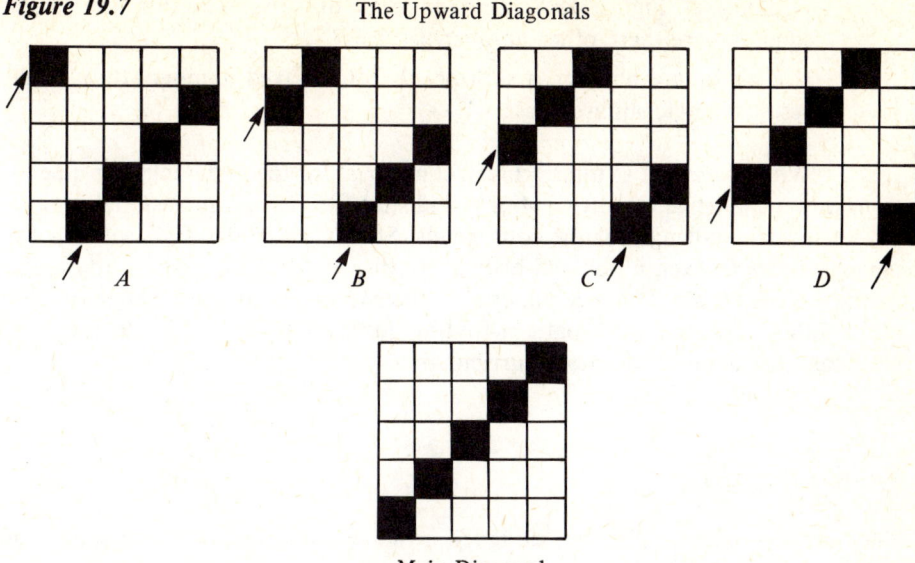

Main Diagonal

The number 4 goes in column 1 row 3, and 5 follows upward. When a diagonal is complete, *drop down a box.*

The number 6 is placed in column 3 row 3. Now finish diagonal *D*.

Then you follow the same pattern, drop down a box, and continue until all upward diagonals are complete.

Check your work with that of Figure 19.8. There is a definite pattern to the odd-order squares that requires careful attention to the upward diagonals. When it is learned, the work becomes a good deal easier. This is not the only pattern that yields magic squares, so some students will find valid squares in a different manner. Much pattern work is available for students.

Figure 19.8

17	24	1	8	15
23	5	7	14	16
4	6	13	20	22
10	12	19	21	3
11	18	25	2	9

▶ Looking at Figure 19.8, find patterns of squares within the larger squares. Are there other number patterns?

If each square number is subtracted from a fixed number (100), is the result a magic square?

What starts out as interesting drill material for the underachiever quickly turns into a challenge worthy of your gifted students. Three dimensional squares pose a special challenge for the courageous. Students can also find patterns for magic squares of even-numbered orders. If you would like to follow up on this work, there is ample reference material at the end of the chapter. Magic squares are another rich mine of pattern-finding ideas, leading to many areas of mathematics common to school curriculum.

19.4 In Conclusion

The activities selected here are designed as a sampling of an endless supply of paradoxes, puzzles, and games. All of these activities have direct application to secondary mathematics and are not merely seen as recreation. In addition to those considered, you might like to examine:

1. The golden rectangle
2. Goldbach's conjecture
3. The mathematics of musical scales
4. The four color problem

If each of these is explored, you will soon find a wealth of pattern ideas that will be pertinent to your lessons. The most important pattern is the one you establish when you use activities like the ones in this chapter. That pattern should enable you to add important, interesting experiences that will enhance the everyday work of your mathematics students.

We close with a familiar puzzle.

$$x = y \quad (x, y \neq 0)$$

Multiply by y: $\quad xy = y^2$
Subtract x^2: $\quad x^2 - xy = x^2 - y^2$
Factor: $\quad x(x - y) = (x - y)(x + y)$
Divide: $\quad x = x + y$
Substitute x for y: $\quad x = 2x$
$$1 = 2$$

Something is wrong somewhere! What a nice time students can have trying to find out. Perhaps they will better remember the caution about dividing by zero.

Footnotes

1. Marlow Sholander. "Convergence," *Historical Topics for the Mathematics Classroom.* 31st Yearbook. Reston, Va.: National Council of Teachers of Mathematics, 1969, pp. 432–434.
2. Martin Gardner. *Martin Gardner's Sixth Book of Mathematical Games From Scientific American.* San Francisco: W. H. Freeman, 1971, pp. 29–30.

For Investigation and Discussion

1. Select an activity from Martin Gardiner's book (see references) that can be used for pattern-finding and describe how it is to be used.
2. Outline the steps you would take to teach students how to use the "clipped-off" graph that results from an attempt to solve 7, 9, 12 jug problem using the "graph computer."
3. Explain why the search for pattern is an important process in a mathematics class.
4. Construct a lesson plan whose objective is to provide practice with the skill of addition of polynomials using a third-order magic square.

For Further Reading

Books

Charosh, Mannis, ed. *Mathematical Challenges.* Reston, Va.: National Council of Teachers of Mathematics, 1965.

Court, Nathan. *Mathematics in Fun & Earnest.* New York: New American Library, 1961, pp. 172-178.

Gardiner, Martin. *Martin Gardiner's Sixth Book of Mathematical Games From Scientific American.* San Francisco, Ca.: W. H. Freeman, 1971.

Hill, Thomas, ed. *Mathematical Challenges II—Plus Six.* Reston, Va.: National Council of Teachers of Mathematics, 1974.

Mott-Smith, Geoffrey. *Mathematical Puzzles for Beginners and Enthusiasts,* 2nd ed. New York: Dover Publications, 1954.

Schaaf, William. A Bibliography of Recreational Mathematics, Vols. 1, 2, and 3. Reston, Va.: National Council of Teachers of Mathematics, 1970 (Vol. 1), 1970 (Vol. 2), 1973 (Vol. 3).

Periodicals

Arcidiacono, Michael J. "The Magic of Manhattan,' *The Mathematics Teacher.* Vol. 68 (January 1975), pp. 59-60.

Brown, Stephen I. "From the Golden Rectangle and Fibonacci to Pedagogy and Problem Solving," *The Mathematics Teacher.* Vol. 69 (March 1976), pp. 180-188.

Brumfiel, Charles. "Using a Game as a Teacing Device," *The Mathematics Teacher.* Vol. 67 (May 1974), pp. 386-391.

Hammel, Thomas Ray and Ernest Woodward. "Developing Mathematics on a Pool Table," *The Mathematics Teacher.* Vol. 70 (February 1977), pp. 154-163.

Troccolo, Joseph A. "Instant Insanity—A Significant Puzzle for the Classroom," *The Mathematics Teacher.* Vol. 68 (April 1975), pp. 315-319.

For Further Reading on Magic Squares

Books

Ball, W. W. R. *Mathematical Recreation and Essays.* New York: Macmillian, 1962, pp. 193-221.

Fults, John Lee. *Magic Squares.* La Salle, Ill.: Open Court, 1974.

Kraitchik, Maurice. *Mathematical Recreations.* 2nd ed. New York: Dover Publications, 1953, pp. 142-192.

Periodicals

Arnott, David. "Magic Squares," *Mathematics Teaching.* No. 48 (Autumn 1969), pp. 26-30.

Atkinson, Thomas P. "Guided Discovery with Magic Squares," *The Arithmetic Teacher.* Vol. 22 (April 1975), pp. 288-292.

Freitag, Herta T. and Arthur H. Freitag. "Magic of a Square," *The Mathematics Teacher.* Vol. 63 (January 1970), pp. 5–14.

Frisinger, H. Howard. "Mathematics and Our Founding Fathers," *The Mathematics Teacher.* Vol. 69 (April 1976), pp. 301–307.

Sawada, Daiyo. "Magic Squares: Extensions into Mathematics," *The Arithmetic Teacher.* Vol. 21 (March 1974), p. 183–188.

Williams, Horace E. "A Note on Magic Squares," *The Mathematics Teacher.* Vol. 67 (October 1974), pp. 511–513.

Swetz, Frank. "Mysticism and Magic in the Number Squares of Old China," *The Mathemathics Teacher.* Vol. 71 (January 1978), pp. 50–56.

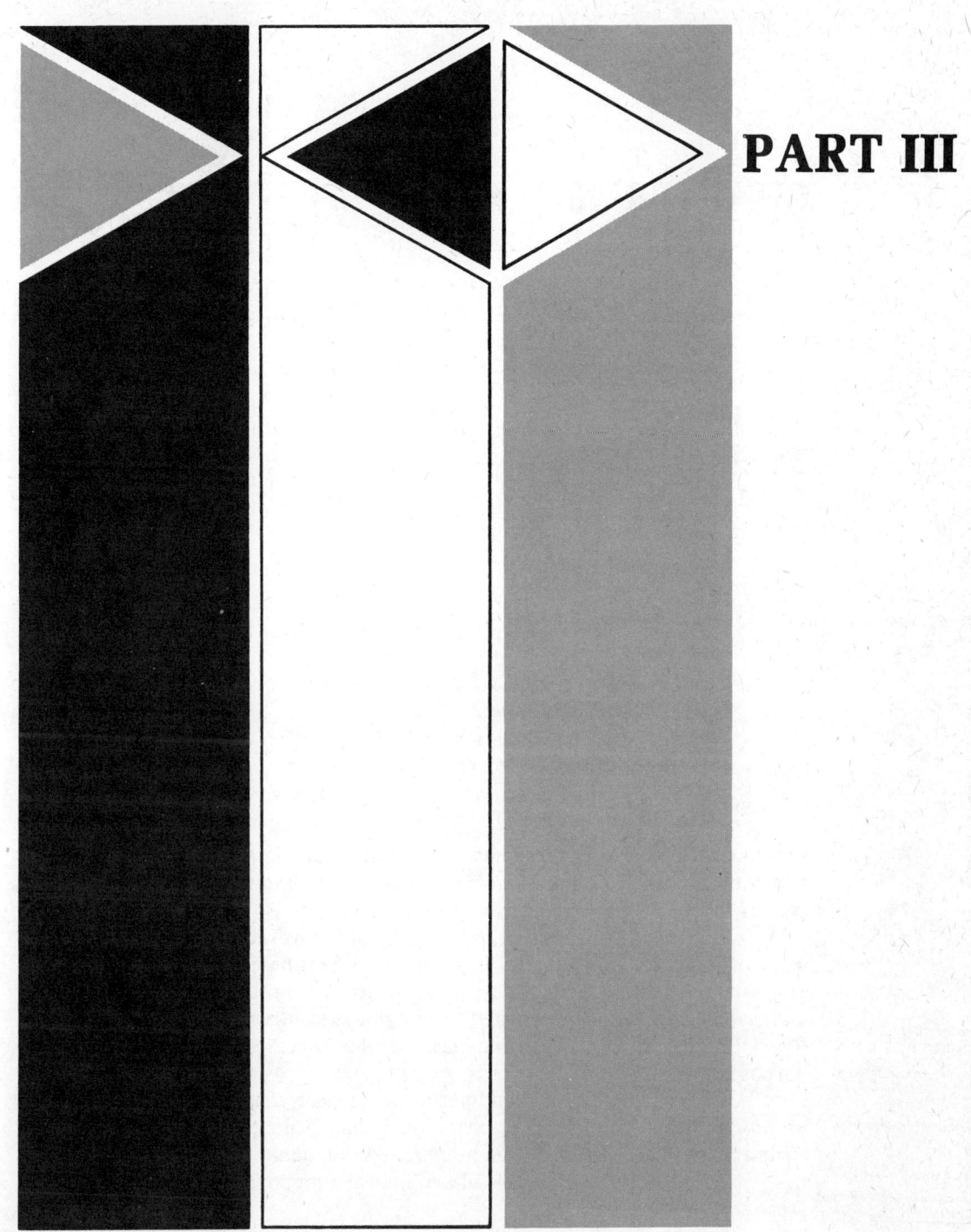

PART III

Measuring Progress in Mathematics

CHAPTER 20

Evaluation

How can a teacher tell how effectively the goals of mathematics instruction are being achieved in his classes?

How can he determine how well each student is doing in trying to accomplish all the tasks established for a given course?

Indeed, how can a teacher provide for continuous improvement and growth in his own ability as a teacher of mathematics?

In attempting to answer these questions, among others, the teacher must make many judgments. He becomes involved in a process known as evaluation, a vital part of the entire teaching-learning situation.

In the early chapters, a good deal of space was devoted to the establishment of goals for mathematics instruction. While these objectives served as a guide for the development of a program of instruction, they also form the basis upon which criteria may be created for judging the outcomes of such instruction. Evaluation begins with a clear statement of what is being evaluated and for what purpose.

Only when objectives and purposes are clearly in mind, can the question of *how* to gain the desired information (what evaluative techniques and instruments shall be used) be given attention. What can a teacher do to carry out this "judging" activity in as careful and logical a manner as possible? There is a great deal.

20.1 Testing

When teachers think of evaluation, they tend to think of testing and marking. The tests are generally paper and pencil affairs that require the students to solve a number of problems and do a number of examples. These problems and examples reflect the work that has been completed and is being evaluated. The tests are given to determine just how much the student has been able to accomplish. In addition, it provides the teacher with evidence that will be considered when a student's mark for the grading period, term, or year must be determined. Testing and marking are activities that are fraught with danger. The one quality that teachers should concern themselves with when carrying out these processes is simple humility.

You can estimate for yourself the importance of marks to students by carefully observing their actions the next time you return graded test papers. The feelings of elation and depression aside, watch how student interest wanes as soon as he has seen the magical number at the top of his paper and has explored every possible avenue for increasing his score. How many times have you been in a classroom in which a test is returned to students and, in the process of "going over" the problems, the teacher is heard to repeat, 'But John, surely you should pay close attention as we examine problem 5. I believe you had it wrong!" So powerful is the concern with the grade that, once it is known, interest vanishes.

While many deplore this emphasis upon marks, it still exists. Our students gauge themselves by these scores and formulate opinions about their abilities and potential in a given school subject on the basis of them. It is not often that we find a student who says, "Yes, I am doing poorly in math, but I really love it anyway." Quite the opposite is usually the case. We tend to select as our favorites those subjects in which we do well. This may be a stronger cause and effect relationship than the converse: We tend to do well in those subjects we like most.

We can exert an important influence on the feelings of students about marks, but this is a difficult task. For now, let us understand that since grades are of such significance to our students, we must handle marks carefully and with humility. Marks may ultimately influence student career choices. We know that marking is a risky process at best. We are always open to question, but we do our best to be fair with our students. There are very definite ways in which we can reduce our margin of error, however; and we now turn our attention to some of these.

Making Tests 20.2

Purpose

The chief evaluation instrument of most teachers is the teacher-made pencil and paper test. While there are many alternatives to these tests, which will be considered shortly, let us focus upon the construction of an effective pencil and paper test. What can you do to enable yourself to make the best of all possible tests? Everything begins with a consideration of what you are trying to accomplish. What are you testing for? Is it mastery of given skills? Is it the ability to solve problems? Is it a test of appreciation? These questions and any others that may apply in a given situation must be clearly answered.

Content

Once our purpose is identified, we turn to the content to be covered. For most of us, it is difficult to construct questions, exercises, and problems. The few minutes required to list all of our content to be covered results in an invaluable beginning of a plan for the test to be made.

Here is a list of content to be covered, made by a teacher who is preparing a test on percent:

1. Convert percent to decimal and common fraction.
2. Convert decimal and common fractions to percent.
3. Solve proportions.
4. Find percent of a number (percentage).
5. Find what percent one number is of another (rate).
6. Given a percentage (base), find the whole.

These skills and concepts will be tested by a number of questions of different types. Some may be straight computation, others may require organization of information first. This brings us to the next step in the process: constructing the questions.

Questions Required

From our topic list, we can see that some questions are best suited to straightforward computation questions, while others lend themselves to verbal problems. If we make a table listing the kinds of questions to be constructed for each topic, we can more easily decide on how many questions of what type are needed (Table 20.1). Such a table enables you to be sure that you will include all desired topics and also identifies the number and kind of items required.

Table 20.1 Table of Topics and Types of Questions.

Topic	Type of Question		
	Straight Computation	Verbal Problem (Familiar)	Verbal Problem (New Situation)
Convert percent	4		
Convert fractions-decimals	4		
Proportion	1	1	1
Find percentage	1	1	1
Find rate	1	1	1
Find base	1	1	1

Test Items

How shall the test items be made up? Common sense provides some guidance: Questions sould have but one correct response, should fit within the framework of your test plan, and should meet the purposes for which they were created. But what of the level of difficulty? How can we be sure before the students take the test whether or not a given item is too hard or too easy?

One interesting and effective idea is contained in a publication of the Educational Testing Service designed especially for teachers.[1] Although we cannot determine for present use the difficulty of items, over a period of time we can accumulate information to ease the construction of future tests. There must be a trial and error period when student responses are analyzed so that a teacher can build up a collection of items and a reservoir of information about the relative difficulty and effectiveness of each. Not only is the process simpler than could be hoped for, but it is a valuable learning situation for students as well.

When a test has been scored and returned, the papers are arranged in order of scores from the lowest to the highest. The pile is then split into two equal halves consisting of the "highs" and the "lows." (This is an approximation method for quick results.) Assign any "middle" papers to each group at random. If there is an odd number of students, hold out the middle paper and do not count it. Distribute the papers to the class so that the right-hand side of the room gets the "high" papers and the left-hand side gets the "low." If one student is left out (the discarded middle paper when the total number of papers is odd), you might make him scorekeeper at the chalkboard. You now tally on the board by a show or hands the number of highs who got an item right, as well as the number of lows, by taking each test item by turn. When all the responses are tallied, the teacher and the students calculate two scores that the Educational Testing Service pamphlet refers to as the *success* score and the *discrimination* score, which are defined as follows:

H = the number of highs getting the item right
L = the number of lows getting the item right
$H + L$ = *success* (the total number getting the item right)
$H - L$ = *discrimination* or the "high-low difference"

In 10 to 20 minutes you will have completed a close approximation of what is known statistically as an item analysis. Of course, if we use standard procedures to compute this, or if we followed the procedures described here without student help, the required time would make the process forbidding. This approximation is quick, easy, and provides good information. At the same time, students are active participants in the entire process, adding to their understanding of how scores are arrived at and how test items can be judged. They have a better understanding of the entire process, as well as of how their performance fits into the overall scheme of things. But of what importance are the calculated results? A rule of thumb is provided in this same pamphlet: Divide the number of students present by 10 and round off to the nearest whole number. If the discrimination score of an item exceeds this number, it has satisfactory discrimination. For example,

In a class of 32, 11 highs and 7 lows got an item right. Hence, the *discrimination* is $H - L = 11 - 7 = 4$. The rule of thumb says $32 \div 10 = 3.2$; round off to 3. This item is a good discriminator since it exceeds 3.

What does it mean for an item to be a good discriminator? One of the objectives in constructing questions is to make up items that will be answered correctly by those who know and incorrectly by those who do not know. A test item is telling you little about the relative achievement of students if everyone answers either correctly or incorrectly. This is not applicable to tests designed for purposes other than mastery of a unit of work and marking. If you were to design a test for the basic multiplication facts, you would have little interest in discrimination, expecting 100 percent mastery of all students. But if you are trying to determine how much has been learned about a particular unit and how well the students compare, the discriminating power of each item is an index of how well the item is doing the job for which it was intended. On a single test administration, if an item should fail to discriminate, it should be discarded. However, it may be worth while to examine and possibly test the item again if it looks like a reasonable item. Results with small groups sometimes vary greatly. At any rate, you now have information about the discriminating power of each item. If an index card file is made with each item listed on a separate card, this information can be recorded on the back for reference. For example, if an item given in a test in September, 1976, has a discrimination score of 5, you would write the following on the file card:

    Discrimination 5   9/76

But is the item difficult or easy? We have not as yet considered this aspect. The *success* score (H + L) that we computed enables us to make an assessment of this factor. For the sample item we have just considered, the success score was 11 + 7 = 18. If we compute what percent this is of the total class (32), we have a good gauge of the difficulty of the item—in this case about 56%. If we think in terms of 90% as indicating items that are too easy and 30% as indicative of items that are too hard, we find 56% in an in-between range from which we would like most of the items to come. (This *success* score is sometimes called a "difficulty index.")[2] There is some difference of opinion among experts as to how many items there should be, of what difficulty they should be, and in what order they should appear in a given test. Many believe that you can achieve maximum reliablity and dispersion of scores "if every item in the usual sort of multiple-choice test is answered correctly by somewhere between 60% and 70% of the students tested."[3]

Whatever the case, a strict arrangement of questions from easier to harder often results in difficulties; once a student fails to answer the last questions, the item-analysis figures are no longer suitable. If he quits and does not reach the question, we cannot say for sure whether a student could have answered a given question or not. One way to avoid this situation might be to cycle questions as to difficulty. For example, if we employed a cycle of three, we have a question, followed by a slightly more difficult question, again followed by a slightly more difficult question. The fourth question returns to the difficulty level of the first, and so on. In this way, we prevent the frustration level of the student from building to the point where he "drops out" of the test. Generally, a *success* index of 50-60% is recommended for all items.

The *success* score is also entered on the back of the item card to add to your stored information about it. In this way you have a ready-made file of items, with difficulty index and discriminating index available at a glance. After a few years of operation, you should have at your fingertips a rather large collection of tested items that will greatly facilitate the construction of future examinations.

These scores may also provide the teacher with diagnostic-type information about the class that may well influence future planning. For example, if items had generally low success scores, then examine the items carefully to determine if the area in question should be retaught in class. Of course, a decision would be based upon the cause for the low success score. It may well be that the question itself is poorly constructed.

Validity and Reliability 20.3

Whether the tests you construct are reliabile and valid are basic questions to be asked of all tests. As a matter of fact, an important difference between standardized and teacher-made tests is that the standardized test has undergone procedures designed to evaluate its reliabilily and validity. This is usually accomplished by using a sample population of students and by studying how closely the test results match student performance on other criteria–grades, other tests, teacher evaluation, and so on. Does your test measure what it is supposed to measure? If it does, it is a valid test. If the students took the test again, would they come out with the same score? If they would, the test is reliable. In this instance, reliability refers to consistency. Of course, these questions are seldom anwsered with yes or no. What we generally try to determine is the degree of validity or the degree of reliability present in the test we have before us. Although the time required and the complication of computing these statistics is too burdensome for most teachers, much information is available to enable the interested teacher to carry out the calculations.[4]

There are some guidelines that may be used in trying to determine how valid and reliable standardized tests are. These will be considered later. Suffice it to say here that a careful look at the item will help you to determine if it will do its intended job.

Construction of Items 20.4

The writing of good test items is a difficult, skillful, creative task. Teachers often talk about the impossibility of writing objective questions to test complex mathematics concepts or skills, and they are not far from wrong. Professional test makers have developed many ingenious questions that appear in published examinations, and these examinations are an excellent source of questions for the teacher. Whether it be to test recall of facts or to demonstrate the use of concepts learned, some simple guidelines can help in the difficult task of constructing questions.

Keep the question language simple enough for students to understand; otherwise you will find that you are testing language rather than mathematics. When you have constructed an item, ask yourself if the question may be interpreted in more than one way. If it can, it is in need of revision. Ambiguous statements foul the test purposes. These are the two most important ideas to keep before you as you make up questions. Avoid the use of lengthy statements and double negatives, and be careful that the information in one question doesn't provide the correct answer to another.

By and large, if you keep out ambiguities and maintain the use of straight-forward language without "tricks" of any kind, you will have the best chance of constructing items that will do as you intend. There are interesting collections of items and evaluative comments available to help you.[5] The use of these, together with the published tests, offers the teacher a rich source of ideas.

The use of teacher time is an important variable in the construction of tests. While an essay test requires much more time when it is being scored than does a short-answer test, the latter requires a good deal more time in the construction phase. With the various techniques that can be used to refine this test, the time question eventually resolves itself in favor of the short answer. In the long run, it may well be worth any additional initial effort.

20.5 Scoring

Mathematics teachers frequently assign different weights to the items that make up a given test. This is one reason for the wide disparity of grades given to the same paper by different teachers of mathematics. It is not uncommon for teachers in a graduate course, grading the same test paper, to find the range of grades given to this paper will frequently exceed 30 points, with scores running from as low as 40% to as high as 80%. Some of this variation can be accounted for by the different weights teachers assign to the test items. It would seem that if test items could be constructed of equal weight, a big step would be taken toward making the teacher-made test more objective.

When we consider if a test is objective or subjective, we do not refer to the appearance of the test items—multiple choice as opposed to essay—but rather we refer to the scoring process. If all people who score the test give it the same mark, the test is high in objectivity. If, on the other hand, the marking of the paper varies with the teacher doing the scoring, then that particular test is of a subjective nature.

The New York State Regents Examinations are a good example of tests that are becoming more objective. The tests are scored by the local teachers and then checked by the appropriate state official. Frequently there is a disparity in the two grades. Lately, however, those constructing the tests have been creating items that are more objective. Hence, most teachers will score the papers in the same way and arrive at virtually the same grade. If teachers would construct items that bear equal weights and contain only one correct response, they too would move in the direction of creating more objective tests. Essay questions may also fit this definition of objective, provided that an ideal response can be constructed with which all papers may be compared. If this results in consistency of scoring regardless of who the rater is, we may then call the essay test an objective one.

20.6 Other Evaluation Techniques

All our attention, thus far, has been devoted to the use of pencil and paper tests. Let us now focus on other ways to assess student behavior and teacher effectiveness.

Observation

In a paper on evaluation, Dr. Marvin Taylor makes the point that tests are not the most widely used evaluation technique.[6] He claims that observation is probably more common. There is much to support this point. In the daily work with students, teachers are constantly acting and reacting to what is happening among their students. In fact, one of the important qualities of the successful teacher is his sensitivity to what is happening to students as the work develops. Observation is indeed a primary evaluation tool. Taylor goes on to explain that teacher observation may be assisted by making use of check lists. There are published check lists available that will enable us to accumulate valuable information about a student's behavior.[7] In addition, these check lists also minimize our tendency to allow our personal involvement to influence our observations. Thus, the information gathered may be more accurate and certainly more fair.

Interview

Disruptive behavior, lack of sucess, and disinterest are all common partners of the learning process in school classrooms. The interview is one of the ways in which teachers can gain important information in trying to help youngsters. It is sometimes surprising how the genuine concern of the teacher for a student as expressed in a personal interview often may be a step in the right direction for a student in trouble. There is a marked difference in the tone of an after-school interview when a student is told to "stay after school" as a means of punishment and when a student is asked to meet with a teacher after school because the teacher is concerned about apparent student difficulties. It may well be that several brief interviews will be necessary before a student will "open up," since we cannot force him to provide information or accept us as a helping agent.

Cumulative Record

On of the first places to look when students are experiencing difficulty is the cumulative record. A source of constant surprise is how many students in junior and senior high schools are working with the disadvantage of an undetected physical defect. Despite all the usual school examinations and precautions, we still find health problems that have remained hidden. Poor eyesight, faulty hearing, or other handicaps may well reduce the student's effectiveness in school to the danger point; and time does not seem to make a difference.

Be sure to find out if those of your students who are not achieving are not bearing the burden of some physical problem.

Sociogram

Sometimes social problems may be at the root of student difficulties. An effective, but somewhat time-consuming, device to use in this area is the sociogram.[8] The students are asked to indicate on paper or an index card the three members of the class they would most like to work with for some purpose that is germane to the work of the class. (The class will be divided into small work groups for skill work, project work, or other such activity.) The diagram and charts that result from organizing the data collected are called sociograms. They show the student's choices, as well as whether the selection was a first, second or third choice (Figure 20.1, see page 328). These charts give the teacher quick information about the popularity of students, the isolated students, and any class cliques. Of course, the information must be used with wisdom, but the acceptance of one student for another is an important factor in class conduct. The total rejection of a youngster by his classmates may well be as responsible for a lack of success in school as is partial eyesight.

Figure 20.1 Sociograms.

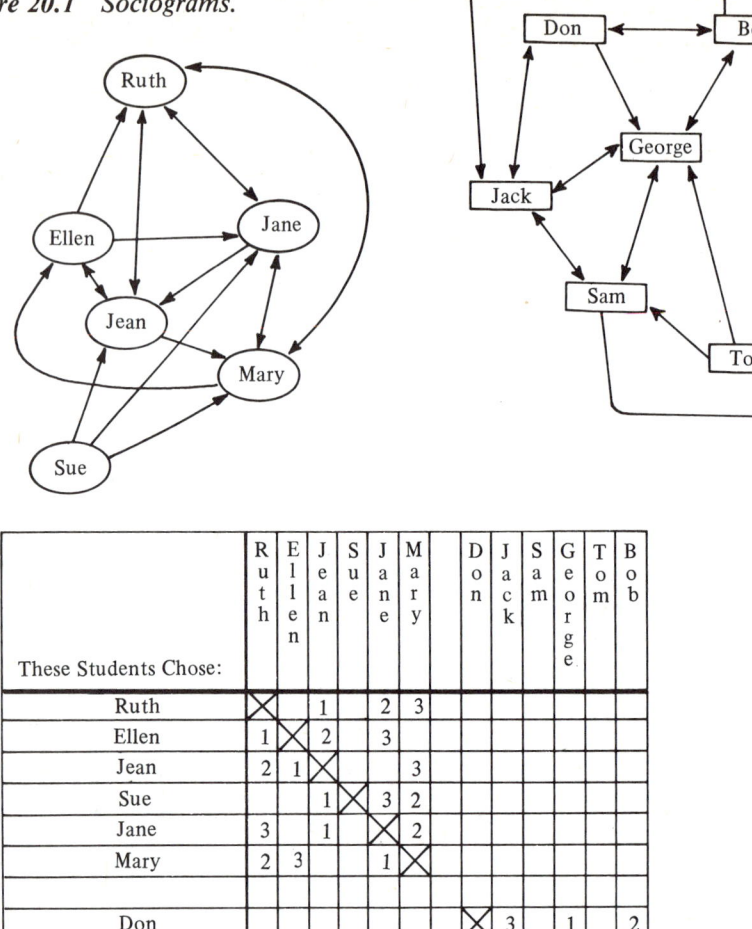

Questionnaires, Rating Scales, and Interest Inventories

Questionnaires, rating scales, and interest inventories may assist the teacher in appraising factors like attitude towards mathematics, aspiration levels, and personal interests. In general, they may add information to the total picture of the child. These devices, more than any of the others, must be used carefully. Often students respond to the questions or statements on an attitude scale the way they think the teacher would like them to respond. It is also possible for the reverse to be true; that is, students may conceal their feelings and perhaps offer as responses the opposite of what they feel the teacher would like to see. In addition, interpreting the data gathered is no simple task, whether the instrument be published or teacher-made. But clues can accumulate about youngsters that may in the long run add up to some explanation for behavior and offer a possible beginning for providing assistance.

The chief purpose of all these evaluation techniques is the collection of information about a youngster to round out the total picture we have of him. We are assuming that there is a direct relationship between how much we know about a youngster and our ability to help him. If the net gain of all these procedures is the realization that the student should be referred to a guidance counselor, or physician, then this too would have made it worth while. One additional area of valuable assitance for teachers and students is the standardized tests.

Standardized Tests 20.7

A standardized test differs from the teacher-made counterpart in many ways. To begin with, published tests are usually constructed so that administration and scoring of the test are done in accordance with very specific instructions. To offer some sense of the thoroughness of the process by which the test is created, the National Council of Teachers of Mathematics yearbook on evaluation states that

> ... a good published test is usually the result of highly scientific construction involving advanced pretesting on appropriate populations: item analyses for discrimination and difficulty; extensive review and editing to produce terse, unambiguous phrasing; and meticulous scrutiny by mathematicians for soundness and national curricular appropriateness.[9]

Add to this the creative talents and experience of the test maker and you begin to get a notion of what is involved. In the yearbook just mentioned, it is estimated that one form of a 40-minute standardized test would cost from $5000 to $10,000 to construct.

Published tests are generally of three basic types: diagnostic, ability or aptitude, and achievement. Sometimes it is difficult to tell one from another because the content of the tests seems similar. Carefully reading the test manual (most standardized tests have an accompanying manual that contains statistical and informational data about the test and its construction), as well as examining the questions, would help in finding out just what type of test is at hand.

Standard Error

Despite the careful development of these examinations, the results must be used with great care. It is easy to make serious mistakes. It is only natural to want a specific number to use as a description of the achievement level or ability level of a student. How convenient to say that a particular student is operating at a 6.3 grade level! There is the ring of finality about it. Unfortunately (or perhaps fortunately), no test has yet been constructed that offers such accurate labels.

If we were to be interested in the *true score* of the child on a given achievement test, we must seek out the *standard error of the test scores*. There are a number of different standard errors that are reported in the manual, e.g., standard error of test scores, of averages, and of differences. We are now concerned with the standard error of test scores. Let us take a case in point:

John takes an algebra achievement test. He gets 33 of 50 items correct. Bob gets 40 items correct. The standard error of the scores is 4.

What do the results show? Evidently Bob is much higher in achievement than John. He has scored seven points higher on a 50-item test. If this were a teacher-made test and if percents were used, John would get 66 percent whereas Bob would score 80 percent. The difference is substantial, but let us look at the standard error. It tells us that John's true score lies anywhere from 29 to 37—four points above and below his test score. In fact, it tells us even more: It says that of all the possible questions available to test achievement in this area, if we continue to select samples of 50 and retest John over and over, he would score between 29 and 37 two out of three times. What's more, if we were to use two standard errors (eight points), John would score between 25 and 41 on the repeated tests 95 out of 100 times! Thus one standard error would place John's true score from 29 to 37.

Some standardized tests report scores as a band rather than as a specific number of points in order to call attention to the importance of this standard error. If we look at Bob's score and the standard error, we see that his true score is the band from 36 to 44 (Figure 20.2). Since his band and that of John overlap, it is recommended that teachers do not regard the scores of these boys as "really different."[10] This is true despite the large difference in percent scores!

Figure 20.2

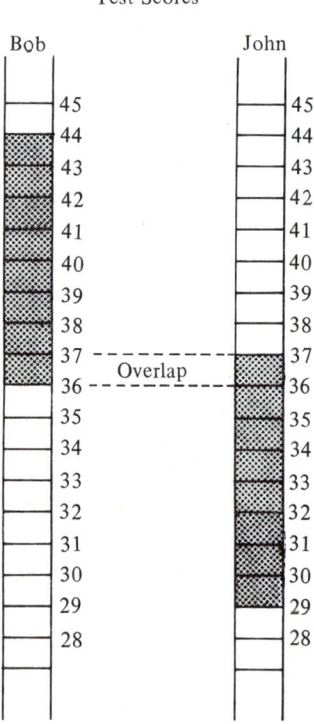

To be clear about the implications of this we must fully understand the standard error. The only error being referred to is that of sampling—the items chosen for the test. Would the student get the same score if 50 different questions were asked about the same subject?

We have completely ignored errors that may be introduced by bias in item selection, mistakes in scoring, the effect of weather, personal problems, and attitudes. It is rather sad to observe how some test scores have the status of a brand upon a student, especially in light of all these possible error factors. Once again we find that humiltiy becomes an important factor in the use of these standardized test scores. When it comes to teacher-made tests, infinite wisdom is required!

We can use the scores of our tests to determine student success with our course if, over the period of a year, we administer many tests to the students. Thus, we happily do not have to rely upon a single measure. Generally, a student who is superior will consistently score higher over the year so that we are in better position to make a judgment than we would be with a single such score. If you would like a quick estimate of the standard error of the test scores of your own tests, you may want to use Table 20.2.

Table 20.2 Estimated Standard Error of Test Scores.*

Number of Items	Standard Error	Regardless of Test Length	
		When the Score Is:	Standard Error Is:
< 24	2	0 or perfect	0
24–47	3	1 or 2 points from 0 or 100%	1
48–89	4	3 to 7 points from 0 or 100%	2
90–109	5	8 to 15 points from 0 or 100%	3
110–129	6		
130–150	7		

*Modified from *Short-Cut Statistics for Teacher-Made Tests,* 2nd ed. Educational Testing Service, 1964, p. 16.

Validity-Reliablity

Earlier we had considered two all-important criteria that should be applied to any test: validity (does the test measure what it is supposed to) and reliability (if a student takes the test again will he get the same score). Standardized tests are generally carefully checked for these two characteristics.

Validity is usually determined by checking against some other criterion, a criterion always open to question. Sometimes grades in the subject may be used. At other times aptitude or ability scores may form the basis for comparison. The concept of correlation is employed in order to arrive at a coefficient of validity. Thus, if the scores on the achievement test in question seem to reflect the order of the students with respect to grades, we may find the coefficient of validity to be around 0.50. If there was no relationship at all, the coefficient would be about 0.00. If those who scored high on the achievement test scored low in grades, and vice versa, the validity coefficient might turn up at −0.50. For a rule of thumb, validity coefficients that are considered satisfactory will run from about 0.40 to 0.65. It is also common to find that validity has been determined by referring the test questions to a jury of experts who render an opinion as to whether or not the items appear to test that which is intended. This is called *face* or *content validity* and is often used in addition to the correlation validity procedures described previously.

Reliability is concerned with the consistency of the test. Since it is easier to make a consistent test than a valid one, reliability coefficients are expected to be higher than those of validity. Most standardized test makers are not satisfied with reliabilities that are less than 0.90. Teacher-made tests may be expected to demonstrate reliablity coefficients between 0.60 and 0.80. Earlier it was indicated that continued testing provides the stability required to use the test scores as indications of comparative achievement. Because of this, you can increase reliability scores simply by increasing the number of items. Once again we find that it is necessary to look beyond the statistics. A widely used formula for computing the reliability coefficient is the Kuder-Richardson Formula 21:

$$\text{Reliability} = 1 - \frac{M(n-M)}{ns^2}$$

where M is the mean, n is the number of *items,* and s is the standard deviation.[11] The Educational Testing Service publication contains a table that will quickly provide approximate reliabilities.[12] This may be a handy guide for your tests.

Marking

All of these various statistical techniques of analysis that are applied to standardized tests point up the need for the intelligent use of test results. You have seen the questions that may be asked of tests carefully standardized by experts. If you take the time required to approach your problems of test construction in the way that these professionals have, you would improve your tests greatly. Hence, it seems that your tests are open to question. Of course, over the period of a year you will have provided students with so many questions that they will tend to separate themselves in terms of achievement; but this is not an automatic process. It will result only from your conscientious efforts and your use of those techniques that can assist you. For example, should your test reliability fall well below 0.60, perhaps you are better off not counting the test at all. Are you prepared to eliminate it? You should be. Yet without computing the statisic, you might never be aware of the poor quality of the test.

As for figuring out marks, while teachers use classwork as a criterion, marks are dependent to a great extent upon test scores. These are the same test scores that vary greatly when different teachers score the same paper, the same test scores that are open to the serious questions just discussed: reliability, validity, standard errors, and other influences. Nevertheless, many teachers still say that they will be completely objective and average test scores, and that shall be the student's mark! Have all these other contaminating forces been considered? The averaging process itself is open to question. Although it may seem somewhat presumptuous in a book for mathematics teachers, let us briefly look at this example:

John takes 3 tests:

Test 1	10 items	8 correct	80%
Test 2	5 items	1 correct	20%
Test 3	15 items	12 correct	80%

What is John's average? It seems simple enough to find out:

$$\begin{array}{r} 80 \\ 20 \\ 80 \\ \hline 180 \end{array} \qquad 3\overline{)180}^{\,60}$$

His average is 60%.

Do you agree with this? I hope not since it is incorrect. This student was tested on 30 items of which he got 21 correct. We therefore compute his average as follows:

21 out of 30

$$\frac{21}{30} = \frac{7}{10}$$

His average is 70%.

In this one simple case, we have a 10% discrepancy in average. Is it necessary to once again call for humility in marking?

Marks are all important to our students. It seems that they are working for the mark rather than the learning, which is, after all, what school is supposed to be about. What would happen to students and teachers alike (and parents?) if all marks were suddenly banished from schools? What a beautiful thought to contemplate! Walter Mitty will forgive us. Until the day arrives when we can manage to get marks out of our way, let us make the best possible use of them, and put them to work for us. We know students respond better to reward than to failure so let us be generous with marks. The notion that a student tries harder if you grade him down would seem to contradict everything psychologists would have us believe about motivation. Nothing succeeds like success. If marks are an indication of success, let's use them to advantage. One thing is sure: We will receive few complaints from parents if we grade on the high side. Since the process is a stab in the dark at best, give all students the benefit of the doubt. This is the best way to minimize unwanted side effects of marks. Perhaps then the satisfaction of achievement will center on what has been learned, rather than on some number or letter on a piece of paper.

Footnotes

1. *Short-Cut Statistics for Teacher-Made Tests,* 2nd ed. Pamphlet No. 5, Evaluation and Advisory Service, Educational Testing Service, Princeton, N. J., 1964, pp. 6–12.
2. Jack C. Merwin. "Constructing Achievement Tests and Interpreting Scores," *Evaluation in Mathematics,* 26th Yearbook. Reston, Va.: National Council of Teachers of Mathematics, 1961, pp. 61–65.
3. *Short-Cut Statistics for Teacher-Made Tests,* 2nd ed. Pamphlet No. 5. Evaluation and Advisory Service, Educational Testing Service, Princeton, N.J., 1964, p. 10.
4. *Short-Cut Statistics for Teacher-Made Tests,* 2nd. ed. Pamphlet No. 5, Evaluation and Advisory Service, Educational Testing Service, Princeton, N.J., 1964, pp. 30–37.
   Also see: Jack C. Merwin. "Constructing Achievement Tests and Interpreting Scores," *Evaluation in Mathematics,* 26th Yearbook. Reston, Va.: National Council of Teachers of Mathematics, 1961, pp. 61–68.

5. See the following:

    Jack C. Merwin. "Constructing Achievement Tests and Interpreting Scores," *Evaluation in Mathematics,* 26th Yearbook. Reston, Va.: National Council of Teachers of Mathematics, 1961, p. 47-51.

    "The Evaluation of Mathematical Learning," In Part 5 of *Emerging Practices in Mathematics Education,* 22nd Yearbook. Reston, Va.: National Council of Teachers of Mathemtics, 1954, pp. 339-409.

    Making the Classroom Test. Pamphlet No. 4, Evaluation and Advisory Service, Educational Testing Service, Princeton, N.J., 1959, pp. 17-23.

6. Marvin Taylor. *The Process of Evaluation.* Unpublished, Queens College of The City University of New York, 1966, p. 2.

7. Donald M. Medley and Harold E. Mitzel. "Measuring Classroom Behavior by Systematic Observation," *Handbook of Research on Teaching* (N. L. Gage, ed.) Skokie, Ill.: Rand McNally & Co., 1963, pp. 247-328.

8. Helen Hall Jennings. *Sociometry in Group Relations,* 2nd ed. American Council on Education, 1959.

9. Sheldon S. Meyers. "Publishing Evaluation Materials," *Evaluation in Mathematics,* 26th Yearbook. Reston, Va.: National Council of Teachers of Mathematics, 1961, p. 98.

10. *Short-Cut Statistics for Teacher-Made Tests,* 2nd ed. Pamphlet No. 5, Evaluation and Advisory Service, Educational Testing Service, Princeton, N.J., 1964, p. 16.

11. For a quick method of calculating the standard deviation, see: *Short-Cut Statistics for Teacher-Made Tests,* 2nd ed. Pamphlet No. 5, Evaluation and Advisory Service, Educational Testing Service, Princeton, N.J., 1964, p. 23.

12. *Short-Cut Statistics for Teacher-Made Tests,* 2nd ed., Pamphlet No. 5, Evaluation and Advisory Service, Educational Testing Service, Princeton, N.J., 1964, p. 31.

For Investigation and Discussion

1. List factors that complicate the task of testing and marking. Discuss the implications of each factor for evaluation procedures.

2. Make up a pencil and paper objective test on the topic of ratio and proportion. Carry out the steps indicated in the text: identify purpose clearly, list all content to be tested, construct a table of topics and question types, and construct suitable items.

3. Describe procedures you might use to test the validity and reliability of the test you constructed for problem 2.

4. Describe evaluation procedures used by teachers other than pencil and paper tests. Explain each procedure, its purpose, and its use.

5. Divide your class into small groups in order to work on a variety of topics otherwise impossible to explore as a single group. Arrange this grouping using the sociometric device known as a sociogram. (Use a sample class of students or your own methods class.)

6. Explain the major differences that exist between teacher-made and standardized tests.

7. In this chapter the statement is made that although two students' scores on a standardized achievement test may differ by seven items (out of total of 50 items), the "true ability" of the students may be equal. How is this possible?

8. Select a standardized achievement test in mathematics. (See listing in the National Council of Teachers of Mathematics, 26th Yearbook: *Evaluation in Mathematics.*) Secure a copy of the test and test manual. Describe and interpret the test validity, test reliablity, and standard error of the test scores.

For Further Reading

Books

Braswell, James S. *Mathematics Tests Available in the United States.* Reston, Va.: National Council of Teachers of Mathematics. 1972.

Buros, Oscar K. ed. *Mathematics Tests and Reviews: A Monograph Consisting of the Mathematical Section of the Seven Mental Measurement Yearbooks (1938-1972) and Tests in Print II (1974).* Gryphon Press, 1975.

Butler, Charles H. and F. Lynwood Wren. *The Teaching of Secondary Mathematics,* 5th ed. New York: McGraw-Hill, Chap. 7, 1970.

Hedges, William D. *The Testing and Evaluation for the Sciences.* Belmont, Ca.: Wadsworth, 1966.

National Council of Teachers of Mathematics, 22nd Yearbook: *Emerging Practices in Mathematics Education.* Reston, Va.: The National Council of Teachers of Mathematics, 1954, Part 5.

National Council of Teachers of Mathematics, *Evaluation in Mathematics.* 26th Yearbook. Reston, Va.: The National Council of Teachers of Mathematics. 1961.

Weaver, J. Fred. "Evaluation and the Classroom Teacher," *Mathematics Education,* 69th Yearbook. National Society for the Study of Education, 1970, Part I, pp. 335-366 (distributed by University of Chicago Press).

Periodicals

The Arithmetic Teacher. Vol. 21 (January 1974). (The focus of this issue is evaluation.)

Crouse, Richard and Carl Jacobson. "Testing in Mathematics—What Are We Really Measuring?" *The Mathematics Teacher.* Vol. 68 (November 1975), pp. 564-570.

Epstein, Marion and Sheldon Meyers. "How a Mathematics Test is Born," *The Mathematics Teacher.* Vol. 51 (April 1958), pp. 299-302.

Foreman, Dale I. and William A. Mehrens. "National Assessment in Mathematics," *The Mathematics Teacher.* Vol. 64 (March 1971), pp. 193-199.

Kinsella, John K. "Evaluation of Student Learning in Secondary School," *Bulletin of The National Association of Secondary School Principals.* Vol. 43 (May 1959), pp. 125-128.

Lankford, Francis G., Jr. "What Can a Teacher Learn about a Pupil's Thinking through Oral Interviews?" *The Arithmetic Teacher.* Vol. 21 (January 1974), pp. 26-32.

Payne, Joseph N. "Giving the Student a Part in His Evaluation," *The Mathematics Teacher.* Vol. 50 (January 1957), pp. 77-78.

Sawyer, W. W. "Some Thought on Examinations," *Mathematics Teaching.* No. 69 (December 1974), pp. 51-53.

Stover, Donald W. "Testing and Grading: Procedures for Improved Student Motion," *The Mathematics Teacher.* Vol. 70 (September 1977), pp. 498-503.

Swadener, Marc and D. Franklin Wright. "Testing in the Mathematics Classroom," *The Mathematics Teacher.* Vol. 68 (January 1975), pp. 11-17.

Taba, H. and E. I. Swain. "A Proposed Model in Evaluation," *Educational Leadership.* Vol. 20 (October 1962), pp. 57-71.

Thompson, Giles B. "Test, Marks and All That," *Mathematics Teaching.* No. 65 (December 1973), pp. 54-55.

Williams, S. Irene and Chancey O. Jones. "Multiple Choice Mathematics Questions—How Students Attempt to Solve Them," *The Mathematics Teacher.* Vol. 67 (January 1974), pp. 34-40.

Pamphlets

Educational Testing Service. Evaluation and Advisory Service Series:
- No. 1: *Locating Information on Educational Measurement: Sources and References.*
- No. 3: *Selecting an Achievement Test: Principles and Procedures.*
- No. 4: *Making the Classroom Test: A Guide for Teachers.*
- No. 5: *Short-Cut Statistics for Teacher-Made Tests.*

CHAPTER 21

Epilogue

We have come a long way. Indeed, after 20 chapters of text, it would seem that everything of importance that had to be written was written; and this is probably the case. But perhaps there are some simple ideas that may be briefly mentioned-the kind of ideas that often elude us because of their simplicity.

For example, have fun in your mathematics classes. Make it an enjoyable place to be for both yourself and your students. We have seen the fruits of the "if its hard its good" kind of approach in the fact that so many people in our society have a deathly fear of numbers in any form. As you organize the work of your classes, maybe you should ask yourself if you are building in enough opportunities for purposeful enjoyment. There was a time when amateurs worked with mathematics strictly for the pleasure it brought them. Are we too serious about the work that goes on in mathematics classes today?

In addition, don't fuss if students misuse words or if their statements are not models of logical clarity. Try to keep in mind that teachers do business in ideas and that words and symbols are merely tools for the communication of the ideas. They are not the end product in itself. If students have some difficulty, work with what they mean instead of what they may say. We lose so many creative thoughts because the way in which students may present these is faulty. This is not their loss alone. Often we lose the student for mathematics altogether. How many times have you seen the push of a teacher for a correct statement drive an original thought from the mind of a child, with the result that the student begins to feel that what he does know is incorrect?

Finally, when we feel excited about what is happening in the mathematics class, when we feel that the mathematics consideration of the moment is a most stimulating one, we should let this be reflected in our actions in the room. How catching is genuine enthusiasm! What better way to create excitement and joy about mathematics than to exhibit just such reactions as we work with our students?

Being a teacher is about the most important job you can do in our society. You will carry out all your work with the world's most precious possession: its young people. On top of that, when teaching is done in the field of mathematics, the importance is multiplied tenfold, for mathematics is itself one of man's finest creations. It is living proof of some of the wonderful things that can come from the minds of humans, as well as a most influential force in twentieth century society. In a world in which work of significance is difficult to find, those who decide to teach mathematics are to be envied. How proud they must be!

It has been the purpose of this book to help those who make mathematics teaching their career to function a little better, with an eye toward greater satisfaction for both teacher and student. If the ideas presented seem to be almost prescriptive in nature, it is not because of a desire for imitation. On the contrary, the ideas were presented in specific fashion in order to make them crystal clear to the reader. Once goals have been clarified, it is hoped that teachers will glean from the ideas enclosed here the desire to move out on their own and create more challenging and meaningful experiences for students than have found their way between these covers. In this, and in all else you may do as a teacher of mathematics, I bid you good luck!

INDEX

Air supply, mathematics of, 24–27
Algebra,
  equations of transformation, 229
  experiments in, 9–12, 98–107
  inequalities, 69–75
  introduction to, 98–101
  as a language, 102–104
  linear functions from circle rolling, 276–282
  linear programming, 178–184
  multiplication of binomials, 260
  patterns in, 274–294
  planning unit in, 8–13
  polynomials, 179–182
Allendoerfer, Carl B., 247
Applications, use of, 15
Area,
  growth of, 58–62
  as a model for distance, 130–134
  of polygons with fixed perimeter, 57
  of rectangle, 129
  to represent factors, 283
  of sectors of a circle, 210
  of trapezoids, 134
  of triangles, 58, 129
Arithmetic mean, 194
Averages, 34

Bell, E. T., 97, 148, 237
Binomial distribution, 215
Boehm, George A. W., 217
Brahe, Tycho, 175

Calculus,
  antiderivative, 142
  central problem of, 137
  differentiation, 134–139
  integration, 141–147
  introduction to, 134–139
  intuitive introduction, 130–134
Circles,
  experiments with, 60–61
  and line relationships, 92
  properties of, 81–83
  rolling circles for linear functions, 276–282
  tangent, 157
Circle graphs, 28
Circular functions, 151
Circumference of Earth, 81–83
Commission on Mathematics, 124, 150
Computers,
  role in society, 217
  simple programs for, 219–220
  use with Monte Carlo methods, 216–217
Congruence, lesson plan in, 16–17
Conic sections, reflection properties of, 158–166
Construction in design making, 64
Copernicus, Heliocentric Theory of, 175

Definitions, how to teach, 109
Dienes, Z. P., 239
  multibase blocks, 218
Directed numbers
  introduction to, 44–45, 265–267
  operations on, 267–270
Discovery learning, finding patterns, 254
Distributive law, 123, 283
Division of large numbers, 30
Domain, 74–75

Eclipses, 154–157
Einstein, Albert,
  ideas on aging, 84
  Theory of Relativity, 175
Ellipses, 176–177
  construction of, 162
  locus definition of, 161
  reflection properties of, 161–163
Energy conservation, mathematics of, 34–36
Equality axioms, 106–109
Equations,
  with fractions, 80–81, 279
  linear, 41–42, 85, 103–109
  quadratic, 114–125
  with radicals, 84–85, 89–90, 93
Eratosthenes,
  circumference of Earth, 81–83
  sieve of, 258
Experiments,
  in algebra, 9–12, 98–107
  from diagrams, 101
  motion, 38–44
  patterns from, 274–276
  in probability, 208–210
  simple science, 98–105
  from tables, 104
Exponents, 25–26
Euclid, 46
  geometric model of reality, 173–175
Euclid's Elements, 173–174
Euler, Leonhard, 170–173
Evaluation,
  cumulative record, 327
  implication of marks, 320–321
  interview, 327
  marking, 332–333
  observation, 326–327
  questionnaires, rating, scales, inventories, 328–329
  sociogram, 327–328
  standardized tests,
    construction of, 329
    standard error of, 329–331
    validity-reliability of, 331–332
  teacher-made tests,
    construction of, 321–326
    item construction for, 325–326
    scoring, 326
    validity-reliability of, 325

Factoring,
  devices for, 119, 122
  difference between two squares, 119–120
  trinomials, 121–124, 286–289
Factors as area of rectangle, 283
Fehr, Howard, 218
Finite arithmetic, 117
Fitzgerald, William M., 98
Formulas, 30, 42
  areas of polygons, 58
  distance to horizon, 89, 90
  from experiments, 40, 100
  listing of, 43
  significance of, 43
Functions,
  described as variation, 289–294
  introduction to notation for, 71
  periodic, 148–149
  trigonometric, 232–235

Galileo, 133, 177
Gardiner, Martin, 310
Gaskell, Robert E., 169
Geometric models of multiplication, 128
Geometry,
  area of polygons, 57–62
  circles, 60–61, 92, 81–83, 157
  congruence, 16–17
  of eclipses, 155–156
  interactions of theorems and physical laws, 49–50
  of light rays, 46–50
  non-Euclidean, 173–175
  parallel lines, 51–54
  proof, 247–251, 301–303
  similar triangles, 94–95, 155–156
  tangents, 90–95
  topology, 170–173
  transformational, 62–65, 230–231
Grades, marking on a curve, 212–217
Graph theory, 173
Graphs, 34, 40
  of area and volume growth, 59–60
  circle, 28
  from experiments, 100
  finding slope, 265
  inequalities,
    one-dimensional, 70
    two-dimensional, 71–72
  introduction to,
    bar, 188–189
    circle, 190
    line, 190
  multiplication tables, 264–265
  speed-time, 128–130
  triangular grid for jug problems, 309–312
Group, properties of, 224–227

Hadamard, Jacques, 247
Haldane, J. B. S., 61
Heron, 48

Horizon, distance to, 88–90
Hyperbolas,
  construction of, 164–165
  locus definition of, 163
  reflection properties of, 163, 166
Identity element in multiplication, 87
Inequalities, 181
  axioms for, 74
  formal solutions, 73–76
  informal solutions, 71–73
  linear, 69–76
  one-dimensional graphs, 70
  two-dimensional graphs, 71–72
Integers,
  introduction to operations on, 265–267
  operations on, 267–270
  the set of, 45
Instantaneous speed, 137–139

Kepler, Johann,
  three laws of motion, 175–176
Klein, Felix, 248
Kline, Morris, 175, 177–178
Konigsberg Bridges, 170–171

Learning,
  classroom freedoms, 18–20
  principles of, 7–8
Least common multiple, 80
Leibniz, G. W., 140
Light, speed of, 86
Light rays,
  geometric theorems and, 49
  mathematics of, 45–54
  parallel lines and, 52–54
  reflection of, 46–50
Limit, 138–139, 140–141
Linear equations,
  formal solutions, 104, 106–109
  solution of, 41–42, 85, 103–109
  solutions by language, 105
  solutions using equality axioms, 106–109
Linear functions, 44
  unit plan for, 8–13
Linear programming, introduction to, 178–180
Locus, conic sections, 159–165
Low achiever, use of computers with, 221

Magic squares, 312–316
  construction of odd-numbered order, 314–315
  patterns of, 314–316
  use in algebra, 313
Mathematical symbols, meaning and importance of, 42
Mathematics,
  of air supply, 24–27
  of dieting, 75–76
  of energy conservation, 34–36
  and environment, 3

as language, 3
language of science, 97–110
of light rays, 45–54
of living things, 56–76
models of reality, 168–184
used in prediction, 42
of space exploration, 78–95
teaching objectives of, 2–5
as a tool, 112–126
of water conservation, 28–30
Matrices, 173, 229–230
Mean, arithemetic, 194
Measurement,
   conversion of units, 86–88
   metric, 30–34
   place in curriculum, 33
Metric system, 30–34
Metrics, 41, 75–76, 87
   meaning of prefixes, 33
Monte Carlo methods, 216–217
Mosteller, Frederick, 216
Motion experiments, 38–44
Motion laws, 128–139
Motion problems, 31–32
Multiplication of large numbers, 30

Negative numbers (*see* Directed numbers)
Networks, 170–173
Newsom, Carroll V., 168–169
Newton, Isaac, 140
Numbers,
   basic facts, 261–265
   finding the LCD, 262–263
   odd-even, 255–257
   perfect squares, 258–261
   prime-composite, 257–258
Number line,
   to show additive inverse, 267–268
   use with signed numbers, 45
Numeration systems, 218–219

Operations, unary, 117

Parabolas,
   construction of, 159–160
   locus definition of, 159
   reflection properties of, 158
Paraboloid, 158
Parallel lines, applications of, 51–54
Pascal's Triangle, 215
Patterns,
   in algebra, 274–294
   in experiments, 40, 99, 274–276
   in formulas, 279–280, 281–282
   in geometry, 296–305
   of magic squares, 314–316
   in multiplication tables, 261–265
   in numbers,
      odd-even, 255
      perfect squares, 258–261
      prime-composite, 257–258

Percent, 26, 28–29, 31, 66–69, 195–196
   by formula $br = p$, 68
   introduction to, 66–67
   by ratio and proportion, 67–68
   three cases of, 67
   use in body temperature, 66–69
Perimeter, 57
π (Pi),
   finding the value of, 60–61
   through graphing, 264
Planets,
   periods of, 79–81
   radii of, 78
Planning,
   beginning activities, 14–15
   daily plans, 13–17
   introduction to, 9–10
   unit planning, 8
Playfair's Postulate, 174
Polya, George, 239
Polygons,
   area of, 57–58
   from nature, 56–58
Polynomials,
   introduction to, 282–283
   operations on, 283–286
   visualizations for, 283, 284
Probability, 208–221
   experiments in, 208–210
   informal introduction to, 202
   introduction to, 208–210
   Monte Carlo methods, 216–217
   normal curve, 212–217
   sample spaces, 214–215
   theory vs. practice, 211–212
   tree diagrams, 214
Problem solving, 30
   encouraging insight in, 241–243
   finding a simple equivalent, 243–244
   generalizing, 245–247
   jug-filling,
      general solutions, 312
      using a triangular grid, 309–312
   role of visualization in, 247
   trial and error, 243
   verbal problems
      aids to solution, 240–241
Projects, 76
   on use of electricity, 36
   on water use, 30
Proofs, 247–251
   direct compared with indirect, 301–302
   indirect, 46
      pattern of, 302–303
   introduction through odd-even numbers, 256–257
   rigor and form of, 249–251
   role of diagrams in, 247–248
   significance of, 248–249
   use of analysis in, 251

Proportion (see Ratio and proportion)
Ptolemy, Geocentric Theory of, 175
Pythagorean Theorem, 88
  general proofs, 298–300
  introduction to, 296–297
  proof for 3-4-5 triangle, 297–299

Quadratic equations, 89
  completing the squares, 124
  solution of, 114, 118–125
    by factoring, 119–124
    by graphing, 125
Quadratic functions, 44, 113–126
  graphing of, 124
  of form $y = ax^2$, 112–115
  of form $y = ax^2 + bx + c$, 118–126

Radian measure, 151
Radical equations, solutions of, 84–85, 89–93
Radicals, 114
  operations with, 90
Range, 74–75
Ratio and proportion, 29, 30, 31, 58–61, 81, 82, 94–95, 195–196
  using variations, 293
Reflection, 62, 65
Reflection law, 310
Replacement set, 70
Rotation, 65

Sawyer, W. W., 98, 284
Scientific notation, 25–26, 78, 86
Secants, 92
Series,
  convergent-divergent, 308–309
  sum of, 308–309
Signed numbers (see Directed numbers)
Similar triangles, 94–95, 155–156
Sitomer, Harry, 248
Slope,
  of a curved line, 138
  of a straight line, 135
Space exploration, mathematics of, 78–95
Sphere, surface area of, 93
Square roots, 260
  guess-average method, 115–116
  guess-multiply method, 116–117
Squaring, 260
Standard deviation,
  computation of, 203–204
  use in curved scores, 213–214
Statistics, 31
  introduction to averages, 194
  Chebyshev's Theorem, 205
  collecting data and graphing, 188–193
  decision making, 187–208
  graphs,
    purpose of each type, 191
  market research, 197
  mean, median, mode, 197–201
  measures of dispersion, 203–206
  poll-taking, 195–197
  sampling, 193–196
  selecting proper average, 198–201
Surface area of sphere, 93
Symmetry, 62–65

Tangent circles, 157
Tangent lines,
  to circles, 90–91
  common external, 155–157
  common internal, 155–157
Tanur, Judith M., 216
Tessellations, 56–57
  a special case of area, 303
  with regular polygons, 303–305
Testing (see Evaluation)
Thompson, Sir D'Arcy, 230
Tiling (see Tessellations)
Topology, 171, 173
Transformations, 226–229
  applications of, 230–231
  as matrices, 229
  dilation, 231
  equations for, 228–229
  in geometry, 230–231
  linear, 227
  reflection, 228–229
    on magic squares, 314
  rotation, 228–229
    on magic squares, 314
  shearing, 231
  translation, 65
Transformational geometry, 62–65
Triangle, area of, 58
Trigonometry,
  functions in, 148–149
  ratio to functions, 232–235
  vectors in, 150–151

Units, conversion of, 86–88

Variation,
  applications for, 293–294
  for grouping functions, 289–294
  graphs of, 291–292
  introduction to, 290–291
Vectors in trigonometry, 150–151
Volume,
  growth of, 58–62
  of troposphere, 25–26
Von Neumann, John, 168

Walter, Marion, 63
Water conservation, mathematics of, 28–30
Weaver, Warren, 211
Wilcox, A. B., 169
Willoughby, Stephen, 249

Squares, Square Roots, and Prime Factorizations

n	n^2	$\sqrt{n}$	Prime factorization	n	n^2	$\sqrt{n}$	Prime factorization
1	1	1.000	—	26	676	5.099	2·13
2	4	1.414	prime	27	729	5.196	3·3·3
3	9	1.732	prime	28	784	5.292	2·2·7
4	16	2.000	2·2	29	841	5.385	prime
5	25	2.236	prime	30	900	5.477	2·3·5
6	36	2.449	2·3	31	961	5.568	prime
7	49	2.646	prime	32	1,024	5.657	2·2·2·2·2
8	64	2.828	2·2·2	33	1,089	5.745	3·11
9	81	3.000	3·3	34	1,156	5.831	2·17
10	100	3.162	2·5	35	1,225	5.916	5·7
11	121	3.317	prime	36	1,296	6.000	2·2·3·3
12	144	3.464	2·2·3	37	1,369	6.083	prime
13	169	3.606	prime	38	1,444	6.164	2·19
14	196	3.742	2·7	39	1,521	6.245	3·13
15	225	3.873	3·5	40	1,600	6.325	2·2·2·5
16	256	4.000	2·2·2·2	41	1,681	6.403	prime
17	289	4.123	prime	42	1,764	6.481	2·3·7
18	324	4.243	2·3·3	43	1,849	6.557	prime
19	361	4.359	prime	44	1,936	6.633	2·2·11
20	400	4.472	2·2·5	45	2,025	6.708	3·3·5
21	441	4.583	3·7	46	2,116	6.782	2·23
22	484	4.690	2·11	47	2,209	6.856	prime
23	529	4.796	prime	48	2,304	6.928	2·2·2·2·3
24	576	4.899	2·2·2·3	49	2,401	7.000	7·7
25	625	5.000	5·5	50	2,500	7.071	2·5·5